Who Really Won the Battle of Marathon?

This edition is dedicated to the memory of Dimitris Kollias, a good friend who contributed in various aspects of our research and who sadly passed away a few weeks before the release of the book.

Who Really Won the Battle of Marathon?

A Bold Re-appraisal of One of History's Most Famous Battles

Constantinos Lagos and Fotis Karyanos

Translated by John Carr

Pen & Sword
MILITARY

First published in Great Britain in 2020 by
Pen & Sword Military
An imprint of
Pen & Sword Books Ltd
Yorkshire – Philadelphia

ISBN 978 1 52675 806 4

A CIP catalogue record for this book is
available from the British Library.

Printed and bound in the UK by TJ International Ltd,
Padstow, Cornwall.

Pen & Sword Books Limited incorporates the imprints of Atlas,
Archaeology, Aviation, Discovery, Family History, Fiction, History,
Maritime, Military, Military Classics, Politics, Select, Transport,
True Crime, Air World, Frontline Publishing, Leo Cooper, Remember
When, Seaforth Publishing, The Praetorian Press, Wharncliffe
Local History, Wharncliffe Transport, Wharncliffe True Crime
and White Owl.

For a complete list of Pen & Sword titles please contact

PEN & SWORD BOOKS LIMITED
47 Church Street, Barnsley, South Yorkshire, S70 2AS, England
E-mail: enquiries@pen-and-sword.co.uk
Website: www.pen-and-sword.co.uk

Or

PEN AND SWORD BOOKS
1950 Lawrence Rd, Havertown, PA 19083, USA
E-mail: Uspen-and-sword@casematepublishers.com
Website: www.penandswordbooks.com

Contents

Acknowledgements

We would like to thank the following individuals and organizations who made this edition possible:

- Manolis and Christos Takidellis of Menandros Publishing House, Athens, for publishing our book in Greek under the title Μάχη του Μαραθώνα. Η Ανατροπή.
- Costas Gerardos and Plaisio Computers S.A., for sponsoring the English translation of the Greek edition.
- John Carr, for his translation and editing of the book.
- Mirela Terzakis, for her contribution to the translation of the bibliographical notes.
- Philip Sidnell, Matthew Jones and Mat Blurton of Pen & Sword Books for seeing the book through to print.
- Iannis Nikou, for permission to use his painting 'Ancient Athenian Warriors' ('Αρχαίοι Αθηναίοι Πολεμιστές') on the book jacket.
- Assimakis Katsiaris and Nikos Kalogeropoulos, for creating maps and drawings for the book.
- Jeff Vanderpool, for permission to use his photographs of Marathon.
- Dr Denver Graninger, for information on the unpublished ancient inscription at Marathon.
- Spyros Zagaris, former Mayor of Marathon (Greece).
- Lydia and Costas Carras.
- Pantelis Vatakis.
- Emmanuel Mikroyannakis.
- The Ephorate of Antiquities of Eastern Attika.
- The National Archaeological Museum of Athens.
- The Acropolis Museum, Athens.
- The British Museum, London.
- The Staatliche Museen zu Berlin / Johannes Laurentius.
- The American School of Classical Studies at Athens (ASCSA).

- The British School at Athens (BSA).
- The École Française d'Athènes (EfA)
- The Deutsches Archäologisches Institut (DAI), Athens.

NB – all dates in this book are BC unless specifically recorded as AD.

Abbreviations

AA	*Archäologischer Anzeiger*/Deutsches Archäologisches Institut. Berlin: de Gruyter.
AC	*L'Antiquité Classique.* Brussels.
AΔ	*Αρχαιολογικό Δελτίο* (*Archaeological Bulletin*).
AE	*Αρχαιολογική Εφημερίς. Περιοδικόν τῆς ἐν Ἀθήναις Ἀρχαιολογικῆς Ἑταιρείας* (*Archaeological Ephemeral*).
AJA	*American Journal of Archaeology*: The Journal of the Archaeological Institute of America. Boston (Mass.): Boston University, Archaeological Institute of America.
AJPh	*American Journal of Philology.* Baltimore (Md.): Johns Hopkins University Press.
AntClass	*L'Antiquité Classique.* Brussels.
Antichthon	*Journal of the Australian Society for Classical Studies.* Sydney (Australia): Macquarie University, Australian Society for Classical Studies.
APA	American Philological Association.
ARV	J.D. Beazley, *Attic Red-figure Vase Painters*, Oxford, 1962.
AthMitt	*Mitteilungen des Deutschen Archäologischen Instituts, Athenische Abteilung.* Berlin: von Zabern.
ASCSA	American School of Classical Studies in Athens.
BSA	*Annual of the British School at Athens.* Athens; London: British School at Athens.
CAB	International Centre for Agricultural Bioscience International.
CJ	*The Classical Journal.* Ashland (Va.): Randolph-Macon College, Department of Classics, Classical Association of the Middle West and South.
CPh	*Classical Philology: A Journal Devoted to Research in Classical Antiquity.* Chicago (Ill.): University of Chicago Press.
CQ	*Classical Quarterly.* Oxford: Oxford University Press.

CSCA	*California Studies in Classical Antiquity.* California: University of California Press.
CW	*Classical World.* Pittsburgh (Pa.): Duquesne University, Department of Classics, Classical Association of the Atlantic States.
GRBS	Greek, Roman and Byzantine Studies. Durham (N.C.): Duke University, Department of Classics.
HZ	*Historische Zeitschrift.* München: Oldenbourg.
IG	Inscriptiones Graecae.
JHS	*The Journal of Hellenic Studies.* London: Society for the Promotion of Hellenic Studies.
MMJ	Metropolitan Museum Journal. New York (N.Y.): Metropolitan Museum of Art. Turnhout: Brepols.
Π*AE*	Πρακτικὰ τῆς ἐν Ἀθήναις Ἀρχαιολογικῆς Ἑταιρείας. Ἀθήνα. Ἀρχαιολογική Ἑταιρεία.
PCPhS	*Proceedings of the Cambridge Philological Society.* Cambridge: Cambridge Philological Society.
REA	*Revue des Etudes Anciennes.*
REG	*Revue des Etudes Grecques.* Paris: Les Belles Lettres.
SCO	*Studi Classici e Orientali.*
SEG	*Supplementum Epigraphicum Graecum.*
TAPA	*Transactions and Proceedings of the American Philological Association.* Baltimore (Md.): Johns Hopkins University Press.
ZPE	*Zeitschrift für Papyrologie und Epigraphik.* Bonn: Habelt.

Translator's Introduction

In all military history the 490 battle of Marathon has been an unfailing member of the list of the key battles of the world, up there along with Thermopylai, the Milvian Bridge, Tours, Agincourt, Trafalgar, Waterloo, the Somme and Stalingrad. Marathon is considered epochal because, in the view of the vast bulk of historiography, it halted what could have turned into a Persian invasion of Europe that could well have strangled Greek civilization, and by extension European culture, in its cradle.

Other aspects of the battle also appeal to a Western mind. Marathon was a victory for local democracy and independence over an attempted foreign-imposed autocracy. The present obsession with political correctness cannot (and should not) obscure the undeniable fact that it was also a victory of Europeans over alien Asiatics who had no business being in Greece in the first place. And the great majority of narratives stress that even though the fight was an unequal one, the righteous 'few' prevailed against the foreign hordes. This narrative, in fact, appears to be the chief attraction which the battle has for scholars. It owes its dramatic effect to appearing to confirm the instinctual view that defence against unprovoked aggression is the noblest form of military action. Defence generally carries a connotation of 'rightness' against the presumed 'wrongness' of aggression. Setting aside the vexatious question of what 'right' actually means, it appears that Marathon is one of those battles that reinforce the popular prejudice that the people with right on their side however few, will somehow always win, if not physically, then in the grand firmament of historical glory.

Someone who picks up a book titled *Who Really Won at Marathon?* is thus likely to experience a cultural shock of sorts. The initial reaction is likely to be: why, the Greeks, of course – everybody knows that. No-one, of course, disputes this. The 'who' in the title refers not to which side won but to whom on the Greek side the ultimate victory in a very hard-fought encounter can really be attributed. Was it the Athenian and Plataian hoplites, given the credit from Herodotus to the present day? Or were other factors, so far unreported and unrecognized, the real movers in the action that saved Athens and its newly-minted democratic polity and paved the way for the city's – and Greece's – 'golden age'?

It was this question that motivated Constantine Lagos, a lecturer in the Hellenic Air Force Academy, and researcher Foris Karyanos to re-examine and re-evaluate the entire vast and often contradictory corpus of works on Marathon in search of clues.

Herodotus, our earliest source for the battle, is undoubtedly authentic but disappointingly spare on just what happened in those chaotic hours on the Marathon plain north of Athens on an early September day in 490. In his *Histories* he devotes at most a dozen or so lines to the action – a mere summary. To be sure, other ancient writers stepped in to fill in what appeared to be awkward gaps in Herodotus' account; but whereas Herodotus had the supreme advantage of gleaning facts from veterans of the battle, the others had to necessarily view it through the distorting mists of up to several centuries. Which really has left no-one satisfied from that day to this.

In Herodotus' day historiography was only just beginning to emerge from the Homeric tradition in which the actions of gods and heroic men, and their capacity to inspire and teach, was far more important to the listening public than a dry chronicling of what happened and on what date. Herodotus was not interested in a mere journalistic blow-by-blow account of Marathon – the trend that dominates most historiography today – but in the wider scheme of how it affected great power relations and the future course of Athenian society. He was not a war correspondent but a supremely capable travel and feature writer whose interests ranged far and wide; the technical details of a military campaign were of little use to him. He was a cultural, not a military, historian. The ultimate significance of the battle, rather than a tactical and strategic treatise, was his chief concern.

Of course, that could not satisfy later readers with a more specific interest in strategy and tactics. It was left to Roman-era writers, long after the event, to put some flesh on the bare bones that Herodotus supplies. Cornelius Nepos, in the first century, provided a wealth of previously unknown detail, including the assertion that it was the Persians who opened the battle with a cavalry charge – appearing to contradict Herodotus' venerated report that it was the Greeks who charged first 'at a run'. Nepos' sources are unknown, so there is no sure way of determining the accuracy of the claim. Starting in the early nineteenth century cohorts of mainly British and German travellers and amateur archaeologists visited Marathon to see for themselves the lay of the land and render their own judgements as to what actually took place on that memorable day in 490. In the twentieth century a vast number of professional investigations by British, Greek, German and American archaeologists added to the burgeoning corpus of Marathon studies, but without really throwing much extra light on key issues, such as where the Athenian camp was located and where exactly the Persian defeat turned into a rout. It is fair to say that despite the ongoing welter of scholarship, we still may well know less about the battle of Marathon than Herodotus did (and, for his own reasons, omitted to mention).

Into this scholarly maze stepped Lagos and Karyanos, who can be credited with formulating a new reconstruction of the battle that differs in a few radical respects from the traditional ones. The most striking difference is their theory that the time-honoured image of the 'few' Greeks fending off the 'many' Persians is an exaggeration; what Herodotus and the great majority of ancient writers failed to mention were the Athenian light-armed troops who must have accompanied any hoplite force into battle. Lagos and Karyanos attribute this lack of mention to simple class bias. The hoplites were soldiers well enough off to afford their own armour and weapons, and hence belonged almost exclusively to the upper classes, as did those who wrote about their feats of arms; anyone of the lower orders who wished to fight was given second-class light-armed status. Thus taking the number of light-armed into account, the Greek force at Marathon – traditionally numbered at 10,000 Athenian and 1,000 Plataian hoplites, would actually have been considerably larger, perhaps up to 30,000, which would greatly shorten the odds against victory.

As Lagos and Karyanos relate in the climax of the book, these light-armed men consigned to the shadows of history were the ones who actually turned the tide of the battle in a way that took the overconfident Persians totally by surprise.

Of course, their reconstruction is a theory only, but they have marshalled an impressive array of evidence in its favour. The subsequent history of Athens also argues powerfully for the decisive role of the light-armed *thetes* (the lowest social class) in the Athenian victory. After the battle the *thetes* suddenly found themselves with political power in the democratic polity, a change that very likely reflected their climactic combat role that would have been grudgingly acknowledged by the aristocratic hoplite class. And it may not be too much to claim that the subsequent expansion of the Athenian democratic polity proved fertile ground for the city's classical golden age in the fifth century.

So who really won at Marathon? The answer supplied by Lagos and Karyanos may surprise us.

JC

Chapter 1

The Empire Strikes Back

In 499 the Greek cities of Ionia in Asia Minor that had been subjects of the Persian king, Darius I, rebelled against him. After six years of hard fighting the Ionian Revolt was quenched in blood and smashed. The only two cities of mainland Greece that had aided the Ionians, Athens and Eretria, were thus next on Darius' attack list. Hippias, the former tyrant of Athens who was expelled from the city in 510 and living in Darius' court, connived with the Persians for his return to power and the overthrow of the newly established Athenian democracy. However, the first Persian expedition to Greece in 492 under Mardonius came to grief in Macedonia after the fleet was destroyed off Athos. Mardonius broke off his campaign aimed at southern Greece and returned to Asia with whatever men he had left.

This, however, did not deter the Great King, who at once ordered a fresh expedition to be readied. By the summer of 490 the new Persian fleet, numbering a great many warships and transports, was ready. At the same time the Persian expeditionary force was put together, consisting of 20,000–30,000 combat soldiers, a large number of auxiliaries and some 1,000–2,000 cavalrymen with their horses. Datis and Artaphernes were appointed to command the expedition, while Hippias, the deposed tyrant of Athens, acted as adviser.

In 491, the year before the new expedition against Greece, the Great King demanded 'earth and water' from the Greek cities. Few dared refuse, among them Athens, Sparta, Plataia, Eretria, Karystos and Naxos. In the spring of 490 the fleet set sail from Asia, possibly touching at Rhodes and Samos, and headed for the Cyclades islands. Naxos, refusing tribute, was destroyed by the Persians. After that, the remaining Cyclades submitted to Datis without a fight. Thus by the summer of 490 the whole Aegean area was under the Persian thumb. Finally the Persians landed on mainland Greece and took Karystos; at the end of summer they moved on Eretria which, despite a heroic resistance of six days, fell to the Persians through treachery.

The punishment of Eretria was exemplary: its temples were burned and its people massacred.

After Eretria the Persians moved on their next objective, Athens. The natural terrain features of Marathon, especially its shoreline, led the Persians to choose it as the landing point at Attica. The Persian landing at Marathon proceeded smoothly, with the Persians securing control of the greater part of the Marathon plain. They did not, however, plan to stay there but to proceed with all speed to Athens. They were unable to move forward because the Athenians, who knew of the Persians' movements, blocked the critical Brexiza pass at the southern end of the plain. The Persians were thus prevented from moving on Athens at once, a development that turned out to be crucial to the progress of the battle of Marathon and the subsequent Persian defeat. It became quickly apparent that the Athenians would not give in, with the result that Hippias' importance was minimized and he was pushed to the sidelines. The Persians knew they would have to meet the Athenians in battle at Marathon, where the verdict of arms would be delivered.

I: Preparing the campaign

1. Introit

In the three decades of the reign of Darius I (521–486) that preceded the battle of Marathon in 490, the Persians carried out a great number of campaigns, almost all of them victorious. The relatively few failures were caused by extraneous factors to do with mostly natural phenomena rather than defeat in pitched battle. But even in those cases the Persians were able to avoid total catastrophe thanks to competent staff planning.[1] One typical case is the expedition to Scythia in 513; even though the Great King[2] failed to bring the European Scythians to heel, he succeeded in managing a tactical withdrawal of his army.[3] Moreover, his general Megabazus seized Thrace with part of the Persian expeditionary force – the first European portion of territory which the Persians annexed.[4] Thus the claim that Darius' army returned in triumph from its expeditions, as Aischylos makes his chorus say in the *Persians*, is not far from the truth.[5]

The years of Darius' reign coincided with the apogee of Persian military strength and the period of its most efficient organization in the two centuries that the Achaemenid dynasty ruled. In 490 the Persian Empire stretched from Europe and North Africa all the way to India.[6]

Darius is estimated to have ruled over some 70 million subjects,[7] at a time when the Athenians – his main adversaries in Greece – numbered a mere 30,000 citizens in a total population of 150,000–170,000.[8] Despite the sheer extent of his domain and its immense population, Darius was the first ruler of a multi-ethnic empire who was able to mobilize a large number of his subjects in a relatively short time. The Persians also had amassed considerable experience in managing campaigns, especially in staff work. Thus the Persian staff was able to plan complex operations far from the main centres of the empire.[9] Under Darius Persian battle tactics, which had begun to develop under Cyrus the Great (559–530), had been perfected. These were based on coordinating infantry and cavalry attacks on the enemy, with the latter as a striking force.

Darius conscripted men from all corners of the empire, but his elite units were those of ethnic Persians and Medes. The great majority of the imperial infantry was made up of light-armed soldiers whose main weapon was the bow. While the Persians had other foot soldier specializations for various battle tasks, their strongest arm was the cavalry.[10] In 490 the best horsemen in the empire were the Persians, Medes and Saka. These last were Asian Scythians, subjects of the Persians, who as nomads were more familiar with cavalry tactics than anyone else in the empire. We can be sure that the expeditionary force that Darius sent to Greece in 490 included units of these infantry and cavalry forces. The subject peoples were compelled to supply the Persian army with considerable manpower.[11] They fought with their own weapons, being assigned special tasks in accordance with the customs of each people. The Persians did not train any of their subject peoples in tactics foreign to them. The Greeks of Ionia and Aiolia, as well as the Phoenicians, had a strong naval tradition, and so they provided the empire with warships and crews. Thus the army of the Persian Empire consisted of separate units with their own structure, organization, training and mission. An outside observer would get a clear impression of the multi-ethnic army from the differences in battle gear and weaponry.[12] However, the Persians had succeeded in organizing and harmoniously unifying these multifarious units into a whole. In fact, Persian commanders took full advantage of this variety, ensuring that many different specializations and talents could be used. This way the Persian army was ready at any moment to undertake campaigns anywhere from the steppes of modern-day South Russia, to the North African deserts and the jungles of India.

2. Building the fleet

After suppressing the Ionian Revolt in 494, the Persians assayed their first expedition to Greece in 492. The drive was thwarted by a violent storm that smashed the fleet off the Athos peninsula, so no progress could be made south of Macedon. Almost at once Darius began preparing another expedition to Greece. The loss of an entire fleet was just a short-term obstacle for the Great King; such were the massive economic resources of the empire that he could replace the lost ships in a short time. Preparations proceeded feverishly, with hundreds of ships built and thousands of men recruited, not to mention horses and supplies requisitioned, until the spring of 490. Herodotus writes that Darius ordered the coastal cities paying tribute to him to build two types of vessels, the 'long' ships and the horse transports.[13] The former were troop transports that would ferry the invading force to Greece, while the horse transports would handle the cavalry.[14] According to Herodotus the Persian fleet that sailed in 490 numbered 600 triremes.[15] Most scholars believe that this referred to the troop carriers only, excluding the horse transports and supply ships.[16]

We cannot be sure of the accuracy of Herodotus' number, however, as he uses it as a generic figure to describe Persian imperial fleets in other passages.[17] Plato writes that the Persian fleet which invaded Greece in 490 consisted of triremes and transports;[18] but he differs from Herodotus in the number, putting it at no more than 300, or half Herodotus' figure. Yet neither is Plato trustworthy, as he places the number of Persian troops at 500,000; there is no way a force of this size, or even a portion of it, could have been transported in 300 vessels. Cornelius Nepos says that the Persians had 500 ships, though without distinguishing between triremes and transports.[19] Regardless of the figures given by each ancient source, what seems certain is that the fleet was a combination of both types of ship, plus supply vessels, although we cannot obtain an accurate number from any source.[20] Modern scholars are also divided on the issue. Hammond goes with Plato's figure of 300;[21] Balcer goes even lower, putting the number of triremes at between 200 and 300.[22] Most, however, would seem to accept Herodotus' figure of 600.[23]

From what Herodotus tells us about Xerxes' fleet which sailed to Greece ten years later, in 480, most of the ships in the invasion of 490 must have been Phoenician. The rest were probably an assemblage of vessels from Karia, Kilikia, Lykia, Cyprus, Egypt, Ionia and Aiolis, as was the case in Xerxes' expedition.[24] According to Herodotus, the fleet that sailed for Greece in 490 was joined at Rhenaia, on Delos, by 'the Ionians and Aiolians'.[25] This would indicate that the crews manned their own ships.[26] The Ionians, Aiolians, Cypriots and Karians had participated in the Ionian Revolt,[27] after the crushing of which those groups – despite their grave human and material losses – were compelled to supply men and ships for the invasion of Greece. Herodotus also mentions that the Parians contributed to the fleet with one trireme.[28] Quite possibly the other Cyclades islands also contributed, as Herodotus reports that when the Persians overran them, they recruited the local manpower into their expeditionary force.[29]

3. Size and composition of the Persian expedition

All ancient sources indicate that the army that Darius launched against Greece in 490 consisted of powerful infantry and cavalry forces. As it had to be transported by sea, it must have been somewhat smaller than that which Xerxes marched overland ten years later. Darius probably had little trouble getting the army together; he was able to pick the best fighters out of the hordes he could recruit from the vastness of his domain. But from which areas did these men come? Herodotus names Persians, Saka and Medes in the land army, and Phoenicians, Ionians, Aiolians and Cycladians in the navy.[30] The Persians, who were the dominant ethnic group in the empire, manned the elite units of both the infantry and cavalry.[31] The Greeks believed that the Persians called all Scythians Saka,[32] and especially those that were their subject peoples.[33] They were redoubtable horsemen, and as such an asset to the Persian army, and only secondarily used as foot soldiers.[34] Herodotus also makes a general mention of the Medes in the army, though later writers imply that all the soldiers were from Media.[35] That would be far from the truth. Of course, there would have been a good number of Medes in the army, as the commander Datis himself may have been a satrap of Media and probably a Mede himself (see below).[36]

If in 490 Datis was indeed the satrap of Media, we may have an inkling of the ethnological make-up of his army. Sekunda estimates that Datis would have exercised supreme military command west of Mesopotamia and hence in command of the forces remaining in Asia Minor after the Ionian Revolt.[37] After the failure of that insurrection, Darius could well have extended Datis' jurisdiction, as satrap of Media, to the Asia Minor coast. To carry the hypothesis further, Darius may have considered the expeditions of 492 and 490 an extension of the crushing of the Ionian Revolt rather than a completely new campaign.[38] It is thus likely that Datis' army contained elite Persian, Mede and Saka units that had fought the Ionians a few years previously, and after the end of the revolt had remained in Asia Minor as occupation forces. To these will have been added other men from Media, which was Datis' main region of governance.

Neither do our ancient sources agree on the size of the Persian army that attacked Greece in 490. Herodotus makes no attempt at numbering it, beyond the very general observation that 'the foot soldiers were many and well-supplied'.[39] Later ancient writers, however, hazard guesses ranging from 80,000 to 600,000 men,[40] the low end of this range coming from Lucius Ampelius.[41] Then we have an epigram attributed to Pseudo-Simonides referring to the Athenians at Marathon who confronted – or killed – 90,000 Persians.[42] Cornelius Nepos says there were 210,000 Persians at Marathon in a combat capacity, of whom 200,000 were foot soldiers and 10,000 horsemen.[43] Pseudo-Plutarch hikes the number of Persians to 300,000, a number repeated by Pausanias and Souda.[44] Plato and Lysias inflate the figure yet more, to half a million, while Justin gives us the rather incredible figure of 600,000.[45] Without knowing just how some of these writers came by their figures, we may dismiss them as exaggerated. It is possible, however, that in their computations of the number of soldiers they included auxiliary personnel and ship crews which, if taken together, would outnumber the combat troops several times over. In the second century AD, Aelius Aristides figured that the wildly differing estimates of the Persian army at Marathon given us by the ancient writers were themselves proof of a huge number.[46] He himself declines to give us his own estimate, saying merely that the troops were so many that they could have 'flooded Athens'.[47]

Scholars up to the end of the 18th century based their estimates of the size of the Persian force on what they got from ancient literary sources.

It was the British historian William Milford who in 1795 considered that Nepos' figure was too large for such numbers to be transported by sea, though Milford himself did not hazard a guess at the real figure.[48] The British scholar William Leake in the early nineteenth century was perhaps the first to try and arrive at an estimate;[49] writing in 1829, he based his figure on the objective criterion of how many men he believed would have been ferried from Asia to Greece by the Persian fleet. He concluded that not more than 30,000–32,000 Persian infantry and cavalry would have fought at Marathon; add the auxiliaries and ship crews, and the number could rise to 177,000.[50] Yet Leake's figure for the combat troops is much lower than the lowest of the ancient figures. Besides, in 1838, nearly a decade after Leake published his findings, another British scholar, George Finlay, pushed the figure yet lower, to 24,000.[51]

The questioning of ancient reports of the number of Persians in the invading force reached a peak at the close of the nineteenth century with the appearance of the discipline of military historiography.[52] First among the exponents of this were mainly German writers, who rejected the figures of the original sources for the important battles of antiquity, including Marathon. They believed they could assess the Persian strength in 490 on the basis of findings from archaeological excavations in what had been the main centres of the empire. Some of these historians also personally examined Marathon, at the spot where they believed the battle took place, and described the physical surroundings to see how they would have affected the battle's tactics and outcome. Led by Hans Delbrück, these researchers suggested new criteria for estimating the size of the Persian force. The result was a set of figures even lower than those of Leake and Finlay; in 1887 Delbrück would claim that no more than 10,000–15,000 Persians fought at Marathon.[53] In 1920 the same historian would halve that estimate to a mere 4,000–6,000![54] Delbrück's figures influenced other German scholars such as Mayer, Kromeyer and Busolt, and began to seep into the works of more conventional non-military specialist writers. Thus at the close of the nineteenth century virtually no contemporary authority accepted the figures for the Persian force quoted by the ancients.

Yet these very low figures by military historians came under challenge in the early twentieth century by researchers of the battle of Marathon who considered them unrealistic in their turn.[55] Herodotus writes that 6,400 Persians fell on the battlefield,[56] almost all them combat troops fighting in the front line.[57] As we shall see, this figure is considered reliable, and alone would debunk Delbrück's overly low estimate.[58] Research in more recent decades has turned up new data on the issue, which when combined with the critical examination of older estimates gives us an expeditionary force of 20,000–30,000 men.[59]

Some authorities, such as Hammond, suggest an approximation of 25,000–30,000,[60] though Berthold would reduce that to 20,000–25,000.[61] Scott puts the number of front-line Persian fighters at Marathon at between 20,000 and 30,000, basing his figure on the number of Persian dead and the carrying capacity of the Persian fleet, which Scott numbers at 600 ships.[62] Similar estimates are put forward by Hignett (20,000 foot soldiers)[63] and Lazenby (24,000).[64] The latter bases his calculation on the assumption that a typical trireme of the period could carry up to forty combat soldiers;[65] thus the 600 ships mentioned by Herodotus would have ferried 24,000 men. However other scholars consider that the Persian triremes may have been modified in order to carry a larger number of troops. This could have been done by removing rowers and thus making up more space for combat soldiers.[66] Additionally, other types of vessels besides triremes may well have carried fighting men as well;[67] for example, cavalrymen and their auxiliaries could have travelled with the horse transports.[68]

The Persian army was organized into units of one thousand (*hazarabam*), of which ten formed a *baivarabam* (corresponding to a modern division – *tr.*). Sekunda deduces from this fact that if, say, 20,000 troops manned the Persian front line at Marathon, they would have comprised two *baivarabam* of 10,000 men each.[69] The theory appears plausible, as the Persians seem to have organized their army on the decimal system, even down to the smallest units.[70] That might also explain the presence of two Persian commanders; according to Sekunda, Datis and Artaphernes could each have commanded a *baivarabam*, or division, on the front line.

The majority of modern scholars accept a figure of 20,000–30,000 men on the Persian side, though a stubborn minority holds out for lower than 20,000, say, 12,000–15,000.[71] Yet these low numbers appear unrealistic in the light of Xenophon's assertion that an army which invades Attica would need to have more men than the number of Athenians in a position to bear arms.[72] Xenophon cited the Peloponnesian War (431–404), in which the Spartans and their allies invaded Attica many times. Yet his analogy holds up for 490. As we shall see, the Athenians could field not only 9,000–10,000 hoplites (heavy-armed foot soldiers) but also a considerable number of light-armed troops which some authorities say outnumbered the regular hoplites by as much as two to one. Though the light-armed Athenians lacked the training and equipment of the hoplites, they were a military force to be reckoned with. The weapons of many were in no way inferior to those of their Persian opponents. Certainly the Persians had intelligence of how many troops the Greek city-states could field, supplied by Greek exiles in Darius' court.

Echoing Xenophon, in the twentieth century first Sotiriadis and then Hammond argued against the view that the Persian army at Marathon numbered just a few thousand combat troops, on the grounds that the Persians would not have dared to attack Athens and Eretria with a force smaller than those cities could put up.[73] According to Strabo, the Eretrians had some 3,000 hoplites, a figure generally agreed to be right.[74] Yet they also had light-armed troops of unknown number, but almost certainly greater than the number of hoplites.[75] Thus in 490 the combined military strength of Athens and Eretria totalled 12,000–13,000 hoplites, and a rather larger number of light-armed troops.[76] Moreover, the Persians had no way of knowing whether the Athenians and Eretrians would fight separately or on a common front. We may assume that Persian planning was based on the second, more difficult, scenario. The Persians also must have considered the possibility that Sparta would come to the aid of Athens and Eretria. Sparta had powerful military forces and the best fighting men in Greece. The Persians could not know in what strength the Spartans would rush to the aid of Athens and Eretria; therefore they would not have been so foolish as to attack Greece with a mere few thousand soldiers when their potential foes might well be in a position, for all they knew, to array tens of thousands against them.[77]

The first of the more recent writers to attempt to calculate the number of Persian cavalry in 490 at Marathon was Leake, who arrived at 6,000–7,000.[78] This estimate remains the largest so far published after the ancient authors.[79] The next largest numbers have been proposed by

Kontorlis (5,000) and Dionysopoulos (3,000).[80] According to Sekunda, the Persian cavalry numbered no more than 2,000, units of 1,000 each being placed at each wing.[81] Munro supposes that for an infantry force of 25,000, some 5,000 horse would be enough, but he considers that the Pesian cavalry was only 1,000, without explaining how he came by it. [82] Berthold came to a similar conclusion, that 5,000 horsemen would be enough for a force of 20,000–25,000 infantry that he believed the Persians fielded at Marathon; however, he adds that because of the limitations on ferrying horses by sea, the cavalry at Marathon numbered 1,000 or less.[83] Most recent commentators accept Berthold's view, and converge on a rough number of 1,000.[84]

Those scholars who assert that the Persians had a relatively small number of men at Marathon also tend to assume that the cavalry, too, was not numerous.[85] Most put the number of horsemen at 200 or even less. However to Drews, a specialist in the cavalry of the ancient Near East, 200 is far too low. He bases this conclusion on Herodotus' assertion that as the Persians in 490 pinned hopes for victory on their cavalry, the Great King ordered horse transports to be built to ferry it to Greece.[86] Herodotus twice mentions that Darius gave orders for horse transports to be built, in order to show how important cavalry was to the expedition.[87] Herodotus' second such reference, in fact, mentions only the order for horse transports and not warships. A force of a mere 200 horsemen would hardly justify such preparations on the part of the Persians. Moreover, such a small force would not have overly worried the Athenians.[88] Drews' estimate is that the Persians fielded about 1,000 cavalry. In 511 the Athenian tyrant Hippias had hired a similar number of horsemen from Thessaly as mercenaries.[89] Herodotus claims that at that time the power of the Persian Empire was such that Darius probably had never heard of Athens.[90] If this claim stretches credulity, it indicates that the Greeks believed Darius at the apogee of his power disdained Athens and all the Greek city-states. If the tyrant of Athens could hire 1,000 horsemen, could not Darius have the ability to raise a force of at least similar, if not greater, size, despite the problems of transporting it?

We may conclude, then, that the Persians could not possibly have sailed against Greece in 490 with less than 20,000 combat troops. Our estimate is that the army consisted of at least 25,000. Correspondingly, the number of cavalry must be established at 1,000 at least, and most probably more, perhaps up to twice that number.

4. The Persian commanders, Datis and Artaphernes, and Hippias' involvement in the campaign

After the Persian fleet came to grief off Athos in 492, Darius stripped Mardonius of his command, and hence did not appoint him leader of the 490 campaign.[91] Herodotus implies that Darius blamed Mardonius for the disaster that befell the first expedition;[92] yet that same Mardonius became the most trusted adviser of Xerxes when he mounted the throne, which indicates that Darius kept him within the circle of his trusted officials.[93] If Darius had indeed believed Mardonius to be responsible for the Athos disaster, he would not only have relieved him of command but executed him as soon as he set foot back in Asia. During the 492 expedition Mardonius had been wounded in a skirmish with the Brygians in Macedon.[94] Thus he may not have recovered fully in order to lead the new campaign. Our ancient sources are vague on just why Mardonius was not in command of the 490 expedition against Greece. Scott makes the interesting observation that Darius was reluctant to allow any commander to exercise campaign command for more than a year, whether successful or not.[95] It is thus possible that Mardonius was sidelined for that reason rather than any failure or wound.

Darius appointed two officials, Datis and Artaphernes, to command the new expedition.[96] Why two commanders were appointed instead of one remains a mystery, as well as the reason for their separate powers. Neither is it clear from our extant sources whether one outranked the other, or both had equal status. It would have been risky, one feels, for Darius to send out two equal-ranking commanders. In fact, some ancient writers mention only Datis as the commander and are silent on Artaphernes.[97] But even those who mention both men tend to imply that it was Datis who had primacy in the giving of orders, on the grounds that his name always precedes that of Artaphernes, whereas in alphabetical order the opposite would be true.[98] Herodotus writes of specific actions taken by Datis during the campaign, but none by Artaphernes.[99] The conclusion, then, is that Datis exercised supreme command over the expeditionary force. Artaphernes was a relative of Darius' (as will be seen later), though secondary in overall command, Datis must therefore have enjoyed the confidence of the Great King to a large degree.[100]

As we have seen, Datis was very likely the satrap of Media when Darius assigned him to command the 490 expedition. Lewis has published the text of a clay tablet discovered in the ruins of Persepolis that includes the name Datiya (Datis).[101] It may well refer to the same Datis of 490, as the text indicates that this Datiya was an important member of Darius' court and one of his highest-ranking officials. The tablet says that in 494 Datis returned to Persepolis from Sardis, where he could quite possibly have been putting down the Ionian Revolt. Datis had two sons, Armamithres and Tithaeus, who in 480 commanded cavalry units during Xerxes' invasion of Greece.[102] The fact that ten years after Marathon these sons of Datis held important posts in the Persian army indicates that they will not have been very young at the time, so in 490 Datis would already have had grown children. We learn no more of Datis from Persian sources. But the writings of Herodotus and other ancient authors paint us a picture of a capable military commander as well as a clever diplomat.[103] Though history has since indelibly associated his name with the Persian disaster at Marathon, Datis had scored notable victories in the Cyclades and Euboia. Even his defeat at Marathon could be attributed not so much to his own mistakes as to the Greek battle plan that was ahead of its time. Probably no Persian military commander would have been able to foresee and successfully deal with the Greek tactics in the battle of Marathon.

We know very little about the second Persian commander, Artaphernes. Herodotus introduces him as a nephew of Darius and son of the satrap of Lydia, also named Artaphernes, who had played a leading part in suppressing the Ionian Revolt.[104] His son was yet another Artaphernes, who a decade later would march with Xerxes in the next invasion of Greece.[105] Thus father, son and grandson shared the same name. The eldest, the satrap of Lydia, according to Herodotus had unfinished business with the Athenians. In 507/6 he had received an Athenian mission at his headquarters at Sardis; the Athenians wanted to seal an alliance with the Persian Empire.[106] Before that could happen, he told his visitors, the Athenians would have to grant 'earth and water' to Darius. We don't know exactly what this symbolic ritual entailed, but probably it was a ceremonial way of recognizing the Great King as suzerain.[107] Darius shunned making alliances with foreign nations, as he considered them all inferior, but was prepared to act jointly with them if they offered 'earth and water'.[108] To successfully complete their mission, the Athenian envoys performed this ritual before Artaphernes, who represented the Great King. On the envoys' return to Athens, however, the citizens disavowed their action, with the result that Darius and Artaphernes were affronted.[109]

Yet in 501/0 another Athenian mission met Artaphernes at Sardis. By then it had transpired in Athens that Hippias, the city's deposed tyrant, was trying to get Darius on side to claw back power. The task of the Athenian mission was to reassure Artaphernes that Athens had friendly feelings for the Persian Empire. But during the meeting Artaphernes bluntly told the Athenians to take back Hippias; the demand was refused.[110] Thus, twice in the space of a few years, the Athenians had defied Artaphernes. Worse was to come. In 498 Athens sent help to the Ionian Greeks who had rebelled against the Persian yoke.[111] A combined force of Athenians, Eretrians and Ionians put Sardis to the torch, including the temple of Kybele, a deity which the Persians particularly revered; only the citadel of Sardis, defended by Artaphernes and his guard, held out against the Greek attack.[112] From then on the Athenians became Artaphernes' worst enemies.[113] He may well have insisted on his son Artaphernes being one of the commanders of the punitive expedition in order to avenge twenty years of slights at Greek hands.[114]

According to Pausanias, Artaphernes the Younger commanded the Persian cavalry at Marathon.[115] If this is correct, then we have some indication as to his age: the duties of a cavalry commander would require that he be in good physical condition and relatively young. However, in 490 the younger Artaphernes would have been a mature man, as ten years later we find his own son and namesake in command of a part of Xerxes' army consisting of Lydians and Mysians.[116]

The elderly Hippias, the deposed tyrant of Athens, also had a part in the expedition.[117] He seems not to have held any official post in the Persian army but to have been there to advise its commanders. The Persians made a practice of taking along leading personalities from the lands they were about to attack, where some of them would have held power in the past.[118]

This shows a high standard of operational organization and planning, in both the military and diplomatic spheres. From what Herodotus tells us, it appears that Datis and Artaphernes faithfully followed Hippias' advice, to the point at which the reader might conclude that he was in fact the unofficial leader of the expedition.[119] That, of course, could not be the case.[120] But it shows how much importance the commanders attached to Hippias' advice, presumably on the orders of Darius.

Hippias' presence in the Persian force in 490 suggests that, apart from his advisory role, the Persians could have been planning to restore him to power in Athens. They seem to have believed that his physical presence there would ensure Athens' peaceful surrender.[121] Herodotus, however, is ambiguous when it comes to how the Persians would have employed Hippias in conquered Athens. The ancient historian claims at one point that Darius planned to enslave the Athenians and carry them off to the Persian Empire;[122] yet elsewhere he says that the Persians intended to reinstate Hippias in power at Athens.[123] One way of reconciling these two apparently contradictory statements is to presume that Herodotus meant that if the Athenians were to surrender without a fight, their city would be spared and Hippias would be back in power. In such a case the bulk of the Persian force would have remained in Athens in order to use Attica as a base of operations against other Greek city-states that had refused to grant 'earth and water'.

But if the Athenians were to resist, as had the Eretrians, the Persians intended to raze the city and carry off the Athenians captive to Asia.[124] In such a case, one imagines, the reinstatement of Hippias would be impossible, as there would no longer be an Athens for him to rule. Hippias' role in the campaign as a tyrant-in-waiting for Athens under Darius' thumb would make sense only if the Athenians were prepared to voluntarily accept him and not resist the Persians. Regardless, however, of whatever plans the Persians might have had for a subjugated Athens, Hippias' presence had mainly diplomatic and propaganda value, to send a message to the Greeks that the Persian operation was a 'just' one with the basic aim of restoring Hippias' 'legitimate' rule that had been terminated in 510 with his expulsion from Athens, and not necessarily to destroy the city.

II: The Aegean becomes a Persian lake

1. Earth and water for the Great King

According to Herodotus the disaster that befell the Persian fleet off Mount Athos in 492 was what decided the Persians to try another sea route two years later.[125] The plan that Darius' staff officers worked out before the 490 expedition involved an approach to mainland Greece via the Cyclades. According to the plan, the islands would be approached and occupied one by one, and thus the Cyclades would become imperial territory to secure the shortest and safest route between Asia and Greece. The islands would serve as ideal supply points for any force the Persians planned to send against Greece in future. Moreover, the conquest of the Cyclades would have propaganda value as showing that the Persians had got over the effects of their failure at Naxos ten years before.[126] After taking the islands, the plan was for the fleet to sail on to Eretria and Athens, to be occupied by the troops on the ships.

But Darius' aim was wider; a year before the expedition, in 491, he had sent heralds to the Greek city-states demanding the ritual 'earth and water'.[127] These diplomatic initiatives by Darius on the eve of and during the campaign tend to confirm the view of the ancient historians that the Great King not only wished to punish the Athenians and Eretrians for aiding the Ionian rebels, but to occupy all the cities of Greece.[128] However, many researchers have pointed out that the Persian expeditionary force of 490 was too small to overrun all of Greece. This view, though, does not take into account the important advantages the Persians would gain by taking Athens and Eretria. The conquest of these cities would give Darius bases from which he could set out to seize the rest of the Greek cities in separate campaigns.[129] With Athens and Eretria fallen, morale in the other Greek cities that refused 'earth and water' to Darius would crumble. As a result, they would change their tune and accept Persian suzerainty, as so many others already had done before 490. Thus Datis – or whoever was commander – could begin the subjugation of all of Greece with new reinforcements from Asia and in collaboration with those Greeks who already were vassals of the Great King.

Most Greek city-states, in fact, did submit to Darius,[130] beginning with the island of Thasos.[131] Those cities that refused to knuckle under were a distinct minority, viz. Delos, Naxos, Karystos, Eretria, Plataia, Sparta and of course Athens. The two last-named cities were the most important of the refusers, and the only ones which we know expressly rejected the Great King's demands.[132] Herodotus writes that when the Athenians and Spartans heard out the Persian heralds and their 'earth and water' demand, they put the envoys to death at once; the Athenians threw the Persians over the *barathron*, a steep cliff outside the city limits where condemned criminals were similarly executed,[133] while the Spartans cast their visitors down a well. These more or less simultaneous actions by the Athenians and Spartans against the Persian envoys indicate that they were the result not of the momentary passion of an enraged populace but very likely the outcome of previous contacts between the two cities' authorities.[134] Pausanias asserts that it was Miltiades, later to serve as one of the ten Athenian generals at Marathon, who was chiefly responsible for executing the Persian envoys.[135] As we will see, Miltiades was very active in Athenian politics during the crisis, and proposed ways of meeting the Persian threat. He thus could very well have been the man who suggested hurling the envoys off the cliff.

Plutarch and Aelius Aristides claim that among the envoys was a Greek interpreter whose job it was to translate Darius' demands to the Athenians.[136] This man was not executed with the Persian heralds but put on trial.[137] Despite his status as a mere interpreter with no involvement in policymaking, he was sentenced to death and led to the *barathron*. He was convicted for collaborating with the enemy, thanks to his job, against the Greeks. He was also judged worthy of death for misusing the Greek tongue in the service of Darius.[138] The execution of the Persian envoys who were on official diplomatic business was a serious moral lapse by the standards of antiquity.[139] Yet the act indicated the determination of Athens and Sparta to fight the Persians to the death, leaving no room for any negotiations.

Regardless of the defiant stand of these two city-states against Darius, the Greeks were starting to feel the first consequences of his wrath before it came to armed blows. When the Aiginetans offered 'earth and water' to the Great King, the Athenians regarded it as an intent to join the Persians in the attack on Greece.[140] At that time the Athenians and Spartans had organized a punitive strike against Aigina to prevent it joining Persia.[141] The operation had been a success. A Spartan expeditionary force occupied Aigina, took several of its leading citizens hostage and delivered them to the Athenians.[142] This way Athens made sure that Aigina would be neutralized and not be able to offer the Persians any help when the Persian fleet appeared off mainland Greece.[143] The neutralizing of Aigina by those Greeks determined to resist Darius cannot mask the fact that the Persian ultimatum had another purpose besides that of subjugating the Greek cities. The Persians knew that not all Greeks would accept the 'earth and water' demands, and thus there would be a rift between the accepters and the rejecters. Given the intense rivalry among the Greek city-states, armed conflict along those lines might well have broken out just before Datis' expedition, easing the conquest of Greece. This *divide et impera* strategy of Darius was one characteristic of his empire's able diplomacy.[144]

The start of preparations for a campaign by Datis and Artaphernes would have been known to the Athenians who would have had a keen sense of impending danger. The arrival of the Persian envoys with Darius' ultimatum simply confirmed their fears. But the envoys' execution signalled that the Athenians' decision to fight without prior negotiation was irrevocable. A chasm of blood with the Great King had yawned open and no negotiation could bridge it. According to Aelius Aristides, when Darius heard about what the Athenians had done to his envoys, he was so enraged that he ordered shackles to be manufactured, numbering more than the estimated Athenian population.[145] These shackles would be used on the Athenians who would be thus led before Darius after the capture of Athens. It is possible that Aelius Aristides exaggerates here. Yet it is also possible that the Athenians feared that Darius intended to carry them all off to Asia in chains, as he had with the surviving Eretrians.[146] To the Athenians, however, the shackles would prove quite unnecessary, as they would either win the battle or die trying.

2. The Persian fleet in the eastern Aegean

In 491, after Darius himself had inspected Datis' and Artaphernes' expeditionary force at Susa, the troops left for the Aleian plain in Kilikia, which had been chosen as the assembly point for boarding the ships that would sail for Greece.[147] By the end of the winter of 491/90 the assembly was complete. The ports of Kilikia teemed with the ships of the Persian fleet including the horse-transports and the long warships. The task of the long ships was to both carry infantry and to protect the slower transports from possible attack by Greek warships during the crossing. By spring 490, with the sailing season at hand, the Persian fleet was ready to sail into the Aegean.

The Persian Empire, the greatest power the world had yet seen, was about to unleash on Greece a powerful military juggernaut consisting of masses of well-equipped infantry and cavalry, commanded by the ablest officers the empire could boast. The staff had well-defined aims which they planned to put into effect as soon as the army reached Greece, thanks to intelligence from local informers.[148] At the time the majority of Greek cities had submitted to Persia, as a result of Persian diplomacy; some, in fact, had actually gone to war with others that had not.[149] All this would have convinced an impartial observer in 490 that Darius would wreak his vengeance on the Athenians and Eretrians without too much trouble, and then set out to conquer Greece.

Herodotus reports that Samos was the Persian fleet's first stop in the Aegean.[150] Some modern scholars, however, claim that it touched first at Rhodes;[151] they refer to a passage from the *Lindos Chronicle* recording a siege of the city by 'a powerful force of Darius headed by Datis' that aimed to subjugate Greece.[152] This same document says that some Rhodians fled to refuge in the island's mountains and others to Lindos. Datis besieged Lindos but failed to take it, so he signed a truce with the inhabitants and left Rhodes. The *Lindos Chronicle* thus gives the impression that the city escaped Persian occupation, which is scarcely possible. Most likely the Lindians accepted Datis' terms of surrender, avoiding a massacre, and later dressed up the event as a military victory. If the Persians did attack Rhodes in 490, then Darius could have used Datis' expedition to take the Dodecanese as well.[153]

If we cannot be fully sure that the Persian fleet touched at Rhodes, we are quite certain that it did arrive at Samos. This island throughout antiquity was a strategic nexus for any fleet sailing into the Aegean from the Asian shores and headed for the Cyclades or mainland Greece.[154] Its indigenous black pine was considered excellent ship repair material. It was no accident that the great powers in control of the Aegean in ancient times maintained their largest naval stations on Samos.[155] In 490 Samos had been under Persian control for thirty years.[156] Its people had been among the first to rise against the Persian occupation in the Ionian Revolt; but in 494 the crews of fifty triremes that Samos had contributed to the Ionian rebel fleet defected to the enemy on the eve of the crucial battle of Lade.[157] This had been the result of secret collusion between the upper classes of Samos and the Persians, who thus spared the island the bloody vengeance they visited on the other Ionian rebels after crushing the revolt.[158] Thus when the Persians landed on Samos they had no need to carry out any military operation. Leaving Samos, the fleet bypassed Ikaria, where there were no port facilities, and set course for the Cyclades.[159]

3. The Persians seize the Cyclades and Karystos

It was not the first time that the Cyclades were the scene of Persian military operations. Almost a decade earlier, in 499, Aristagoras, the tyrant of Miletos; Artaphernes the Elder, the satrap of Lydia; and Persian admiral Megabates had moved against Naxos with a force of 200 triremes carrying Ionian and Persian troops. Darius had given his blessing to the expedition planned by his subordinates.[160] In 490, with a force three times as large, the Persians again attacked Naxos first. Though the Naxians in 499 had successfully resisted the siege, this time they fled to the mountains, despairing of any defence. The Persians captured any Naxian they could find and burned the city and its temples.[161]

The Persians reserved a harsh punishment for the Naxians; we don't know whether it was in retaliation for some Naxian resistance or whether it was in revenge for the resistance of nine years before.[162] The Naxians had taken no part in either the Ionian Revolt or in the burning of Sardis.[163] Consequently, they would not have been considered 'enemies' of Darius who had to be chastised. The clear message to all Greeks that the Great King sent through the destruction of Naxos was that they had to submit: either they capitulate voluntarily, or face disaster and death as the Naxians had.[164] Herodotus says that after Naxos the Persians intended to attack 'the other islands', without saying which.[165] The only specific move he records is the fleet sailing to the islet of Rheneia off Delos. The terrified Delians had already fled to neighbouring Tenos to seek refuge in the hills. As soon as Datis heard of that, he ordered the fleet to move to Rheneia rather than Delos proper. He sent a message to the inhabitants that they could return to Delos and that Darius had promised they would not be harmed; the people returned to their homes. A Persian mission set foot on Delos to burn 300 talents' worth of libations at the Temple of Apollo to honour the god.[166] By this Datis seems to have wanted to assuage the feelings of the Ionians serving in the Persian fleet.[167] He also may have wanted to gain the approval of the Greeks by displaying respect for their religion, employing a carrot-and-stick policy.[168]

Except for the events at Naxos, Rheneia and Delos, Herodotus gives us no more information on the Persian moves in the Cyclades. It is certain that all fell under Persian control, as we understand from Herodotus' statement that when the Persian fleet left Delos and sailed towards Euboia, it 'touched at the islands' to recruit manpower and take hostages.[169] By recruiting islanders the Persians had two aims: first, to man the fleet with experienced crews who knew well the waters and coasts of mainland Greece; and second, to keep the Cycladians docile, as their recruited men were also in effect hostages.[170] We don't know if the Cycladians contributed ships to the Persian fleet. Herodotus mentions just a single trireme given voluntarily by Paros.[171] Very likely the Persians left garrisons on their new island conquests.

The relatively swift overrunning of the Cyclades would tend to confirm Herodotus' assertion that 'the islanders' had offered 'earth and water' to Darius' heralds before the Persian fleet appeared.[172] It is intriguing that most of our information about the Persian conquest of the Cyclades in 490 comes not from Herodotus but from Aischylos, in whose play *The Persians* the people of Paros, Naxos, Mykonos, Tenos, Andros and Melos are all listed as Darius' subjects.[173] The conquest of the Cyclades is also attested from the contributions in ships and men which various islands gave to Xerxes' expedition ten years later. Naxos and Paros were the most important island states of the Cyclades and were among the strongest and wealthiest powers of Greece. In 500 the Naxians were able to field a hoplite force of some 8,000 men. Despite this asset, however, they were unable to stem the forces of Datis and Artaphernes. The fact that the Cyclades caved in relatively easily argues for the view that the Persian plan was effective and the expeditionary force strong and well-organized.[174] The summer of 490 was already underway when the Persian fleet sailed from the Cyclades heading for mainland Greece. As Krentz notes, the Persians left behind a 'double' column of smoke soaring into the skies: one rose from the smouldering ashes of Naxos and the other from the sacrificial altar of Apollo on Delos.[175] Scott interprets the message that Datis intended to send to the Greeks refusing to submit: 'We are not ruthless barbarians; submit to us and we will respect you and your gods; we only punish those who resist us.'[176]

The Greeks did not know where the Persians would strike first after their fleet sailed from the Cyclades. The mystery cleared a few days later when the Persian ships appeared off Karystos at the southern end of Euboia. The invaders disembarked there without meeting resistance.[177] They sent messengers to Karystos demanding men for their army and hostages. The Karystians refused, saying they would not fight their neighbours the Athenians and Eretrians. On receiving this reply the Persians began their siege of Karystos, burning the surrounding crops. According to Herodotus, after an initial skirmish the Karystians accepted the Persian demands.[178] The sight of the massive Persian army before the walls may well have melted the Karystians' resolve to resist. By seizing Karystos the invaders secured a large and safe supply base for the fleet's operations against mainland Greece. The place had another advantage in that it was equidistant from Eretria and the coast of Attica. The Persians thus felt that they could stage a surprise attack on either Eretria or Athens with equal facility.[179]

4. The siege and sack of Eretria

The capitulation of Karystos brought the realities of war closer to the Athenians and the Eretrians. Everyone awaited the next move of the Persian fleet, which turned north after leaving Karystos, when it became clear that Eretria was the next target. The move was logical in that Eretria was the weaker of the two Greek cities that were in the invaders' sights. It is axiomatic that an army which has the initiative and confronts two enemies would tackle the weaker one first. So far the Persians had carried out their campaign impeccably, leaving nothing to chance. But the Athenians, their main adversaries, had not been inactive. In the face of imminent enemy attack they actively sent the Eretrians aid when they asked for it, by despatching their *klerouchoi,* or settlers, to Euboia as a military reinforcement.[180] According to Herodotus, the *klerouchoi* arrived at Eretria before the Persian fleet. Herodotus numbers that force at 4,000 Athenians who lived on lands around Chalkis.[181] Elsewhere, Herodotus says that a similar number of *klerouchoi* had settled on lands that Athens seized from Chalkis after defeating it in battle in 506.[182] The men were therefore either the same original settlers or their sons whom Athens sent to succour the Eretrians in 490.[183] As Chalkis was close to Eretria, they could move there in a short time.[184]

In 490 Eretria was the chief city-state of Euboia since its main rival, Chalkis, had been utterly defeated by Athens several years earlier.[185] In 498 Eretria had sent help to the rebelling Ionians, an event that argues for some considerable power.[186] Plato is thus quite credible when he avers that at the time of the battle of Marathon the Eretrian soldiers 'were among the most renowned in Greece and not a few in number'.[187] Yet despite that reputation, it would appear that the Eretrians quailed before the imminent Persian attack. Instead of joining with the Athenian *klerouchoi* to resist the attack, the thought of the Persians swarming ashore made many Eretrians consider abandoning the city and fleeing to the mountains, as many of the islanders had done.[188] Some aristocrats toyed with the idea of surrendering the city and ancient sources imply that they conspired to aid the enemy by lowering the morale of the citizens.[189] In the end the Eretrians decided to shut themselves within the city walls and fight from there. It was a move that handed the initiative to the Persians. In a state of despair the Eretrians daily waited for the Persians to appear before their walls. Even those most determined to resist knew that they would not last long. In this situation the Athenian *klerouchoi* would be powerless to do anything; therefore Aischines, a local dignitary, advised them to leave Eretria and save themselves in order to defend their own city when the time would come.[190] If the Eretrians had any confidence that they could withstand the imminent Persian assault they would have enrolled the Athenian *klerouchoi* in their ranks rather than sending them away.[191] The latter crossed the Euboic Gulf, setting a course north of where the Persian fleet was operating and may even have begun the attack on Eretria, and landed in Attica at Oropos.[192] Thus the *klerouchoi* evaded contact with the Persians and suffered no losses. Their aim was to reach Athens and join the Athenian army;[193] but as we shall see, these men undertook an important special mission in Attica, joining up with the Athenian army only at Marathon.

The Persian forces hit the shore of southern Euboia simultaneously at three points: Tamynai, Choirea and Aigilia, from where they would advance on Eretria.[194] Older studies place these three locations at some distance from Eretria; Tamynai, for example, was believed to be some twenty kilometres away.[195] But more recent research indicates that the three landing places, named by Herodotus, were closer to Eretria than was previously thought.[196] The places where the Persians chose to land indicates that they planned the operation with meticulous care, with the aim of occupying Eretria in the shortest possible time. Herodotus says specifically that the Persian cavalry went ashore at Euboia, but makes no mention of how it could have been employed operationally.[197]

The Eretrians were grossly outnumbered, and thus Herodotus' claim that they were able to resist the Persian siege for six consecutive days comes as a surprise.[198] Many defenders fell at the city walls; the attackers also suffered serious losses. The Persians attacked with great vigour, indicating that Datis was willing to sacrifice many troops just to seize Eretria as soon as possible. Of course, that wasn't his sole objective, as Athens would be next. On the seventh day Eretria was betrayed by two of its leading citizens, Euphorbos and Philagros, who either secretly opened a postern gate to let the Persian hordes in, or deliberately abandoned a section of the wall they were charged with defending.[199] The Persians surged into Eretria, took the people captive and put the temples to the torch in retaliation for the burning of the Temple of Kybele in Sardis.[200] Plato claims that the Eretrians resisted for only three days, after which they were all captured.[201] Those few who escaped were caught in an efficient dragnet operation in which all the Persian troops moved in a single line, one man next to another, covering all the territory of Eretria, and effectively ensnared the fugitives.[202]

After depositing their captives on the islet of Aigilia in the south Euboic Gulf,[203] the Persians set sail for the shore of Attica. The Eretrian captives would remain on Aigilia under guard until after the battle at Marathon, when the retreating Persian fleet would pick them up and transport them to Asia as human booty to display to Darius.[204] The voyage as far as the Asia Minor coast and then overland to Susa would have been a severe ordeal, if we credit Philostratos, who claims that half the Eretrians perished on the way.[205] The survivors were led in chains before the Great King, who treated them leniently. Though he nursed resentment over the Eretrian support of the Ionian Revolt, he appeared satisfied at the sight of the hapless captives and did not penalize them. Darius ordered that they be resettled at Arderikka in Kissia.[206] As for Eretria, it was rebuilt in the middle of the fifth century by its neighbours the Styrians.[207]

Datis and Artaphernes, on behalf of the Great King, had duly punished one of the Greek cities that had rashly defied him by aiding the Ionian Revolt and burning Sardis. Now the chief target was Athens. The summer of 490 was about to draw to a close.[208] The Persians knew that the time for military operations was running out, that they would have to be on their way back to Asia within several weeks at the latest. Though Athens would not be as easy a target as Eretria, Persian morale was high. The city would fall quickly, either through battle or treachery, as had happened with Eretria.[209] So far the campaign had enjoyed one success after another, and there was nothing on the horizon that could cast a dark cloud over the Persian plans.

III: The Persians land at Marathon

1. Setting foot on Attic soil

Plato tells us that as soon as the Greeks heard that Eretria had fallen to the Persians, they were paralysed with fear.[210] This fear must have been felt especially by the Athenians, as they well knew that the Persian army, the weapon of the Great King's revenge, would now strike at their own city. In the back of their minds they may well have feared that within a few days Athens might cease to exist. Everything they had worked hard for would be lost. The public and sacred buildings in the Agora and on the Acropolis would fall into ruin, the pretty parks and gardens of Athens would be reduced to ashes. Families would be torn apart; the men, their wives and children would either be slain or become slaves in the depths of Asia, with no hope of ever returning to Attica. For almost the past ten years, though the Athenians had fretted over the coming clash with Darius, life had proceeded normally; in fact, impressive strides had been made in the arts and letters. Above all, they had begun to experience an altogether new lifestyle: they learned what it meant to live free, to hold their fate in their own hands without it being determined by a king, a tyrant or a few aristocrats. Now all that might well be about to end, and in the cruellest and most abrupt way. Yet the fear that gripped the Athenians when they heard of the fate of Eretria soon gave way to fury at the invaders who had entered their land to destroy their lives.[211] This sentiment provided the motive force for the Athenians to prepare to meet Datis' army when the time should come.

After occupying Eretria the Persians remained there inactive for a few days. Following the siege and sacking of the city, they would have needed a brief respite for rest and reorganization.[212] The staff officers, aided by Hippias, were finalizing the plans to land at Attica and march on Athens. It is clear that the invaders had a well-thought-out plan to occupy the city. As soon as their fleet had entered the Aegean they had left the Greeks wondering about their next moves. Even now at the eleventh hour, when the Athenians were aware that the Persians were on their doorstep, they still didn't know just when or where the enemy would step onto Attic soil.

A seaborne landing operation by a large army such as that commanded by Datis presupposes a suitable shoreline approachable by the ships and the troops on them. The sea near the shore would need to be very shallow for a good distance out, so that the landing troops could wade ashore with relative ease. On the other hand, the water further out would need to be deep enough to allow the ships to approach as near as possible. The ideal location for such an operation would be a sandy beach without shoals to endanger man or vessel. The beach would also need to front a wide plain where the land assault on Athens could be prepared. As soon as the troops could be organized on the plain, and supplies and fresh water secured, then the attack on Athens could get underway.

In all the coastline of Attica, two locations meet the aforementioned requirements; the beach at Marathon in northeast Attica and the beach of Phaleron south of Athens.[213] The Marathon shore is about eleven kilometres long, and that of Phaleron some four kilometres. Both beaches at the time were sandy and without rocks that could hinder a seaborne landing. Behind these beaches stretched plains with ample supplies and fresh water, enough to meet the needs of a large army and its many horses. The Persians would be able to form a temporary camp after landing and prepare for the march on Athens. The hinterland of Marathon is the plain of the same name, just as at Phaleron, where the plain is now covered by the southern suburbs of Athens. Phaleron would appear to be a wise choice for the Persians. The centre of Athens, the Agora, was just ten kilometres away, whereas Marathon was forty-two kilometres distant.[214] There were no natural barriers between Phaleron and Athens that would hinder an invading army. On the contrary, the mountain mass of Mount Pentelikon interposed between the city and Marathon.

In reality, however, the apparent advantages of Phaleron were disadvantages for an attacking army. The short distance from Athens would favour the defending Athenians who could quickly field a counter-force. An army, however powerful, is at its most vulnerable while landing on an open beach, especially when the enemy is in an entrenched position nearby. The Persians had cavalry, whose disembarkation would be a time-consuming business, and could only occur when control of the shore was secured. A few years before, in 511, a Spartan force had landed at Phaleron in order to seize Athens and topple Hippias' tyranny only to be decisively trounced by Hippias' army.[215] Yet before that, as far back as 546, ex-tyrant Peisistratos had staged a surprise landing at Marathon, defeating the force sent to stop him and occupying Athens.[216]

One of the great ironies of history involves Hippias, who played an important part in both of those prior actions. In 546 he had joined his father Peisistratos in the successful Marathon landing, while in 511 he had commanded the force that defeated the Spartans at Phaleron. In both cases Hippias had won, first on the offensive and then on the defensive. As fate would have it, fifty-six years from his first military operation at Marathon, Hippias would be there again. If anyone in 490 knew which parts of the Attic shoreline were best for a seaborne invasion, that man was Hippias, now guiding the Persians. Would he be lucky a third time? The final decision was made to land at Marathon. Phaleron must also have been under consideration, as after the battle the defeated Persians would attempt a landing there.

2. The place: Marathon in 490

To be able to analyse the Persian tactics before and during the battle at Marathon, we need to examine why they chose this location to start their move on Athens. We know the general characteristics of Marathon in

490 thanks to descriptions by ancient writers and more recent historical, archaeological and geological research.

Marathon is situated in northeast Attica.[217] In ancient times the district was bounded by Rhamnous to the north and Prasiaiai to the south. Its shoreline extends from the Kynosoura[218] promontory to the northern limits of today's Nea Makri. About halfway along the shoreline, at the present-day location of Aghios Panteleimon, a small inlet divides it in two.[219] The northern half is the beach of Schinias,[220] and the southern half, Marathon beach. This inlet at Aghios Panteleimon was probably formed by the Charadros River that once seems to have flowed into the sea at that point. The Kynosoura promontory protected almost the whole of Marathon Bay from the strong northerly winds that are typical of the eastern Attic climate towards the end of summer.[221] According to geological studies, the shoreline to the south of the inlet has not changed much since antiquity;[222] however, that of Schinias was probably a few hundred metres more inland than it is today.[223]

The principal main physical characteristic of Marathon is the extensive plain, about 9.5 kilometres long and 4.8 kilometres wide. In the east the plain meets the South Euboic Gulf, while spurs of Mount Pentelikon form its boundaries in the other directions.[224] These are Drakonera to the northeast, Stavrokoraki to the north, Kotroni to the northwest, Aphorismos to the southwest, and Agrieliki (or Agriliki) to the south. The heights form a crescent around the Marathon plain, the main extensions of which are Vranas in the northwest and Ano Souli in the northeast, where the modern town of Marathon is now. The plentiful springs running from Mount Pentelikon assured a ready supply of fresh water by means of a river and a few streams that flowed to the sea. This water was adequate even in the summer, when other watercourses in Attica were dry.[225] The main springs were the Makaria, Mati and Drakonera, which fed the Charadros (or Oenoe) River, the sole river in the plain. Until recently the Charadros split into two streams, the Skorpio (or Sechri) and the Kainourgio (New). In addition, the Marathon plain contained two marshes, the Great Marsh in the northeast and the Lesser Marsh, or Brexiza,[226] in the southwest. Recent geological studies show that in 490 the Great Marsh was a lagoon morphing into a swamp.[227] The Lesser (or Brexiza) Marsh also existed during antiquity since it began to form in the third millennium.[228] The Lesser Marsh was mostly drained during the 1930s, but it is possible to locate its extent with some accuracy in the southern part of the Marathon plain.[229]

Ancient literary sources say that the wider area of Marathon contained four separate communities: Marathon proper, Probalinthos, Oenoe and Trikorynthos (or Trikorythos).[230] In classical times these towns, or *demes*, belonged to a unified administration called the *Tetrapolis*, the origins of which are unknown. According to Stephanos Byzantios, the original name of the Tetrapolis was Hyttenia, as one of the deities that were worshipped in the four communities was named Hyttenios, which probably was connected with the Tetrapolis.[231] Yet this was not the chief deity worshipped at Marathon, as the administrative and religious centre of the Tetrapolis seems to have been the local shrine of Dionysos.[232] We know of the shrine and its function mainly through classical-era inscriptions, as its precise location remains unknown to this day.[233] The Marathon communities seem to have been towns in name only; we might better describe them as large villages.[234] The *deme* of Marathon was probably an exception, as in classical times it had enough of a population to be a town, especially as the majority of the people of the Tetrapolis were citizens of it. This emerges from the Assembly of the Five Hundred in Athens, where the *deme* of Marathon had ten deputies, Probalinthos five, Oenoe four and Trikorynthos just one.[235] Moreover, the *demarch* (head man of the *deme*) of the Marathonians was the chief official of the local Tetrapolis administration, as he was charged with officiating over the sacrifices attending the religious rituals of the time.[236] Thus it may be that the wider area of Marathon took the name of its main *deme* which would have been the only proper town.[237] The citizens of the Tetrapolis belonged to two Athenian tribes, the Aiantis (Marathon, Trikorynthos and Oenoe) and the Pandionis (Probalinthos).[238]

Many researchers have tried to locate the remains of the ancient *deme* of Marathon, suggesting various possible locations. Almost all, however, agree that it was in a different place than the modern town of the same name.[239] Most have concentrated on two areas: Vranas, which lies among the heights of Stavrokoraki, Kotroni and Agrieliki; and Plasi, three kilometres to the south near the coast. Both places have yielded up concentrations of ancient potsherds, portable objects and building foundations.[240] Archaeological excavations tend to favour both sites, showing that Vranas and Plasi were inhabited in classical times.[241] The evidence indicates that the settlement at Plasi flourished in the Archaic period, and Vranas in the Classical period. It is possible, then, that in Archaic times the *deme* of Marathon was located at the Plasi site and later moved inland to the Vranas.[242] One could speculate that this move took place in the aftermath of the battle of Marathon after the Persians destroyed the Plasi site.[243]

There was very likely already a small settlement at Vranas that was amalgamated with the Marathon *deme* after 490. Archaeological evidence also shows that the Plasi site continued to be inhabited into Classical times, though less in area than before.[244] This might explain why Ptolemy in the first century AD listed Marathon as a part of 'Inland Attica' rather than 'Coastal Attica'.[245] In that century Marathon was probably identifiable with the Vranas site, which was some four kilometres from the coast and hence could qualify as 'inland' rather than the 'coastal' Plasi. However, Greek archaeologist Vasileios Petrakos suggests that the Marathonians at the time of the battle lived mainly in farming homesteads scattered over the plain, and did not form the pattern of a typical Attic town.[246] In such a case the *deme* of Marathon would have covered a large area including the Plasi and Vranas sites as well as the land in between.

Though some progress has been made in trying to determine the precise location of the Marathon *deme*, the locations of the other members of the Tetrapolis remain unknown, as so far no unmistakable remains of their public buildings have been found. But the few references in ancient writings, the discovery of inscriptions, excavations of burial grounds and the few remains of edifices that have come to light all suggest possible locations. Thus most researchers would place Oenoe in the gorge that is now called Ninoi, two kilometres west of today's Marathon town.[247] Here, near a Frankish-era tower, traces of Classical and Hellenistic habitations have been found, possibly belonging to ancient Oenoe. One of the main finds is an extensive Roman-era public building that some have identified with the 'Pythion' of Marathon, known from literary and epigraphic sources; others believe it was connected to a spring that is still nearby.[248]

In the wider area there is a cave inside which a shrine to Pan operated; Pausanias mentions it, and it appears to have been within the bounds of Oenoe. As for Trikorynthos, scholars place it north of the Great Marsh, in a place that has yielded archaeological relics dating from prehistoric times right up to the Byzantine era.[249] Archaeologists place the prehistoric citadel of Trikorynthos on a hill near the Makaria spring.[250] The remains of a proto-Helladic (3000–1900) settlement have been found near the present-day Olympic Rowing Complex. The same location has yielded up later remains of human habitation, from the Geometric to the Roman eras. These include a large Classical-era cemetery that probably belonged to Trikorynthos and was in use at the time of the battle of Marathon.[251] Probalinthos, lastly, is placed by scholars at the south end of the Marathon plain in the present-day districts of Valaria, Brexiza and Xylokeriza.[252] In the last-named location a Classical-era grave stele has been found with the names of Probalinthos citizens on it.[253] This would place Probalinthos, or a part of it, in that place. Moreover, on the basis of the method of geographical description by Strabo, Probalinthos would have been the southernmost community of Marathon.[254]

In ancient times the plain of Marathon was one of the most fertile in Attica, cultivating mainly wheat.[255] Its farming output was relatively high in relation to its population, and much of it would have been routed to Athens.[256] It is also quite possible that the Marathonians cultivated fruit and vegetables for the Athens market, much as they do today. Marathon may not have had many fruit trees, whose produce would have been for local consumption only.[257] Vineyards would have been scarce, as few ancient sources mention any, and there is no mention at all of local wine.[258] This may read strangely, as we know that Dionysos, the god of wine, was the main deity worshipped in the Tetrapolis. But the fertile Marathon plain would have been better for growing wheat, a more important staple for the people than grapes.[259] The cultivation of the vine at Marathon, in fact, began much later, after the establishment of the modern Greek state in the nineteenth century when some of the marshes were drained.[260] The wider area of the Tetrapolis also included a lot of grazing land, mainly at the base of the mountains. Stockbreeding seems to have been highly developed in Marathon in ancient times.[261] The bull emblem of the Marathon *deme*, besides commemorating the myth of Theseus' seizure of the 'Cretan bull' in that area, could also have been a reference to local stockbreeding.[262] A fifth century inscription probably intended to honour the Athenians who fell in the battle refers to the plain as *portitrophos*, or 'bovine-nourishing'.[263]

3. Why did the Persians pick Marathon?

The Marathon shoreline had several natural advantages for a Persian amphibious landing. There would be ample food supplies stored in homes for the invaders to use. The Persian horses would have plenty of grazing ground in the wide and fertile plain, while the scattered farmsteads would provide drinking water from their wells.[264] Thus the problems of supply would be solved for the Persians.[265] There was also, however, a political dimension to the choice of Marathon as a springboard for the attack on Athens. Herodotus hints that it was Hippias who advised the Persians to land there.[266] As we have seen, in 546 he had been with his father Peisistratos on an identical campaign; even at the young age of about twenty-three, Hippias had advised his father to re-enter Athens and regain power after his second exile.[267] As Hippias had helped plan that operation at Marathon, many years later he was in a position to offer the Persians the benefits of his own experiences. The Persians in 490, like Peisistratos in 546, sailed to Attica from the Eretrian coast. Peisistratos had met no opposition to his landing, while his forces had joined those of his Athenian supporters at Marathon. His political foes had delayed moving against him, doing so only after learning that he was on his way to Athens. The counter-marching defenders had encamped at Pallene, near the temple of Pallas Athene. Peisistratos pounced on them as soon as they finished their midday meal as they were either sleeping or playing dice, and decisively routed them. Peisistratos returned in triumph as tyrant of Athens.[268]

We do not know the size of the force that Peisistratos landed at Marathon in 546, though it would have been much smaller than the Persian force. It would have consisted of a sizeable body of infantry and probably cavalry, as Peisistratos' Eretrian allies could field some of the best cavalry in southern Greece.[269] His landing at Marathon was in fact the paradigm for all the factors involved in disembarking a large military force and preparing for a march on Athens. Hippias would have been well aware of how it could be done, and probably believed that many Marathonians supported him, not only because they had helped his father but also because the Peisistratid tyranny had done much for the small farmers who were a majority in the area. Hippias certainly hoped for a welcome from the Marathonians in 490.[270]

Herodotus attributes the Persian decision to land at Marathon to the fact that it was not far from Eretria and that the terrain was suitable for cavalry operations. If the Persians had picked Phaleron they would have had to sail all the way around Cape Sounion, a voyage of many hours that would have exposed the fleet to attack by the Athenian navy. The Athenians would also have been given time to entrench themselves at Phaleron, depriving the invaders of the advantage of surprise. The Persians, moreover, were not fans of sea voyages and memories will have been fresh of the destruction of their fleet off Mount Athos two years before. Most of the ships in the Persian fleet were Phoenician. Though the Phoenicians were a maritime people, they would not have been familiar with the waters around mainland Greece. Even in the summer, Greek seas can be plagued with dangerous currents and winds making navigation difficult.[271] A voyage from Euboia to Phaleron would encounter strong winds and currents. Thus Herodotus' belief that the Persians picked Marathon because of its proximity to Eretria – some 18 nautical miles – rings true. It would greatly shorten the Persians' trip to Attica.

Herodotus also notes that Marathon appealed to the Persians because their cavalry could operate easily.[272] Kratinos, a fifth century comic writer, calls Marathon 'a perfect place for cavalry'.[273] Yet an ancient commentator on Plato disparages Marathon as 'stony, unfit for horses, and full of mud, swamps and ponds'.[274] This observation, which contradicts Herodotus and Kratinos, has been used by some modern scholars to argue that the Persians made a mistake in choosing Marathon, which turned out to hinder the use of their cavalry during the battle.[275] The assertion by the commentator on Plato does contain some truth, as there were marshes and ravines at Marathon in ancient times.[276] But it avoids mention of the extensive plain which was, according to Herodotus and Kratinos, suitable for cavalry. Hippias was experienced in the use of cavalry in warfare; in 511 he had hired 1,000 Thessalian horsemen who repulsed the Spartans at Phaleron, and had cut down all the trees in the area to enable the horsemen to operate.[277] Hippias may well have urged a landing at Marathon also because he knew that the cavalry would have a free field of operations there.[278]

Besides the aforementioned advantages, Herodotus would have been aware of more reasons why the Persians picked Marathon. Yet his basic arguments have been rejected by some twentieth century scholars, who claim that the 'real' reasons remain unknown as the Persians landed at Marathon despite knowing that the area was not suitable for an advance on Athens. Their sole explanation is that Marathon was chosen in order to draw the Athenian army away from the city so that the Persians could sail round to Phaleron and seize the unguarded city from that direction.[279] Such a conclusion appears to be based exclusively on Herodotus' narrative, ignoring the physical advantages Marathon would have offered. The adherents of this theory seem to be unaware of the fact that the Persians had planned their attack on Athens with great care. As we have seen, they achieved all their strategic objectives, quite possibly on schedule. After careful thought they would have decided on Marathon as the best place from which to launch an attack. Hippias, for his own reasons, may well have concurred. But almost certainly the Persian staff would have examined the issue from all angles before the decision to land. And there may have been other factors unknown to us.

One factor which would have weighed heavily with the Persians was that their tactic would cause problems for the Athenians' defence strategy. It seems scarcely possible that their aim was to draw out the Athenian army and sneak round to take Athens by surprise. But, once at Marathon, the Persians left the Athenians two alternatives: either shut themselves up behind their walls,[280] or march out to meet the invaders in a pitched battle. In the first case the Athenians would be obliged to leave the rest of Attica at the mercy of the enemy; worse, they would give up the initiative. The Eretrians had chosen to defend themselves within their walls, leaving the terrain to the Persians, and had been destroyed. Moreover, if the Athenians remained behind their walls, the Spartans would be unable to help.[281] At any rate, it was of little concern to the Persians what the Athenians might do, as they were confident that their superior numbers would overcome any resistance on their way to the city. They imagined that at the mere sight of the great army the Athenians would capitulate without a fight.[282] But if they chose to fight, their defeat would be certain. Datis and Artaphernes might well have wished for the latter, as victory in battle would give them a prestige greater than if they had merely besieged Athens and taken its surrender.

The Persian move on Athens, as we shall see, came very close to success. But it was to be catastrophically derailed by one characteristic of the environment at Marathon which the Athenians would use to great effect and which was ignored by the Persian commanders to their detriment.

4. Persian operations at Marathon and the Athenians' first line of defence

The writer known as Pseudo-Plutarch reports that as soon as the Persians landed at Marathon and set up their camp, Datis 'declared war' on the local people.[283] Lending weight to this assertion are passages by (the real) Plutarch and the writer called Pseudo-Demosthenes that Datis' forces ravaged the area.[284] This would likely include the Tetrapolis and its member-communities. Excavations in the Marathon plain tend to confirm some damage inflicted around 490.[285] Yet such a claim vitiates the theory that most Marathonians supported the ex-tyrant's regime and were friendly towards Hippias, and therefore would welcome him even with a Persian escort. What could have happened is that even if Hippias believed he would be welcomed back, once the Persians saw that it would not happen they moved to intimidate the locals into avoiding any action that might hinder their campaign.

Possibly Datis sent an ultimatum to the people of the Tetrapolis demanding their cooperation, and when they either refused or did not reply, attacked their towns. In such a case the Marathonians would be expected to flee.[286] This would suit the Persians, as crowds of local men, women and children would seek shelter at Athens, on the way spreading fearful reports of the size of the enemy hordes and possibly exaggerated stories of their killings and depredations. These crowds of refugees, swelled by other people in eastern Attica, would hinder any Athenian expeditionary force that might march out from Athens and quite possibly deal a blow to the soldiers' morale.

The Athenians could not have had prior knowledge of where in Attica the Persians would land; for all they knew, it might be at Phaleron. Herodotus appears to have it right when he says that the Athenian army set out from the city as soon as word arrived of the Persian landing at Marathon. A careful study of the evidence reveals the source of the Athenians' information about the movements of the Persian fleet. The aforementioned 4,000 Athenian *klerouchoi,* after leaving Eretria to its fate, undertook to monitor the enemy's movements and constantly inform the authorities at Athens.[287]A few days before the landing the *klerouchoi* had been at Oropos, heading south to join up with the Athenian army. They used the northeast Attica coast road from Oropos to Athens, which afforded them a view of the Eretrian coast across the water.[288] They would thus have been in a position to observe the hundreds of Persian ships in the southern Euboic Gulf. They would not have needed news of the fall of Eretria, as the destruction of the city, marked by palls of smoke, would have been quite visible. Within a few days – maybe not more than three – as soon as the Persian fleet headed for the Attic coast the *klerouchoi* would have been able to determine just where it was going to land – the bay of Marathon. They would have immediately relayed the news to the Athenian authorities.[289]

We may speculate that the *klerouchoi* were instructed to remain within sight of the probable landing spot to act as observers and possibly form a front line of skirmishers to prepare for the arrival of the Athenian army. The *klerouchoi* could also have been charged with preparing the ground for the Greek expeditionary force. One such main task would be to scout around for a suitable campsite for thousands of Greek troops and make sure that it had access routes and fresh water sources, plus ease of access to farmsteads for food supplies. So it's probable that the Athenians were receiving intelligence in real time before the Persians even set foot at Marathon.[290]

Relatively few men will have been entrusted with the task of monitoring the Persian fleet as it sailed from Euboia to Marathon. Very likely most of the Athenian *klerouchoi* – perhaps aided by the people of the Tetrapolis and other communities in northeast Attica, including the *deme* of Rhamnous[291] – took over other duties. Most of the local manpower would have gone into planning an initial line of defence and preparing the logistics for the Greek army. We presume that with the phrase, 'As soon as the Athenians were informed of the news [of the Persian landing at Marathon], they went to help those already at Marathon', Herodotus indicates that there was already a body of men at Marathon to whose aid the Athenians rushed with their expeditionary force.[292] It cannot refer, as some scholars believe, only to the people of Marathon or the local conscripts of the four communities who stayed to await the arrival of the Athenian force.[293] As we have seen, in 490 the population of the Tetrapolis was far too small – a few hundred men at most – to be able to put up resistance to the Persians, and therefore could not have made up the body of men that Herodotus implies the Athenians went to help.[294] The Athenian staff knew that the occupation of the communities of Marathon, perhaps with the exception of Probalinthos, could not be prevented. They would fall to the Persians before the Athenian army could get to the area. It is therefore reasonable to suppose that the men who were already at Marathon, whom the Athenians would reinforce from the city, were the some 4,000 Athenian *klerouchoi*, possibly joined by the local conscripts.

The biggest risk for an amphibious invasion force landing in enemy territory is a counterattack at the time of landing. The defender seeks to hit the attackers at their most vulnerable, striking the landing craft with long-range weapons as they approach the shore. The Persians, however, encountered no opposition when they landed at Marathon, which shows that even if the *klerouchoi* were in the area, which we believe they were, they would not risk tangling with such a large attacking force. The Persians occupied the Marathon plain with ease, gaining an initial advantage over the Athenians. Even though unopposed, the landing must have been a difficult and complicated business because of the sheer number of ships and the need to disembark cavalry as well as infantry. Getting horses off the vessels onto a shore lacking dock facilities would have been no easy matter, and was possible only after full control of the shore was secured.[295] A few days before, the cavalry had been landed at Eretria, therefore we may assume the Persians had some experience of this type of task; nonetheless, it would still be time-consuming. After the procedures of landing, the next step was to secure the whole Marathon plain and arrange for the camp to be set up in preparation for the march on Athens. Most commentators reasonably suppose that the Persians needed one or two days rather than hours for the purpose.

Some writers have questioned why the Persians did not hasten to secure the routes from Marathon to Athens right after their landing.[296]

Noah Whatley attempts to explain such strange inertia on the part of the Persians by presuming that it would make no sense while the army was still in the process of disembarkation.[297] It could be done, on the contrary, when disembarkation was complete, as the whole force would be required.[298] Whatley also says that there was no strategic pass such as Thermopylai that an attacker would need to secure for an unopposed move on Athens.[299] We believe that view to be mistaken. The Persians would ultimately fail at Marathon because they failed to secure the Brexiza Pass at the southern end of the Marathon plain that was the sole exit point on the road to Athens.[300]

The Persians, of course, had no intention of remaining at Marathon after their disembarkation was completed and supplies secured. Athens was the prime objective, to be attacked by all the available forces. But the plan was held up by the appearance of an Athenian force, likely made up of the *klerouchoi* and local conscripts at precisely the route the Persians would have to take through the Brexiza Pass. As a result, the invaders postponed an immediate move and stayed in the Marathon plain to see what would happen. If the Athenians refused to give in, there would be a fight at Marathon. This initial hurdle to the planned Persian march on Athens was no accident; it indicates the Greek state of readiness even before the Persians landed, and the speed and accuracy of the intelligence they had about the enemy's movements after the destruction of Eretria.

5. Hippias: a marginal figure

When the Persians set fire to the temples of Eretria and eliminated its population, they knew well that news of such brutality would quickly reach the Athenians and the other Greeks, and strike fear into them. Possibly the Persians resorted to such measures specifically to hurt Greek morale, especially among their main foes, the Athenians. The message was clear: the Eretrians' fate or an even worse one awaited the Athenians unless they capitulated unconditionally and without resistance. Some information is available from several ancient sources that claim that immediately after the sacking of Eretria, Datis sent an ultimatum to Athens warning the city that it could expect worse than the Eretrians had suffered if they did not give in.[301]

It appears, however, that the fate of Eretria had an effect opposite to what the Persians intended. The Athenians figured that even if they did surrender, they would not escape Persian vengeance. They thus had no other choice but to fight to the last. Either they would win or all die fighting. During those tense days the Athenians seem to have come to the conclusion that the Persians' real goal was to destroy their city and not merely to restore Hippias to power. This in turn deprived the tyrannophile party in Athens of any argument in favour of peacefully submitting to Darius and installing Hippias once again as tyrant. This could be why not a single ancient literary source makes the slightest mention of activities of tyrannophiles in Athens who might be presumed to work for Hippias' return prior to the battle of Marathon.[302]

Interestingly, some scholars note that among the expeditionary force that the Athenians sent to Marathon was Hipparchos, the son of Charmos and very likely a grandson of Hippias.[303] In the decade before 490 Hipparchos was considered the leader of the Peisistratid party in Athens. This, however, did not prevent him from exercising considerable political influence in the first years of democratic rule, as in 496/95 he was elected Eponymous Archon.[304] Hippias might well have hoped to meet Hipparchos at Marathon as the representative of a friendly Athenian delegation that would hand him the rule of the city. That, of course, did not happen, and if Hippias' presumed grandson did take part in the Athenian expeditionary force, Hippias would have realized that such a hope of Athenian support was a vain one. Hippias had been away from Athens for twenty years, and must not have been conversant with the new political conditions in the city.[305] The great mass of *thetes* [the lowest class of citizens – *tr.*] who once would have supported him had since benefited from the reforms of Kleisthenes and democratic rule, many of them obtaining land in Chalkis as *klerouchoi*. Yet members of the upper classes as well, once supporters of the Hippias tyranny, had since gained important posts in the democracy and pursued their interests through the new regime.

Herodotus writes that as soon as the elderly Hippias disembarked at Marathon he sneezed, dislodging a tooth that fell onto the beach. Despite a thorough search, he failed to find the tooth and told those who were near him that 'this land did not belong to them and they would not conquer it,' and that 'the only piece of Attica that would be his was the earth that covered his lost tooth'.[306] It's an entertaining story, and Herodotus no doubt employed it to lighten his narrative at a crucial point with a bit of comic relief.[307] Even if the story was authentic and Herodotus heard it from a reliable source, he inserted it deliberately, though its importance was minimal. The historian seems to have wanted to stress that as soon as Hippias set foot at Marathon he realized that he had no real political support left in Athens. On the beach at Marathon Hippias lost not only a tooth but also the whole gamble of a bloodless restoration of his rule at Athens.[308] When the Persians at Marathon saw that the Athenians were determined to resist by force of arms, Hippias ceased to be of any use to them. Significantly, Herodotus makes no more mention of Hippias as a factor in the Persian expedition. The game of politics and impressions was over. The next move now was up to Datis and his powerful army.

Chapter 2

The Athenian Army in 490

The destruction of Eretria by the Persians struck fear and panic into all Greeks. However, the Athenians, the number one objective of Darius' army, had been preparing themselves in time and had taken the necessary measures to meet the looming danger. Though only Sparta and Plataia responded to the Athenians' call for help, the majority of the male population of Athens was mobilized in what ancient Greek writers term a 'pandemia' or 'panstratia'. By the end of summer 490 the Athenian expeditionary force had been formed by a mainly voluntary recruitment of citizens who had been amply forewarned and were prepared to meet the invaders who had landed at Attica.

These men had a high level of morale and a strong sense of duty that motivated them to join up at the critical hour and be sent to Marathon. The Athenian soldiers were not professionals. Only the upper classes served as hoplites, who in 490 numbered about 9,000. But also recruited were light-armed troops, who would have been more than the hoplites, say between 10,000 and 15,000 men. These were thetes, the lowest and most populous Athenian social class. So critical was the hour that Athenian slaves were freed and sent to join the Marathon expeditionary force. The only external help for the Athenians before the battle was sent by the Plataians, who numbered 1,000 or fewer. Thus the Greek force sent to Marathon numbered between 20,000 and 25,000 men, and not 9,000–10,000, as most scholars believe.

Neither were the Athenian commanders professional soldiers. They were members of the upper social class and opposed to the tyranny. The commander-in-chief of the Athenian army in 490 was the Polemarch Kallimachos, under whom served ten generals, one from each Athenian tribe. The ten generals had equal authority; but the one who stood out, thanks to his initiative in preparing the Athenians for war was Miltiades. He was one of the few Athenians of his time who had experience of Persian war tactics; he was a personal foe not only of Hippias but also of the Persians. The Athenians knew he was determined to fight the Persians to the last, and this probably ensured his election as general of the Oineis tribe in 490.

1. Preliminary remarks

News of the Persian landing at Marathon travelled to Athens very quickly. According to Aelius Aristides, as soon as this worrisome event became known the Athenians flocked to their temples to ask for the gods' help in the struggle they knew would come.[1] They did not rely solely on the gods' favour, however, but by applying the maxim that Athene helps those who help themselves, they took immediate practical measures to confront the deadly danger. The Athenians sent their army at once to Marathon to meet the Persians there.[2] Before that happened, they had requested military assistance from the Spartans.[3] We can be certain that these moves were decided by the last Assembly to convene before the battle of Marathon, as we presume that in the few days before the Persian landing the Assembly speaker whose tribe held the Prytany, or presidency, would have called an emergency meeting.[4]

The vote on the urgent measures to save the city indicates that the whole citizen body was involved, as all public affairs were determined by Assembly vote.[5] If the Persians were to seize Athens the citizens would lose their liberty and perhaps their lives as well. This would explain the unanimity behind the decisions, according to Plato, displayed by all Athenian social classes when it became clear the Persians would attack.[6] It is also probably why we hear nothing of any pro-Persian activity by those in Athens who might take advantage of the turmoil to overthrow the democratic regime.[7] We find no mention in our sources of any panic-stricken Athenians who might have fled to the hills to escape the invaders, as occurred in other cities that Datis' army attacked. In the late summer of 490 the salvation of Athens hung on the willing resistance of all its citizens, who had before them the stark choice of victory or death.

A courier by the name of Pheidippides, whom Herodotus calls a *hemerodromos,* or 'day-runner', was detailed to carry the Athenian request for help to Sparta, which some time before had pledged to send military aid to the Athenians whenever they needed it.[8] The runner's task was not to persuade the Spartans to march but to notify them that the time had come for them to do so.[9] Herodotus says Pheidippides addressed the 'Archons' of Sparta, who would have been the Ephors, who were responsible for the conduct of Spartan foreign policy.[10] From what the courier said it was apparent that Eretria had already fallen and Athens was in danger.[11] Yet he appears to have mentioned nothing about the Persian landing at Marathon; therefore, we may place the timing of his mission within the few days between the sack of Eretria and the landing. Pheidippides seems to have been sent to Sparta while the Athenian army was still in the city and in a state of readiness, prepared at any moment to leave for Marathon to meet the Persians. Besides Sparta, the only other city pledging aid to the Athenians was Plataia in Boiotia. One assumes that a courier requesting help would have been sent to Plataia as well. A few years before, Plataia had narrowly escaped destruction at the hands of its main rival Thebes; it had allied with Athens which helped it defeat Thebes. Since then Plataia, faithful to Athens, had essentially become an Athenian protectorate.[12]

The Spartans had their own reasons for standing by the Athenians in their hour of need. In 510 they had toppled Hippias, but soon repented and attempted to restore him to power; in 507 and 506, under King Kleomenes I, they twice invaded Attica to overthrow the newly-minted democratic polity, but failed both times.[13] Yet the Spartans in 490 knew well that if the Persians took Athens it would be the first step towards that Asian superpower's conquest of all Greece, including Sparta. Hence they agreed to provide Athens with military help if it were needed. But when Pheidippides informed the Spartans that the time had come, they claimed religious reasons for not sending a force at once. It happened to be the ninth day of the month, and as the Spartans told the Athenian courier, no army was allowed to march before the full moon.[14] This proffered reason was accepted by many writers of later antiquity;[15] a more modern explanation is that what held the Spartans back was the celebration of the 'Karneia' festival, in honour of Apollo Karneios, a period in which all military operations were banned.[16]

Plato, on the other hand, avers that the Spartans were unable to send a force to help Athens because at the time they were fighting Messenian helots who had rebelled.[17] He adds that when the Spartans finally marched they were too late by one day to participate in the battle, though other ancient sources claim that they got to Marathon three days after the battle.[18] Plato's assertion does not appear to be accurate, yet we must note that even he wonders whether there was some other reason why the Spartans delayed their march. Plato, moreover, does not mention

Herodotus' reason for the delay, though he must have been aware of it.[19] On the other hand, the claim that the Messenians rebelled against the Spartans in 490, thus tying up the latter, finds no support in the available evidence, and modern arguments in favour of that interpretation are not convincing.[20]

2. Hoplites and horsemen in early Classical Athens

The Persian danger mobilized almost all the Athenian citizens who could bear arms. Before the Persian ships landed at Marathon these men already had been formed into the expeditionary force ready to march to meet the invaders. In the late Archaic and early Classical periods the backbone of the Athenian and other Greek armies were the hoplites. At the time of the battle the Athenians had a small corps of cavalry, but the horsemen seem to have fought as foot soldiers. Besides the hoplites, the Archaic Greek city-states fielded light-armed troops who fought with a variety of weapons. Most recent commentators believe that the Athenian expeditionary force at Marathon consisted wholly of hoplites; but as we shall see, a considerable number of light-armed troops fought as well.

At the time of Marathon Athens did not have a professional army.[21] The citizenry undertook the defence of the city with what weaponry it had; the hoplites had little military training and the light-armed soldiers almost none. The commanders and officers, moreover, were not professional soldiers.[22] That is why the commanders of the Athenian army had relatively little authority over their men, while discipline depended largely on the conscience and good sense of the individual soldier.[23] It needs to be emphasized that it was the Assembly that ordered the army to march, and that the army was made up of citizens, hence the commanders were answerable to the Assembly.[24] This was in contrast to the Persian army, whose commanders were answerable to the Great King who appointed them.

Therefore, in all their decisions the Athenian commanders had to take into account the wishes of the citizen-soldiers.[25] In 490 there was no such thing as unquestioning soldier obedience to superiors, as in all modern armies where the subordination of lower to higher ranks is paramount.[26] The Athenian army of the time functioned as a club of equals, whose officers could not arbitrarily make decisions but had to secure the agreement of their men.[27] The only way to gain the confidence of the men was through valour in combat. Thus the Athenian commanders fought in the front line, leading their men forward; the result being that they sustained a disproportionate number of casualties in relation to their men, even when their side won.[28] Such an army would either achieve greatness or disgrace, depending in large measure on its leadership.

In the sixth and fifth centuries the *hoplite phalanx*[29] was the basic military formation adopted by the Greek city-states.[30] The hoplites were heavy-armed soldiers, each of whom wore a breastplate, greaves and a helmet as defensive weaponry. These were made of bronze and sometimes iron. The basic offensive weapon of the hoplite was the spear, which he used to deliver close-order thrusts at the enemy.[31] The hoplite held the spear at all times during a battle, and only in emergencies, such as when his life was in danger, did he throw it at the enemy like a javelin. He used it as soldiers of later generations would use the lance. If a hoplite's spear broke or became useless during an action then he would use his short sword as an offensive weapon. But the use of the sword was not common, and occurred only when man-to-man combat was unusually prolonged. In the battle of Marathon, for example, the sword was used extensively precisely because the fighting was drawn out.

The hoplite's basic defensive weapon was the shield. This was made of thin bronze plate attached to a wooden base, circular in shape and convex. Early shields had a bronze handle attached to the inside and a strap. To hold his shield the hoplite would insert his arm through the strap and grasp the handle. From about 725 onwards two handles appear on shields, one large on the inside centre, the *porpax*, and a smaller one near the rim, the *antilabe*. The hoplite would insert his arm through the *porpax* and grab the *antilabe* with his hand.[32] This innovation enabled hoplites to use heavier shields that would correspondingly lend more protection. This new shield determined the direction of tactics to be used by a hoplite line before and during a battle, as all movements by soldiers in the line depended on how they used their shields.[33] The impression was of a moving wall of metal. Inside the shield was a large leather strap, the *telamon*. When not fighting, the hoplite would carry his shield by slinging the *telamon* over his shoulder so that he would not get tired.

Every hoplite in line carried his shield in such a way as to simultaneously protect his left side and the right side of the hoplite on his left. Thus they could all advance towards the enemy with their shields close together, which gave them cover. This offered protection from the projectiles of the enemy and minimized losses from that quarter before joining battle. When two opposing lines clashed, the hoplites in the front line would strike their shields against those of the enemy while using their spears to stab at the enemy over the shields or through the chinks between them.[34] The battle was decided when one line broke, to be pursued by the victors with spears and swords. This pursuit, however, was always relatively brief.[35] A clash of hoplites was usually a short affair,[36] and serious casualties were rare, even among the losers.[37]

Hoplite tactics depended on the self-discipline of each man.[38] If even one hoplite were to fall back in combat, he would leave the next man unprotected, possibly resulting in a chain reaction as every man did likewise. The first thing a terrified hoplite would do was throw away his shield, whose weight would hinder his flight.[39] Thus the shield, in addition to its defensive function, acquired a symbolic value by which to assess the valour of a soldier. The *ripsaspis*, or 'shield-jettisoner', was not only a coward who threw away his basic weapon (the *hoplon*, from which the term hoplite derives[40]), he ceased to be a hoplite, and worse, was considered a traitor.[41] By his action he was deemed to have exposed to serious danger not only his fellows but also the whole hoplite phalanx and by extension his city, as he could well have opened a breach through which the enemy could enter.

The hoplites fought all together as a unit. Therefore any man who abandoned his position in the phalanx, either to retreat or to surge ahead, would create a break in it. That is why the basic hoplite equipment was the shield. But certainly any soldier who appeared in formation lacking a breastplate or helmet would not be accepted by the officers who had the duty of inspecting every item of the hoplite's equipment.[42] To leave any part of the body unarmoured would render the soldier more vulnerable to death or wounding, which would endanger his fellows and hence the whole line.[43] In the same context no citizen not in perfect health or somehow disabled would be allowed to fight as a hoplite, as they, too, would be liabilities.[44] Beyond the weaponry, a basic quality of the hoplite phalanx was the psychological bond among its members. Every hoplite was highly important for the others, especially those on his immediate left and right.[45] It was thus understandable that hoplites with a common local background, as well as friends and family members, would be placed in the same section of the phalanx.[46] Thus the hoplite line consisted of men of equal importance, so during a battle they could be pulled out of the line and transferred to another sector according to need.[47]

A soldier in a Greek city-state hoplite force had to have the economic means to purchase his shield, helmet, breastplate, and all the rest of his equipment, as it was not provided by the city. These were high-value items made of bronze, which was an expensive material in antiquity. The equipment for a single hoplite took many days of work by several craftsmen. Its cost was therefore considerable, and only citizens with a relatively high income could afford it. Thus the possession of such weapons, usually displayed in peacetime in a conspicuous place in the house such as on the wall above the hearth, was a sign of the family's wealth and influence.[48] An Athenian inscription dated to about 500 mentions hoplite equipment worth 30 drachmai.[49] This must have been at the low end of the scale for such prices at the start of the Classical era.[50] It represented two months' income for the best-paid thetes, the lowest citizen class at the acme of Athens' development.[51] It is worth mentioning that in 484, when the Athenians considered distributing the profits from the large silver deposits that had been discovered at Laurion, they figured them at 10 drachmai per citizen, a not inconsiderable sum for the time.[52]

Most of the information on the Athenians who served in the hoplite army derives from Classical-era sources, and deals with those citizen classes that a century before had been established by the laws of Solon.[53] The more recent reforms of Kleisthenes do not seem to have altered this scheme.[54] The scale of incomes was based on the annual yield of owned land, in dry and liquid produce, the basic unit of measurement being the *medimnos*, or bushel.[55] The wealthiest Athenians, who could produce at least 500 bushels, belonged to the five-hundred-busheller class (*pentakosiomedimnoi*). This was the highest class of Athenian society, which at the time of the battle of Marathon consisted of the landed aristocracy owning extensive estates. Next came the knights (*hippeis*), whose income needed to be at least 300 bushels a year. This enabled a knight to buy and maintain a war-horse, hence the name of the class. A war-horse was a considerable investment, as in peacetime it could not be used for farm work and hence defray its cost.[56]

The third income class was the *zeugitai*, whose annual income was not above 200 bushels. The name suggests to some scholars that it included those farmers who owned enough land to be able to use a pair (*zeugos*) of oxen to plough the fields – that is, they did not manually do the ploughing.[57] Therefore in 490 the class would have included many Athenian farmers owning their own land, even if on a small scale, either in Attica or the Athenian *klerouchies* of Salamis and Chalkis. Recent research, however, indicates that the *zeugitai* did not include most of the small landowners of Athens. It would appear that among the *zeugitai* were those farmers who could produce grains from at least 10 hectares (25 acres) of land worth about one talent, or 6,000 drachmai. That would yield an annual output of over 200 bushels, and thus a typical *zeugites* would have to have adequate acreage for such an output.[58] This would preclude the possession of a small landholding whose harvest was just enough to meet the needs of the household.[59] Such smallholders, therefore could not belong to the *zeugitai*, as they could not produce the necessary 200 bushels, but were relegated to the fourth and lowest class, the *thetes*.[60] This class included others with modest incomes, merchants, artisans, seamen and craftsmen, referred to in the ancient sources as *penetes*. These had steady jobs that could meet their basic living needs.[61] Those who had no property and had to struggle daily to make ends meet were the *ptochoi*, or paupers.[62] These laboured for the better-off Athenian citizens, mostly in manual unskilled labour considered demeaning by other classes of citizen. The standard of living of the *ptochoi*, then, differed little from that of the slaves, alongside whom they often toiled in the fields or on building sites.

Only the three upper classes of citizen were eligible for service as hoplites.[63] The *pentakosiomedimnoi* and knights served in the Athenian cavalry which in the early Classical era numbered just 96 horsemen.[64] This force was engaged mainly in patrolling the coastal areas of Attica. But the Athenians, like all Greeks except the Thessalians, did not employ cavalry as a tactical arm in battle.[65] The horsemen rode to the scene of the battle, each accompanied by a mounted orderly – usually a slave – who had the duties of an equerry. At the scene they would dismount and leave their horses in the care of their orderlies and proceed and fight in the battle on foot as hoplites.[66] The horse could come in useful later, either to flee in case of defeat, or pursue the enemy in case of victory. The Greeks of the Classical era, therefore, did not make any organized or systematic use of the advantages that cavalry could confer on an army. The ancient sources make no mention of any Athenian cavalry at Marathon, or of any action it might have been in.[67] All the *pentakosiomedimnoi*, knights and *zeugitai* fought there as hoplites.[68]

The thetes, in contradistinction to their wealthier fellow citizens, could not afford to buy the equipment of a hoplite and were thus kept out of the ranks. But if an individual thetes could somehow acquire the necessary kit, he could presumably become an Athenian hoplite, as recruitment did not seem to have any class requirements, and we know of no law that could have prevented him.[69] In 490, however, few hoplites would have been thetes, most of whom, if they had managed to put by a small sum, would have used it to better their families' standard of living rather than spend it on a hoplite's weapons.[70]

3. Light-armed troops in Athens in the early Classical period

In the early Classical period only a minority of Athenian citizens could enter service as hoplites or cavalrymen.[71] Even in the middle of the fifth century, when Athens was at the apogee of its power, and democracy in its finest flower, the thetes remained the most numerous of the city's social classes and were unable to procure the weapons a hoplite needed. But this does not mean that they were excluded from Athenian military operations in the Classical period. At the close of the 480s, when Athens began to build a large fleet, many thetes served as oarsmen on the triremes. But before this development, many seem to have fought as light-armed troops in Athenian military operations, as was the case in other Greek cities where men of the lower classes were thus employed.

In contrast to the hoplite who carried a variety of weapons, the light-armed soldier fought mainly with the javelin or bow (as an *akontistes* or *toxotes*). These weapons were inexpensive;[72] moreover, many men would have been familiar with their peacetime use for hunting or guarding their flocks.[73] Those who lacked such experience could participate in battles as slingers (*sphendonistai*) or simple stone-throwers (*lithoboloi*). These last two tasks did not require any financial outlay, and the 'weapons' were easier to use than the javelin or bow. [74] Thus a gradation of light-armed troops evolved, from the javelin-men and archers at the top to the slingers below and the stone-throwers on the bottom rung. [75]

A typical battle of the late Archaic and early Classical periods was based on the hoplite phalanx, but the light-armed troops also had an important part to play. [76] Though the hoplites despised the bow, and the men who used it, they knew that such men were vital to the outcome of a battle. Thanks to their flexibility, light-armed soldiers could move more quickly against the enemy in surprise attacks, carrying out manoeuvres which the heavier-armed hoplites would find difficult. Even more important to the hoplite was the fact that the light-armed troops could protect the flanks and rear from attacks by enemy light-armed troops or cavalry. They could launch long-range projectiles and thus cover the hoplites. When a hoplite phalanx was attacked on its flanks it would break up, as the individual hoplites would then have to fight in bunches, unable to communicate with one another. [77] To prevent this from happening, light-armed formations seem to have been placed on the flanks and in the rear to ward off cavalry and light-armed attacks from the enemy. [78] For example in 479, during the battle of Plataia, the Spartan Pausanias, who commanded the Greek force, asked the Athenians to send him archers to guard the flanks of the Spartan contingent that was under attack from Persian cavalry and in danger of being overrun. [79] Though those men were not hoplites, Pausanias' request shows that their value was recognized, especially in their ability to protect hoplite phalanxes. [80]

Herodotus makes indirect mention of light-armed troops used by the Greek cities in the early Classical era. He implies that Athens used light-armed soldiers as well as hoplites in 507/6, attributing its military victories at the time to the democratic principle of *isegoria*, which motivated citizens to act as free men and repulse their foes, whereas until then they supposedly had been subservient to the tyrants who ruled them. [81] Herodotus probably is referring here to the lower-class citizens who took part in those campaigns after having been given political rights by the reforms of Kleisthenes; their votes in the Assembly had begun to acquire real value. Many modern scholars would concur with Herodotus that the victories of the Athenians in 507/6 were possible thanks to Athens' ability to field a larger army than was usual at that time; the thetes, in fact, must have been recruited.[82] Therefore as early as 507/6, an Athenian army would have consisted of not only hoplites and horsemen, but also many light-armed troops.

Though there are enough references to light-armed troops dating from Archaic times, the writers of the fifth century give sole credit to the hoplites for glory on the battlefield.[83] Herodotus and Thucydides only incidentally mention light-armed soldiers in their accounts of battles. But these admittedly sparse indications, combined with what we can glean from surviving artworks of the time – mainly Attic vase paintings that depict light-armed soldiers fighting alongside hoplites – certify that fifth century armed encounters in Greece did include the light-armed element.[84] Classical-era Athenian writers either played down or avoided mention of light-armed troops, but enough evidence survives to tell us that during the fifty years of the Classical period known as the '*Pentecontaetia*', from 479 to 431, and the Peloponnesian War (431–404), Athenian light-armed troops played a more important role in hoplite phalanx encounters than the ancient literary sources would have us believe.

In 457, during a clash between the Athenians on the one hand, and the Boiotians and Peloponnesians on the other, general Myronides' stone-throwers gave Athens the victory, trouncing some 2,000 Corinthian hoplites near Megara.[85] In 426, during the Peloponnesian War, in a battle between the Athenians and their Akarnanian allies, and the Ambrakiotes and Pelponnesians, it was the light-armed allies of the Athenians who decided the issue.[86] In 424 the Athenian hoplite phalanx was smashed at Delion, mainly by light-armed Boiotians. Thucydides notes that the light-armed Athenian contingent had already left the area at the time, implying that their absence was what cost Athens the battle.[87]

The high point of Athenian light-armed activity, however (from what we know), was their performance at Pylos in 425, during the Peloponnesian War.[88] An Athenian force consisting of archers and oarsmen, armed with whatever they could find, was able to capture hundreds of Spartan hoplites – the cream of the leading families of Sparta – on the island of Sphakteria opposite Pylos. The Athenians at the time had relatively few hoplites at the scene, so the light-armed men can take credit for handing Athens its biggest victory in the war so far. The operations at Pylos showed that the use of basic phalanx tactics was becoming obsolete, and that victory in the field now depended upon combinations of hoplites with light-armed troops, mainly archers and peltasts (from the *peltes,* or small shield).[89] Yet this leaves open the question of why ancient writers avoided mention of light-armed soldiers, even though they played an important part in many encounters before the Peloponnesian War.

Nowhere does Herodotus mention light-armed troops in the Athenian army which marched to meet the Persians in 490. His assertion that at one stage in the battle of Marathon the Athenians lacked archers and cavalry,[90] has led some scholars to conclude that the army at Marathon was exclusively hoplite.[91] But Herodotus was referring to just one phase of the battle, not to the whole encounter.[92] He also makes only incidental mention of light-armed Greek soldiers in the Persian Wars. He seems to have downgraded their importance even in the battles of Thermopylai and Plataia, which otherwise he describes in great detail – in contrast to his summary treatment of Marathon. Yet these few indications are enough to prove the presence of light-armed troops in the Greek armies who fought the Persians in 480/79. Besides a mere mention of them at Thermopylai and Plataia, Herodotus gives us no more details.[93]

Yet there is an important record left by an Athenian who served in the Persian Wars that in one of the battles light-armed troops fought alongside the hoplites. The playwright Aischylos, in his *Persians,* in describing the Athenian action at Psyttaleia that took place simultaneously with the nearby naval battle of Salamis in 480, specifically mentions Athenian archers and stone-throwers.[94] We must not be surprised by Herodotus' account of the same action, which mentions only the hoplites commanded by Aristides.[95] Aischylos' narrative seems to be more convincing than that of Herodotus, as he was an actual eyewitness to events surrounding the battle of Salamis, and he set it down in 472, just eight years later.

It is understandable that the fifth century writers would downplay the contribution of light-armed troops, as the writers themselves belonged to the upper classes. Therefore the fact that Herodotus fails to make specific mention of light-armed troops at Marathon does not mean that there were none. As will become apparent, the view that the Athenians deployed only hoplites at Marathon is one of the more egregious errors committed by writers through the ages. Yet one more category of fighting man known to have taken part in the battle – and on whom Herodotus is also silent – remains to be examined. These men were not hoplites, but their presence at Marathon enables us to draw useful conclusions about the light-armed Athenians who helped defeat the Persians in 490.

4. Freedmen in the Athenian army

Pausanias reports that in 490 the Athenians freed their slaves and recruited them into the army.[96] Thus they fought alongside their former masters at Marathon. Though no other ancient writer mentions anything of the kind, Pausanias makes no fewer than three such mentions, and hence the fact is generally accepted by scholars.[97] He explicitly states that the Athenians freed their slaves before recruiting them.[98] The latter won their liberty before the battle; they were not given promises of freedom later, in case the Athenians were to win. We know from other later cases that when the Athenians and other Greeks needed slaves to fight, they freed them before recruiting them. This was because the ancient Greeks believed that only a free man had the moral courage to fight.[99]

In 490 the Athenians needed the contribution of the slaves in the looming fight for survival. They freed them so they could take their places in the ranks as free men; only thus could they be endowed with the incentive to give their all at the side of the soldiers and not desert at the first opportunity. We remain in the dark about what the status of these freedmen was after the battle – whether they became citizens or metics (resident aliens).[100] In the Classical era a manumitted slave became a metic; citizenship was bestowed only in extraordinary cases. We simply have no indication of the slaves' later status at the time of the battle of Marathon. Scholars who have studied the issue conclude that even if the Athenians had planned to confer citizenship status on the freedmen after the battle, there would have been no time to inscribe them on the tribal lists. This could explain why those freedmen who perished at Marathon were interred not with the Athenian soldiers but with the Plataian allies.

In 490 the number of slaves in Athens was relatively small compared to what it would be at the apogee of Athenian power. Work had not yet begun on a large scale at the silver mines of Laurion, in which thousands of slaves would labour.[101] At the time of Marathon the slaves worked on farms with their masters, or as servants in homes.[102] They were thus familiar members of the household.[103] These generally easy relations between masters and slaves would not have made it difficult for the Assembly to liberate and recruit the latter.[104] It may well have been the first case of freeing slaves in wartime in an ancient Greek state.[105] For the next two centuries Athens would face many more military crises; but in only one more case do we know of slaves being freed before a battle, and that is in 406, before the naval battle of Arginousai.[106] The hasty recruitment of new freedmen in 490 shows how critical the situation in Athens was.

Pausanias credits Miltiades with the decision to free the slaves.[107] But this cannot be strictly true, as the Assembly had not conferred special powers on the general so that he could act unilaterally. However, he could well have been instrumental in persuading the Assembly to pass the act. The motion would first have had to be submitted to the Council of Five Hundred, and then to the Assembly to be approved by a majority of citizens. Any Athenian making such a radical proposal would have had to be especially active in public affairs, and also have the ability of persuading his fellow-citizens of the need for such an extreme measure. Plato has Socrates saying that if any Athenian addressed the Assembly and showed that he didn't know what he was talking about, the Athenians would ridicule and heckle him and force him from the rostrum.[108] If the speaker proved stubborn and refused to leave, the *Prytaneis* (Assembly presidency) would eject him by force. Miltiades, on the other hand, was a clever and persuasive man. The writer of the *Athenian Constitution* says that Miltiades was the political leader of the upper classes ('the nobles and the well-known'), while Aelius Aristides notes his oratorical abilities.[109] Other ancient writers say Miltiades talked the Athenians into taking various preparatory measures to meet the Persian threat; Pausanias may therefore be right in claiming that he proposed to the Athenians to free the slaves and recruit them in their army.[110]

In ancient Greece hoplites and horsemen took their personal slaves with them to war.[111] The slaves carried their masters' provisions and weapons until the time for battle approached. The slave who carried his master's shield (*aspis*) was known as a *hypaspistes*.[112] Well-to-do hoplites had more than one slave to attend to them, but the *hypaspistes* was considered the most trustworthy.[113] On campaign the slaves did most of the work for their masters, such as carrying supplies and weapons, pitching tents and preparing their masters' meals. The duties of the slave, in fact, differed little from those of an equerry in a mediaeval army, or from an orderly in a modern army. There was a difference, however, in that the ancient Greek slave was not a combatant; he fought neither for his master or his master's army. During a battle he stayed in camp in the rear, well away from the action. If the enemy should break through to the camp, the slave would not fight. He might try to flee, but even if captured his treatment would not be much worse than what he was used to. He would simply remain a slave under a different master. A force which overran an enemy camp would usually ensure that the captured slaves were well-treated, as they constituted valuable booty. Yet according to Pausanias' account, the Athenian ex-slaves at Marathon were not mere auxiliaries who stayed safely in the rear but warriors in the front line.[114]

But how would these freedmen have fought at Marathon? Certainly none had the equipment of a hoplite, and it is doubtful whether the Athenian authorities would have been in a position to supply them with large amounts of weaponry. Besides, the freedmen's total lack of training in the arts of war would exclude them from being included in a phalanx. Hoplites might well have objected to their former slaves being deployed with them. Therefore, it is well-nigh impossible for the freedmen to have formed part of a phalanx at Marathon.[115] We assume that they were used as light-armed soldiers, for example, stone-throwers who did not need any special training.[116] The conclusion is that the Athenian army that fought at Marathon included a large force of non-hoplite light-armed troops, and that it would be wrong to assume that only hoplites took part. However, in 490 freedmen were not the only component of light-armed troops in the Athenian army. There was a more numerous component as well.

5. Athenian light-armed troops at Marathon

The Persian attack on Athens in 490 was the most serious threat the city had faced to date, compelling the authorities to take the unheard-of step of freeing and recruiting the slaves. If that extreme measure was adopted it was natural that recruitment would extend to the majority of Athenian citizens who were thetes.[117] Unlike the freedmen, the thetes were registered as members of the tribes, and thus would be easy to conscript into the army.[118] Herodotus reports that the 'entire citizenry' (*pandemoi*) of Plataia, for example, marched to Marathon[119], either as hoplites or light-armed soldiers. If this was the case with the Plataians, then we can reasonably assume that the Athenians did likewise, especially as their city was in the direct line of Persian attack. It would have been odd indeed for the Athenians to leave the thetes behind, especially as they formed the majority of the citizen body, while the Plataians marched en masse. The Athenian army in 490 should therefore have contained many light-armed soldiers of the thetes class, who would be expected to contribute at Marathon in the hour of mortal danger.[120]

A minority of scholars who believe that the Athenian army at Marathon did not include light-armed troops assert that the Athenian commanders planned to confront the Persians with hoplites alone.[121] But as we have seen, Greek warfare of the period did employ light-armed troops whose task was to protect the hoplite flanks from cavalry and light-armed attack;[122] therefore their presence would have been imperative, even if they might end up not being needed at all. Moreover, the Athenian commanders knew that the Persians had a strong cavalry force, against which light-armed troops with projectiles would be more effective than hoplites. If the commanders decided not to take a light-armed contingent, it might have been interpreted as an unwillingness to stop the invader. The conclusion must be that it is erroneous to assume that there were no light-armed troops at Marathon, as such a theory ignores the practice of Greek armies of the time.

Most scholars who assume that there were no light-armed troops at Marathon propound political reasons. There are two theories along these lines: one is that as the Athenian upper classes distrusted the thetes as they were largely supporters of the ex-tyrant and hence could not be risked on the battlefield.[123] But this sounds far-fetched. Though one cannot rule out some thetes being nostalgic for the old regime – just as some of the upper classes were – such an 'explanation' runs up against common sense. It was the Assembly, in which the thetes were a majority, that resolved to resist the Persians and Hippias.[124] If the thetes really wished Hippias to return, what would have been more natural than to vote to negotiate with him, either in the last session of the Assembly or in a previous session? There is evidence, moreover, that immediately after the battle of Marathon the thetes as a class were hostile to Hippias. In 488 the Assembly inaugurated the practice of ostracism which, according to the author of the *Athenian Constitution*, was first used against citizens suspected of having pro-tyrant tendencies.[125]

An ostracism was decided by majority vote, regardless of social class.[126] Hence it was the thetes who as a majority had the controlling votes. The result in 488 firmly demonstrated that the thetes were strongly anti-tyrant, as Hipparchos the son of Charmos, believed to be the head of the Peisistratid faction in Athens, was exiled in the first ostracism vote. One assumes that the thetes' political stance would not have changed much in the space of two years. Another point to note is that if in 490 the thetes did have pro-Hippias proclivities, the hoplites would hardly have dared to go to Marathon leaving them behind in the city. In fact, it is not too much to argue that in such a case the thetes would have willingly opened the gates to the Persians; they might even have marched out to attack the Athenian hoplites from the rear, for all anyone knew.

The second theory in favour of the absence of light-armed troops from Marathon is that the Athenian generals, all members of the upper classes, did not use them because if it turned out that they performed well in battle, their political position at home would be enhanced.[127] In support of this theory we have a statement by Aristotle that Greek cities ruled by oligarchies preferred to hire foreign mercenaries rather than conscript their own citizens.[128] He adds that the lower classes in several Greek cities gained advantages at the expense of the upper classes precisely because the former were recruited to fight wars.[129] Therefore, according to Hunt, this is the reason why the Athenian generals at Marathon used ex-slaves in their ranks; they knew that in case of victory the freedmen would not be in a position to threaten the privileges of the upper classes as they would lack the political power to do so. Even if the freedmen were to become citizens, they would still be on a lower social rung than the hoplites and cavalrymen.[130] Besides, most were aliens, which itself was a serious hurdle against obtaining political power. To recruit thetes, on the other hand, would be to put upper-class dominance at risk.[131] However, after the battle of Marathon the thetes did enjoy a rise in status. The Athenian Assembly acquired a power which it had not had before 490, or if it had, did not use it.[132] From this fact alone we may conclude that the thetes earned their rise in status precisely because they participated in the battle!

Some scholars assert that the Athenians had no archers of their own at Marathon. The basis for this argument is that Attic vase paintings of the late Archaic and early Classical periods depict archers, but in Scythian dress.[133] The archers, then, must have been Scythian mercenaries.[134] An opposing argument claims that the depicted archers are actually Athenians with Scythian equipment, and that Scythian bowmen were never employed.[135] It is conceivable that the Attic vase-painters depicted archers in Scythian garb on purpose as the Scythians had the renown of being the best archers in the Classical era. In this view, the intention was to depict the specialization of the archers, not their ethnicity.[136] Krentz, for one, believes that the archers on the vases are Athenian, adding that the production of such vessels did not cease around 500, but continued on to 490 and perhaps after.[137] He cites that one vase, depicting a hoplite next to an archer in Scythian gear could have been inspired by the battle of Marathon.[138]

If Krentz's view is chronologically correct, we have another factor arguing for the presence of light-armed troops – specifically archers – at Marathon. Around 490 (according to Vos) the images of 'Scythian' archers disappear from Attic vases, or a few years later (according to Krentz). Vos theorizes that in about 500 Athens stopped employing Scythian mercenaries, which is when their images began to be replaced by Greek archers. Our conclusion, drawn from all the above, is that the 'Scythian' bowmen depicted on Attic vases are really Athenians, and the fact that from 490 onwards they are depicted in Greek dress could well be a consequence of the battle of Marathon. In that battle the Athenians had to confront enemy archers in 'Scythian' dress (depicted also on the vases). After the Athenian victory any prestige attached to a Scythian appearance declined, and this was reflected in the vase paintings.

Though all the ancient historians fail to mention the action of light-armed troops and thetes at Marathon, Aristophanes gives us a strong hint in his *Knights* that the thetes fought there. The play's protagonist is *Demos*, an old man who is an allegory for the Athenian Assembly of which the majority are thetes.[139] In the play, *Demos* has fought at Marathon and later taken part in the battle of Salamis as a rower.[140] If only hoplites, or members of the upper classes, had fought at Marathon, then Aristophanes' mention of *Demos* as having fought would have seemed absurd to an Athenian audience.[141] In 424, when the *Knights* was first staged, audiences would have been well aware that all classes had fought at Marathon. Those thetes who had formed the light-armed contingents in the battle also served as rowers in the trireme fleet ten years later at Salamis, just as the play suggests.[142] Some ancient works of art, which according to experts show scenes inspired by Marathon, depict hoplites and light-armed soldiers together.[143] Though emphasis is given to the hoplites, the presence of their light-armed comrades in the field is clearly evident.

There is also archaeological evidence of Athenian light-armed troops, in particular archers, at Marathon. Travellers in the early nineteenth century who visited the area claimed to have found many bronze arrowheads, or to have heard of such discoveries, at the Tumulus of the Athenians.[144] Leake describes them as 'triangular, with a round hole for the arrow shaft, and an inch in diameter'.[145] More recently Yannis Galanakis, the Curator for the Aegean Collections and the Sir Arthur Evans Archive at Oxford University's Ashmolean Museum, asserts that the arrowheads now in various museums around the world purporting to be from the Marathon battlefield have actually nothing to do with the battle; he believes that their origin was elsewhere and that they were sold to credulous buyers through false claims for their 'historicity'. Their purported association with Marathon would fetch a higher price.[146]

Galanakis' assertion appears credible, and there seems to be evidence to buttress it.[147] Yet it is entirely possible that some arrowheads in the British Museum and claimed to have been found at Marathon are the genuine article. Specifically, they include fourteen bronze arrowheads acquired by the British Museum in 1864 from the estate of Percy Clinton Sydney Smythe, the sixth Viscount Strangford.[148] Several years later, in 1878, the museum took possession of eighteen bronze arrowheads believed to have been found by one General Meyrick at Marathon.

In 1906 the museum bought ten iron arrowheads alleged to have been found during an illegal excavation of some 'ancient tomb' at Marathon by a British admiral named Brock in 1830.[149] The museum also has one bronze arrowhead discovered at Marathon and donated in 1959 by the Royal United Services Institute (catalogue number 1959, 0721.4).

The fourteen arrowheads of Viscount Strangford's former collection are of two types. Thirteen of them are of the so-called 'first type'[150] – triangular, with a central aperture to take the shaft; it's a simple type of head, where the blades do not extend beyond the shaft hole. All Meyrick arrowheads also belong to this type. They correspond accurately to Leake's description of the heads he discovered at the Tumulus of the Athenians. It appears therefore that arrowheads of the 'first type' are more common as finds at Marathon.[151] Just one of the Strangford arrowheads is of the 'second type', spear-shaped.[152] There is a 'third type' of head in the British Museum (catalogue number 1959, 0721.4), while a 'fourth type' consists of iron heads allegedly found by Brock in an ancient tomb at Marathon.[153] This 'tomb' could be identified with the Tumulus of the Athenians, the site of many such unofficial explorations.

The 'third type' arrowhead in the British Museum belongs to a Persian type similar to many others found at Thermopylai and the Acropolis of Athens and linked to Persian operations of 480.[154] Four bronze arrowheads found at Olympia belong to the same type, and could well be part of the booty seized by the Athenians at Marathon.[155] The Acropolis of Athens has turned up iron heads of a kind identical to those found by Brock.[156] These 'fourth type' heads were probably on arrows fired by the Persians during the siege of the Acropolis in 480. Indications are that 'third' and 'fourth' type arrowheads were used by the Persians during the Persian Wars.

However, the 'first type' bronze arrowheads that Leake claimed to have found at Marathon, of the same type as the thirteen in the former Strangford collection and the eighteen in the Meyrick donation, are not Persian but Greek.[157] This might lead someone to conclude that they have no connection with Marathon and the battle of 490, based on the assumption that Greek archers did not fight there. But an archaeological discovery shows that the 'first type' arrowhead was used by Athenian archers about 490. An excavation by the British School of Archaeology at Athens at the Vrachos fortification near the village of Fylla in Euboia shows that it was in use by the Athenian *klerouchoi* of Chalkis between 506 and 490.[158] The central building of the complex, Building 3 in the floor plan, appears to have been a barracks for the guard.[159] In Building 2 a triangular bronze Greek-type arrowhead was found, identical to the 'first type' of arrowheads allegedly found at Marathon.[160] It was one of the few relics found on the floor of the Athenian fort at Fylla, probably having fallen just before the fort was abandoned in 490, according to the archaeologists.[161] Indications are strong that these triangular bronze 'first type' Greek arrowheads date to the time of the battle of Marathon.[162]

The 4,000 Athenian *klerouchoi* of Chalkis who according to Herodotus sped to the aid of Eretria could have been among the last to use the fort at Fylla. The archaeologists' findings in Buildings 2 and 3 could well be connected with them. From there it can be surmised that among the Athenian *klerouchoi* who fought at Marathon there were archers. All the aforementioned Persian and Greek arrowheads now in the British Museum belong chronologically to the period of the battle of Marathon, increasing the probability that archers were present in the battle. In the fifth century the Athenians did field a respectable corps of bowmen; in 479, as we have noted, they had gained some renown to the extent that the Spartan commander Pausanias asked for their help in the battle of Plataia. This corps of archers would have existed before Xerxes' invasion of Greece in 480,[163] thus it is fair to assume that they had earned their spurs in a previous conflict, which according to our evidence would have been the battle of Marathon.

Besides the evidence arguing for the presence of archers at Marathon, there is evidence that other categories of light-armed troops also fought there. We know that large numbers of lead slingstones have been found in the area.[164] With a single exception, these projectiles bear no inscriptions or images, which indicates that they were used before the close of the fifth century. At the time the Persians did not use slingers in their armies, in contrast to the Greeks, who had a tradition of them.[165] Greek city-states in the Classical era fielded slingers among their light-armed formations. We know of no other ancient battle fought at Marathon other than that of 490, leading to the conclusion that the slingstones may have been used in the battle. There is other evidence that argues for the possible use of slingers in the Athenian army at Marathon. As we have seen, an arrowhead found at the Fylla fort could indicate the existence of archers; finds at the same site indicate that slingers were there as well. In Room 17 of Building 3 rounded stones were found that could well have been the slingers' ammunition.[166]

The importance of the Athenian *klerouchoi* of Chalkis to research into the role of light-armed troops at Marathon is not limited to what was found in the remains of the fort at Fylla, and the implied signs of archers and slingers. Most latter-day scholars believe that those *klerouchoi* after leaving Eretria crossed over to Attica and joined the Athenian expeditionary force. According to Herodotus there were 4,000 of them,[167] and they would have constituted nearly half of the Athenian army of 9,000 hoplites to whom, ancient writers after Herodotus ascribe the task of stopping the Persians.[168] But that cannot be possible.[169] We know, for example, that those Athenians who became *klerouchoi* were all of the thetes class.[170] Since their establishment in Euboia in 506 a few may have improved their economic condition to enable them to move up to *zeugites*, hence eligible for the hoplite ranks.[171] But in 490 a majority of the *klerouchoi* would not have had that advantage, and so would have had to serve as light-armed troops. To be a *zeugites*, as we have seen, meant that one's holding would have to be able to meet the needs of at least a dozen people; they were not small farmers like the thetes, who would be able to just meet the needs of the family. We can thus conclude that the 4,000 Athenian *klerouchoi* of Chalkis did not, by and large, fight as hoplites, but as light-armed troops.[172]

More evidence supports this interpretation. According to Herodotus, during Xerxes' invasion in 480 the Athenians manned twenty of their triremes with 'Chalkidians'.[173] Ancient authors do not clarify whether they were native Chalkidians or Athenian *klerouchoi*. Most scholars believe the term referred to the latter.[174] Moreover, the crews of twenty triremes would add up to about 4,000, which was the number of *klerouchoi* at Marathon. The great bulk of crews was made up of rowers, who belonged to the thetes class. One could suppose that many if not most of the Athenian *klerouchoi* oarsmen in the twenty Athenian triremes in the battle of Salamis in 480 had fought at Marathon with light arms.

Enough evidence has been adduced, we believe, to make it almost certain that Athenians of the thetes class who fought at Marathon served as light-armed troops, like the newly-freed slaves. Relatively few modern scholars have made that assertion.[175] The various units of freedmen and light-armed thetes share the credit with the hoplites for victory. Even though the freedmen fought in the front ranks, their contribution was ignored by all the ancient chroniclers except Pausanias.[176] The same applies to the lower-class Athenians in the ranks of the light-armed, even though they outnumbered the hoplites. We have already mentioned that the thetes' contribution to victory at Marathon could have been why that class gained in political power in Athens in the years immediately following. It could explain why the author of the *Athenian Constitution* was able to write that just after the victory at Marathon, the *demos* gained 'self-confidence'.[177]

6. The size of the army

A basic problem in studying the battle of Marathon is ascertaining the exact number of Athenians, and secondarily the Plataians, who fought. It was once considered one of the least contestable facts; though Herodotus did not put a number on either side that fought in the battle, Roman-era writers mention some 9,000 Athenian soldiers, or something less than 1,000 men for each of the ten Athenian tribes.[178] This would be consistent with Herodotus' claim that 8,000 Athenian hoplites fought at Plataia just over a decade later.[179] The lower figure for Plataia, indicating a shrinking of the Athenian army in the meantime, could be attributable to the striking growth in the size of the navy in those years. Many members of the Athenian upper classes who formed the hoplite phalanx in 490 did not fight at Plataia in 479, as shortly afterwards they were at Mykale on board Athenian triremes as *epibatai,* or marines.[180] So the number of 9,000 at Marathon undoubtedly refers to hoplites alone, as correctly noted by the ancient sources. Of course, as we have seen, this number cannot have included the light-armed thetes troops and freedmen. As the great bulk of the 4,000 Athenian *klerouchoi* of Chalkis were in the ranks as light-armed soldiers, the figure of 9,000 Athenians at Marathon was not the true total.[181]

This leaves the question of why the false conclusion that just 9,000 Athenians fought at Marathon was allowed to prevail. The figure comes from Roman-era writers, the earliest of whom, Cornelius Nepos, lived in the first century.[182] Later writers possibly copied Nepos. But the weightiest view on the number of Athenians at Marathon comes from Pausanias who wrote in the second century AD. Pausanias specifically concentrated on estimating the total number of Greeks under Spartan King Leonidas I's command at Thermopylai in 480 before they were ordered to withdraw.[183] He wanted to know how many Lokrians served under Leonidas, which Herodotus does not mention, and came to the conclusion that there were more than 6,000. Thus, according to the calculation, Leonidas had 11,200 men at Thermopylai, though Pausanias does not distinguish between hoplites and light-armed troops. But this is a minor fault compared with the mistake he made in assessing the Athenian strength at Marathon. After citing the 9,000 figure he included the freedmen in it, presenting it as the total.[184] That is the prime source of the misconception that lingers until the present day.

We can with some accuracy estimate the number of light-armed troops at Marathon. Scholars believe that in 490 Athens numbered 30,000–35,000 citizens, or roughly 3,000–3,500 per tribe.[185] If the number of hoplites stood at 9,000, then theoretically there would have been 20,000–26,000 lower-class men available for light-armed duties. Most of these would have been eligible for service, as those over the age limit of sixty were relatively few. Pausanias asserts that both the elderly and the very young served at Marathon, but this is almost certainly not correct.[186] Also, there would have been some who avoided conscription either because they were supporters of Hippias or simply too timid.[187] There would also have been some men living in remote mountain areas of Attica who either did not hear of the mobilization order or simply ignored it.[188] The resulting gaps in manpower could have been filled by the mobilized freedmen. As no ancient writer has given us the number of freedmen at Marathon, we can only assume that they were numerous enough, since it would otherwise be hard to justify the radical and risky political move for their manumission and recruitment.[189] Moreover, after the battle the Athenians honoured the fallen freedmen by burying them with the Plataian fallen. The memory of their contribution remained alive at least until the second century AD, to be recorded by Pausanias.

We do not know how many thetes worked the oars in the Athenian navy, which in 490 was much smaller than it would become under

Themistokles a few years later. In 489 the Athenians sailed against Paros with seventy triremes.[190] A year earlier, then, about sixty triremes would likely have been the strength of the navy.[191] A number of thetes would have been held back for service on the ships, even if the Athenians had no intention of using them against the Persian fleet in 490. They would have had skeleton crews, as in ordinary circumstances some 10,000 men would be needed to fully man them. Therefore most thetes serving in the fleet in 490 could well have been transferred to land duties as light-armed soldiers. We may also assume that some light-armed men were kept back as a city guard after the rest of the army marched to Marathon; the 'elderly' and 'very young' mentioned by Pausanias may very likely have been assigned this duty.[192]

Based on what we have said so far, we estimate that at least 10,000 men, and possibly as many as 15,000, served as light-armed troops at Marathon.[193] Van Wees estimates that an Athenian army of the fifth century contained three light-armed soldiers for every two hoplites.[194] This would place the number of light-armed at Marathon at some 13,500, near the median point of our estimate range. Add to these the 9,000 hoplites, and we have a total figure of between 19,000 and 24,000 men, plus the roughly 1,000 Plataians (see below), to give us a minimum of 20,000 and a maximum of 25,000. Several modern writers would agree that the real strength of the Athenian army at Marathon was much larger than the 9,000 cited by Roman-era writers, and that the light-armed troops make up the difference. Milford, for one, puts the figure at between 28,000 and 30,000,[195] Finlay at 22,000;[196] Krentz gives us a possible range of 16,000–22,000.[197] Leake, Lampros and Burn claim 20,000, Sotiriadis 18,000, Munro 15,000 and Beloch 12,000–14,000.[198] Some researchers suspect that ancient writers deliberately understated the number of Greeks at Marathon and correspondingly inflated the number of Persians in order to make the Athenian victory seem that much more impressive.[199] There could well be a grain of truth in this. However, our conclusion is that ancient writers mentioned only the hoplites and ignored the light-armed soldiers simply because they were of no interest.

Herodotus does not say how many Plataians fought at Marathon besides noting that the Boiotian city sent its whole citizenry.[200] The term he employs, *pandemei*, refers to all the soldiery, hoplites and light-armed.

Roman and Byzantine-era writers claim that the Plataians numbered 1,000;[201] more modern writers accept that figure, as they estimate that Plataia would have been able to field about as many men as a single Athenian tribe. In the battle of Plataia, the namesake city contributed 600 hoplites to the Greek side.[202] Krentz accepts the same number at Marathon, a decade before, and adds an equal number of light-armed troops. If correct, the Plataians at Marathon would have numbered about 1,200, not too far removed from the number given by ancient authors.[203]

We estimate that in 490 the Persian and Greek front line troops at Marathon were about evenly matched, with between 20,000 and 25,000 men each. But we must not leave out the tens of thousands of auxiliaries in the Persian army as well as the Persian ship crews.[204] Though they did not belong to combat units, some of them would have been available for arming as light-armed troops in case of emergency.[205] Also, the sheer numbers visible in the Persian camp could well have caused the Greeks to quail at the sight. That could be why the ancient writers stressed that there were far more Persians than Greeks at Marathon. Moreover, the Persians had cavalry, which enhanced their striking power against the horseless Greeks.

There are no indications that the Athenians hired mercenaries on the eve of the battle. Both Peisistratos and his son Hippias had used mercenaries in their campaigns.[206] According to Best, there are many depictions of Thracian peltasts on Attic pottery dating to the late sixth century and early fifth century, showing that Athens very likely had recourse to them.[207] Best speculates that the Thracians could have been hired by the Peisistratids and had remained in Athens after the abolition of the tyranny in 510.[208] Yet by 490 these images had stopped appearing, to be replaced by javelin-men without the *peltes,* or small shields of the peltasts. If those peltasts depicted on the vessels were indeed Thracians, and not – as we have seen in the case of 'Scythian' archers – Athenians in Thracian gear, we have an indication that the Athenians could have stopped recruiting Thracians prior to 490, as Thrace itself had fallen to the Persians.[209]

Common sense also argues against the Athenians' hiring mercenaries; we cannot suppose that mercenaries flocked to Athens to offer their services on hearing that Darius' army was about to attack, as they were salaried men and entitled to a portion of the booty of the defeated force. In 490 few mercenaries would have had many hopes of profiting from serving Athens as chances of defeating the Persian invaders did not seem good. If Athens did not employ either Scythian archers or Thracian peltasts, it is unlikely that it would have used Greek mercenaries. The recruitment of thetes as light-armed troops and the freeing of the slaves were the only solutions open to the Athenians on the eve of the battle.[210]

7. Mobilization at Athens: compulsory or voluntary?

Mystery surrounds the way in which the Athenian army was assembled to meet the Persian invaders in 490. The ancient sources offer very little information about how the Athenian expeditionary force to Marathon was put together. Pausanias writes that the order included the elderly and the very young, as well as the ex-slaves.[211] According to Aelius Aristides the expeditionary force included all Athenians, and the very young, while the older men were left behind to guard the city and its temples.[212] Plutarch claims that 'Athens had no defenders' after the army marched off to Marathon.[213] Though these accounts of the mobilization of the Athenians were written long after the battle, they seem to preserve an authentic tradition of the mass character of the event. The Athenians in 490 had the organizational ability and time available to carry out a complex mobilization. For the past four years, since the Ionian Revolt was crushed in 494, they had awaited Persian revenge.[214] The tears of the Athenian spectators of Phrynichos' tragedy *The Sack of Miletos* were not the result of the evils suffered by their Ionian allies left in the lurch, but the realization that their turn was about to come to experience the Great King's wrath.[215]

Mardonius' expedition to Greece in 492, had it succeeded, would have placed Athens on high alert. The emergency passed temporarily after the Persian fleet was destroyed off Mount Athos and the land forces had to turn back. Yet the Athenians knew it was only a matter of time before a new expedition against them would be unleashed. Thus defence preparations would have continued unabated, indeed speeded up a year later with the arrival of envoys bearing Darius' demand for 'earth and water'. Though the Athenians did not then mobilize, they would have made plans that mobilization would be swift when the time came. The immediate despatch of the Athenian *klerouchoi* of Chalkis to Eretria before the Persians appeared shows that the Athenian authorities had already begun to assign military duties to their citizens. Hammond is likely correct when he says arrangements for a military campaign were already complete by the time the enemy appeared before the walls of Eretria.[216] The heroic resistance of the Eretrians gave valuable time to the Athenians to iron out the last details of the mobilization before it was set in motion.

The ancient writers give us scant information on this mobilization. This leaves the way open for various theories of how the Athenian authorities handled it, based largely on later procedures recorded in ancient sources.[217] Yet these sources, too, can provide only indications, as through the fifth and fourth centuries Athens' military organization underwent changes, affecting the way the mobilization process for a military campaign was conducted. Reliable information on the process begins between 478–431, when Athens assumed a leading role in the Greek world. The rapid rise in Athenian power in the fifth century and the frequent conflicts the city was involved in prompted the development of an efficient mobilization system.[218] But only during and after the Peloponnesian War do we have specific information on how hoplites and cavalrymen were mobilized.[219]

Athenian citizens were mobilized according to both tribe and *deme*, as a result of Kleisthenes' reforms of 508/7. Until then they had been organized on the basis of birthplace in Attica – namely the *diakrioi*, or hill-country dwellers; the *mesogeioi*, or people of the towns and plains; and the *paralioi*, or those who lived along the coasts. Kleisthenes had introduced a more complex tribal system. Each Athenian tribe was to consist of three parts, one each from the hillmen, the plainsmen and the coastal men; these one-third parts were called *trittyes*. The *trittyes* comprising one tribe were normally found in neighbouring areas, though there were exceptions.

The following ten tribes formed the basis of the Athenian administrative system: the Erechtheis, the Aigeis, the Pandionis, the Leontis, the Akamantis, the Oineis, the Kekropis, the Hippothontis, the Aiantis and the Antiochis.[220] All of Attica was at the same time divided into 139 *demes* that functioned as the local governments.[221] Thus every Athenian citizen, regardless of tribe, also belonged to a *deme*.[222] Recruitment was carried out on the basis of both. The roll of citizens, or *lexiarchike grammateia*, was kept in the *demes'* archives, and keeping them up to date was the responsibility of the *demarchs* and another class of official, the *taxiarchoi*. It appears, however, that in mobilization tribal origin played a larger role than *deme* membership, as a soldier was positioned in the phalanx according to tribe.[223] Moreover, when fallen soldiers were buried and commemorated, it was by tribe and not *deme*.[224] The division of a tribe into three *trittyes* was reflected in the army, as the men of one *trittys* seem to have formed a company (*lochos*).[225] After Kleisthenes' reforms every Athenian citizen was expected to fulfil his serious responsibilities to the state, and above all to be mobilized into the army, whenever the state deemed it necessary.

Literary and epigraphic sources tell us that fourth century Athens had the practice of *ephebeia*, in which an eighteen-year-old youth (the age at which he became a citizen) was obliged to serve two years in the military, with duties such as patrolling and guarding the forts on the Attic border with Boiotia and Megaris.[226] We do not know when exactly the *ephebeia* was instituted, though it could possibly have been as early as the time of Kleisthenes' reforms. It gave every young Athenian citizen the chance to acquaint himself with military practice and undergo some basic training in order to equip himself with the skills he might need to fight for his city in the future.[227] In the fourth century the Athenian authorities had the system well in place. In times of peace those citizens who completed their *ephebeia* service were not obliged to serve any more in the military; but in time of war some of the older citizens would be drafted.[228]

How exactly were citizens between twenty and sixty years of age mobilized? The generals of the tribes, along with the *demarchs* and *taxiarchoi* who maintained the citizenship rolls, were responsible for recruitment. It appears that each general picked out of the rolls those men who would be under his command for a specific campaign; this was known as 'list recruitment' (*ek katalogou*).[229] In the fifth century mobilization was effected not on age classification, a practice which began only in the fourth century and was more equitable, but on 'list recruitment'. It enabled the generals to often discriminate against certain citizens,[230] but we may be almost certain that in a time of dire emergency the bulk of citizens were recruited according to need rather than preference.[231]

We do not know how organized the mobilization of light-armed troops was in Classical-era Athens. Were they recruited similarly to the hoplites and horsemen, or did they join up voluntarily and haphazardly? From Thucydides we gather that in fifth century Athens the latter was the rule.[232] Many scholars believe that in 490 the formal mobilization procedures involved only the hoplites, and base the conclusion on the fact that only hoplites are mentioned at Marathon in ancient literary sources. In general, ancient writers, when describing the battles of the fifth century, never put a figure on the Athenian light-armed troops. More modern scholars disagree over whether the thetes were registered in the *lexiarchike grammateia*; they may have been if they had some distinct skill such as archers or javelin-men or peltasts or slingers.[233]

There must have been some way of picking out these men, as many served in Athens' overseas campaigns, and only a certain number could be on board each ship. Thus besides the names of the hoplites, those of some of the light-armed 'specialists' could also have been on the rolls or otherwise known to the authorities. But the poorer propertyless thetes, the *ptochoi*, would probably not have been recruited by list; such men fought either as stone-throwers or with their farm implements, probably operating separately from the main body of the army. Their main duty seems to have been to sabotage enemy installations while the hoplites and specialized light-armed soldiers were facing the enemy.[234] In a pitched battle these men and the light-armed troops would protect the flanks of the phalanx, but the value of the former would be inferior to the latter. The main contribution of the skilled and unskilled thetes was to help with raids on border districts near Boiotia and Megaris. As there seems to have been no formal procedure for recruiting non-hoplites, we assume that they served on a voluntary basis. One such instance occurred in 424, during the Peloponnesian War, in an Athenian expedition into Boiotia.[235] The expedition to Marathon might well have seen many thetes joining up of their own free will.[236]

Nevertheless, there is some evidence that most thetes were compulsorily conscripted for emergency war crises such as the Persian invasion of 490. We know that Kleisthenes' reforms enabled the thetes to participate in elections for the Ten Generals as well as the Polemarch (the titular commander-in-chief).[237] As the most numerous of the Athenian classes, they determined by their votes which of their fellow-citizens would command the army. And if they had that privilege, it would have been absurd for them not to be conscripted, even if on an occasional and voluntary basis.[238] The *demes* would have maintained rolls of the citizens by name, father's name and tribe, just as for the higher classes, as the thetes took part in the meetings of the Assembly and *demes*, and served on juries in the courts.[239] All this argues for the conscription of the thetes in war. In 490, as we have seen, the slaves were freed for service, which could not possibly have been foreseen by Kleisthenes' reforms. That procedure would have been complicated enough, involving the search for available men, their registration, their manumission and induction into the Athenian forces. We assume that the red tape in this case worked.[240] Our conclusion is that if the slaves were able to be processed in order to fight, there would have been little trouble mobilizing the majority of citizens who were thetes, as their names would already have been registered on the state rolls.

The mobilization of 490 involved the majority of Athenian men able to bear arms. If the *ephebeia* was in force at the time, most of those between the ages of eighteen and twenty would already be under arms.[241] But that age cohort made up only a small part of the total army that Athens could field. Its members had as yet no battle experience. Aelius Aristides maintains that the 'very young' were despatched to Marathon; it is more likely that they stayed in the city with the elderly to do guard duty. Many Athenians in 490 would have been veterans of the battles of 507/6, when Athens had beaten back incursions of the Spartans into Attica and halted a three-pronged threat from the Peloponnesians, Boiotians and Chalkidians, and perhaps of the 498 expedition to Asia Minor as well as operations against Aigina in 492.[242] Athens had emerged victorious, most likely thanks to a breadth of mobilization unprecedented in the Greek city-states until that time.[243] Before that time Athens had little experience in mobilizing an army, as most of its battles had been fought by volunteers and foreign mercenaries; there may have been instances of conscription, but they would have involved few men and been limited to clan (an old social unit) or *deme*.[244] This would have been the way in which men were recruited to oppose Peisistratos' move on Athens in 546, when he could count on his supporters in the outlying districts. Whenever Peisistratos required military forces, besides foreign mercenaries and Athenian volunteers, he could draw on men from his home district of Brauron and others in which his supporters lived.

The administrative system resulting from Kleisthenes' reforms was still in its infancy in 507/6;[245] despite the Athenian victories of those two years, we don't know if the practice of 'list recruitment' had yet begun. If it had, the rolls would have been incomplete and inaccurate, as the entire administrative system was still new. If we assume that the Athenian army in 507/6 was primarily a volunteer force, then it says a great deal for its ability, as it was able to defeat stronger forces. In the ensuing years the *demarchs* and the *taxiarchoi* (if they existed) would have brought the rolls up to date each year, adding the names of new Athenian citizens, and so the state administration would have had in place a smoothly efficient mobilization plan. As Athens had been in the Persians' sights since 494, the city must have worked out the optimum mobilization scheme, paying especial attention to the accuracy of the lists of cavalrymen, hoplites and those light-armed troops registered on the rolls.

It is likely that in 490 the Athenian authorities issued a general call to the citizenry to be prepared for mobilization when the crucial hour arrived. Moreover, 'list recruitment' would presumably require some time, and would have been confined to the winter months when plans were made for summer campaigning.[246] In an acute crisis like that of 490, mobilization would have had to be a lot faster. As we have seen, the Plataians mobilized their entire citizen body; it is almost certain that the Athenian mobilization was similar.[247] Though most of the hoplites were conscripted, the bulk of the Athenian army would have been made up of volunteers. We presume that the mobilization process had begun as soon as news arrived that the Persians had sailed to the Cyclades islands. A few weeks later, with the siege of Eretria, the Athenian army would already have taken shape and been placed on high alert.[248]

The ancient Athenian mobilization process was a lot simpler than what it is in a modern army. Horsemen owned their own horses and foot soldiers, whether hoplites or light-armed men, had their weapons at home. Every recruit presented himself on the morning of the day of his conscription with his weapons and a small bag for provisions. Except for the weapons, the recruited soldiers could not be told apart from civilians as they wore not identical uniforms but their own clothes.[249] The wealthier ones brought along their slaves to carry their weapons and provisions. Those recruits living in Athens probably assembled on the Pnyx hill, where the Assembly met.[250] In other *demes* they would gather in the local marketplace or in the precincts of a temple or shrine.[251] Each *demarch* may well have had the right to call together his recruited citizens, as the reforms of Kleisthenes had entitled *demarchs* to call local assemblies.

Every recruit gave his name, father's name and tribe to the *demarch* or *taxiarchos* who acted as a recruiting officer and who checked the name against the rolls. All the recruits of one locality would belong to the same tribe, as did the recruiting officer. On the Pnyx hill, for example, there would be ten tables for registering the recruits of the ten Athenian tribes. Thus registered, each recruit would join his fellow-tribesmen in a designated place. Then groups of recruits from the outskirts would come in from all over Attica to join with the main force. Probably these latter would have arrived in the city a few days before marching to Marathon. No Greek city except Sparta at the time had a special camp where all the army would stay before being called to action. We presume that a large open space in Athens would have been provided for the purpose – possibly one of the gymnasiums. Those men who lived in Athens would have spent the last night at home before marching.

The mobilization of Athens' almost entire citizen body at the end of the summer of 490 was an unprecedented event not only by Athenian but also by Greek city-state standards. We do not know of any previous instance of mass mobilization that would include freed slaves. Some ancient writers, as we have seen, included the very young and the elderly, all of which argues for the view that the majority of Athenian citizens rushed to recruitment. Plutarch, however, is probably in error when he writes that Athens had no defenders when the army was at Marathon,[252] in light of evidence that the very young and the elderly, plus some light-armed troops, must have been left behind as a guard reserve. These men are probably whom Herodotus is referring to when he writes that after the victory at Marathon the troops rushed to aid those in Athens against another Persian landing.[253] The only reason why Plutarch failed to mention them must have been because they must not have been especially effective as fighters.

8. The Athenian command: the Polemarch and Ten Generals

The organization and command of the Athenian army in 490 showed signs of Kleisthenes' reforms of 508/7, plus some later ones in 501/0, as well as retaining older traditions. The main characteristic was that the army commanders were elected; none was a professional soldier. Since 500 the members of each Athenian tribe were headed by one of their number who served as general (*strategos*), elected for one year like the Archons.[254] The office of general predated the creation of the democratic polity, though with duties somewhat different to those established later. Between 500 and 486 the Polemarch shared the command with the Ten Generals; this office was a carryover from very ancient times going back into Athens' mythical past.[255] Before 508 the Athenian military was based on so-called *naukraries*, a system about which we know little, but which involved the office of *naukraros* who would supply hoplites and cavalry. After 508 the duties of the *naukraroi* devolved upon the tribes and new *demes*, though they continued, as their name implies (*naus*, or ship), to be responsible for supplying the Athenian fleet with triremes in the Classical era.

Herodotus describes the authority of the Polemarch as equal to that of the Ten Generals, and adds that he was chosen by lot.[256] Yet we know that the Polemarch was also one of the Nine Archons of Athens, and was elected by the whole citizen body.[257] Until 487 these elected Archons wielded considerable executive power; therefore in 490 the Polemarch outranked the generals. This is borne out by the author of the *Athenian Constitution* who reports that after the creation of the office of the Ten Generals and before 487/6, the Polemarch was the commander-in-chief of the Athenian army. In 490 the Polemarch of Athens was Kallimachos, of whom more will be said later.

Herodotus appears to contradict himself about the office of Polemarch. While giving the impression that his authority was equal to that of each general, he seems also to be aware that the Polemarch did play a somewhat more important role in 490 than he would later in the fifth century, when

Herodotus wrote, and that this role was distinguishable from the others. Herodotus says that the Polemarch led the right wing of the Athenian army at Marathon;[258] in ancient Greece this was the supreme commander's traditional position. Yet the ancient historian fails to precisely define the Polemarch's duties in the battle. This may be because just three years after the battle the office of Polemarch was drastically downgraded to the point at which almost all of his old authority was lost.[259] By the time Herodotus began gathering material for his work in the mid-fifth century, the Polemarch was a mere figurehead.

Between 490 and 440 the Athenians engaged in a great number of military conflicts, more than in all the previous century. In command of the forces that fought these wars were the generals, which helps explain why Herodotus assumed that the situation had been the same in 490. It would seem natural to him that the generals exercised actual command at Marathon, just as in later years. The only ones who could set him right were those same generals who had fought at Marathon and who half a century later would probably no longer be alive.

Most scholars believe that the Ten Generals were elected in one of two ways: either individually by their tribes, or collectively by the Athenian Assembly beginning in 501/0.[260] Yet there is general agreement on the duties of the generals and Polemarch in 490. Until 501/0 the Polemarch would have exercised overall command, with the generals probably as his assistants. Even if the generals were in unanimous agreement about an issue, the Polemarch had the power to overrule them and enforce his own will. But when the Ten Generals began to be elected, either by tribe or the Assembly, their authority was upgraded, even though the Polemarch retained his position as senior officer of the army.[261] Above all, the Polemarch was now obliged to concur with a majority decision by the generals, even if he personally disagreed. Yet we must note an observation by Fornara that even after 500 the Polemarch's view did carry weight, especially if he could employ his prestige and personality to sway the generals into taking a majority decision which he considered correct.[262]

It would appear, then, that at the time of the battle of Marathon the Athenian army displayed characteristics of the reforms of 501/0 but at the same time the Ten Generals were to a degree subordinate to the Polemarch.[263] It was he who had overall responsibility for the army while each general's responsibility was limited to the men of his own tribe. The so-called 'prytany of the day' mentioned by Herodotus[264] apparently refers to the right of each general to exercise overall command for one day in turn. What wider duties that status entailed remains vague. We presume that as the Polemarch retained supreme command, the general-of-the-day undertook larger operational responsibilities than the other generals, in close cooperation with the Polemarch.[265] To use a modern analogy, the general-of-the-day might be compared to an executive officer of today.

The criteria by which the citizens of Athens elected the Polemarch and the Ten Generals – both from the two upper classes of the *pentakosiomedimnoi* and the knights – in the early Classical era are unknown. None of them were professional soldiers. Therefore they would have had to show leadership qualities such as social prestige, facility in public speaking, intelligence and daring.[266] Yet in the election for the Ten Generals that took place in the summer of 490 in Athens,[267] the candidates' political views would have played a large part. There would have been no question of the leaders of the army to be even suspected of belonging to the pro-tyranny faction or of holding the opinion that Athens should negotiate with the Persians and Hippias. We may thus rule out the selection of Hipparchos the son of Charmos, who was considered the head of Athens' pro-tyranny faction. There was simply no room for back-door negotiations with Persian diplomacy as in previous years.[268] Athens needed now not negotiators but warriors. In 490 the Athenians picked their generals from those citizens who they knew were not only worthy men, but willing to fight the Persians to the death.

Of these men who were called upon to assume the leadership of the Athenian army at this critical juncture, we have enough information on only one of them that would enable us to understand why he was elected. This is Miltiades, the son of Kimon, of the Philaidai clan, who was elected general of the Oineis tribe for the year 490/89.[269] All the ancient literary sources set him apart from the other generals for the intelligence and drive which he displayed. His previous record had also been impressive. For more than two decades he had been the governor of the Chersonese in Thrace, an Athenian protectorate.[270] In that capacity he had taken part in many military campaigns that gained him knowledge of the battle tactics of other peoples including the Persians. We know that in 513 Miltiades took part in Darius' expedition against the Scythians under the Great King's orders and in subsequent years he fought off various Thracian tribes and Scythians who attacked the Chersonese.[271] Herodotus does not expressly mention that Miltiades fought the Persians in the Ionian Revolt, but it can be gathered from the context of the narrative. Miltiades' seizure of Lemnos with Athenian cooperation may well be connected with the Ionian Revolt.[272] For years, ever since the Scythian expedition of 513, Miltiades had made no secret of his dislike of Darius.[273] Cornelius Nepos figures that the Great King would have been made aware of this attitude, and logically would have been expected to nurse hopes of eventual revenge.[274]

In 493, while the Persians were snuffing out the Ionian Revolt, they also attacked the Chersonese, which indicates that Miltiades was an enemy of Darius and had thrown his support behind the Ionians.[275] Just before the Persians closed in, Miltiades made his escape to Athens. There, however, he was charged with exercising tyrannical rule in the Chersonese and put on trial, probably in the Areopagus, and acquitted.[276] This judicial *contretemps* does not appear to have dented his reputation among the citizens of Athens; it actually grew after his acquittal. [277] Our sources do not say whether Miltiades occupied any office in the Athenian democratic polity from 493, when he returned, to 490, when he was elected general of his Oineis tribe.[278] But we may be sure that the citizens listened carefully to his speeches in the Assembly, and the magistrates to what he told them privately. Miltiades' years of living next door to the Persians had given him wide-ranging experience in military and political affairs that probably no other Athenian could boast. Between 493 and 490, when Athens was intensely aware of the looming Persian menace, Miltiades would have advised the Athenians on how to prepare to meet this deadly danger, making suggestions to the Assembly that were endorsed.

Playing a large part in Miltiades' election as general was his membership of one of the oldest and richest clans of Attica. Though Kleisthenes' reforms restricted the political power of the old aristocratic families around Attica,[279] these families did retain a certain clout in the Assembly, as several of their members held high office in Athens' newly-minted democracy. According to the author of the *Athenian Constitution*,

Miltiades was the political leader of the city's aristocrats.[280] This shows that he was not simply a wealthy Athenian citizen with some influence over the rest, but a leading political figure who could affect the course of events. That Miltiades was elected to the office of general in 490, a mere three years after his return from the Chersonese, points to his actively canvassing for the position, as he knew that the generals elected that year would be called upon to meet the Persian juggernaut. He would be able to help his city far more effectively as a general than as an ordinary citizen; as a former Eponymous Archon, Miltiades could not run for the office of Polemarch.

Shimron and Lazenby conclude that Herodotus' accounts of Miltiades' activity before the battle of Marathon paint him as a 'capable escaper' rather than a military genius.[281] This may not be far from the truth, as no ancient writer who mentions Miltiades says much on his behalf about the battles he fought in.[282] Yet before 490 he undoubtedly had huge experience; moreover, the ancient sources describe him as very clever and resourceful, citing his seizure of power in the Chersonese by engineering the arrest of the local chiefs.[283] He used similar ingenuity in seizing Hephaisteia, one of the two towns of Lemnos.[284] Of course, sometimes cunning was not enough against a powerful foe. But Miltiades had the ability to judge when to discreetly retire from the scene, to return later when circumstances were more favourable to him.[285]

In addition to his aristocratic background, his military and political talents, and his influence over the Athenians who elected him general in 490, Miltiades was also well known as the biggest enemy of the Persians and of Hippias. If the Athenians were to negotiate terms with Datis, one of those terms might well have been the surrender of Miltiades. Even if the Athenians resisted, the Persians after their victory would have hunted him down and likely executed him. Thus he joined his fate to that of Athens. He also was a personal foe of Hippias, as Herodotus reports that Hippias and his brother Hipparchos had assassinated Miltiades' father Kimon.[286] That opened a great chasm of blood between the two men that could never be bridged. Miltiades could well have felt that the fight against the Great King and Hippias at Marathon was his own personal fight, the chance to pay back his father's murderer.

We can still only speculate about the motivations for Miltiades' resolve in leading his fellow-citizens to repel the invaders. Was it perhaps a love for his home city and for liberty? Was it a hatred of the Persians and Hippias? Was it ego and megalomania, or was it a combination of all of them?[287] In a sense it does not matter much, as all this was by and large known to the Athenians who elected him general. Though they may have been aware that Miltiades was not exactly democracy's biggest fan, they must have been sure that he would fight the Persians and Hippias to the last. What matters for us is that his 'personal war' in combination with his great military experience and abilities raised him to the position of natural leader of the Athenians who fought at Marathon, even though he was just the general of a tribe.[288] This would explain the initiatives that ancient writers attribute to him, initiatives that would ordinarily be the preserve of the Polemarch or all the generals together.[289]

Miltiades' clout, which exceeded that of any other general, led some ancient writers to portray him as issuing orders like some Roman emperor.[290] Until quite recently the erroneous general impression was that Miltiades was the commander of the Athenian force at Marathon. In reality, he did admittedly play a role somewhat wider than what would be expected of a tribal general, but he had no special powers. Miltiades had every right to propose defensive measures to the Assembly, as the ancient writers say, just like any ordinary Athenian citizen. What is important is not that he had a democratic right to make his proposals, but that his communications skills persuaded the Assembly to forthwith take actions that saved Athens.

Herodotus writes that Miltiades was the 'tenth' Athenian general.[291] This has led some scholars to conclude that he had rather more authority at Marathon than the other generals did.[292] Others, however, suspect that Herodotus in this way did not want to signify that Miltiades had expanded powers but pointed him out for his role in the battle of Marathon.[293] Most likely Herodotus merely wished to note that Miltiades, far from having any special position, was the last of the Ten Generals whose turn for one-day command would come, after the other nine. Just before noting the position of Miltiades, Herodotus tells of the departure of the Athenian army for Marathon. The ancient historian could have indicated by this that Miltiades would exercise his day's right of command on the tenth day after the army marched. Herodotus' account also confirms that the actual battle took place several days after the Athenians arrived at Marathon, and as it happened on the very day of Miltiades' right to one-day command.[294]

The special aura surrounding Miltiades in the eyes of the Assembly should not blind us to the importance of the Polemarch. The actions and opinions of Kallimachos distinctly eased Miltiades' freedom of action. The ancient sources indicate that Kallimachos was perceptive enough to see the rightness of Miltiades' views and to support them, even though he was Miltiades' superior.[295] The Polemarch's valour on the battlefield shows that, besides his intelligence and patriotism, he possessed a high degree of personal courage. The fact that the Athenian citizens elected him to the highest military office at a very critical juncture shows that the democratic polity was already working efficiently.

However, we know very little about Kallimachos, who remains a somewhat enigmatic figure. Herodotus mentions only that he hailed from Aphidnai,[296] the home district of Harmodios, one of the assassins of Hippias' brother, Hipparchos.[297] Kleisthenes' reforms had developed that area, whose inhabitants were included in the Aiantis tribe, one of Attica's largest. Local particularist sentiment was strong at the time, and the fact that Kallimachos was from Aphidnai could have worked in his favour to get him elected as the man to repulse the Persians and Hippias. An important archaeological find tends to confirm Herodotus; after Kallimachos' death in battle at Marathon, the people of Aphidnai honoured his memory with a monument on the Acropolis of Athens.[298] It was a marble slab topped by an Ionian capital, 4.68 metres high and supporting a statue of Iris, a messenger of the gods.[299] We do not know if Kallimachos had any special connection with the worship of that deity or whether Iris was picked to symbolize the victory at Marathon and simply placed on Kallimachos' monument.[300] The column features an inscription saying that Kallimachos is the person so honoured.

It may be that Kallimachos intended to raise the monument to Iris himself, and that the citizens of Aphidnai did the job after his death. This monument was found in pieces, along with fragments of other sculptures smashed when the Persians seized the Acropolis in 480. It would seem that it was destroyed with particular fury as being dedicated to the Athenian commander who had trounced the Persians at Marathon a decade earlier.[301] The monument itself indicates that immediately after the battle Kallimachos was revered as Athens' greatest hero. Yet following the conclusion of the Persian Wars this reputation appeared to fade. After 479 the Athenians did not restore Kallimachos' monument, as they did other works of art which the Persians either destroyed or took away with them.[302] And after 470, when Miltiades' son Kimon the Younger rose to prominence in Athenian political life, Miltiades' image as the saviour of Athens began to be promoted.[303] Kallimachos was thus shunted into the margins of historical narrative, and most of what was known about him was forgotten.[304]

A second Athenian general who we know for sure fought at Marathon is Stesileos, the son of Thrasyllos, the only one of the ten who perished in the battle.[305] No source has given us the name of his tribe, and besides his name and patronym, nothing more is known about him. His name appears on two vases dated to the close of the sixth century with the adjective 'good' (καλός).[306] The name was not a common one, and the vase inscription could well refer to the general of 490.[307] If that is the case, Stesileos would have been in his thirties when he fell in battle, as the term 'good' was often given to young men at the end of the Archaic era.

According to Plutarch and Aelius Aristides the general of the Antiochis tribe at Marathon was Aristides, the son of Lysimachos.[308] However, scholars are by no means in agreement that Aristides was actually one of the ten Athenian generals at Marathon.[309] Yet circumstantial evidence points to that; after the battle Aristides gained renown as one of Athens' leading politicians, being elected Eponymous Archon in 489/8.[310] It would be reasonable to suppose that his actions in the battle might have catapulted him to fame a year later. An ordinary soldier would have had difficulty gaining such recognition no matter how bravely he had fought. Therefore the evidence is in favour of Aristides' being one of the ten Athenian generals at Marathon. Plutarch adds several vignettes about Aristides' deeds in the battle, lending credence to his account.[311] He also writes that Aristides and Themistokles fought with their tribes side by side, leading some commentators to conclude that Themistokles, too, was one of the Ten Generals. But Plutarch does not specify what rank Themistokles held at Marathon, whether he was indeed the general of his tribe, the Leontis, or simply an ordinary hoplite who happened to be next to Aristides and his Antiochis tribe during the battle.[312] In 490 Themistokles was about thirty-eight years old and can be expected to have fought at Marathon.[313] But we cannot know if he was a general; neither in Plutarch's *Life of Themistokles* nor in any other work do we have any indication, as we have with Aristides. Themistokles served as Eponymous Archon for 493/2, two years before the battle, but that of course is no proof that he was a general in 490.[314] None of Plutarch's many historian predecessors who provided details about Themistokles record that he was one of the Ten Generals at the battle of Marathon.[315] In fact, the way in which Plutarch's narrative places Aristides and Themistokles fighting side by side – the two would go on to become great political rivals – smacks of sensationalism on the part of the author rather than historical fact. Plutarch also alleges that the glory that Miltiades earned on the battlefield, the 'Trophy of Miltiades', kept Themistokles awake during nights;[316] we could gather from this that Themistokles could boast no outstanding act in the battle that would satisfy his pride, especially not the leadership of his tribe. If he had been a general, we would expect that he would have enjoyed his share of the generals' credit; on the contrary, it was Aristides who was elected Eponymous Archon.

Other men who assumed leading roles in Athenian politics in the 480s could have been generals at Marathon.[317] One such possibility is Xanthippos, who had close ties to the controversial Alkmaionid clan. In 489, just a year after the battle, Xanthippos denounced Miltiades before the Assembly, charging him with responsibility for the failure of the Athenian expedition to Paros.[318] The charges stuck, and Miltiades was convicted by the citizens. Thus Xanthippos had considerable influence over the Athenians,[319] which could have stemmed from service at Marathon, where he could have been the general of his Akamantis tribe.

According to Pausanias, the commander of the Plataians at Marathon was Arimnestos, very likely the same general who led the Plataians in the battle of Plataia in 479.[320] Some scholars consider that Arimnestos commanded the left wing of the Greek line at Marathon, but this appears to be a misreading of Herodotus' assertion that the Plataians were on the far left.[321] However, Arimnestos had no vote in the conclave of Athenian generals, and could have been considered subordinate. There is no indication that either Kallimachos or the generals ever asked him for his opinion on anything. Arimnestos obeyed the Athenian orders and confined his command to his own contingent. To the Athenians, Arimnestos' position was probably inferior to that of one of their own generals, and equal to a *taxiarchos* (see below), if such a rank existed then. After the battle the Plataians honoured their general by placing a bust of him in the Temple of Athena Areia in their city, next to a statue of the goddess. When much later Pausanias visited Plataia he saw the temple and wrote that it was paid for by the share of Persian booty which the Plataians received after the battle.[322]

In 490 there would have been officers subordinate to the Polemarch and the Ten Generals, charged with the duty of relaying orders to the rank and file and ensuring their prompt execution, rather like executive officers. But we are here completely in the dark about who they were or whether they even existed, as our ancient sources mention nothing on the subject. But judging from accounts of operations later in the fifth century, several decades after Marathon, the immediate subordinate of a general was a *taxiarchos*, or brigadier, of whom each tribal unit had one.[323] These officers in peacetime had the task, along with *demarchs*, of keeping up the citizenship rolls; therefore, they played a part in recruitment, though their precise duties in the field are unknown. Perhaps, as we have mentioned, they were executive officers sending orders down the line. Lower down the hierarchy, each of the three *trittyes* of a tribe formed a company (*lochos*), headed by a captain (*lochagos* or *lochageuon*).[324] The author of the *Athenian Constitution* says that the brigadiers appointed the captains.[325] We know of one Athenian officer who probably bore the rank of *lochagos* at the battle of Plataia.[326] This opens the possibility that there could have been other hoplite military ranks, as well as the abovementioned ones, at the battle of Marathon.[327]

The owl, symbol of the Athenian democracy, depicted as a hoplite on an Attic red-figure skyphos of c. 475 BC. (*Louvre Museum, Paris, CA 2192*)

The Faravahar emblem symbolized Zoroastrianism, the primary religion of the Persian Empire. Persepolis, c. 500 BC.

A scene from an Attic red-figure kylix by the 'Triptolemos Painter' depicts a Greek hoplite fighting a Persian archer. (*National Museum of Scotland, Edinburgh, 1888.213*)

A Greek stone-thrower soldier (lithobolos) on an Attic red-figure skyphos of the mid-fifth century BC. (*Kunsthistorisches Museum, Vienna, ANSA IV 1922*)

The greek bronze arrowhead ('first type') found at Fylla is identical to many arrowheads from Marathon. (Source: *J.J. Coulton et al., 112, 6.1., SF 15*)

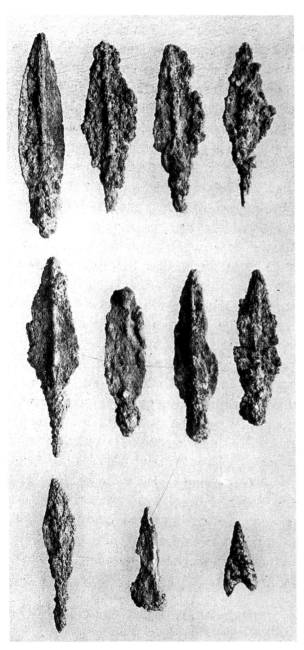

Persian iron arrowheads excavated at the Athens Acropolis and used by Xerxes' archers in 480. They are identical to those Brock reputedly found at Marathon ('fourth type'). (Source: *Broneer, 116, fig. 4*)

A marble portrait of the Roman period found on the Athens Acropolis and considered to be of Miltiades. (*Acropolis Museum, Athens, 2344. Photograph by S. Mavrommatis*)

Aerial photograph of the coast of Marathon with the promontory of Kynosoura and Schinias in the foreground. (*Photograph by N. Daniilidis*)

Aerial photograph of the Tumulus of the Athenians at Marathon. The Lesser Marsh, Brexiza pass and Agrieliki are visible in the background. (*Photograph by N. Daniilidis*)

Brexiza pass (the 'Gates of Marathon'), and the Lesser Marsh, as seen from the coast of Marathon. The 206-metre spur of Agrieliki where the Greek camp of 490 BC is located is in the background (*Photograph by N. Daniilidis*)

Part of the fortifications of the Greek camp at the 206-metre spur of Agrieliki. (*Photograph by Jeff Vanderpool. Published by permission of the Archaeological Ephorate of Eastern Attica*)

The Greek camp at Agrieliki commanded a strategic view of the Marathon plain and Brexiza pass. (*Photograph by the authors. Published by permission of the Archaeological Ephorate of Eastern Attica*)

The view of the Marathon plain from the Greek camp. (*Photograph by the authors*)

Monumental inscription of the classical period on a rock face in the Greek camp at Marathon. This structure is possibly an altar linked to the battle of Marathon. (*Photograph by the authors and Jeff Vanderpool*)

Plaque A10 of the frieze of the Heroön of Trysa in Lykia may depict Miltiades and the other nine Athenian generals leaving the Greek camp at Marathon to fight the Persians. (*Kunsthistoriches Museum, Vienna. Source: O. Benndorf, Das Heroon von Gjolbaschi–Trysa, Jahrbuch der Kunsthistorischen Sammlungen des Allerhochsten Kaiserhauses XI, Wien, 1890*)

A Greek hoplite on an Attic black–figure kylix of the fifth century BC sacrificing a ram just before a battle. (*The Cleveland Museum of Art, Cleveland, 26.242*)

The battle of Marathon on a Roman sarcophagus of the second century AD at the Santa Giulia Civici Musei di Brescia. (Source: *J. Zingerle, 'Relief in Pola', Jahreshefte des osterreichischen archaologischen institutes in Wien, Band X, 157–168, Wien, 1907*)

A fragmentary relief from a sarcophagus of the Roman period probably depicting Kynegeiros attacking a Persian ship during the battle of Marathon. (Source: *J. Zingerle, 'Relief in Pola', Jahreshefte des osterreichischen archaologischen institutes in Wien, Band X, 157–168, Wien, 1907*)

An Athenian hoplite fighting with three Persians on an Attic black–figure lekythos of c. 490 BC. It is likely that this scene was inspired by the battle of Marathon. (*National Archaeological Museum, Athens, 14691*)

A group of Greek hoplites and an archer waiting in a marsh to ambush the enemy. This scene from an Attic black–figure lekythos of c. 490 BC may allude to the fighting in the Lesser Marsh during the battle of Marathon. (*Metropolitan Museum, New York, 26.60.76*)

Scene from an Attic red-figure kylix by the 'Triptolemos Painter' of c. 490 BC showing Greek hoplites attacking Persian cavalry and probably associated with the battle of Marathon. (*National Museum of Scotland, Edinburgh, 1888.213*)

Greek hoplite and light armed soldier fighting side by side against cavalry on an Attic red-figure cup of the first half of the fifth century BC. (*Antikensammlung Staatliche Museen, Schloss Charlottenburg, Berlin, F 2295*)

Reconstruction 1 of the Battle of Marathon. (Source: *J.-J. Barthelemy. Maps, plans, views, and coins illustrative of the travels of Anacharsis the Younger in Greece, during the middle of the Fourth century before the Christian era. London, 1806*)

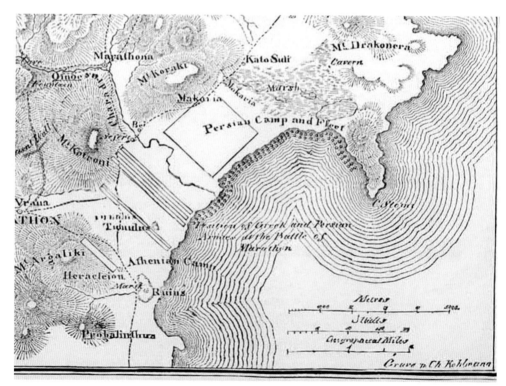

Reconstruction 2 of the Battle of Marathon. (Source: *George Finlay, 'On the Battle of Marathon', Transaction of the Royal Society of Literature of the United Kingdom 3 (1839)*).

A Graeco–Scythian gold horseman appliqué showing a Scythian archer on horseback, his bow and arrow drawn ready to fire. Fourth Century. (*Bonhams. Sale 11597. Lot 245*)

The Temple of Athena Nike at the Acropolis of Athens in a painting by Carl Friedrich Werner, 1877. (*Benaki Museum, Athens, 23956*)

The beach of Schinias where the Persians landed at Marathon. (*Jeff Vanderpool, Marathon*. The Monuments)

The Tumulus of the Athenians. (*Jeff Vanderpool, Marathon*. The Monuments)

Two scenes from the battle of Marathon as depicted in the south frieze of the temple of Athene Nike. (*Acropolis Museum, Athens*)

A Corinthian helmet found in Olympia and inscribed with the name of Miltiades. (*Olympia Museum. Photograph of the Deutsche Archaeologische Institut, Athens*)

Andrew MacCallum, 'View of Marathon' 1874. The main theme of this painting is the Tumulus of the Athenians at Marathon. (*Benaki Museum, Athens, 24524*)

The remnants of the 'Trophy of Marathon' were used as a building material in a medieval tower. (*Photograph by Eugene Vanderpool, 1965*)

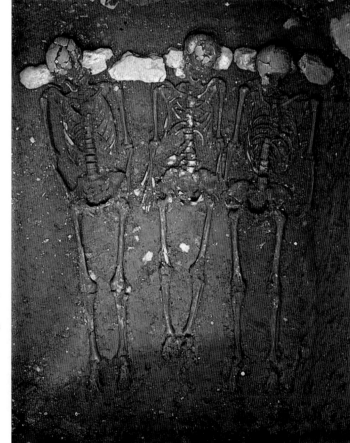

Three of the twenty-one skeletons of the Spartans who were killed in action in 403 BC at Piraeus and were buried at the Kerameikos in Athens. These may belong to the Olympic champion Lakrates and the two polemarchoi, Chairon and Thibrakos. (*Photograph of the Deutsche Archaeologische Institut, Athens*)

Chapter 3

The Athenians at Marathon

As soon as the Athenians heard that the Persians had landed at Marathon, they despatched their expeditionary force there without delay. Pressure from Miltiades was responsible for the swiftness of the reaction; his haste, however, was not aimed at preventing the Persian landing but at seizing the spot that would block the Persian advance towards Athens. This was the Brexiza pass, the first objective of Miltiades' planning. At the same time, measures were taken to supply and administer the force that would meet the invader. Shortly before the Athenian expeditionary force set out, Kallimachos made an offering to Artemis Agrotera for an Athenian victory.

The route that the Athenians took to Marathon is important for the light it sheds on the battle tactics: it followed the regular cart road via Pallene and the Mesogaia to the Brexiza pass. It was the same route that the Persians intended to take in reverse towards Athens. The reason why the Persians stayed at Marathon and did not move forward was precisely because the Athenians had quickly occupied the Brexiza pass and blocked the way. The Athenians encamped on high ground overlooking the pass, where they were safe from Persian cavalry attacks; the Plataians then joined the Athenians in the camp. The Persians were thus compelled to stay in the Marathon plain, and hence the first Greek aim was accomplished; but a large enemy force in the plain could not leave Attica unless defeated in battle. How could the Athenians prevail against a numerically superior and better-armed enemy?

One of the biggest unsolved mysteries of the battle of Marathon is just where both sides encamped before the clash. Our research indicates that the Persians controlled the greater part of the plain and erected the camp for their combat troops, infantry and horsemen, on the flattest part. This was Plasi, roughly in the middle of the plain. Most of the auxiliaries, plus the fleet rowers, remained on the beach at Schinias or on their ships. Ancient sources report that the Greek camp was protected by hills from which they could safely observe the Persians. Herodotus writes that before the battle the Athenians 'lined up at the

Shrine to Herakles'; most researchers think that he refers to their encampment but he could mean that the Athenians arrayed themselves for battle there and that they had originally encamped elsewhere.

Whether the Athenians encamped at the Shrine to Herakles or lined up for battle there, the location of that shrine would be of the utmost importance in shedding light on various aspects of the battle. Many archaeologists have tried to discover traces of the shrine in the hope that it would reveal where the Athenian camp was. Two inscriptions found at Valaria, near the entrance to the Brexiza pass and connected with the worship of Herakles, indicate that the shrine would have been in that area. Revealing in this respect are the remains of the ruined Byzantine church of Saints Theodore at Valaria, where architectural pieces of an ancient temple were part of the stonework.

The camp was in a strategic position controlling the Brexiza pass and enabling observation of the entire Marathon plain and the Persians in it. Its position on high ground gave it a defensive advantage. Our research has discovered that the camp was located on a 206m high spur and adjacent ravine on the north-east slope of Mount Agrieliki. Remains of a provisionally-built but extensive rampart have been found there with traces of auxiliary installations that were put up in haste; moreover, when the crisis passed the structures were abandoned, as evidenced by the lack of permanent remains and ceramics.

The Athenians and Plataians remained in their camp on the 206m spur during the days preceding the battle. The Athenian command occupied the main structure of the rampart, while the thousands of troops of the Greek expeditionary force were spread out over the adjacent slopes. We are led to this conclusion not only by existing evidence but also by new evidence that has come to light. The rampart so far has been largely untouched by human intervention, and a visitor is able to go to where one of the brightest pages of world history was written 2,500 years ago.

I: The March

1. The offering to Artemis Agrotera

Ancient sources connect the Athenians' march to Marathon with the shrine of Artemis Agrotera ('of the Fields') which stood a short distance outside the city limits.[1] According to Xenophon, the Athenians promised the deity that if they should defeat the Persians with her aid, every year they would sacrifice one goat for each one of the enemy they killed.[2] Other sources say this oath was given personally by Miltiades or Kallimachos;[3] Hammond, however, is of the opinion that it was the Athenian Assembly that decided on the oath and Kallimachos as Polemarch was the one to utter it.[4] Reinforcing this view is Plutarch's note that this annual sacrifice to Artemis Agrotera was voted into effect by the Assembly.[5] Moreover, long after the battle when the office of Polemarch had lost almost all of its powers of command over the army, it was this magistrate who formally officiated over the sacrifice.[6]

Kallimachos, however, did not survive the battle; therefore the first of the annual commemorative sacrifices would have been carried out by his successor as Polemarch. Also, when after the battle the Athenians learned how many Persians had been killed (6,400)[7] it would have been impossible to get together that number of goats for Artemis Agrotera every year. So a sort of compromise with the goddess was achieved by which 500 goats would be enough for the annual event.[8] The oldest reference to the durability of this custom comes from Aristophanes, while Xenophon, who wrote a century after the battle, confirms that the custom was kept up.[9]

Krentz believes that Kallimachos swore the pledge to Artemis Agrotera after the army had got into position at Marathon, just before the battle.[10] Others, however, say it took place in Athens; Parke and Dionysopoulos, for example, suggest that the oath was taken on the day the army marched,[11] while Hammond suggests the day of the deity's festival in Athens which according to Plutarch was the sixth day of Boedromion.[12] Hammond believes that was the day Eretria fell to the Persians, two days before the Athenian army marched to Marathon.[13] Parke concurs, though he suggests that the march began on the same day as the festival of Artemis Agrotera.[14] There is certainly a connection between the festival of Artemis Agrotera and the battle of Marathon since the Athenians after 490 annually commemorated their victory on the sixth of Boedromion and not the day of the battle.[15]

Yet the Athenians' offering to the goddess may not have been the result of a mere calendar coincidence. We know that Artemis Agrotera was worshipped as a war deity in Lakonia since Archaic times; just before going into battle the Spartan army would sacrifice a goat to her.[16]

As regards Athens, we have no evidence that she was honoured as a war goddess before 490;[17] thus her fame as a military deity could have spread, and possibly she could have been invoked by the Athenians to hasten the Spartans to their aid. It may be that the pledge was made at her shrine outside Athens as the army was setting out, and Kallimachos would have administered it in full view of the soldiers, as a solemn binding of them all.[18] There would have been enough space, as the shrine is above the extensive area of the Olympieion, and the soldiers would have taken the oath facing the shrine.

The worship of Artemis Agrotera was greatly enhanced in Athens after the battle. In the middle of the fifth century the Athenians built a new marble temple to her, adorned with a wealth of sculpture, that replaced the older sandstone one on the site.[19] Each year on the sixth of Boedromion, the Athenians would celebrate there their victory at Marathon.

2. On the march to Marathon

About two weeks elapsed between the time the Persians took Karystos and their landing at Marathon.[20] During this time the Athenians feverishly worked out possible tactics to employ in case the enemy landed at Marathon or Phaleron. When it became known that Marathon was the objective, the Athenians were prepared to send an army there at once. We gather this from Aristotle and other ancient writers, who claim that Miltiades urged an immediate march to Marathon when news of the landing arrived.[21] For Miltiades to be able to make this proposal, the Athenians would already have completed plans for their defence. Justin, Polemon the Elder and Aelius Aristides all agree on the urgency of Miltiades' request, and that the Athenians could not wait for the expected arrival of Spartan reinforcements.[22] Souda asserts that an unnamed Athenian general suggested that the Athenians wait for the Spartans to arrive, but he was overruled by Miltiades with the backing of Kallimachos.[23] Classical writers such as Aristotle and Demosthenes, who lived relatively soon after the event, confirm that Miltiades took the lead in the defence of Athens from the earliest stage in the Athenian preparations to meet the invader.[24] Aristotle says that Miltiades proposed to the Assembly an immediate march, without the soldiers even taking along rations, and the motion was approved. This, a reference to the so-called '*Decree of Miltiades*', probably means that the army was expected to get its provisions after it encamped at Marathon.[25]

These references indicate that Miltiades was already highly influential at Athens, and throws some light on how the army would be provisioned.[26] It also demonstrates Miltiades' clear impatience to set out immediately. However, he knew well that the Athenians would not be able to forage for supplies in the Marathon plain and homesteads that would be in Persian hands. Thus they would need a supply line from the rear. Miltiades request that the Athenians march without provisions is not for the three-day rations that each one had to have with him (see below) but the train of supply transport. If the supply carts set out for Marathon together with the army, they would obstruct its swift march, seriously setting back the time schedule.[27] Aristotle goes on to say that Miltiades told the Athenians that they would re-provision themselves at Marathon. If this is true, then it was probably the first time in Athens' history that the provisioning of an army was done by the state.[28] Miltiades must have had a clear idea of just where to camp at Marathon, a place where he knew that a supply train could reach the army's rear after it had camped there.[29]

Ancient literary sources reveal the pressure that Miltiades piled on the Athenian Assembly to get the army moving with the least possible delay. The oldest such reference occurs in Aristophanes' *Wasps* in the phrase 'setting out at once'.[30] This play was staged in 422, nearly seven decades after the battle.[31] A century after the battle Isokrates said the Athenians went to Marathon on the same day the Persians landed.[32] Polemon the Elder goes so far as to say that Miltiades was in such a hurry that he would even have the troops run all the way![33] This writer and sophist attributes the haste to 'acute danger'[34] that must of course refer to the Persian landing. Yet there must have been some other reason for the hurry; Miltiades would not have believed that, however fast the army marched, it could stop the Persian landing, as a large part of the Persian force would be already ashore by the time it got there. Neither could he hope that the Athenians would be able to defend the Tetrapolis. He rather planned on blocking the Persian advance on Athens by bottling up the enemy on the Marathon plain. The Persians, for their part, certainly had the intention of moving on Athens as soon as the landing process was completed and laying siege to the city as they had to Eretria.

The only route the Persians could take was through the Brexiza pass at the southern end of the Marathon plain that leads to the plains of Mesogaia.[35] The Athenians would have been able to effectively block this pass, the only place on the route to Athens where they could have done it. If the Athenian army was too late in securing positions at the Brexiza pass before it was seized by the Persians, it would have to either do battle in the Mesogaia plains or withdraw to Athens. Miltiades knew or sensed that if the Athenians took on the Persians in the open plain where the latter had the advantage, it would mean defeat. In such a case the Greek flanks could not be protected by natural terrain features and would be exposed to destructive attacks by the Persian cavalry. If, on the other hand, the Athenians chose to hole themselves up behind the walls of Athens, the Persians would be there in a matter of hours and immediately begin a siege, closing off all routes to the city. In that case not even the Spartans would have been of much help. After either a battle or a siege, Athens would fall to the enemy just as Eretria had. Miltiades' strategy was to quickly march to secure the Brexiza pass before the Persians could move south.[36] There is evidence that by now he had worked out a comprehensive strategy for the encounter at Marathon.[37]

In the Athenian army were a few horsemen; besides the Polemarch and the generals, many well-to-do Athenians had horses. But the great bulk of the army marched behind their commanders on foot.[38] The different classes of soldiers bore equipment according to their means; the hoplite had a helmet, breastplate, greaves, a shield, two spears and a sword. We don't know how the hoplites packed their equipment on campaign; it would appear that the weapons were tied to the shield by leather straps, and thus portable.[39] But the hoplites themselves did not carry their weaponry; those and other provisions were carried by the hoplites' personal slaves. However, as we have seen, in 490 many Athenian slaves had been freed for service at the front as light-armed troops. We speculate that these men could have had the task of carrying their former hoplite masters' equipment all the way from Athens to Marathon. Scholars in the past believed that even the less-well-off *zeugitai* would have had personal slaves to carry their weapons, but more recent opinion holds that they probably had beasts of burden to carry the loads.[40] Horses, mules and donkeys, unlike carts, could move at the same pace as the foot soldiers. and the poorer hoplites could have had such animals with them.[41]

Almost all the thetes on campaign served as light-armed soldiers, carrying a bow and small arrows, or a javelin or a sling. Some had a short sword strapped on or a hunting knife.[42] Some may have worn helmets, but most used an animal-hide cap that would offer some limited protection in a combat situation.[43] In the Athenian army of 490, as we have seen, the poorest *ptochoi* would have not been able to afford any real weapons; they either took with them farm implements or nothing at all. They would be expected to fight with whatever came to hand, either farm tools, cudgels and stones, or by picking up the weapons of anyone who had fallen near them, friend or foe.

During the fifth century every Athenian who set out on campaign had with him a small bag, the *gylion,* containing three days' rations.[44] These would consist of wheat or barley bread, and salted foods (*opsa*) wrapped in vine leaves. The *opsa* of the poorer soldiers would consist of garlic, onions, olives and cheese, while their better-off comrades would enjoy more expensive fare such as figs, smoked meat and fish.[45] The vine-leaf wrapping could preserve the salted *opsa* for several days. Such fare required no cooking and could be consumed on the march.[46] But it could last no longer than a few days, and on an extended campaign cooked food would be needed. Wine was a basic staple of an ancient Greek army on the march.[47] The better-off would have their own flasks with expensive wine, preferably from Chios, while the rest had to make do with Samos or Thasos wine, or cheaper local varieties. Athens in the Classical era was not famed for the quality of its wine, and therefore we can presume that the flasks of the men in 490 contained mostly local wine; the poorest soldiers probably had to drink the worst quality wine that had the taste of vinegar.

As far as we know the Athenians had no ceremony for departing soldiers as in Sparta, where the women publicly handed the shields to their male relatives with the injunction to return either 'with your shield or on it'. Some Attic vase paintings of the fifth century seem to show departing hoplites receiving their weapons from either their father or older male relative, and sometimes from an elderly woman, probably the mother.[48] This procedure seems not to have been accompanied by any other gesture apart from a handshake.

The hoplite and light-armed citizens and freedmen would at first have followed the course of the Ilissos river. On the east bank of the river, about a kilometre from the city limits, stood the shrine of Artemis Agrotera. The army would have made a brief halt there, and as we have seen, Kallimachos would have carried out a sacrifice together with a pledge and a prayer for victory. When the march resumed, the men passed in front of the shrine and proceeded northeast. The tramp of their feet would have mingled with the rush of the water in the Ilissos river. One can imagine the commanders in front, silent and pensive, considering the dangers ahead. No doubt many high-flown patriotic speeches had echoed in the Assembly, but every soldier knew that resistance to the enemy was much easier said than done.

We may also imagine some general riding up and down the column urging the *taxiarchoi* and the junior officers to pick up the pace. This man would probably have been Miltiades. He was not particularly liked by most Athenians who suspected him of having ruled Chersonese as a tyrant and because he had escaped the death penalty in his recent trial thanks to his aristocratic friends. Some soldiers may well have inwardly cursed him as he rode past them, yet they also would have felt a degree of admiration for him. He was over 60, and yet here he was, displaying the energy of someone in his twenties![49] Everyone in Athens knew that such a man as Miltiades, a mortal enemy of Darius and Hippias, would never consent to discuss capitulation terms with the Persians. There was a lingering suspicion among the Athenian citizenry that some of the wealthier men would have been prepared to surrender the city; but Miltiades, they knew, was not one them. His fellow Oineis tribesmen had elected him their general a few weeks before on the strength of his indisputable leadership qualities.[50] Ever since his return to Athens he had been haranguing the Assembly on the Persian threat, and had been heeded precisely because, besides his oratorical talents, he was the one who best knew that threat. He had been the only one who had argued that the Persians could be repulsed only if the Athenians prepared with a cool head, seized the initiative and acted with alacrity instead of taking refuge behind the walls. If Miltiades rode along the column of the Athenians marching to Marathon few soldiers would have cheered him as he passed by them, except for his own men of the Oineis tribe.[51] Miltiades would probably not have noticed this as he rode to join Kallimachos and his fellow generals in the front of the long column.

3. The route of the march

No historical account of the battle of Marathon makes any mention of the route the Athenian army took to get there. Yet the issue has its importance, as the precise location of the Athenian camp at Marathon – to this day unknown – would directly depend on the route taken.[52] If we knew where the Athenian camp was, we could estimate where the Persians had encamped and also where the clash took place, assuming it was somewhere between the camps.

Scholars present us with two alternatives for the route of the march. The first, the Pallene route, proceeds through the Mesogaia plain between the heights of Hymettos and Pentelikon, continues east of the present-day town of Nea Makri and approaches the Marathon plain from the south. As today, the road was during antiquity the main connection between Athens and northeast Attica. For much of its route it passes through the flattish fertile Mesogaia plain; excavations have uncovered sections of an ancient road that wheeled vehicles could traverse.[53] This would have been an obvious route for the army and the supply trains following in its wake.

The second alternative, the Pentelikon route, winds over the mountain of the same name. In fact, the route could consist of three separate paths starting at what are today the northern suburbs of Athens.[54] The first path starts at Kifissia and proceeds over the western spur of Pentelikon to Stamata, where it forks into two smaller paths, the one leading through the Aulon valley to the small plain at Vranas, and the other through the Oenoe canyon – near the present municipality of Marathon – to the area known as Beis between the heights of Kotroni and Stavrokoraki.[55] Sir James Frazer, a British scholar specializing in the geography of ancient Greece, in the late-nineteenth century described the two paths as stony and irregular. The second path starting at present-day Ekali ran across the south of Pentelikon to Rapentoza and over to Vranas. According to Frazer this path was especially hazardous and generally avoided by the locals.[56] A third path began at Kifissia, went through Ekali and ended up at Vranas, following the Dionysos and Rapentoza streams. For the last 3.5 kilometres it became very narrow.[57]

The route along the paths from Kifissia and Ekali to Marathon turns out to be some five kilometres shorter than that through Pallene. Yet it was hardly suitable for an army on the march, either that of the Athenians towards Marathon or that of the Persians towards Athens, especially if the latter had cavalry.[58] In some places these mountain paths were so narrow that they could only be traversed single file. Parts of the route were on an incline and along the rims of crevasses and cliffs; horses and carts would find it impossible to traverse. Yet despite the formidable difficulties an army would face in those conditions, the bulk of nineteenth and early-twentieth century scholarship took it for granted that the Athenians used the Pentelikon route. As all these paths end up at Vranas, it was natural for researchers of the battle to assume that Vranas is the area where the Athenians encamped in Marathon in 490. Therefore, they figured, the battle itself must have been fought nearby.

In 1838, however, George Finlay definitely ruled out the Pentelikon route, insisting that any route other than that via Pallene which, after all, was much more passable than Pentelikon and the only one negotiable by wheeled carts, would be impractical.[59] Finlay argued that the Athenians knew that the Persians, with their considerable army and cavalry force, would use the Pallene road to march on Athens, and therefore it would make sense for the Athenians to block them there.[60] The British historian also believed that Peisistratos had taken the same route to Athens in 546, defeating a force sent to stop him at Pallene.[61] Another consideration backing up Finlay's conclusion is that while it would be possible for the cavalry-less Athenians to take the Pentelikon mountain route, the Persians, because they had cavalry, would certainly not use it; moreover, the hilly terrain would give the Athenians a defensive advantage, something the Persians knew. Therefore, there could be no thought of taking to the mountain, especially as it would leave the Pallene and Mesogaia route free for the Persians.[62] According to Finlay, since travellers of his time reached Marathon via the Pentelikon route, they tended to assume that the Athenian army would have done the same.[63] Those travellers recorded that parts of the path over the mountain were paved with shaped stones, lending the impression that the path was an ancient road.[64] There is no longer any trace of those stones, while students of ancient Greek road-building rule out the road's existence in 490.[65]

Though Finlay's arguments seem to be convincing, the great majority of nineteenth century scholars dismissed them, except for German historian Ernst Curtius and Greek scholar Ioannis Typaldos.[66] Only towards the close of the nineteenth century did Frazer revive Finlay's arguments,[67] which received rather wider acceptance in the first half of the twentieth century.[68] After the 1960s the theory gained more acceptance still, with more elements added.[69] Thus Berthold avers that the Greeks followed the Pallene route in order to protect as much of Attica as possible from the invaders; the Mesogaia in particular had great economic and strategic value for Athens.[70] An Athenian army could also protect the coastal communities from Persian sea raids and secure provisions from the inland communities. The Mesogaia towns also supplied many Athenian fighting men, most of whom can be presumed to have joined the army en route to Marathon. The army's presence would also lend the locals a sense of security, especially those who had to flee their homes at Marathon to find refuge farther south.

The great majority of modern writers conclude that the Athenians took the Pallene route to Marathon. Yet there are adherents of the Pentelikon theory.[71] Notably, one of these is Nicholas Hammond, who in 1930 walked the distance from Athens via Pentelikon and figured that the Athenians would have managed it.[72] He cites his experiences as a British liaison officer with Greek partisans during the 1941–44 German occupation to conclude that the ancient Greeks would have been equally adept at using mountain paths to move men.[73] But Burn and Berthold counter-argue that the analogy between the Athenians at Marathon and twentieth-century Greek partisans is a false one; the Pentelikon paths would simply have been too narrow and difficult for any large army to traverse, and halts would have been frequent. Hammond, on the other hand, says that not only did the Athenians use that route, but the Persians intended to use it as well.[74] Against this, however, Green sets the aforementioned point that use of the Pentelikon route would have left the easier Pallene route wide open for the Persians to march unopposed through the Brexiza pass.[75] Hammond later conceded that the Pallene route was a possibility, as on a map in one of his publications about the battle of Marathon he places the Athenians at Valaria near Brexiza, indicating that they got there via Pallene.[76]

We decided to check the Pentelikon route for ourselves, and we must agree with Finlay and Frazer that the mountain paths even today are all narrow and hard to negotiate.[77] The environment of the mountain, moreover, is ideal for an army to defend itself against an enemy climbing up from Marathon, and thus if the Persians attempted the route they would meet with disaster in the defiles.[78] We may speculate that only some Greek foot couriers and reconnaissance teams could have used the Pentelikon paths.[79]

It is thus almost a certainty that the Athenian army, considering the sheer difficulty of the mountain route and the need to accommodate thousands of men and pack animals, took the coastal Pallene route to Marathon. Today it corresponds to Mesogeion Avenue as it goes through Aghia Paraskevi and then becomes Marathonos Avenue going through Pallene (now Pallini), Pikermi and Nea Makri to end up at Marathon. The plain of Marathon is entered from the south through a pass flanked by the sea on the right and the Agrieliki height on the left. The pass is about 1.5 kilometres long and about 1.2 kilometres wide. As we have seen, until the 1930s the pass was narrower still, as much of it was taken up by the Lesser Marsh, so named in contrast to the Great Marsh at the northern end of the Marathon plain.[80] The area is known as Brexiza. The Lesser Marsh existed at the time of the battle and the water line in the southern coast of Marathon was approximately where it is today.[81] So the ancient route through Brexiza must have been at most 200 metres wide, narrowing to a few dozen metres where the pass debouches into the plain; today's Marathonos Avenue runs exactly over that narrow stretch, reaching Valaria at the southern end of the plain.[82]

Herodotus reports that the Plataians arrived at Marathon to find the Athenians already there; therefore, they did not go to Athens first to join their allies and march together. Plataia is in Boiotia, just past the Attic border northwest of Marathon. The most likely route of the Plataians, then, would have been via Acharnai and then over the Pallene route that the Athenians took. Of course, an alternative way over Pentelikon cannot be ruled out. The Plataians did not have more than about 1,000 men and maybe less, and lacked cavalry. Such a small number would not have had undue difficulty negotiating the mountain paths. Cornelius Nepos, however, in contrast to Herodotus, writes that the Plataians went to Athens first and marched to Marathon together with the Athenians. It is possible to combine the two accounts and suppose that the Plataians went to Athens first, found that the Athenians had already marched, and followed in their tracks. We must remember that the Athenian decision to march was a hurried affair, and there was no time to wait either for the Spartans or the Plataians.

The distance from the city of Athens to Marathon, some 40 kilometres, could have been covered in half a day.[83] We consider that when the Athenians reached the southern end of the Marathon plain the Persians had not yet completed their landing at Schinias beach. The appearance of Athenians was the reason why the Persians stayed in the plain and did not advance to the Mesogaia and the Attic hinterland. The Athenians not only knew exactly where they would encamp at Marathon; they had seized a strategic point blocking the progress of the Persian army and offering considerable protection against enemy attack, especially by the cavalry. The appearance of the Athenians threw the Persians' initial plans into disarray and forced them to remain in the Marathon plain and clash with the Greeks there.[84]

Yet, even if we assume that the Greeks attained their initial aim of blocking the Persian advance south, their position was still inferior to that of their opponents. A large enemy force had assembled on the Marathon plain that had no intention of withdrawing without a fight. It was up to the Greeks, though, to choose the time and method of the first attack. The big problem for the Greek commanders was how to prevail against a numerically superior foe that had a strong cavalry arm as well as other advantages.

II: The Opposing Armies

1. The Persian camp

Some ancient sources say that the Persians had set up a camp at Marathon, but give no more details about exactly where the camp was or what it comprised.[85] Nepos writes that after their defeat in the battle: 'the Persians withdrew not to their camp but to their ships'.[86] Pausanias, the first student of the archaeology of the battle, in the second century AD reported finding what he considered traces of the Persian camp. In particular, at a spot northwest of the Great Marsh, he found some spaces hewn into the rock that he thought would have been horse shelters: 'above the lake are stone cradles for Artaphernes' horses and traces of his tent on the rocks'.[87] Pausanias would presumably have got his information from the locals.[88] However, the spaces hewn into the rock were simply traces of stone quarrying in the surrounding foothills.[89] After the battle a legend appears to have arisen about a treasure trove that the Persians had hidden at or near their camp; but this can be safely discounted, as well as the recent theory that the camp was at today's Kato Souli, based solely on the rock cuttings.[90]

Pausanias also recorded that he saw close by 'a lake of which the greater part was marshy'.[91] Today there is a small salty lake called Drakonera near the adjacent hill southeast of the Great Marsh. In Pausanias' time there was indeed a lagoon that was marshy in places and whose water was salty where the sea entered; over time the Great Marsh was formed, and Drakonera appears to be the remnant of the larger body of water that Pausanias saw.[92] About 300 metres southeast of Drakonera, the shoreline of Schinias beach begins. The consensus of opinion is that the Persians landed at Schinias and moored their ships alongside one another;[93] the Kynosoura promontory would have served as a windbreak for the ships moored at Schinias. The crews would have been placed in readiness to depart for Phaleron in case the Athenians were defeated or capitulated.[94] That could explain why the ships were able to sail away quickly after the Persian defeat. If the ships had been drawn up on shore, almost certainly the Greeks would have been able to seize many more than the seven Herodotus relates.[95] Between Schinias beach and the Great Marsh the sand rises into a ridge where today there is a pine wood. Geological studies reveal that a ridge existed at Schinias also in ancient times, and it is possible that pine trees were there as well. This may explain Pausanias' claim that the Persians 'landed at a grove'.[96]

The Persian force included a cavalry arm which, as soon as it landed, would have begun reconnaissance patrols in the immediate area.[97] These patrols would also have served to deter any Greek attempt to oppose the landing. Their task was made easier by the lack of any Athenian cavalry. First to be occupied would have been the town of Trikorynthos, as nearest to the coast at Schinias. The communities of the *demes* of Marathon and Oenoe would have had the same fate;[98] however, the invaders seem not to have taken Probalinthos, as in that case they would have dominated the Brexiza pass as well.[99] Probalinthos, as we have seen, was at the southern end of the Marathon plain and a key point on the route to Athens. We assume that as the Persian cavalry patrols probed southwards towards Probalinthos and Brexiza, they saw a considerable Greek presence taking up the northeast foothills of Agrieliki dominating the Brexiza pass.

The men whom the Persians saw blocking their way were the 4,000 Athenian *klerouchoi* of Chalkis, perhaps joined by men from the Tetrapolis. After presumably coordinating their moves with the Athenian authorities, they had taken up a position at a height overlooking Brexiza as soon as the Persian fleet had come into sight and it had become plain that it was heading for Marathon.[100] The defenders were some seven kilometres south of Schinias and constituted the first serious obstacle to the Persian plan to march south. Within a matter of hours after the *klerouchoi* occupied the position, the Athenian main force turned up to further secure the position.

The Persians would have perceived their tactical disadvantage at Brexiza, and their commanders thus decided that the battle would have to be waged at Marathon. This realization would have forced them to move their combat units away from Schinias and into the plain, and to secure the towns except for Probalinthos.[101] As masters of the whole plain, the Persians would have been able to pick the best place for a camp. They did not give up their original plan to move on Athens through the Brexiza pass, but hoped to draw the Greeks into a fight beforehand or intimidate them into surrendering.[102] It would have made no sense to keep the combat troops on the beach and far from the enemy. Neither would the Persians have set up their camp anywhere near the Great Marsh, as it would present obvious difficulties.[103] Far better to camp on the plain itself, especially as the Athenians had no cavalry and therefore were in no position to mount a surprise assault. The Persians pinned great hopes on the size of their army and the awe it would strike into the hearts of their foes.

Herodotus says that the Greeks decided to line up about eight stadia (1,500 metres) from the Persians, indicating that the latter were already well inland. We believe that the distance Herodotus mentioned was the minimum between the Greek lines and the nearest Persian units. As we shall see, the Greeks positioned themselves at Valaria in front of the Brexiza pass; 1,500 metres away, the Persians would have been at today's Plasi.[104] This latter location is the flattest part of the Marathon plain, and until the twentieth century it lay between the streams of Skorpios and Kainourgios, both outlets for the Charadros river.[105] We have no way of knowing whether the beds of those streams – indeed of the Charadros itself – were at the same place in ancient times, though most researchers place them rather to the north of where they are today.[106] At the end of the summer of 490 those watercourses would have been either very low or dry, and hence little if any hindrance to the Persian moves. Their banks, in fact, might have acted as ramparts against any attack by the Greeks.

The Persians usually erected rough battlements around their camps while on campaign; these were made of logs in front of which was a defensive trench.[107] We may assume that this was done at Marathon, as we know it was done ten years later at the Persian camps prior to the battles of Plataia and Mykale.[108] The Persian ships could have brought plenty of timber across from Euboia, and the soft soil at Plasi would have been suitable for digging the trench round the camp. This was intended for the combat infantry and the cavalry; there was obviously no need to bring up the bulk of the auxiliaries and the fleet rowers who would be expected to remain on the beach or on board ship, prepared for any eventuality.[109]

At Plasi, as mentioned above, remains have been found of a settlement that was inhabited from prehistoric to Classical times. Many believe it to be the location of the *deme* of Marathon at the time of the battle. The settlement would have come under Persian control in the days leading up to the battle, as the Persian camp lay thereabouts. One can assume that the inhabitants fled, and the empty houses served as Persian billets. Near this ancient settlement at Plasi is the Aghios Panteleimon coast, where a small inlet could have served as an anchorage for some Persian ships.[110] This way the Persians could have been supplied by sea closer to the camp. And those ships could be used as a defence of the Persian camp in case of a Greek surprise sea attack.[111]

2. Ancient references to the Athenian camp

Though Pausanias took pains to try and ascertain the location of the Persian camp at Marathon, he seems not to have tried to look for the Greek camp.[112] That there was a Greek camp is confirmed by other ancient writers. Herodotus provides the earliest mention in two places in his history, where he writes of a Shrine of Herakles as being where the Athenians were before the battle. In the first he states that 'the Athenians were arrayed at the shrine of Herakles when the Plataians arrived to aid them'.[113] In the second instance, Herodotus says that after the battle, when the Athenians returned to their city they took up position at the shrine of Herakles at Kynosarges after having left the other shrine of Herakles at Marathon.[114]

After his first mention of the Shrine of Herakles, Herodotus relates the arrival of the Plataians and some events that occurred before the battle, apparently confirming that the Athenian camp was located at the area of the shrine. All modern scholars accept this account. However, we should point out that the verb that Herodotus uses to describe the Athenian positioning – *tetagmenoi*, a participle of *tasso* – in relation to the Shrine of Herakles indicates an order of battle rather than an encampment; in other parts of his history he employs the same verb to describe an array for imminent battle.[115] Moreover, Herodotus in the second reference does not explicitly say that the Athenians had encamped at the Shrine of Herakles at Marathon, whereas he does say so for Kynosarges. This means that the Athenians could have lined up for battle at the Shrine of Herakles and not encamped there beforehand. If this interpretation is correct, Herodotus' second reference may be that after the battle of Marathon the Athenians left for Phaleron straight from the battlefield and the Shrine of Herakles, not their camp. The fact that Herodotus, after mentioning the Shrine of Herakles and the Athenian line-up, narrates events that surely took place in the camp the previous days may be attributed to his wish to present events outside strict chronological order, a method which Herodotus often employs, sometimes abruptly.[116] We should point out that even if the Shrine of Herakles marks the Athenian line-up, their camp would have been close by. Any discoveries therefore relating to the camp or the shrine could determine the Athenian position.

Of course, the presence of the Athenian camp at the Shrine of Herakles cannot also be ruled out. In such case it would have been impossible for the whole Greek army to camp inside the area of a small shrine;[117] therefore theories have arisen such as the shrine being the headquarters of the army while the troops camped outside, or that the shrine was within the Greek camp, or whether it was in the rear as a depot for the supply trains.[118] Cornelius Nepos makes no mention of any such shrine, though he fills in a gap left by Herodotus in describing the terrain of the battlefield and probably also of the camp. According to Nepos the Athenians positioned themselves 'in the foothills opposite the enemy' and were 'sheltered by high hills' from the enemy cavalry.[119] This account by Nepos clearly refers to the battle array and not to the camp. Yet immediately beforehand he also avers that 'the Athenians encamped in a suitable place', logically connecting the camp with the battle order and the 'high hills'.[120] Aelius Aristides tends to confirm this interpretation when he says that before the battle the Athenians observed the Persians from a height.[121] The implication is that the Athenian camp was on an elevation.

Besides the ancient writers, an ancient art work supports the view that the Athenians were on a height. This is Plaque A10 of the relief on the Trysa Heroön in Lykia, which depicts a line of ten hoplites moving downhill.[122] The seventh hoplite in the line is clearly the leading figure, as he is the only one facing the viewer. He is also distinguished from his fellows by his helmet which bears three plumes, while the other helmets have just a single plume. This soldier is pictured as beckoning to the three last men in the line to follow the others. According to American art historian and archaeologist Evelyn Harrison, the image is that of Miltiades who had also been depicted in a mural of the battle of Marathon in the Poikile Stoa in the Agora of Athens.[123] Ancient sources say that such a scene was included in the mural; Aischines states that Miltiades had been pictured as urging the Athenians on to fight the Persians.[124] Aelius Aristides agrees with Aischines and adds the detail that Miltiades did this by beckoning the Athenians to follow him.[125] The figure of Miltiades on the mural of Poikile Stoa may have been identical with that of the main figure on Plaque A10 on the aforementioned relief on the Trysa Heroön. Nepos writes that the mural depicted Miltiades and the other nine generals,[126] so one can suppose that the plaque image is of the ten generals as they leave the Athenian camp to face the Persians, as in the Poikile Stoa mural. Harrison supposes that an eleventh figure at the end of the line, and lower than the rest, represents a Plataian soldier on his way to help the Athenians.[127] Pseudo-Demosthenes describes a similar scene with the Plataians on the mural.[128] There is therefore a strong case for identifying the figures on the plaque with those on the mural, i.e. the ten figures representing the Athenian generals of the battle of Marathon.

The Trysa Heroön was built in the early fourth century,[129] and hence could well have been inspired by the mural of the battle in the Poikile Stoa of Athens of a century earlier (c. 462/1).[130] This latter work was carried out three decades after the battle, when many of the veterans, eyewitnesses of what was depicted in the mural, were still alive. Thus, we can vouch for the authenticity of the details in the Poikile Stoa and the later Trysa Heroön.[131] Plaque A10 of the latter, in fact, appears to render a likeness of the physical environment of Marathon at the place where the Athenians encamped: the six soldiers preceding the figure that likely represents Miltiades are moving downhill, an indication that the Athenian camp must have been on ground significantly higher than the plain where the Persians had encamped.

Even without the pictorial evidence we have just cited, it would be hard to believe that the Athenians encamped in the open Marathon plain for several days, and not in a location that would have offered some protection from the invaders.[132] If they had done so they would have been sitting ducks for the Persian cavalry.[133] We know, moreover, that ancient Greek armies on campaign avoided setting up camp on flat ground; they preferred heights that would provide a natural defence, enhanced by basic fortification works.[134] In 479, for example, the Greeks at Plataia before the battle encamped in the foothills of Mount Kithairon, from where they could observe the Persians in the plain below.[135] In the days preceding the clash, whenever the Greeks probed into the plain they were attacked and pushed back by Persian cavalry.[136]

The lay of the land at Plataia is similar to that at Marathon; moreover, before the battle at Plataia the Greeks had encamped in a grove of trees on the slopes of Kithairon, at a spot known as the 'Monument of Androkrates'. Plutarch reports that the land there was very difficult for the Persian

horse to negotiate but by the same token ideal for an infantry defence.[137]
This description ties in with that of Cornelius Nepos in his account of
the Marathon battle. Plutarch says that Arimnestos, the Plataian general,
picked the ground at Plataia in 479; it may not be too much to suppose
that Arimnestos – according to Pausanias also the commander of the
Plataians at Marathon[138] – recalled the details of Marathon in choosing
where the Greeks would build their camp at Plataia. It was probably no
accident that Nepos and Plutarch gave similar descriptions of the ground
where the Greek camps were erected.

To summarize, the ancient sources strongly indicate that the Athenian
position at Marathon was located on some high ground, most likely the
foothills of one of the heights around the Marathon plain, from where the
Athenians could observe the enemy goings-on. The Shrine of Herakles
was either at the Athenian camp or near to where they lined up for
battle. Recent scholars and archaeologists have made it a priority to try
and locate this shrine, as it would pinpoint exactly where the Athenians
encamped and by extension, just where the battle took place.

3. The search for the Shrine of Herakles

Until the mid-twentieth century the academic community was almost
unanimous in concluding that the Athenian expeditionary force marched
from Marathon via the mountain route over Pentelikon. Based on that
assumption they placed the Shrine of Herakles at the logical end of the
route, which is the small plain at Vranas.[139] Some identified the shrine's
location with that of the post-Byzantine monastery of Saint George that
stands on a small eminence at the southwest side of Vranas.[140] But most
of the other researchers suggest that the site was about 500 metres to the
south, where there stands another post-Byzantine church, that of Saint
Demetrios, in the northwest foothills of Mount Agrieliki.[141]

At this site, the Greek archaeologist Georgios Sotiriadis tried to find
the remains of the Shrine of Herakles, as well as the Greek camp. In
the 1920s he carried out some small-scale and superficial digging around
the church of Saint Demetrios; his work appeared to bear fruit in 1929
when he discovered what he believed to be traces of an 'ancient terraced
enclosure' about 100 metres to the north of Saint Demetrios in the foothills
of Agrieliki.[142] Sotiriadis published his theory that the enclosure was an

exercise ground for the youth of Marathon, where athletic contests were held in honour of Herakles (the 'Herakleian Games', see below) whose shrine would not be far away. For years he searched in vain for traces of the shrine. Yet he remained convinced that the enclosure had some connection with the Shrine of Herakles, and believed it was there that the Athenians set up their camp. But in the 1950s and 1960s, the American archaeologists Pritchett and Vanderpool, after extensive investigation of Sotiriadis' work, ruled out any connection of the site with the battle of Marathon and debunked the Greek archaeologist's theories, going so far as to say the remains were not even ancient.[143]

Despite Sotiriadis' ultimate failure to unearth the site of the Shrine of Herakles, his work threw some light on other sacred shrines that could have existed at Marathon at the time of the battle. A farmer gave Sotiriadis a fragment of an inscription from a boundary stone of a shrine to Athene dated to the first half of the fifth century which he had found in his field close to Saint Demetrios.[144] Sotiriadis searched the find spot and discovered close by the remains of an enclosure containing the foundations of a building with rooms and some movable relics. Though the building was shown to have been an ancient shrine, nothing more came to light about which deity it belonged to.[145] Judging from the boundary stone, he assumed it was of Athene.[146] Continuing his search, Sotiriadis found yet another enclosure about a kilometre distant. It contained potsherds as well as pieces of a statue of an enthroned deity which he also attributed to Athene.[147]

Ancient literary and epigraphic sources reveal that a Shrine of Athene Hellotia stood at Marathon.[148] Sotiriadis believed that one of the shrines he excavated was that of Athene Hellotia, but most other archaeologists disputed his theory. They based their argument on the fact that ancient sources connect the Shrine of Athene Hellotia with the marsh (*helos*) of Marathon;[149] consequently, the remains that Sotiriadis unearthed were more than two kilometres away from the nearest marsh (the Lesser, or Brexiza, Marsh), which is likely to be the 'Marsh of Marathon'.[150]

Despite Sotiriadis' extensive efforts at Marathon, the problem of locating the Shrine of Herakles was no nearer a solution. But the discovery of two fifth century inscriptions connected with the worship of Herakles at Marathon – the first archaeological finds that certainly have something to do with the particular shrine – revived hopes that its site may be found. The two inscriptions were discovered within a short distance of each other at the southern end of the Marathon plain. The content of the older one, dated to 490/480, consists of the selection procedure for the officials of the 'Herakleian Games'.[151]

> *At Marathon the games of Herakles will be organized by thirty men (the athlothetai)... they will be elected of the present, three from... each tribe, of those who pledged at the shrine to help the progress of the games to the best of their ability... not under thirty years of age... these men shall take the oath at the shrine... over the sacrificial victims. As overseer there will be....*

The large number of officials involved – thirty – seems remarkable, as does the fact that representatives of the ten Athenian tribes were among them. It would appear that the 'Herakleian Games' at Marathon had yet to hold their first event, and that the above-mentioned inscription was a document for their establishment. The inscription specifically states that the games would begin after Athenian citizens from the ten tribes gave their formal pledges at the Shrine of Herakles. Therefore, the games were not merely of local but pan-Athenian importance.

Such high-level events were not common in Athens of the Classical era. It appears, then, that the Athenians attached a high level of importance to the 'Herakleian Games' of Marathon;[152] indeed, these games attained pan-Hellenic prestige in the first half of the fifth century. Pindar, for example, says that athletes from other Greek cities participated in the 'Herakleian Games' and that silver cups were awarded to the winners as they were to the victors in the Panathenaian Games.[153] Vanderpool believes that these Marathon games were held under the aegis of the Archons of Athens;[154] if true, it would tend to confirm that the Athenian *deme* was involved, and hence they were a commemoration of the victory at Marathon. As will become apparent, the battle was the cause of the Athenians holding special festive events in honour of the deities believed to have contributed to their victory, such as Artemis Agrotera and Pan. It would have been logical to honour Herakles, too, as another divine helper.

The pledge of the Athenians to institute the 'Herakleian Games' at Marathon, as evidenced by the above-mentioned inscription, shows that the events had a direct connection with the battle. There was probably a worship of Herakles already in place before 490,[155] as some ancient sources claim that the people of Marathon were the first Greeks to honour the deity in that way.[156] Marathon was central to the Herakleid myth, as the place where the sons of Herakles found refuge from persecution by Eurystheus,[157] who lost his life there.[158] If there had been such a festival for Herakles before 490,[159] then the Athenians later would probably have honoured their fallen of the battle by means of funeral games involving all ten tribes. And these games might be identified as the 'Herakleian Games'.[160]

It is therefore likely that the pledge recorded in the first inscription of the 'Herakleian Games' was given by the Athenian army at Marathon, either before the battle or immediately after it. In the former case, the Athenians would have been performing an offering to Herakles in the hope of victory; in the latter, they would have been heaping honours on him in thanks. The fact that the selection of officials would be from among all who gave the pledge leads us to the conclusion that they would have comprised all the men who had fought, hence the selection would have taken place after the battle. Arguing for this view is also the reference in the inscription that Athenian citizens of all tribes were present; this could not have been by pure chance, as the inhabitants of the Tetrapolis belonged to just two of those tribes. Marathon, moreover, was relatively isolated from the main Attic population centres. Therefore, an occasion for the presence of all the Athenian tribes was the expedition of 490.[161]After the Persian repulse, the Athenians sped to Phaleron to beat off an expected Persian attack there; but the enemy, seeing resistance, withdrew.[162] With the Persian danger gone, the Athenians would have returned to Marathon in order to bury their fallen and those of the enemy.

We believe that the games in honour of Herakles were instituted at Marathon after the Athenians returned from Phaleron. The first inscription of the 'Herakleian Games' appears on the reverse of a stele bearing an older and unrelated inscription dated to the late-sixth century.[163] This fact shows that the former inscription was made in haste and in line with the extraordinary circumstances we have seen. The

Athenians probably recorded the institution of the 'Herakleian Games' in 490 on a stele which they happened to find in the Shrine of Herakles at Marathon as they didn't have time to order a new one.[164]

The first inscription of the 'Herakleian Games' was found in 1930 in the area of Valaria, near the entrance to the Brexiza pass, far from Vranas where earlier investigators had looked for the Shrine of Herakles. Vanderpool speculated whether the shrine might have been very close to where the stele was found.[165] In 1940, on a visit to the site, he found little except pieces of ancient building marble.[166] These fragments had been known since the late-nineteenth century, when Curtius and Kaupert had noted them on the map 'Marathon' of the *Karten von Attika* series. They were cited as being to the south of the small Byzantine church of the Saints Theodore.[167] Vanderpool said the stele was found 'a few metres south of the marble pieces' that Curtius and Kaupert had noted.[168] This is about halfway between the church and the north edge of the Lesser Marsh.[169]

In 1966 Vanderpool published his theory that the Shrine of Herakles should be looked for at Valaria, based on the discovery of the 'Herakleian Games' inscription.[170] It appears that Vanderpool had informed others of his theory in the meantime, as a year earlier another distinguished American archaeologist, William Pritchett, had published his view that the findspot of the aforementioned inscription is unrelated to the location of the Shrine of Herakles.[171] According to Pritchett its stele belongs in the category of so-called 'wandering stones', that had been moved from their original position and used as building material; it could have come from anywhere in Marathon. Nevertheless, Vanderpool in his 1966 publication of the first inscription of the 'Herakleian Games' definitely pinpointed the location of the shrine at or near Valaria.[172] A year later, the French epigraphist Louis Robert asserted that the inscription had been found *in situ*, thereby buttressing Vanderpool's position about Herakles' Marathon Shrine.[173] Pritchett replied in a publication in 1969 repeating his assertion that the stele at Valaria had been re-used in antiquity and could have been among the materials used to build the Saints Theodore church, which is why it was found in the vicinity.[174] In the same article Pritchett argued that the Shrine of Herakles must be sought far from Valaria, in the wider area of Vranas. In 1972, six years into the running controversy over the location of the Herakles Shrine, Greek archaeologist Spyridon Marinatos disclosed a second inscription connected with Herakles which he had unearthed at Marathon, specifically at Valaria, very near where Vanderpool claimed the first stele had been found.[175] Marinatos' find thus reaffirmed Vanderpool's theory, which Pritchett in the end conceded.[176]

The second inscription to do with the 'Herakleian Games' is dated to the mid-fifth century, a few decades after the first.[177] Its first line describes an offering to Herakles of some precious object by an unnamed victor: 'To Herakles, this for him to be glad ... dedicated for the victory in the Herakleia Empylia'. Greek archaeologist Stephanos Koumanoudis was the first to identify the term 'Empylia' with the 'Herakleian Games', a view now endorsed by almost all experts in Greek epigraphy.[178] It would appear that Herakles was worshipped in the district as 'Herakles Empylios' ('Herakles within the Gates'), which throws some light on where the shrine could have been. The term derives from *pyle*, or gate, which could not apply to any of the *demes* of Attica, as none was fortified in Classical times.[179] It therefore could apply to some natural feature resembling a gate near the shrine. Koumanoudis and others interpret the word as a clear reference to the Brexiza pass.[180] This pass, the southern entrance to the Marathon plain, is indeed narrow; moreover, until the 1930s much of it was covered by the Lesser Marsh making it even more narrow. Hence the connection of the term 'Empylios' with the pass would be logical.[181]

A line from Pindar supports the view that the Shrine of Herakles was located in a narrow pass, or in the original words, 'in a recess of Marathon'.[182] Additionally, a line of a fifth century epigram recorded in an inscription honouring the fallen Athenians of the battle at Marathon says that the Athenians formed up at the 'gates' holding their spears.[183] Koumanoudis holds that the phrase does not refer to the gates of Athens[184] or have any metaphorical meaning,[185] but refers to the 'natural gates' of Marathon, which would be the Brexiza pass. From this Koumanoudis concludes that the term 'Empylios', meaning 'within the gates', shows that the Shrine of Herakles would have been within the Brexiza pass; the second line of the epigram for the fallen at Marathon contains the term 'coast' (*anchialos*), which according to Greek epigraphist Angelos

Matthaiou could well refer to the east side of the Brexiza pass which abuts the sea.[186] The conclusion would be that the Athenians lined up at the Shrine of Herakles at the 'natural gates' of Marathon. The discovery of the two above-mentioned inscriptions at Valaria, and the reference to 'gates' in the later one, have convinced many recent scholars that the shrine was located in front of or in the Brexiza pass and that this was also the area of the Greek line-up in 490.[187]

Writers such as Hammond, Burn and Pritchett, who earlier had placed the Shrine of Herakles at Vranas or the foothills of Mount Kotroni abandoned their theories and accepted Vanderpool's view.[188] Burn does concede that Vanderpool's position for the Athenian army makes strategic sense. The position of Valaria in the Brexiza pass was ideal for blocking a Persian advance on Athens. The idea, however, is by no means new. As early as 1838 George Finlay, basing his conclusions on the lay of the land and common sense, had placed the Athenian army and the Shrine of Herakles in the foothills of Agrieliki in the Brexiza pass.[189] But the bulk of academic opinion at the time preferred Vranas as the place for both. Finlay's view was largely ignored for the next 130 or so years, as the search took a wrong course. It took the discovery of the two aforementioned inscriptions to define the likely site of the shrine and the Athenian camp.

The marble pieces found by Vanderpool near where the first inscription was unearthed seem to have come from some ancient temple.[190] Though Vanderpool stopped short of actually claiming that the fragments were part of the Shrine of Herakles, other modern researchers have been less cautious.[191] The view that the shrine and the Byzantine church occupied the same spot has been gaining in strength, though the issue is still unresolved, as the marble fragments have yet to be dated with any accuracy.[192] Further investigation would be needed to throw more light on the subject. It would need to be ascertained whether the pieces were *in situ* when they were used to help build the Byzantine church, or whether they were carried there from some other location. The investigation would be a complex one, as pieces of other ancient edifices have been found at Valaria that could have come from any number of shrines in the wider area, such as the shrine of Athene Hellotia or the shrine 'of the Egyptian Gods' near the spot called 'Nisi', dated to Roman times.

Until such time as archaeologists can definitely locate the Shrine of Herakles, either at the Saints Theodore church or elsewhere, we may make certain observations. Though the position is just a few hundred metres from the foothills of Agrieliki and within the 'gates of Marathon', i.e. the Brexiza pass, it is in the southern part of the Marathon plain. It would seem inconceivable that in 490 the Greeks would encamp at the present site of Saints Theodore or in the wider Valaria area; that way they would have been in danger of a Persian cavalry attack at any moment. Logic would have dictated that they set up camp anywhere else but the open plain.[193] As we have already noted, ancient Greek armies avoided stopping at flat land and sought encampments on high ground for defensive purposes. Given that the Persians at Marathon had a strong cavalry force, this tactic would have been imperative for the Athenians.

Nunnus writes that there was a shrine inside an olive grove at Marathon, leading to more recent speculation that it refers to the Shrine of Herakles.[194] Other ancient sources also mention such a grove.[195] If the Athenian army did encamp at such a place, then the grove would have afforded protection to only a small part of it; besides, the Greeks would have been easy targets for Persian archers, or the Persians might set fire to the trees. Something similar occurred ten years later in 480, when the Persians fired flaming arrows at and torched the wooden defensive wall which the Athenians had built on the Acropolis.[196] Nepos says the Athenians took defensive measures at Marathon by forming up in 'the foothills of steep heights'. It would appear obvious that the foothills of Agrieliki would have given better protection to the Athenians than any grove, large or small, in the plain below. And even supposing that the Shrine of Herakles was indeed at Valaria where the ruins of Saints Theodore are now, it does not necessarily follow that the Athenians encamped there. Herodotus in his account could well have mentioned the shrine as the place where the Athenians did not set up camp but lined up for battle.

4. The position of the Athenian camp

Ancient literary and epigraphic sources, as well as more recent research by scholars and archaeologists, converge on the conclusion that the Athenians and Plataians encamped in the general area of northeast

Agrieliki. The strategic importance of the position is clear, as it offers an unimpeded view of the Brexiza pass through which the Persian army had to march on Athens. The foothills of Agrieliki, as we have seen, would have been the site of the Greek camp, a short distance from where they lined-up for battle.

Mount Agrieliki consists of two peaks, 557 and 361 metres high respectively, plus a spur of 206 metres.[197] This last is separated from the first two by a gully that descends to the northeast foothills. This rocky spur is an extension of Agrieliki into the southern part of the Marathon plain, right above the entrance to the Brexiza pass.[198] The spur's northern side is steep; almost vertical in places; hence the spur can be accessed only from the gentler southeast slopes, by an uphill path running along the gully for about 300 metres.[199] Most of northeast Agrieliki is sparsely covered, mainly by pine trees. On the side, however, where the gully debouches into the plain, there is an extensive grove of hundreds of wild olive trees (*agrielies*) which have given their name to the mountain.[200] The subsoil here does not contain marble and the schist rocks are not as hard as the rocks of the mountain itself; hence wild olive trees would have found more favourable ground than elsewhere on the mountain to take root, irrigated by rain water running down the gully.

This lay of the land seems to have been unchanged for thousands of years. There is every reason to suppose that wild olive trees abounded here in ancient times as well. Recent experience with brush fires has shown that even after a devastating fire, such as that of 1994 when all the trees in the area were burned, they somehow start growing again within a few years.[201] If the Shrine of Herakles was inside the grove of wild olive trees, as many ancient sources indicate, it could have been at the start of the gully that separates the two peaks and the spur of Agrieliki. The gully could also have been the 'recess' that Pindar mentioned.

Important archaeological evidence comes to the support of the terrain to buttress the view that the Athenian camp, and perhaps the Shrine of Herakles, were in this part of Agrieliki. In January 1838 George Finlay read a paper to London's academic community – published the following year – in which he claimed to have found antiquities at the site relating to the Athenian camp. He assumed that some ruins found at the Brexiza pass had belonged to the camp, as well as a 'Hellenic (ancient Greek) wall' of some height 'running up' the side of Agrieliki.[202] Finlay claimed these were the remnants of the Greek camp of the battle of Marathon. Yet his discovery failed to ignite any real interest, as it was universally assumed that this camp and the Shrine of Herakles were at Vranas, not Agrieliki.

During the 1920s and 1930s, Sotiriadis carried out small-scale probes on the northeast side of Agrieliki. He reported finding some ancient ruins, among which the most important was the 'ancient Greek wall' running up the mountain that Finlay had mentioned first.[203] This was an ancient rampart crowning the 206-metre spur,[204] and Sotiriadis explored it for the first time in 1926.[205] The following excerpt from Sotiriadis' report shows that he was impressed with the size of the ruins:

> *These walls were revealed clearly and undeniably along the whole length of the ancient citadel, as soon as I reached the crown of the height… They were clearly of [ancient] Greek construction, two metres thick, with the exterior well preserved to a small height. The wall is preserved in three places along the long ridge, forming a perimeter of about 300 metres. The fourth side, the one looking towards the Marathon plain, to the east and northeast, was never built up as there had been no need to. The side of the height here is too steep. The same is observable in the walls of all ancient citadels where the steepness of the height renders any walling unnecessary. The entrance to the citadel must have been from the narrow southeast side, as the wall is unbroken everywhere else.*[206]

Sotiriadis believed that on the 206-metre spur he had discovered a Mycenaean era settlement with its 'Acropolis' on the highest point, which continued to be in use in later centuries.[207] In his first report, Sotiriadis mentioned that he found many 'ancient Greek' (Classical period) potsherds, as well as some from the Geometric and Mycenaean periods.[208] In later articles, however, he clarified that he found those relics only inside a small cavern within the enclosure of the rampart near its southeast corner, adding that most of them were of the Classical era.[209] Sotiriadis' main reason for supposing that the rampart at 206 metres had been raised in Mycenaean times was that, as he wrote, 'the construction of the walls indicates that era'.[210] Influencing him, however, was the fact that in the plain near the foothills of Agrieliki he had previously unearthed a tholos-tomb containing a gold cup.[211] As this was proof that the Marathon plain had been inhabited in Mycenaean times, he supposed that the citadel of the settlement would be nearby, and the nearest such location was the 206-metre spur.[212]

However, Sotiriadis' conclusions did not convince other archaeologists. In subsequent years new research was carried out on the northeast side of Agrieliki and its fortification by Wrede, Pritchett, Vanderpool and McCredie. They gave detailed descriptions of the rampart and stressed the fact that it was built carelessly,[213] unlike what would have been expected for the acropolis of a citadel.[214] The stones were not dressed, and appear to have been placed without particular care.[215] At no point was there evidence of mortar or any connecting substance, and neither did the archaeologists discover any trace of foundations or of a gate, not to mention soldiers' living quarters.[216] The ground within the perimeter is rocky and uneven, just like the ground outside.[217] All the evidence points to a hasty and provisional construction, lacking anything that might improve conditions for any soldiers stationed there.

Sotiriadis appears to have used no scientific criterion for his view that the Agrieliki rampart dates back to the Mycenaean era, and no subsequent archaeologist has been able to endorse it. Moreover, they have failed to find a single datable potsherd within the enclosure of the rampart or outside;[218] only McCredie claimed to have found a few crude fragments that cannot be dated.[219] Sotiriadis said he discovered the Classical-era potsherds, and a few of earlier ages, inside the small cavern within the enclosure of the rampart. The fact that nothing similar was found outside the cavern might suggest that any human activity for a long time took place only there. Vanderpool notes that the potsherds could throw light on when the cavern was used, but not the fortification.[220] Yet the rampart itself was a large construction and the absence of potsherds from its surface is puzzling. A much smaller construction stands at the summit of Mount Stavrokoraki opposite Agrieliki, dated to the fourth or third century; it may have been a watchtower built there so that its guards could monitor the Marathon plain and transmit signals to the Athenian garrison at Rhamnous.[221] This small work is a mere six metres in diameter, enough to accommodate five or six men. Nevertheless, the

American archaeologist Merle Langdon found at least one dateable pottery fragment in that restricted space.[222] In contrast, the Agrieliki rampart is some 300 metres in circumference and would have been occupied by a relatively large number of soldiers. Yet not a single datable potsherd has been found there.[223]

Though every archaeologist who examined the site after Sotiriadis flatly disputed his theory of its purpose and date,[224] they were unable to come up with a convincing alternative theory.[225] Pritchett and Vanderpool believed that the rampart resembled similar structures in Attica dating to Hellenistic times.[226] The German archaeologist Walther Wrede rejected Sotiridadis' 'Mycenaean' dating for the rampart, but did not offer an alternative dating; instead, he speculated that it could have served as a refuge (*Fluchtburgen*) for the inhabitants of Marathon in case of hostile attack.[227] But McCredie, after careful examination of the rampart, ruled out any such function on the grounds that such defensive works were not built in Attica in ancient times.[228] He points out that even assuming the impossible, that such a rampart had been built to protect the local populace from an attack, it would have had to be far from any strategic points an enemy might seize. Yet it is located precisely at a strategic spot, as it commands the only passage from the plain of Marathon to the Mesogaia. Consequently, it would have been a prime objective for any army heading into Attica from Marathon.[229] Hanson does not rule out the existence of such refuges for threatened populations in Attica, but agrees that if any did exist, they would have had to be far from strategic points.[230] It follows that if the people of Marathon did take refuge on the rampart of Agrieliki, they would have been putting themselves in harm's way, as the position would be literally on the front line of hostilities.[231] We may therefore rule out the function of the ruin as a refuge.

The archaeologists who followed Sotiriadis in exploring the foothills of Agrieliki failed to find any datable pottery fragments, thus ruled out (apart from Wrede) the possibility that any settlement was once there, not to mention the *deme* of Marathon, the most important in the Tetrapolis.[232] Yet they seem not to have taken into account Sotiriadis' description of some other ruins on the 206-metre spur, beneath the rampart, but less significant. Finlay mentioned in 1838 the existence of 'terraces' on northeastern Agreliki that had probably served as installations of the Athenian camp;[233] these were probably identical to what Sotiriadis described as 'remnants of the Marathon *deme* settlement'.[234]

The 206-metre spur on the northeast slope of Agrieliki is the most strategically important spot at the southern end of the Marathon plain, offering a view of the whole plain and controlling the Brexiza pass. The rampart occupies the most suitable place for this. It would serve as protection for any force guarding the route from Marathon to the Mesogaia.[235] It could not be accessed from the north, as the slopes are too steep; the sole access would be from the southeast, via a quite negotiable footpath.[236] This is strong evidence that the fortification was the basic defensive work for an army facing attack from Marathon. Though extensive in area, its construction appears to have been hasty, which argues that it could have been put up under severe time pressure with no thought for whether it could be used in the future as a permanent fortification.

The rampart on Agrieliki was never a part of Attic defence planning, as it was not included among the better-organized forts that the Athenians maintained on a permanent basis in the Classical period.[237] No source mentions such a fortification in the Marathon area. As the rampart in question was not built for a formal purpose, it would follow that it was built in response to some serious military emergency such as an enemy army attempting to go through the Brexiza pass. The lack of potsherds and any trace of an edifice within the wall argues for the structure being built and manned in a hurry, for a short period of time, and being abandoned after its purpose was served. Though much money and effort were expended on its construction, after the emergency passed there would have been no more use for it.

We know of just two instances in ancient times where military exigencies would have led to the construction of the type of rampart on Agrieliki. These are Peisistratos' landing at Marathon in 546 and the Persian landing in 490.[238] In the former case, according to Herodotus the Athenians sent out to resist Peisistratos did not reach Marathon but encamped at Pallene where they were defeated. Hence it is impossible that the rampart was built by Peisistratos' foes.[239] The Athenians of 490, however, did indeed reach Marathon; the 206-metre spur of Agrieliki is at the end of the route via Pallene that the army took, as any more progress would have taken them into the Marathon plain which the Persians controlled. But given its large size, the rampart would not have been intended for just a few soldiers as observers; moreover, it seems to have been connected to other installations lower down the slope.[240] The rampart would have been the most impressive fortification, though not the only one on the 206-metre spur of Agrieliki.

A careful analysis of the evidence of the rampart on the northeast slope of Agrieliki argues in favour of it having been connected with the Athenian encampment in the days before the battle of Marathon. Its mode of construction was provisional, and carried out in a very short time. Yet the rampart cannot be considered an unimportant work, as the wall is 300 metres in circumference and consists of hundreds of tons of rock. At the end of summer 490 thousands of Athenian soldiers occupied that location. The work could well have gone up in a short time if the labour was well-organized. Ancient sources indicate that the Athenians were quite skilled at such projects, as attested by Thucydides, who reports that in 425 the Athenian garrison at Pylos was fortified by a wall that took just six days to build, and without any special tools.[241] The Athenians did it with their bare hands. The wall at Pylos, also, was not a provisional structure like the wall at Agrieliki but intended to be more permanent, as hand-carried mud was used to cement the stones. The Athenian army at Pylos numbered a few thousand men, but so effective was the wall that a much larger Peloponnesian force proved unable to dislodge it.[242] The Athenians at Marathon in 490 would have had the men and resources to build an equally effective wall.

Pritchett, after examining the relatively sparse evidence on ancient Greek temporary camps, cites ancient sources to conclude that their walls were made of undressed stone with no mortar material.[243] Timber and thorny branches would have been placed atop the walls to boost their defensive qualities. Pritchett notes that the same technique is employed by Greek shepherds today to protect their sheepfolds.[244] The walls proper, however, were only slightly over a metre high. With McCredie and other scholars, Pritchett propounds the view that this type of rampart is an example of the *herkos*, or barrier, that according to ancient sources the Greeks erected around their temporary camps.[245] These same authorities, however, reject earlier suggestions that the *herkos* included upright poles and a trench in front of the rampart, of the kind used by the Persians in the Persian Wars and later by the Romans.[246] The Persians and Romans, however, in their campaigns almost always encamped on level ground, unlike the Greeks who encamped on hilly terrain and as a consequence were forced to use whatever rough materials came to hand. These materials were stones and wood, assuming there were trees in the vicinity, and anything else.[247] The Greeks did not dig trenches around their positions because the rocky ground did not permit it.[248]

Though in Attica, as we have seen, Classical-era fortifications have been preserved that were manned on a permanent basis by Athenian troops, no provisional rampart has been located of the time of the Persian Wars. Some have been detected, on the island of Patroklos and in Korone, dating to the early Hellenistic period. Excavations have shown that they were put up by the expeditionary force of Ptolemy II sent to help the Athenians during the Chremonidean War (267/61).[249] Because they appear to have been in use for a long time, these installations could be considered long-term in that they contained buildings that were probably dormitories for the troops, cookhouses, water cisterns and other facilities. As there seems to have been no great change in the methods of building military camps between the Classical and early Hellenistic eras, the later fortifications were built in the same way as the earlier ones; the evidence shows that the field camps in the Chremonidean War differed little from Classical camps except for the addition of some more or less permanent buildings. According to McCredie, the Ptolemaic camps in Attica were built hastily on an eminence and had walls 2.5 metres thick. Though not much higher than a metre, the walls offered adequate protection.

By combining Classical and Hellenistic literary sources with the evidence of the Chremonidean War camps in Attica,[250] it becomes clear that the rampart on the northeast spur of Agrieliki was part of an ancient temporary military camp. The walls are almost as twice as thick as their height.[251] The thickness probably enabled timber and twigs to be placed on top in what was the usual *herkos* construction of antiquity. These common features shared between the rampart of 206-metre spur and the Ptolemaic camps in Attica led McCredie to label the former as '*a small fortified camp*'.[252] As Sotiriadis noted, the rampart may have been hastily built, but it was strong. It had to be built as quickly as possible as the

Persians could have attacked at any moment. There was no time to make mortar or dress the stones. The principle of the *herkos* would have been similar to that of a street barricade of more recent times – a stopgap measure to delay an attacker as much as possible rather than serve a defensive purpose. Sotiriadis and later archaeologists found no gateway in the fortification, just an entrance opening on the southeast side of the wall;[253] this would argue for the existence of a provisional rampart rather than a more permanent installation.

There is no known fortification work from the Marathon period in Attica. Yet the Athenians did build one in Euboia, which gives us insights into dating the Agrieliki rampart. This is the fortification at Vrachos, near the village of Fylla. As we have mentioned, this was built and used by the Athenian *klerouchoi* of Chalkis until 490; of interest is the fact that not only is the fort contemporaneous with the battle of Marathon, but the men who built and used it could have helped build the Athenian camp at Marathon. The two structures are remarkably similar. Both were built on a rocky ridge or spur (130 metres high at Fylla,[254] 206 metres high at Agrieliki), while the northern approaches are rocky and steep and the southern approaches more usable. Both were built to enable the garrison to observe the plains below, the Lelantine plain in Euboia and the Marathon plain in Attica. Both are arranged in a rough oblong shape, with the southern wall longer than the eastern and western ones; also in both cases the southern wall is lower than the others, while there is no northern wall, as there was no need for one, since there was an unassailable cliff edge.[255] Both ramparts were built of stone gathered locally.[256] There are differences, however, in that the Fylla fort contained structures that could have been sleeping and living quarters and the stones were laid carefully, indicating that it was a long-term installation. The Agrieliki rampart, on the other hand, contains no trace of a building. The strong similarity between the two structures is no accident, and leads us to conclude that they were built at about the same time. As we have seen the Fylla fort was built between 506 and 490.[257] The *klerouchoi* who left it then, possibly went to Marathon and began building the Agrieliki rampart.

Ancient sources imply that the ancient Greeks were not overly careful about where they made their temporary camps while on campaign, and therefore the signs of hasty construction at Agrieliki would be justified, even on the grounds of lack of time. Whatever the soldiers found at hand, whether rocks or wood or thorny branches, was useful material. The Athenian camp at Marathon would have been made up of many tents scattered over the slopes of Agrieliki that of course have left no traces.[258] Most of the men, however, would have slept outside the tents, some on leather mattresses stuffed with straw and others on the ground.[259] The men would have had their weapons with them at all times, as there was no separate armoury in the camp.[260] The Athenians and Plataians were always with their arms, even when asleep. There was also probably a place set apart for assembly where the soldiers would have been informed of various issues. There would have been sentry posts outside the camp, with some temporary structures for them near the main fortification.[261] Here, however, we enter into speculation which future research into the battle of Marathon and the attendant conditions may well clarify.[262]

None of the surviving ancient literary sources on the battle of Marathon record the rampart on Agrieliki. It is possible, however, that it is mentioned in one of four epigrams that are believed to have been inscribed on a cenotaph in Athens, probably at the *Demosion Sema* (Public Cemetery), which some scholars believe honoured the fallen Marathon warriors.[263] According to Matthaiou, these epigrams included references to places where the stages of the battle took place. The first line of the fourth epigram states that one phase occurred 'in front of a defensive wall [*herkos*]'.[264] Matthaiou believes it refers to either the precinct of the Shrine of Herakles or that of Athene Hellotia, as in his words, 'no source refers to any kind of defensive wall at Marathon'.[265] We suppose, however, that the '*herkos*' of the epigram might well refer to the rampart on Agrieliki and not to the wall of a shrine's precinct.[266]

In 1838 Finlay, as we have seen, published his theory that before the battle the Athenians encamped on the northeast slope of Agrieliki.[267] A map drawn under his direction shows the camp as an oblong, part of which includes the rampart on the spur.[268] The map shows that Finlay not only knew of the fortification, but also believed it to be part of the Greek camp which covered a wider area on the height. Finlay also claimed that the Athenians were on a high point from where they could have a good view of the Persian army and fleet.[269] Though most nineteenth century scholars rejected Finlay's view on the location of the Greek camp, a small minority adhered to it as having the advantage of common sense, though they had as yet no concrete evidence. Most of the latter were German historians, the first of whom was Ernst Curtius, who propounded the theory that the Athenian camp must have overlooked the 'southern passage' – i.e. Brexiza – to enable the Athenians to block the Persian advance.[270] Then there was Eduard Meyer, who in 1901 wrote that the camp would have been on a height near the southern part of the Marathon plain, or what we would call northeast Agrieliki.[271]

In the early 1920s, Johannes Kromayer endorsed the view of his co-patriots, and in fact specifically placed the camp as overlooking the Brexiza pass and on the '200 metres spur of northeastern Agrieliki', i.e. the 206-metre spur.[272] He also noted that the steep, almost sheer face of the northern slope of Agrieliki would have protected the Athenians from Persian cavalry attacks and from archers, whose arrows would not have been able to reach so high. What seems remarkable is that Kromayer reached his conclusions not after any personal investigation of the site but after studying the maps in the *Karten von Attika*. Yet instead of marking the site of the Athenian camp according to his own description, in his own maps he placed it farther down the slope, south of Saint Demetrios, to the north looking towards the Marathon plain. To him, that seemed the most suitable position for an army to be able to block the Brexiza pass.

Kromayer may be said to be contradicting himself here, which is attributable to the fact that he did not visit the site himself but sent an associate, Veith, to do the investigating. It is doubtful whether Veith took the trouble to climb the 206-metre spur of Agrieliki, and hence may well have concluded that the Greek army encamped on the north slope of the mountain, a conclusion that Kromayer took at face value. If Kromayer had gone to Marathon he would have confirmed what he wrote by discovering the rampart. He published his theory in 1921, only five years before Sotiriadis 'discovered' the rampart and wrongly identified it with a Mycenaean-era acropolis. Kromayer's theory seems to have influenced his younger colleague and compatriot Hermann Bengtson, who placed the Athenian camp 'on a spur of northeast Agrieliki'. We may note that northeast Agrieliki has only one spur (206-metre spur).[273]

Petros Themelis, another Greek archaeologist who has excavated Marathon, places the Greek camp 'between roughly the foothills of Agrieliki and the Brexiza marsh, in order to control the sole passage from Marathon to Athens through which the Persians could move…'.[274] His colleague Stefanos Koumanoudis considers that the Shrine of Herakles was located at the site of the church of Saints Theodore at Valaria.[275] However, he also places the Greek army before the battle right at the base and to the east of the 206-metre spur, inside the Brexiza pass. This would be a few hundred metres south of where he considers the shrine was and exactly beneath the rampart of the 206-metre spur. Christos Dionysopoulos places the Greek camp approximately where Kromayer did, but in a somewhat smaller area.[276]

The aforementioned proposed locations of the Greek camp of 490 are very close to the 206-metre spur. However, none of these, either north of the 206-metre spur, looking towards Marathon or east towards Brexiza, would have been suitable for a military camp. It would have been impossible, for example, to set up camp on the steep slopes where Kromayer and Dionysopoulos said. The terrain would simply have been too difficult to accommodate a large military force. Moreover, the Greeks would have been vulnerable to Persian archer attacks from the plain.[277] There are historical cases where Greek armies encamped near mountains or in their foothills suffered crushing defeats.[278] The positions suggested by Themelis and Koumanoudis could have been suitable for a large army, as being on low land and in the open, but by the same token would be open to Persian cavalry attacks. The conclusion must be that the Greeks actually did set up camp at the 206-metre spur but on its highest points which they fortified.

None of the archaeologists who examined the northeastern Agrieliki position or considered that the Greek camp was in the vicinity suspected that the rampart had been part of the camp itself. Probably they were influenced by the writings of Sotririadis who, as we have seen, drew a thoroughly wrong conclusion; they investigated the site purely in terms of the 'Mycenaean' context, to determine whether it was or was not of that era. Though the universal conclusion was that the ruin was not Mycenaean, archaeologists did not pursue the issue further.[279] The issue should have been whether the rampart was or was not part of the Athenian camp in 490, but no one set this question.

Investigations at the 206-metre spur were carried out before 1966 when Vanderpool published the theory that the Greeks drew up for battle in front of the Brexiza pass.[280] However, it was only after Marinatos published the contents of the second epigram of the 'Herakleian Games' in 1972, and Koumanoudis wrote in support six years later, that this theory was adopted by most researchers of the battle of Marathon. If the Greeks lined-up in front of the Brexiza pass, it would make sense that they had encamped on northeastern Agrieliki, as both locations were strategically close to each other for defensive purposes. However, when this theory gained ground, all examination at the rampart on the 206-metre spur had stopped; there seems to have been no attempt at re-examination in the light of new findings.[281] Any scholars who do re-examine the ruins of the rampart may well discover evidence confirming not only the location of the Greek camp but also of the Shrine of Herakles, through findings such as those which Finlay and Sotiriadis located.[282] Nearby the rampart the remains of the sentry posts that the Athenians must have set up around the camp may be unearthed.[283] It is worth noting that while visiting the site we happened to come across an interesting find. A few dozen metres beneath the rampart, on the face of a marble bedrock has been carved an official and monumental ancient inscription which was unknown and unpublished. Two lines can be discerned:

$$[...]MIAKA\Theta EI\Lambda H\Pi TAI$$
$$[...]\Pi TOY$$

According to epigraphists it probably dates to the fourth century and is the first – official – rupestral inscription recorded anywhere in Eastern Attica. The letters are quite large for an Athenian inscription and it is certain that it was the work of a skilled slate cutter.[284] This makes it an exceptional discovery and its position shows a likely link to the Greek camp of the battle of Marathon. The bedrock bearing the inscription is also carved in the shape of an altar. We cannot preclude the possibility that the inscription is commemorative of the battle; in such a case it could have been carved at a particular spot in the Greek camp that in 490 was considered to be important.

The fact that no ancient source mentions the rampart on northeastern Agrieliki should not necessarily discourage further research. These sources concentrate exclusively on the monuments the Athenians put up after the battle and on the tombs of the fallen. The camp, naturally, falls into neither category, with the exception of the Shrine of Herakles which, however, seems to have been abandoned before the end of the Classical era.[285] We know that the chief interest of visitors to Marathon in ancient times was to see the tombs of the fallen Greeks rather than the remains of their camp and the Shrine of Herakles.[286] This is true for even such an observer as Pausanias, the most famous traveller of antiquity, visited Marathon in the second century AD and reported on the tombs of the Athenians and Plataians (and freedmen), the cenotaph of Miltiades and the 'Trophy of the Battle', as well as some traces which he believed were of the Persian camp.[287] He searched in vain for where the Persians were buried, but as far as we know did not look for either the Athenian camp or the Shrine of Herakles. There is a logical explanation for this apparent omission, as both appear to have been in the Probalinthos district, which was abandoned as a settlement in the first century AD. When Pausanias visited in the next century, Probalinthos was uninhabited, which may explain why he failed to mention anything in that area.[288]

Nevertheless, there are signs that the presumed Athenian camp on the northeastern Agrieliki spur did have visitors after the battle. In the small cavern within the perimeter of the rampart, Sotiriadis, as we mentioned, located Classical-era potsherds. These were mainly black-figure, and were probably made specifically for devotional rather than everyday use, as the former were most likely to be left in a cave. This raises the possibility that a small shrine could have been in the cavern. It brings to mind a passage in Herodotus, who reports that a few days before the battle, when Pheidippides arrived at the Athenian camp from his mission to Sparta, he told the Polemarch and the generals of a curious incident during his mission. He said that as he was crossing Mount Parthenion in Arkadia he came across a figure that was half-man and half-billy goat who promised the runner he would help the Athenians against the Persians if they agreed to worship him.[289]

This of course refers to Pan, who was worshipped in caves in ancient Greece. The battle of Marathon was the occasion in which the cult of Pan was introduced to Attica, and gained widespread acceptance, as a cave in the Acropolis was used for it.[290] The Tetrapolis of Marathon was one of the earliest places where Pan-worship was introduced, mainly in the cave at Oinoe.[291] It may well be that if and when archaeological excavations at the Agrieliki site are resumed, it will be found that the worship of Pan in Attica began in the small cavern in the rampart – even before the battle – and spread to Athens. The site would also have been in devotional use for some time after 490.[292]

The connection of Mount Agrieliki with the battle of Marathon may not be limited to what was found on the 206-metre spur. Near it is a taller peak of 361 metres, where in 1933 Sotiriadis discovered a small stone structure of about a square metre.[293] An initial investigation turned up a thick layer of ash and charred animal bones. Inside the ash and among the stones he found vessels and potsherds, most of which he dated to 'the Geometric and later Hellenic years'.[294] Sotiriadis believed that the structure served as a sacrificial altar used by the shepherds whose flocks grazed on Agrieliki, as he considered that the fragments were those of offerings given by poor people. Later archaeologists attached no great importance to the site,[295] except for Langdon who investigated the altar, found potsherds of the Geometric and later periods and concluded that the site was the scene of sacrifices to Zeus Ombrios ('Rainmaker') to pray for rain in the Marathon plain.[296] Though it appears that the altar began to be used in the Geometric era, it remained in use for a considerable time, as evidenced by the potshreds discovered. Sotiriadis believed there was some connection with the 206-metre height, as both are linked by a footpath. It is possible that the soldiers in 490 could have used this altar for sacrifices, to pray not for rain but for victory in the imminent clash with the Persians.

The northeast slope of Agrieliki overlooking the Brexiza pass, along with the spur at 206 metres and the altar at 361 metres, as well as the gully separating them, constituted the general area where the Athenians and Plataians encamped a few days before the battle.[297] The gully effectively protected some thousands of men while allowing them access to provisions from Mesogaia in the rear.[298] As we have seen, the gully narrows at its southeast end, which offers the sole access, or Pindar's 'recess'. The narrow point offered security in that it enabled the Athenians to control anyone entering or exiting the camp. Spies could therefore be excluded, while sensitive information would not go out to the enemy. Today the spot of the Greek camp is covered with wild olive and pine trees and the same may well have been true in ancient times; this may be the 'grove of Marathon' that some writers connect with the presence of the Greek army.

The location offered good protection against the Persians, as it would have been impossible for the Persian cavalry to operate on that sloping and stony ground; only a few horsemen would be able to make it up the path, and slowly at that. In such a case they would easily have been neutralized by the Greeks, who also had an unrestricted view of the whole Marathon plain and of any Persian operations in it. Above all, they commanded the Brexiza pass and the route to Athens. Finlay speculates that before the battle the Athenians stationed troops in the pass to block the expected enemy advance, and that the *klerouchoi* had erected provisional defensive works there after arriving before the main force.[299] Finlay's theory appears to be realistic, and it cannot be ruled out that the Greeks had built defences in the pass as well.

The area covered by 300 metres of wall on the Agrieliki spur would have accommodated only a small part of the Greek force;[300] therefore, it could have housed the staff, consisting of the Polemarch, the Ten Generals and perhaps the Plataian general, along with a small guard. The senior officers would doubtless have convened at a spot offering the best view of the enemy to enable them to decide on their moves.[301] Thus, the rampart may have served in fact as the 'headquarters' (*Strategion*) of the Greek force,[302] but also as the strongest point of defence in the camp in the case it suffered a Persian attack.[303] For more on the latter theory see the following chapter.

Chapter 4

Awaiting the Barbarians

As both sides encamped in the wider area of Marathon, the Persian commanders hoped that the mere sight of their vast army would scare the fight out of the Greeks. As part of a campaign of psychological warfare they appear to have sent the Athenian commanders a demand for surrender; they may also have believed that supporters of the deposed Hippias were working towards surrendering Athens peacefully. The occupation of the strategic 206m spur by the Greeks resulted in ten days of inaction; the main responsibility for this lies with the Athenian commanders, who had to decide whether or not to give battle to the Persians. The delay worked to the Persians' advantage as each passing day harmed the Greeks' morale. The Persians, who wanted a clash as soon as possible, provoked the Greeks constantly, including the despatch of the ultimatum. This Persian move, together with the news that the Spartans would not be marching at once to the Athenians' aid, triggered a conference of Athenian generals to decide what was to be done.

The conference resulted in a deadlock. Those generals who wished to avoid a fight with the Persians probably preferred to stay on the 206m spur to wait for the Spartans to turn up. Miltiades, seeing a negative climate developing, canvassed Kallimachos in favour of an immediate encounter; he swayed the Polemarch by outlining a battle plan that showed how the Athenians and Plataians could beat the Persians even without Spartan help. What this plan was remains a major mystery of the battle. Those generals in favour of an immediate move gave their individual days of command to Miltiades; this enabled him to fully brief all the soldiery on the details of his battle plan. The Persian ultimatum was rejected, and when Miltiades' formal day of command as head of the Oineis tribe arrived, he ordered the Greeks to descend from their rampart on Agrieliki and form up to meet the Persians in battle.

1. Effects of inaction on Greek morale

In ancient times when two armies faced one another, battle was rarely joined immediately. War is, after all, a nasty business for most people, and it is logical for conflict to be put off as long as possible. Apprehension before a battle is even greater when the commanders and soldiers of an army have not fought their particular opponent before, and therefore have no prior experience to call on. This is Whatley's view of what happened at Marathon in 490 when Greeks and Persians confronted one another before the battle.[1]

The two nations had clashed a few years before on the battlegrounds of the Ionian Revolt, but the Ionians and Aeolians had no military experience; the Athenian force that had sailed to help them in 498 had met a Persian force, but it had been of poor combat value, unlike the elite forces of the Persians who were now opposite them at Marathon. Yet the Persians also lacked knowledge of the Athenians, who were not the Asia Minor Greeks they had fought and beaten more than once in the past. Therefore there seems good reason to believe that, as Whatley suggests, the delay in the clash of arms at Marathon is attributable to indecision and hesitancy on both sides.

Though this position appears to be a sensible one, the Persians would have had no reason to delay the clash with the Greeks. The morale of their troops was high and they sought to bring their campaign to a quick and victorious conclusion. Those who would benefit from delay were the Athenians, who would thus gain valuable time before the expected arrival of the Spartans. Some scholars, however, theorize that the Persians were wholly responsible for the delay that could have been part of a tactical plan to pin down the Athenian army at Marathon while a quick commando-type operation would be launched against defenceless Athens. Arthur Munro, a British historian, first floated this theory in 1926;[2] he speculated that the Persian landing at Marathon might have been a mere diversion designed to keep the Athenians occupied at Marathon while the main Persian fleet would sail to Phaleron direct from Eretria. The force that was to disembark at Phaleron would consist of a large part of the infantry and all the cavalry. In this reasoning, Datis would have had no reason to immediately attack the Athenians at Marathon as he would be waiting for Artaphernes' operations at Eretria to be completed, whereupon both commanders could work in concert, Datis at Marathon and Artaphernes at Phaleron.[3] This theory, as we shall see analytically in Appendix IV, contains several flaws and weaknesses. No ancient literary source mentions anything of the kind; on the contrary, they stress that it was the Persians who desired an immediate clash with the Athenians, disembarking their full infantry at Marathon and cavalry force for that purpose.[4]

Part of Whatley's theory that both sides were hesitant at first to clash rests on the fact that the Athenians occupied a strong position in the days before the battle, as Finlay had first claimed in 1838.[5] The Persians would have found themselves unable to proceed southwards from the Marathon plain through the Brexiza pass and towards Athens, as the Greeks had taken up positions on Agrieliki overlooking the pass. As we have seen, Finlay supposed that the Athenians encamped at northeastern Agrieliki before the Persians had completed their full disembarkation.[6] Thus the Athenian presence served to effectively trap the Persians in the plain, forcing them to delay action. So, according to Finlay, the Athenians – first the *klerouchoi* and then the main force – on the northeast Agrieliki foothills halted the planned Persian advance through Brexiza towards Athens.

However numerous the Persians were, they would not attempt to force the pass as long as the Greeks held the overlooking height. The consequences could be disastrous, as the Persians learned in 495 during the Ionian Revolt; an army of 30,000 of their men had been marching to take Pedasos, the capital of Karia, when a Karian force ambushed them while they were negotiating a narrow pass and wiped them out.[7] The Karians had thus made excellent use of natural terrain features. This relatively recent experience would have made Datis and Artaphernes extra cautious when it came to marching through narrow passes such as the one before them at Brexiza. Neither would the Persians have countenanced attacking the elevated Greek position. Thus the theory that the Athenians encamped at the northeast side of Agrieliki were the obstacle to the planned Persian move through the pass seems to be the most sensible explanation of why the two sides at Marathon waited so long before doing battle.

The Greeks, then, were responsible for the pre-battle delay. They would decide when and where to fight the Persians, though it is admittedly a paradox that the numerically smaller force would impose its will on the larger one at Marathon. No ancient source fixes the exact number of days that elapsed between the arrival of the Athenians and the commencement of battle. Most modern scholars place the interval between seven and ten days. Also, Herodotus implies that some days passed between the time the Athenians decided to fight and the day of battle. Herodotus calls Miltiades the 'tenth' general, which may indicate that he held the 'prytany [i.e. command] of the day', on the tenth day (the day of the battle, as it turned out) from the time the Athenians set out from the city. It is quite probable, then, that the Athenians spent up to ten days encamped on Agrieliki.[8] As the Persians could not effectively attack the height the Greeks occupied, there could be no fight. In the days before the battle Datis might have hoped that the Athenians would capitulate peacefully, perhaps through the treacherous efforts of Hippias' followers. The Athenians, on the other hand, would have been waiting for the Spartans to arrive with reinforcements. In the event, neither happened: the Athenians did not surrender to Datis and the Spartans did not arrive in time for the battle.

Though it would appear that a delay in giving battle would suit the Greeks better than the Persians, the precise opposite was in fact true. The days of inactivity must have seriously eroded the morale of the Athenians and Plataians. Since their arrival and encampment on the northeast slopes of Agrieliki, they would have had a full view of the Marathon plain below them, teeming with tens of thousands of foot soldiers and cavalrymen constantly moving to and fro; in the distance they would have seen the disconcertingly large Persian fleet and its crews lined up at Schinias beach. The fighting men would have been indistinguishable from the mass of auxiliaries and ship crews, and it would have been understandable if all of them were viewed as front-line combat troops which the Greeks would soon have to encounter. The hubbub of this great mass would have been audible to the idle defenders on the Agrieliki spur;[9] there would have been dozens of ships seen plying between Euboia and Attica ferrying supplies for the Persians.[10] Datis' fleet was the biggest that had ever sailed into Greek waters so far; no Greek had ever before seen its like.[11] The sight of it is sure to have dampened morale among the Athenian and Plataian soldiers at Marathon. The only similar force they had heard of was the thousand ships that had taken the Achaians to Troy!

Aelius Aristides, however, says that the sight of the mass of men, horses, dogs, ships and everything else that made up the Persian force, far from striking terror into the Athenians, gave them 'a pleasant anticipation' as they considered that all before them would soon be theirs.[12] Though this may sound far-fetched, there could have been a reason for that. Aelius Aristides composed his panegyric speech a full six centuries after the battle, portraying the Athenians on the eve of the battle rather unrealistically as 'fearless heroes' sure of victory. In reality, however, the feelings of the Greeks would have been very different; common sense dictates that the sight of such a multitudinous foe was far from pleasant. Herodotus seems to acknowledge this by writing that half the Athenian generals shrank from fighting such a superior-looking adversary.[13] In response to this sentiment Miltiades told Kallimachos that if there was any more delay, the effect on Athenian morale would be disastrous, and that there was a real risk that the Athenians would give up without a fight.[14] Well might the average Greek soldier quail at the thought that 'all Asia' had come to attack him.[15] The presence of the Persian cavalry would have had a sobering effect on the Greeks. We know that in 479 the Persian cavalry at Plataia had made probing attacks on the Greek positions to try and draw out the Greeks to battle.[16] Those skirmishes not only had caused some casualties; they had also damaged Greek morale. Similar tactics may have been used at Marathon, judging from the account of Cornelius Nepos, who reports that the Athenians took specific protective measures against the Persian cavalry, either by encamping in a grove of trees or erecting an abatis (barrier) before their position.[17]

Before the later battle at Plataia, every time the Greeks attempted to stake out positions in the plain they were attacked by Persian cavalry.[18] At Marathon, however, no such action has been recorded. It seems that the Athenians effectively protected themselves by encamping on a height, in combination with a wooded grove or abatis. Almost certainly they did not move from their position until the day of battle; their defensive measures would have deterred any direct threat from the Persian cavalry. Yet it is quite possible that some small groups of Persian horse would have probed as far as they could below the Greek position, possibly hurling insults at the Greeks above and challenging them to come down and fight.[19] That happened at Plataia, where the Persian squadrons rode up to the foothills of Mount Kithairon and taunted the Greeks as 'women'.[20] Such provocations might well dent the morale of the Athenians and Plataians forced into inactivity in their positions.

Not much is known about the daily routine of the Greek soldiers in their temporary camp. Certainly in the days leading up to the battle they would not have been inactive; there were plenty of duties to carry out, such as building up the rampart as well as sentry and patrol duty, cleaning their weapons and preparing their meals.[21] The rest of the time they could spend as they liked,[22] sleeping or eating, chatting or playing dice.[23] The soldiers had no fixed posts inside the camp, while those with tents would generally share them.[24] But too much spare time would have had a detrimental effect on Greek morale, as giving them too much time to brood on the deadly threat faced by them and their families. Freedom of movement within the camp, moreover, would create ideal conditions for the spread of unconfirmed rumours that would be easily believed.[25] The men on Agrieliki would doubtless have been told that Spartan reinforcements would turn up within a few days, but it would have not done much to assuage the fear and anxiety that mounted with each passing day. Would the Spartans ever arrive? Would they come too late? The great mass of the enemy was milling in the plain below, plainly visible and audible. And even if the Spartans were to come up in time, brave as they were, would they and the Athenians and the handful of Plataians be able to overcome this sea of humanity below them?

In addition to the anxiety generated by the view of the enemy, living conditions in the Greek camp deteriorated, especially where resupply was concerned. Each soldier leaving Athens and Plataia took with him rations for just three days. It may be that the Athenian *klerouchoi* and the inhabitants of the Tetrapolis had brought some supplies for the main Athenian expeditionary force to find when it arrived. But it all would have been exhausted in a few days. The supplying of the army would then have had to be by supply train – pack animals and oxen pulling carts loaded with sacks of flour and jars of water. The supplies being brought in could have included millstones, cooking utensils, medicines and tools for building fortifications.[26] Even though there was ample water in the Marathon plain, the Athenians would have had a water shortage, as the spot on Agrieliki where they encamped seems to have been dry.[27]

Even if there had been a spring nearby, it would have been inadequate to meet the needs of thousands of men. The position occupied by the Athenians and Persians was picked according to strategic and security considerations. The northeast side of Agrieliki is dry in summer, in contrast to the foothills where a spring at Megalo Mati feeds a stream that runs into the Lesser Marsh.[28] This source even today sends large quantities of underground water to Brexiza, even in the summer. About a kilometre to the north, where the Tumulus of the Athenians now stands there was a stream called the Sehri (or Skorpio river). The soldiers at Agrieliki, however, did not have access to these water sources, as the Persian cavalry controlled the plain.[29] Thus water will have been among the supplies reaching the Athenian rear by supply train.[30]

A Greek soldier of the period on campaign consumed about 840 grams of grain or bread, one-tenth of a litre of preserved food, one-quarter of a litre of wine and about 2.5 litres of water a day.[31] This corresponded to about 3.8 kilos.[32] If we suppose that 20,000–25,000 men in the Greek expeditionary force were at Agrieliki, they would need between 76 and 95 tons of supplies a day, or between 830 and 1,050 mule loads.[33] In those critical days all the mules and carts in Attica would have been requisitioned by the Athenian authorities.[34] Besides, the supplying of the Athenian camp would not have been direct from the city but from some closer points in the Mesogaia plain, for example Pallene, that could have been the assembly point for all supplies coming from Attica. A mule therefore could make several journeys a day between the supply depot and the camp. But even assuming all of the above, to supply the Greek force at Marathon would have been a colossal task for the Athenian authorities.

Additional problems were presented by how to protect the supply trains between the Mesogaia and Agrieliki from enemy attacks. During the Median Wars the Greek supply trains were always prime targets for the Persians. Herodotus, in his account of the battle of Plataia, often mentions Persian attacks on Greek soldiers trying to get water from nearby streams and springs. A few days before that battle the Persians had scored a signal success by ambushing a large 500-mule supply train carrying provisions for the Greek army over Kithairon, killing or capturing all the personnel.[35] Herodotus writes that as a consequence of the Persian cavalry raids the Greeks had no access to water and were unable to get supplies from the rear.[36] A decade earlier at Marathon, the Greeks would have been especially careful to protect their supply convoys; very likely the convoys would have approached Agrieliki from what is today Nea Makri, avoiding the Brexiza pass. This would have been because the road that runs through the pass to Agrieliki would have made the convoy vulnerable to Persian surprise raids. Rather than risk their supplies through Brexiza, the Athenians would have used other paths to the camp or perhaps made their own.

On the northeast slope of Agrieliki there is a road that may well have been made in antiquity, running parallel to the road through Brexiza but at a height above it.[37] This road is up to three metres wide, and seems well-built, as there are several stone structures at the sides. It was able to take wheeled vehicles, but its purpose remains a mystery, as the main road through Brexiza runs a few score metres below. The road begins at the southwest foothills of Agrieliki, in the area of today's Nea Makri and ends near the top of the rampart on the 206-metre spur. It does not seem to have any connection with either the Brexiza pass or the Marathon plain. It could have been used as an alternative route in case of danger on the main Brexiza route. At some points on the road are ancient marble quarries, leading to speculation that it could have been constructed in antiquity for the transport of marble. It is equally likely that the road was cut out in 490 for the purpose of safely supplying the men in the camp, and subsequently used for the marble quarries.

All this demonstrates the great difficulties that would have been encountered in supplying the Greek troops at Marathon. The average soldier would have had access to relatively scant provisions, barely enough for his daily needs. Besides the Persian threat and supply issues, other problems must have plagued the Greek force. The stationing of a large number of men in a restricted space such as the 206-metre spur of Agrieliki for several days in late summer temperatures would have threatened their hygiene, another factor in lowering morale. The Persians, on the contrary, had the whole Marathon plain from which to collect water and provisions; besides the local communities, their fleet in the Euboic Gulf would have brought in more. Thus the Persian morale would have been higher than that of the Greeks. But the Persians did not want to delay the clash; they wanted the suspense to end, either through the capitulation of the Greeks or through a battle which they were confident they would win.

2. Athenian generals deadlocked

Assuming that the drawn-out inactivity on the part of the opposing armies at Marathon would benefit the Persians more than the Greeks, it would seem that the Persian commanders realized it and tried to make use of it. Diodorus reports that after sacking Eretria, Datis delivered an ultimatum to the Athenians demanding their surrender in return for forgiveness for the destruction of Sardis; however, if they were to resist they would suffer a fate worse than that of the Eretrians.[38] Plato adds that Datis informed the Athenians that not a single Eretrian escaped the Persian dragnet after their city was sacked.[39] Though Plato does not mention any demand by Datis for Athens' capitulation, the messaging undoubtedly occurred in the days between the destruction of Eretria and the battle at Marathon. The assertions of both writers strengthen the theory that Datis communicated with the Athenian commanders before the battle, demanding surrender. Some scholars believe Diodorus and Plato refer to the same ultimatum,[40] which in any case would have been delivered to Kallimachos, the Athenian commander-in-chief, and not to the city authorities, namely the Boule of Five Hundred, which in turn would have informed the Assembly before the army marched. According to Herodotus, after the execution of Darius' envoys before the 490 expedition, it would be a long time before the Persians sent any more heralds to Athens.[41] Hence any ultimatum from Datis would have been sent to the Greek camp. Diodorus adds that Miltiades, who was already at Marathon, undertook the task of replying to Datis' heralds.

This brings us to a factor that has not been fully addressed by scholars so far, regarding the function of Athens' democratic polity while the army was at Marathon. As the great bulk of the army consisted of Athenian citizens, in effect the Assembly was located in the Marathon camp. Theoretically the Athenians could have carried on political business in the camp, debating and voting on issues while the elected leaders could continue carrying out their duties. Of course, the assembled soldiers were not only citizens but also a fighting force that had to be combat-ready at all times. Thus one assumes that from the moment the army left Athens, all political activity was suspended, possibly ordered by the last Assembly to meet a few days before. Military matters were now paramount, and the decisions would be made by the Polemarch in collaboration with the ten generals. It would thus have made no sense for Datis to have sent his ultimatum to Athens, most of whose citizens had left anyway; he would have sent it to the Greek commanders on Agrieliki.

Some researchers believe that the Persian ultimatum triggered a conflict of opinions among the Athenian generals about what to do.[42] It is a logical conclusion, though also playing a part in the generals' hesitancy would have been the Spartan reply to Athens' request for aid. When Pheidippides arrived at Marathon from his mission to Sparta he conveyed the news that the Spartans could march only after the next full moon. This would be only a few days away, but in the Athenian camp every hour counted. The Athenian commanders would be expected to have been aware of the religious rituals of their Spartan allies, and should not have been surprised at the fact that the Spartans could not march at once. Nevertheless, those generals who were against engaging the enemy could have been hoping that the Spartans would override their religious rules and hasten to Athens, perhaps accompanying the courier.[43]

On receiving Datis' ultimatum and the news that the Spartans would delay their march, the Athenian generals under great pressure met to decide what to do. The conclave ended in stalemate, as half the Athenian generals urged an immediate attack on the enemy and the other half opposed it.[44] This threw responsibility for a decision on Kallimachos, who would thus have the tie-breaking vote. He therefore listened carefully to the arguments of both sides. At that juncture Miltiades took it upon himself to urge Kallimachos to adopt the position of those in favour of battle. Obviously, the five dissenting generals stuck to their guns, and none of them would change his view.

According to Herodotus, the five generals not in favour of a battle considered that the Athenian army was outnumbered.[45] On setting out from Athens, these men might well have wished to fight the invader, but one look at the size of the Persian force, plus the news that the Spartans would take time to arrive, could have made them change their minds.[46] The ancient historian does not tell us what the dissenting generals' alternative plan was, if any. We may safely rule out a suggestion to return to Athens to organize the defence there, as it would lead to a siege, and then capitulation to, or conquest by, the Persians. It is also highly improbable that the five dissenters expected the Persians to withdraw without a fight while the Athenians held the height on northeast Agrieliki. Some light on this problem could be shed by Nepos and Souda. The latter writes that before the Athenians marched, an unnamed general suggested that they wait until the Spartans turned up, when they could all march together; Miltiades, however, along with Kallimachos persuaded the Athenians to march at once and not wait for the Spartans.[47] Nepos, for his part, says that Datis wanted to get at the Athenians as soon as possible, before the Spartans could appear.[48] These two citations seem to point to the dissenting generals pinning their hopes on the Spartan presence before giving battle.

Common sense appears to be on the side of Nepos and Souda, though their historical accuracy remains uncertain. It is very likely that Miltiades talked the Athenian Assembly into approving a march to Marathon at once. Then, when the army got there and fulfilled its initial mission of blocking the Persian line of advance, half of the generals saw what a formidable force they would be up against, and opposed a quick clash until the Spartan reinforcements could turn up. They might also have argued that the Greeks had already seized strong defensive positions on spur 206-metre of Agrieliki, threatening the planned Persian line of march on Athens; therefore the Greeks could afford to play a waiting game, safely in their position, until the expected Spartan arrival.

One newly-discovered piece of evidence buttresses the view that the five dissenting generals had another plan. This is the fact that the rampart on Agrieliki was not walled on its north side, as the height there fell off abruptly to a 200-metre cliff. [49] The walled section on the southwest side, where the bulk of the Athenians were encamped, shows signs of having been built stoutly enough to resist an enemy attack from that quarter. On the south side of the 206-metre spur ruins have been found that could be the remains of further fortification in 490.[50] It is clear that the rampart at the top would have served as the last line of Athenian defence in case the Persians seized the Brexiza pass and the foothills of Agrieliki.[51] In such a case the defence of the rampart would not have lasted very long under a concerted attack, but it could have given the Athenians just enough time until the Spartans came.

We could suppose that the alternative, if any, proposed by the dissenting generals was that the Agrieliki rampart should be held at all costs, taking advantage of the terrain and the simple yet strong fortification. A reference to this could be found in Nepos, who writes that the argument in the Athenian command was over whether to 'get behind the walls' or fight.[52] This, of course, could imply that the term 'walls' means the walls of Athens, and that the dispute broke out in Athens before the army marched. Yet Herodotus clearly states that the argument occurred in the camp at Marathon; therefore, though Nepos appears to be wrong about where the argument took place, he is right about the content. We thus conclude that the term 'behind the walls' must refer to the Agrieliki rampart and not the walls of Athens. The dissenters considered that the Athenians had more chance of winning in a strong defensive position rather than fighting in the open plain against superior numbers and probably being defeated.

Herodotus clearly records that as long as the Athenian force remained inactive, the higher the probability it would not go into action. He terms the attitude of the dissenting generals 'the worse' of the two choices, concluding that any more delay would have worked in the Persians' favour.[53] As we have seen, however, he does not record any alternative plan proposed by the dissenters. He admittedly was not present at the battle, and therefore his view may well not be objective, as it appears to support that of Miltiades and the other four generals urging a clash. Gathering material for his work in Athens much later, Herodotus must surely have been apprised of the dissenting stance, but it is remarkable that he accepts as undoubtedly right the choice of Miltiades and his supporters, and condemns the other side as wrong. But an objective observer would not necessarily conclude that to delay the fighting was injurious to the Greek side. Some writers assert that the most sensible course of action for the Athenians would have been to await the Spartans and go into battle thus reinforced.[54] Herodotus' negative view may have derived not from any judgement of the rights or wrongs of the views but simply from the detrimental effect of the delay on Greek morale. The days before the battle saw a war of nerves between the two sides, a war that the Greeks were starting to lose. Any more delay could have reduced Greek morale to nothing and led to their surrender to Datis.[55]

Miltiades, thanks to his keen perception and years of experience leading men into combat situations, was quick to perceive the dropping morale in the Athenian camp. Fearing the possibly disastrous consequences of any more delay, he hastened to tell Kallimachos of his concerns. According to Herodotus, Miltiades warned Kallimachos that declining morale in the ranks could well lead to a surrender to Datis and the restoration to power of Hippias in Athens, all without a fight.[56] At no point, however, does Herodotus indicate that there was any danger from treachery by pro-Hippias men in the army or back in Athens. Even if we suppose any such elements among the soldiery did not harm morale, they could have taken advantage of the situation for their own ends.[57]

3. Miltiades persuades Kallimachos to give battle

In Herodotus' account, the deadlock among the Athenian generals was broken when Miltiades talked Kallimachos into voting in favour of immediate battle. Even though most scholars accept the account in the *Athenian Constitution* that the Polemarch in 490 was the commander-in-chief of the Athenian army, he could be overruled if a majority of the ten generals disagreed with him.[58] For example, if a six-to-four majority prevailed among the generals on any issue, the Polemarch could not override them, and had to go along. Although since about 500 the Polemarch was no longer the supreme commander but simply the first among equals, he could still carry weight with the generals.[59] In the crucial conclave that took place in the camp at Marathon the generals were tied, making Kallimachos the tie-breaker, not because he had any special influence but simply because his vote could tilt the verdict one way or the other.[60] That is why Miltiades appealed personally to him. What seems to have escaped the attention of many scholars is the fact that the Ten Generals had already convened on the issue of whether or not to give battle, and Kallimachos had not been present. This indicates that the powers of the Polemarch were separate from those of the generals, and that he could be effective only in case of a tied vote among them.

Miltiades confronted Kallimachos, appealing to him in dramatic terms to endorse those generals in favour of a fight with the Persians. Though Herodotus quotes some passages from the exchange, we don't know if the meeting was private or if the generals were present. Bearing in mind that Miltiades had assumed a key role in the proceedings and had worked closely with Kallimachos, his prestige and perhaps his persuasiveness may well have moved him to approach Kallimachos on his own initiative after the deadlocked generals' meeting without the others being present, especially the dissenters. Herodotus' phrase is: 'Miltiades went to him [Kallimachos] and said …' Of course, there was no way Herodotus could have recorded the actual words uttered, but set down what his sources may have remembered or what he thought would have been said:[61]

> *It now depends on you, Kallimachos, either to see Athens subjugated or maintaining its freedom, and to leave behind you, as long as human beings live, such a name against which not even Harmodios and Aristogeiton could leave […]*
>
> *I come to you with an explanation of the way in which events may turn out in our favour, as you are precisely the one on whom the issue depends. We ten generals are divided in our views; some expect us to give battle, while others advise against it …*

Evans quite correctly notes that Herodotus sensationalized the meeting of the two men, as he did with the meeting between Eurybiades and Themistokles on the eve of the battle of Salamis.[62] We believe that the meeting took place within the precincts of the walled camp on the 206-metre spur of Agrieliki. We can imagine them standing at the rampart surveying the whole Marathon plain teeming with the enemy. In the distance they would see the massed Persian ships on the beach at Schinias and the Kynosoura promontory. They would have been able to gaze over the sea at Euboia and perhaps make out the waterfront at Eretria. Miltiades and Kallimachos, like the rest of their soldiers, would often have looked into the distance, probably with foreboding. Below and to the right was the Brexiza pass, through which the Persians would have to pass on their way to Athens, something which the Athenians and Plataians had to thwart at all costs. We may suppose that many Athenian soldiers saw Miltiades and Kallimachos in conversation, with Miltiades the more animated, and the Polemarch mostly silent but asking curt questions. The expressions on the two men's faces would have told the soldiers that something was going on that would have a huge effect on their lives. When the conversation was finished the Polemarch would have nodded as a sign of agreement that the time for battle had come. Kallimachos 'agreed with Miltiades and voted for battle' as Plutarch says.[63]

On closer examination we believe it was hardly possible for Kallimachos to have been swayed by such words of Miltiades that Herodotus records. The speech would have been better suited, say, during the last Athenian Assembly session before the army marched than to a talk with the Polemarch. All that Miltiades is reported to have said was already known to Kallimachos; it did not include any specific arguments that would have persuaded him to fight at once rather than wait for the Spartans. Quite likely Miltiades would have pointed out the waning morale in the army, urging a clash as soon as possible. Kallimachos also would have been aware of the morale situation. Miltiades' words therefore would have contained some key point touching on some practical issue. In such a case Miltiades would not have employed flowery rhetoric to convince Kallimachos, but instead would have outlined, clearly and decisively, a comprehensive plan with which to emerge victorious without Spartan help.

The Polemarch seems not to have put forward any objections to Miltiades' words. Unfortunately, Herodotus omits any reference to what Miltiades had worked out as a battle plan. To this day, the lack of mention of a plan remains the biggest mystery of the battle, spawning several putative reconstructions by scholars over the past couple of centuries. Herodotus does not report a single word uttered by Kallimachos during the meeting. Though he acknowledges the Polemarch's assent, he does not think it necessary to quote him. We would have liked to see some record of what Kallimachos said in those critical minutes when the fate of Athens and all Greece hung in the balance.

4. Miltiades as 'operational commander'

Kallimachos' assent to the urgings of Miltiades was the event that set in motion the battle of Marathon. From the moment the decision was made, it is reasonable to assume that the Athenians sought to clash with the Persians at the earliest opportunity. Yet Herodotus informs us that nothing happened for an undetermined number of days more. During that time those Athenian generals in favour of battle voluntarily gave up their assigned rotating days of command to Miltiades. As we have seen, each general was entitled to the 'prytany', or operational command over the whole army, for one day.[64] Plutarch writes that it was Aristides who suggested that the other generals give up their 'prytany' days to Miltiades, and certainly Kallimachos must have consented.[65] It follows that Miltiades' own day of command would have been some days distant; as Herodotus says that the battle took place on what would have been Miltiades' 'prytany' anyway, and in the end he did not need the assigned days of the other generals, we conclude that there were still some days of delay after the crucial meeting between Miltiades and the Polemarch. Herodotus' mention of Miltiades as the 'tenth general' suggests that Miltiades' 'prytany' would fall on the tenth day after the march from Athens. This argues for the Athenians having waited in place for ten days before doing battle.[66]

No ancient literary source tells us just why the other Athenian generals agreed to give up their 'prytany' days to Miltiades. A common-sense explanation would be that having overall command, Miltiades would be able to work out battle tactics and brief the whole army accordingly, not just the men of his own tribe. Such planning would hardly be possible in the single day of his own 'prytany' and just before combat. Herodotus' story is the strongest piece of evidence that Miltiades was the guiding mind behind the Greek tactical planning. However, he gave the order to advance on his own tenth day and not before. One might speculate that the four generals who gave their command days to Miltiades – and Kallimachos who consented to this – did it not because they thought he had any great abilities, but so that they wouldn't be blamed in case of defeat. That, however, is most unlikely as in case of defeat Kallimachos would take the blame anyway, followed by the general on whose command day the defeat occurred, regardless of whether he had handed his 'prytany' to Miltiades or not. Of course, if the Athenians had been vanquished at Marathon there would have been no recriminations simply because there would have been no Athens and no-one to act as accuser.

We conclude that Miltiades waited until his own command day to order the army into action from Herodotus' detail that only those generals in favour of battle gave Miltiades their command days.[67] It was therefore a voluntary concession on their part, and not binding on all the commanders. The five dissenting generals would not have handed over their own command days, and neither could the Polemarch make them change their minds. Thus an opposition of sorts continued to exist among the Athenian generals, despite the fact that battle had already been decided, and the dissenters had to go along. That would explain why Miltiades waited until his own command day, when he had undisputed operational command, to give the order for battle.

Scholars have come up with three possible explanations of why Miltiades put off a battle for so long.[68] The first is that he employed the time to brief the Athenians and Plataians on the battle tactics he planned to apply;[69] to inform several thousand men would have taken some time.[70] It is a plausible theory, though it would not have been the main reason for the delay. The second theory, that the Athenians were waiting for Spartan help,[71] seems less plausible, as Pheidippides had already returned from Sparta to inform the army that the Spartans would march only after the full moon. Miltiades would have had no reason for further delay on that count. The third theory is that Miltiades waited until his own day of operational command so that he and his family could reap the credit of victory.[72] This does sound credible, and Miltiades may well have acted partly out of personal motives.

We believe, however, that Miltiades was moved not by ambitions of personal glory but by the desire to do what was legal; being granted four days of command by four generals was well and good, but it may not have been strictly legitimate and might well have later been considered illegal. As the division of opinion among the generals had gone quite deep, Miltiades could not risk even the smallest setback on the day of battle. All the Athenian soldiers knew which generals had which days of overall command, and if Miltiades dared to order a clash with the Persians on what was not ordinarily his 'prytany', there was a risk that a portion of the army would not approve. It is conceivable that some soldiers might have disobeyed the order to attack either on the grounds that they considered Miltiades' command irregular or simply thought up some excuse not to fight; they could have argued that since Miltiades was not in lawful command on certain days, they were under no obligation to follow his orders. At the same time any supporters of Hippias in the army would have had a convenient excuse to hold back.

In the Athenian army of the time, unlike a modern army, discipline was not enforced by the commanders but depended on the self-discipline of each soldier.[73] Of course the Athenian citizens could not do what they liked, since they respected the authority of the officials they elected. Yet no citizen of the Athenian democratic polity was prepared to unquestioningly obey any order, as they considered the law to be above all. In case an official order involved breaking the law, the citizen was obliged not only to disobey but to report it to the authorities. Normal democratic procedure may have been suspended in the Athenian camp, in order for the Ten Generals and the Polemarch to be able to do their jobs, but the laws of the city still applied even in those critical days. In this light, some generals' voluntary giving up their command days was probably quite illegal. Miltiades, then, wisely waited until his own 'prytany' day arrived to initiate action, otherwise he might have had a problem getting the troops to fight as he planned. The prestigious right wing of the Athenian lineup probably was not the preserve of any one tribe – though there is some evidence that it was of Aiantis – but may have been occupied by the tribe whose general had the 'prytany' for that day.[74] Miltiades thus made sure he was procedurally correct in those critical days until he personally could lead the Athenians and Plataians into battle.[75]

Diodorus writes that Datis in his ultimatum claimed that Athens was his by right, as he purportedly was a descendant of Medos, the son of Medea and Aigeus, a legendary king of Athens.[76] According to Datis' story the Athenians unlawfully expelled Medos, who was forced to flee to Asia, where he became king of the region named after him as Media. On those grounds Datis considered himself the rightful owner of Athens,[77] whose inhabitants were obliged to surrender the city to him. The Athenian commanders rejected the claim, and Miltiades replied to it by saying that if Medos, an Athenian, had founded the kingdom of Media, then it was Media that should be subject to Athens, and not the other way round![78]

On the day on which Miltiades exercised overall legitimate operational command, he gave the order for the Athenians to leave their camp and move downhill to the plain where they would be arrayed against the Persians. The mural of the battle of Marathon in the Poikile Stoa in Athens seems to have recorded this moment when Miltiades issued his orders.[79]

Another part of the mural depicted Kallimachos pursuing the enemy. Miltiades is thus featured in the opening stage of the battle, while Kallimachos is pictured in a later stage when the Persians were on the run.[80] This pictorial separation on the Poikile Stoa wall painting tends to confirm ancient literary sources who reported different duties for both men: Kallimachos had primacy as the Athenian commander-in-chief, while Miltiades, though exercising the 'prytany' was still a subordinate. Thus Kallimachos could not have been portrayed as obeying one of his generals, even Miltiades who had planned the tactics to be used in the imminent clash with the Persians.[81]

Chapter 5

The Battle of Marathon as Seen
by Recent Scholars

The fragmented and scattered information we have about the battle of Marathon from the ancient sources has left open several key questions about the time and place it was fought. Researchers have formulated many theories about the battle based on the literary, historical and archaeological evidence available to them. These theories can be classified into five groups, based on how the opposing forces were deployed before the battle. They can be represented as five basic reconstructions. The most realistic of them (Reconstruction 5) was first published by the American archaeologist Eugene Vanderpool, and is gradually finding favour with other recent scholars, who, however, have little more to add.

Over the past two centuries scholars have been trying to piece together the tactics of both sides and the progress of the battle. Yet today major unsolved issues remain. Most attempts lack originality and are mere re-workings of former theories; as John Evans, a leading student of the battle of Marathon, has commented, 'it is difficult to suggest an original reconstruction of the battle.' Since the first theories were published in the early-nineteenth century, there have been many permutations. While earlier scholars concentrated on drawing conclusions from ancient sources, chiefly Herodotus, more recent scholars have included wider archaeological and geological findings in their theories.

Thus some of the early assumptions about how the battle was fought that appeared to be self-evident have been discarded as new evidence has come to light in recent decades. Some writers have changed their minds about how the battle was fought on the basis of these new discoveries.

Introduction

Many students of the battle of Marathon over the past two centuries have attempted to reconstruct its phases as well as the tactics followed by both sides. Yet serious questions remain to the present day. There has been a multitude of theories, a few of which are original but most are versions of older views.[1] The reconstruction attempts that have seen the light of day so far can be roughly classified into five types, based on how the scholars see the position of the opposing armies forming up before the clash. Since the first such attempts in the early-nineteenth century, there has been a wide variation in theories. While the earlier scholars worked solely with the ancient sources, more recent writers also take into account the results of archaeological and geological research in the wider Marathon area. Thus some views on the battle which used to be taken for granted have since been discarded by the findings of recent decades. Some scholars have changed their minds completely about what they believe happened on the basis of this more recent research.

The five reconstruction categories

Writing in 1982, Van der Veer published his classification of attempts to reconstruct the battle. He named three categories; his A, B, and C categories[2] correspond to our groups 1, 2 and 5 immediately below. We have added two more, 3 and 4, which postdate Van der Veer's article.

Reconstruction 1 (Van der Veer A)

The Greeks formed up at the entrance to the plain at Vranas, with their hoplite phalanx between the foothills of Kotroni and Agrieliki. The Persians lined up opposite the Greeks, with the beach behind them. The Persian line stretched from the entrance of the Brexiza pass to Plasi near Mount Stavrokoraki. The two sides clashed initially at Valaria, where the Tumulus of the Athenians would be raised.[3] The Persians and Saka broke through the Greek centre and pursued it back towards Vranas. At the same time the Athenians and Plataians on the wings attacked the Persians on their fronts, driving them back. Thereupon the two Greek wings joined up and about-faced towards Vranas, catching up with the Persians who had been pursuing the Greek centre. In this part of the plain the Persians were trapped and neutralized. Then the Athenians and Plataians chased the two Persian wings to their ships and clashed again with the Persians who were trying to board them.

This is the earliest attempt to reconstruct the battle of Marathon and begins with J.D. Barbie du Bocage, a French geographer and mapmaker who drew the maps for J-J. Barthelemy's *Voyage du Jeune Anacharsis en Grece*. Bocage's map on the battle of Marathon is dated 1798 but was published for the first time in 1806 in an English edition of Barthelemy's book.[4] Bocage records there that he based his map on material published by visitors to Marathon as well as ancient authors. He depicted the presumed initial positions of the opposing forces, but did not follow up later phases of the battle with more maps. However, his map led the way for others to follow in his path. Prokesch von Osten, who visited Marathon in 1825, tried to reconstruct the battle along the lines of Bocage's map.[5] The first complete such theory on the reconstruction of the battle was advanced by Leake in 1829.[6] His narrative was generally accepted as authentic by many later scholars, but after about 1960 this dominant narrative began to lose its force.[7]

According to Reconstruction 1, then, the Athenians and Plataians formed up on a narrow strip of land between the heights of Kotroni and Agrieliki; this high ground would protect their wings from Persian cavalry attack. The retreat of the Greek centre is believed to have occurred in the direction of the plain at Vranas, which the adherents of this theory identify with the *mesogaia* mentioned by Herodotus. This is where the encirclement and neutralization of the Persians and Saka by the Greek wings is presumed to have occurred. Subsequently, there was a general Persian retreat to the ships, with the Greeks in pursuit. Those scholars who accept Reconstruction 1 and assume that the Persian ships were lying at Schinias also assume that many of the fleeing Persians fell into the Great Marsh and were drowned.

Though such an interpretation appears to take account of the physical lay of the land at Marathon, it contains serious proven flaws. It is based on the assumption that the Shrine to Herakles, and hence the Athenian camp, were in the vicinity of Vranas. But as we have seen, most modern researchers place the shrine elsewhere, namely at the Brexiza pass and the north-east foothills of Agrieliki. Another error lies in the assumption that the Athenian army marched to Marathon by the mountain route over Pentelikon, and another assumption that the Persians planned to march on Athens by that same route. It would thus appear that the Persians decided to confront the Greeks at Vranas instead of following the easier route by way of the Brexiza pass and through Pallene to Athens. It hardly needs pointing out, however, that if the Greeks had decided to hold the Vranas position they would have been committing a grave error in leaving the Brexiza pass wide open for the Persians to march through. According to this reconstruction the Greeks would have attacked from west to east and would have had the sun in their eyes. No responsible commander would have ordered such an attack [tr.]

Reconstruction 1 cannot be considered reliable, as it leads to erroneous conclusions about where the battle took place and unfolded. It has, in fact, greatly fallen out of favour, and in recent years only a minority of researchers support it. Yet not long ago it entered the limelight again, as several media outlets and in particular television documentaries on the battle of Marathon present Reconstruction 1 as the 'real picture'.[8] The theory was publicized even more in 2010, when much international interest centred on the 2,500th anniversary of the battle. Most of the reporting in the global media revolved around the assumptions of Reconstruction 1.

Reconstruction 2 (Van der Veer B)
The Greeks formed up in front of the north-east foothills of Agrieliki, with their backs to the high ground. Their two wings were not protected by any physical terrain features. Opposite the Greeks, the Persians formed up in a straight line stretching from the foothills of Kotroni in the north almost to the coast. The initial clash occurred in the general area where the Tumulus of the Athenians was later raised; the fallback of the Greek centre was towards either Vranas or the Brexiza pass – and here the proponents of this reconstruction differ. In the latter version, the encirclement of the Persians and Saka in the centre occurred right at the entrance to the pass.

Reconstruction 2 was first published by George Finlay in 1839.[9] He based his theory on the assumption that the Athenians marched to Marathon via the coast road, and suggested that Cornelius Nepos' 'high hills', beneath which the Athenians lined up, are the foothills of north-east Agrieliki. The Greeks took this position in order to monitor the way to Vranas and the coast road to Brexiza and the *Mesogaia* simultaneously.

Noted supporters of this scenario include Sotiriadis, Meyer, Kromayer, Schachermeyr, Hignett, Pritchett, Marinatos, Lazenby, Steinhauer and Dionysopoulos.[10]

Finlay judged the Shrine to Herakles, along with the Greek camp, to have been on the lower slopes of northeastern Agrieliki and the Brexiza pass. More recent writers, however, accepting the theory popular in the nineteenth and early-twentieth centuries that the shrine occupied the site of the church of Saint Demetrios at Vranas, placed the camp of the Greek army at that point, about two kilometres west of Brexiza. The same difference of opinion applies to where the Athenians and Plataians positioned themselves before the battle. While Finlay placed the Greek line from the coast to the north-east slopes of Agrieliki, later scholars placed it also at Agrieliki, but extending from Saint Demetrios to the entrance to the Brexiza pass.

Hence most of the adherents of Reconstruction 2 place the Shrine to Herakles at Vranas, though recent archaeological research has disclaimed this theory. Also, by that theory the Greek wings would not have been protected by any high ground. Another weakness of Reconstruction 2 is that it leaves unclear in which direction the Greek centre retreated under pursuit by the Persians and Saka – towards Vranas or Brexiza?[11] The assumption is that the retreat would have been in the direction of the foothills of Agrieliki.[12] But that would have been a dead end, as the ground there rises very sharply; the Athenians would have been hemmed in before their compatriots on the wings had the chance to push back the enemy on their fronts and join forces to move on the Persians from the rear.[13] In conclusion, Reconstruction 2 has serious flaws which damage its reliability.

Reconstruction 3
Reconstructions 1 and 2 were criticized in 1894 by Amédée Hauvette-Besnault, a French archaeologist. In their place he offered a third theory that he believed combined the positive elements of the other two.[14] According to Hauvette-Besnault, the Greeks formed up between Kotroni and the coast, with the Persians between Stavrokoraki and the coast. The Greeks had initially assembled at Vranas (in line with Reconstruction 1), but on the day of battle they moved over to the

north-east slopes of Agrieliki and lined up perpendicular to the coast (as in Reconstruction 2).

This theory at first found a few adherents, but was quickly forgotten. Only in 1988, nearly a century later, did Hammond bring the theory back from obscurity by publishing his conclusions that were very similar to those of Hauvette-Besnault.[15] In Hammond's view, the Greeks at first lined up along the north-east Agrieliki foothills, as in Reconstruction 2, with the Persians opposite. They thus stayed in position for several days, as neither side wished to initiate a clash. At night both sides settled down in place, though each night the Greeks would creep closer to the enemy position, with the result that when the day of battle dawned, they had shifted about a kilometre from their original position at Agrieliki. They then would be between Kotroni and the sea, some 1.5 kilometres from the Persian position at Stavrokoraki.

To remain undetected by the enemy the Greeks gradually crept forward behind the shelter of a movable wooden abatis. So successful was this tactic that on the morning of the battle the Greeks were able to surprise the Persians, who (improbably!) had no idea they were so near. On the basis of this reconstruction, the Greeks formed up in the centre of the plain, with no protection afforded by natural high ground. The retreat of the Greek centre took place in the Marathon plain, in what Herodotus terms the *mesogaia*, to be followed by the action on the wings.

Reconstruction 3 thus attempts to resolve several issues unresolved by its predecessors such as in which direction the Greek centre retreated and where exactly in the plain the battle was waged. Yet on balance it seems less reliable than Reconstruction 2, based as it is on the arbitrary view that the Greeks moved forward at least a kilometre in open and unprotected ground without any attempt by the Persians to hinder them. Almost certainly, if the Greeks had attempted such a thing they would have been attacked in the open plain. Even if the Persians did not choose to launch a frontal attack, they could have hammered the unprotected Greek flanks with infantry and cavalry that would have enjoyed a free field of action. Hammond's theory that the Persians were surprised thanks to the mobile abatis stunt cannot hold up, as that tactic was completely unknown in antiquity; it comes as no surprise, then, that Hammond's reconstruction has found few supporters.

Reconstruction 4

The Persians lined up in front of the southern edge of the Great Marsh all the way to the sea at Schinias. The Greeks had initially formed up at Valaria, where the Shrine to Herakles was located. However, on the day of the battle they moved some five kilometres into the Marathon plain to face the Persians. The Greek line extended from the coast through the plain to Stavrokoraki. It was the Greeks who opened the action by charging the Persians, who appear not to have expected it, as the Persian line did not move during the Greek charge. In the ensuing clash near the Great Marsh, the Persians and Saka pierced the Greek centre and sent the Athenians in that sector into retreat. At the same time the Greek wings overcame the Persians in their sectors at the edge of the Great Marsh; those Persians driven back by the Greek left fell into the marsh, while those driven back on the right retreated towards Schinias and the ships.

At that point the Greeks on the right and left about-faced, joined up and encircled the Persians and Saka who had broken through. After defeating the enemy in the plain, the Greeks turned and chased them into the Great Marsh and towards Schinias, where they were pursued up to the ships themselves while attempting to board. Meanwhile, the Greeks who had been pushed back in the centre continued their withdrawal to the point at which the Tumulus of the Athenians would later be raised. There the withdrawal halted, but the men did not return to the fight.

This reconstruction is the most recent one, having been published in complete form by Nicholas Sekunda in 2002.[16] Some of its premises, however, were formulated by Eschenburg in 1886.[17] It is based on two persuasive pieces of evidence: the position of the 'Trophy of Marathon' and the discovery of bones presumed to be of the Persian dead.[18] Both of these were close to the edge of the Great Marsh, and hence Sekunda's interpretation presumes that all the main phases of the battle took place there.[19] However, it is the only reconstruction that does not place any phase of the battle at the site of the Tumulus of the Athenians. Sekunda, though acknowledging that arrowheads used in the battle were found in the Tumulus' earth, claims that this earth was taken from the 'real' site of the battle five kilometres away near the Great Marsh. He fails to explain, however, why the Athenian dead were buried so far from the presumed battlefield. Moreover, his theory comes into conflict with Thucydides and Pausanias on where the fallen Athenians were buried.[20] Also, according to this reconstruction, the Greeks in the centre retreated in the plain, and therefore the *mesogaia* that Herodotus refers to must be that location.

Reconstruction 4 would appear to be the most original of those we have considered so far; however, like its predecessors it has plenty of serious flaws. Firstly, it assumes that the Greeks would have been in control of the whole Marathon plain before that battle, and that the Persians would somehow voluntarily have restricted themselves to a small area around the Great Marsh and Schinias beach. Secondly, it assumes that the Greeks would have covered the five kilometres from Valaria (the presumed site of the Greek camp) to their final line-up just before the Great Marsh without being harassed by the Persians, especially the cavalry which would have had the run of the open plain. These two objections alone make Reconstruction 4 a rather unrealistic proposal.

There is not much of a bibliography on Reconstruction 4, as it has been propounded relatively recently. However, it appears to be the basis for Krentz's theory of the battle tactics employed as regards the positions of the opposing armies before the clash.[21] He differs from Sekunda, though, in how the battle got started; he believes that the Greeks did attack 'at a run' with the aim of preventing the Persians from deploying their cavalry. Krentz claims the Greeks charged for about 1.5 kilometres (eight stadia) to stop the enemy horse from attacking. According to him, the cavalry at that time was stationed north of the Great Marsh (at today's Kato Souli). From that point, Krentz's and Sekunda's theories largely coincide.

The Greeks might just possibly have been able to run at the enemy in the way Krentz supposes, if we accept his theory that the hoplite's weaponry in 490 was somewhat lighter than was once believed.[22] Krentz does, however, acknowledge a potential serious flaw as he describes the Athenians' run at Marathon as unprecedented for them. Yet he believes Miltiades could have persuaded them to perform that reckless action over a distance of 1.5 kilometres, without having had any previous experience of that kind, and in the face of Persians prepared for battle.[23] We may discount this as scarcely possible, as each Athenian hoplite enjoyed a certain degree of freedom, and did not automatically obey the orders of a superior as in a modern army, especially if he believed the order to be absurd. What Krentz suggests would have been rejected outright by the Athenians as leading to certain disaster. Thus, again, Reconstruction 4 cannot be considered as a valid attempt to describe the battle

Reconstruction 5 (Van der Veer C)

The Greeks lined up in the area of Valaria between Agrieliki and the coast of Marathon in front of the pass at Brexiza. The line would thus have blocked the whole pass. The two ends of the line were protected by natural obstacles; the left by the foothills of northeastern Agrieliki and the right by the sea. The Persians formed up opposite them, about 1.5 kilometres distant, and about 500 metres north of where the Tumulus of the Athenians later went up. According to this reconstruction, the battle took place in the general area of the Tumulus. When the clash began, the Greeks in the centre fell back towards the Brexiza pass, pursued by the Persians and Saka, while the Greeks on the wings successfully overcame the Persians on their fronts. Whereupon the two Greek wings joined up and about-faced to move on the attacking Persians and Saka. The join-up occurred while the two wings were approaching. In the ensuing struggle the Greeks overcame their foes and pursued what was left of them to the ships at Schinias, fighting even at the ships.

Reconstruction 5 was published by Vanderpool in 1966; essentially it's a variation of Reconstruction 2 as Finlay had thought it up, with the difference that whereas Vanderpool places the Greeks in front of the Brexiza pass, Finlay places them on the north-east slopes of Agrieliki.[24] Adherents of Reconstruction 5 include Themelis, Koumanoudis, Burn (with reservations), Shrimpton, Van der Veer, Pritchett and Matthaiou.[25] Most of these are archaeologists with experience of excavating at Marathon and are in a position to know the physical characteristics of the terrain. The theory finds support in the archaeological record, such as the Tumulus of the Athenians and the discovery at Valaria of two inscriptions mentioning the Herakleian Games and suggesting the existence of the Shrine to Herakles in the vicinity. In Herodotus' narrative the Shrine of Herakles is intimately connected with the battle, either as the location of the Athenian camp or where they lined up. Even if they didn't form up at the shrine, they must have done so not far way, as they cannot have been too far from their camp. All evidence points to the Persians' intending to force the Brexiza pass on the way to Athens; the encampment of the Greeks on the slopes of Agrieliki and at Brexiza was, according to this reconstruction, what foiled the Persian plan.

The Greek formation was thus adequately protected by physical terrain characteristics that would have prevented flank attacks by the enemy cavalry. The theory that the Greeks lined up in front of the Brexiza pass is buttressed by an epigram on the fallen of Marathon, which says that the Athenians stood before 'the Gates' and 'on the coast'.[26] These 'Gates', as we have seen, can be identified with the Brexiza pass, just east of which is the sea.[27] The reference to 'Gates' is also connected with the adjective *empylios* ('within the Gates') that is recorded in the second Herakleian Games inscription and which, as we have seen, would indicate the location of the Shrine of Herakles within the Brexiza pass.[28]

Most supporters of Reconstruction 5 agree with Vanderpool's placement of the two sides before the battle, though there is some disagreement about where the Greeks encamped at first. On the map accompanying his work, Vanderpool locates the Shrine to Herakles – and hence the Athenian camp – at Valaria, among the ruins of the church of Saints Theodore.[29] Koumanoudis, however, has published a map showing the Greek force at the north-east base of Agrieliki, theorizing that the Greeks encamped there before the battle, and not at the Shrine to Herakles at the site of the Saints Theodore church.[30] Van der Veer, in one of his maps, places the shrine at the base of the 206-metre spur of Agrieliki, where Koumanoudis places the Greek camp.[31]

According to the adherents of Reconstruction 5, and setting aside the differences of opinion over the exact location of the Athenian camp, the battle opened at Valaria, where the Tumulus of the Athenians would later be raised. Then the Persians and Saka drove back the Greek centre and pursued it towards the *mesogaia,* or near present-day Nea Makri. This is the only reconstruction that confirms Herodotus' mention of the *Mesogaia* as the extended eastern Attic plain that is still called *Mesogeia.* It is what the Brexiza pass guards from the north. Yet no-one presumes that the Greek withdrawal reached the pass itself, as all the evidence indicates that the attacking Persians and Saka were surrounded on the Marathon plain before they could reach the pass. Vanderpool supposes that the Greeks clashed with the Persians at Brexiza, after which the Greeks chased the Persians into the Great Marsh and to Schinias, killing many.[32] Scholars such as Themelis, Van der Veer and Pritchett would concur.[33]

Yet such a manoeuvre as Vanderpool suggests would have been impossible. We suspect that he attempts to reconcile two conflicting theories: though he was the archaeologist who published crucial evidence showing that the Shrine to Herakles stood at the south end of the Marathon plain at the entrance to the Brexiza pass, he also found the remains of the 'Trophy of Marathon' at the north end of the plain five kilometres away.[34] Therefore he placed the Athenian camp and initial line-up at the southernmost point of the Marathon plain at the Brexiza pass, but presumed that the main phase of the battle was conducted near the Great Marsh. Despite this problem, however, Reconstruction 5 is based on strong evidence. It is no accident that it has gained popularity in recent years as the most realistic of the reconstructions posited so far. Yet it fails to adduce more evidence for its validity.

In the next chapter we present our own reconstruction of the battle of Marathon, the result of our own research while taking into account older studies as well as more recent critical ones. It has much in common with Reconstruction 5, but includes data that are published for the first time.

Chapter 6

Reconstructing the Battle of Marathon

Our reconstruction of the battle of Marathon is based on existing evidence as well as new material resulting from our research. It puts forward factors hitherto unknown, towards a completely original yet quite realistic account of how the battle unfolded. It agrees with much of what Herodotus wrote, while taking into account other literary, archaeological and topographical evidence. As presented in our reconstruction, the battle developed in two phases. In the first phase we describe how the Greeks descended from their camp overlooking the Brexiza pass, as outlined in Reconstruction 5 and lined up in Brexiza. The Greek centre was weaker and not as well-armed as the wings. This provoked the Persian attack involving the whole corps of cavalry and part of the infantry against the weak Greek centre. The controlled withdrawal of the light-armed Greek line drew the elite Persian units towards the Greek rear.

In the second phase we describe how the attacking Persian cavalry and infantry were drawn into a trap at the Brexiza pass and then massacred in the Lesser Marsh. At the same time the Greek hoplites on the wings threw back the Persians opposite them at the spot where the Tumulus of the Athenians would later go up. However, they did not pursue the Persians in their sectors but wheeled inwards to join up and block the retreat of the Persians in the centre who found themselves entrapped. These Persians came under attack from thousands of light-armed Athenian troops and freedmen and were massacred. Some Persians managed to escape the Greeks' trap, only to blunder into a Greek ambush by the ships. Helping us in our reconstruction are the maps of Marathon by Curtius and Kaupert included in their Karten von Attika, as these are considered the most reliable, especially as they depict the terrain before the extensive draining of the marshes in the 20th century and hence are more useful than modern maps.

A Phase I: the battle begins

On the day that the Persian fleet sailed from the shores of Eretria to land the forces of Datis and Artaphernes at Attica, the 4,000 Athenian *klerouchoi* of Chalkis had left Euboia and were already in northeast Attica. They may well have joined up with men from the Tetrapolis and the *deme* of Rhamnous, which lay sixty stadia (about eleven kilometres) distant from Marathon.[1] When the men saw the Persian ships sail in the direction of Attica, they knew an invasion was imminent. The news was despatched to the authorities at Athens, who without delay set in motion a pre-arranged plan to send the Athenian army to Marathon. The threat of invasion forced the Athenian *klerouchoi* as well as the inhabitants of the Marathon community to leave the plain. The local noncombatants would have fled already, but men able to bear arms would have stayed; together with the *klerouchoi* they took up strategic positions on northeastern Agrieliki, next to the southern end of the Marathon plain and far from Schinias beach, where the Persian ships were approaching. From their vantage point on Agrieliki the Athenians were able to monitor the Persians' movements and inform Athens of the rapid developments.

While keeping an eye on the invading forces, the men on Agrieliki examined the terrain, picking the 206-metre spur as a stronghold that would enable them to survey the entire enemy force while providing a rampart against a Persian attack. The Athenians knew that the hilly nature of the spot would hinder the Persian cavalry and obstruct the movements of the infantry. The position also had the advantage of unhindered access to the rear echelons, the Mesogaia plain and Athens. The main benefit to the Athenians, however, was that the position in the northeast foothills of Agrieliki blocked the Persians' route through the Brexiza pass in the direction of Athens. In this manner the Athenian *klerouchoi* and local people would avert the danger of what had happened to Eretria a few days before, when the invaders had marched right up to the city walls. Now at Marathon, the Persians for the first time faced the probability that they would have to fight a pitched battle with a Greek army.

The Athenian *klerouchoi* and locals did not have to wait long for the main body of the Athenian expeditionary force to arrive. On the same day that the Persians disembarked, the Athenians left Athens and in a matter of hours, marching via Pallene and the Mesogaia, arrived at the northeast slopes of Agrieliki. They found the *klerouchoi* and locals eagerly awaiting them, and encamped on the 206-metre spur. At once they began to fortify the place as best as they could. Probably on the following day the Plataians turned up. Over the next few days the Greeks completed their rough rampart on the spur of Agrieliki and other defensive works.

The Persians, on landing at Schinias, at once moved to secure most of the Marathon plain and the settlements of the Tetrapolis. They most likely destroyed those communities, possibly because the few inhabitants who had not fled either resisted or refused to cooperate. But they would have soon learned that the pass leading to the Attic hinterland and Athens was held by the Greeks who were encamped right above it. Thus the Persians proceeded cautiously to a short distance before the Greek camp and set up their own camp at Plasi, about 2.5km from the northeast slopes of Agrieliki, where the Athenians and Plataians were. The Persian army faced the Brexiza pass, which was its prime objective if the operation at Marathon was to prove successful.

It is quite likely that before the onset of battle Datis called on the Greek commanders to surrender, and that the call was rejected. Datis would then have known that the decisive encounter would take place at Marathon. He may well have begun provocative movements designed to lure the Greeks down from the spur to fight, lining up his soldiers in the plain beneath it and sending flying squads of cavalry close to the Agrieliki foothills to both reconnoitre the position and intimidate the defenders. The Greeks' morale must have taken a plunge as they saw how large a force the Persians had while they themselves remained motionless. The Athenians and Plataians, moreover, were having supply problems, and the promised Spartans were still nowhere to be seen.

There were other factors harming morale, such as rumours that Athens was about to capitulate to the Persians and that Hippias would be returned to power. The Athenian generals and the Polemarch worried about the effect of such rumours, yet could not seem to agree on the best way of countering the enemy offensive. Some generals favoured staying put in the Agrieliki area to await the Spartans' arrival, after which they could fight the Persians all together. The others urged a quick clash without waiting for the Spartans, concerned that plunging morale in the Greek ranks could lead to an unconditional surrender. Miltiades, the general with the greatest influence in the army, favoured the latter solution. He carried with him Polemarch Kallimachos and thus gained a majority vote for an immediate attack. Those generals who had voted for an attack gave their own operational command days to Miltiades, who now had the responsibility of deciding what to do. But wishing to keep his actions within the letter of legality, he waited until the day that his own tribe, the Oineis, assumed its turn to command and he could legitimately take over. He used the intervening time to plan tactics and brief the men on what they were to do.

As the day of the Oineis command dawned, the Athenians and Plataians prepared for battle. The men had breakfast while the senior officers presided over the traditional religious rites necessary before any battle.[2] Then the army, under the command of Kallimachos and guided by Miltiades, marched in line down from the camp at Agrieliki, into the plain to where the Lesser Marsh bordered the plain itself. The point at which the path met the Lesser Marsh is now traversed by Marathonos Avenue at the point where the Nea Makri Health Centre stands today. The Athenians and Plataians descended from Agrieliki in file formation, with the Aiantis or Oineis in front and the Plataians bringing up the rear. The Greeks continued marching for a few hundred metres over the solid terrain at Brexiza, along the route now taken up by Artemidos Street, Marathonos Avenue, Phidippidou and Kallimachou Streets, and leaving the Lesser Marsh behind.

Within minutes the head of the column reached the area where most researchers believe the Shrine to Herakles was located, near the present remains of the Saints Theodore church.[3] There the men formed into a hoplite phalanx, as each man who arrived was placed next to his predecessor. When the Greek line was complete it was about 1,600 metres long; starting at the foothills below the 206-metre rampart, where Anemonas Street now ends, and extended down through a narrow ravine to the Saints Theodore church at Kallimachou Street, ending up at the coast, about where Marathon Arka and Themistokleous Streets are today. This way the whole Greek force physically blocked the way through the Brexiza pass.[4] The left of the line at Agrieliki was held by the Plataians, while the Athenian Aiantis or Oineis tribes held the right, almost at the sea. In between were the Athenians of the other tribes. The Polemarch was stationed in the place of honour on the right wing. The line at which the Lesser Marsh met the plain is now occupied by Herakleous Street, marking the closest the rear of the Greek line could get to the marsh. Ahead of the Greeks stretched the Marathon plain, while the northern limit of the Lesser Marsh lay behind. The Greeks thus blocked the Brexiza pass without, however, being hindered by marshy ground.

As the Greeks descended from the high ground to form up, the Persians became aware of the movement at once. It was clear that the Greeks were preparing for battle. For several days the Persians had tried to lure the Greeks into coming down to fight, but without success; now, however, the Greeks were finally entering the plain. The experienced and battle-hardened Persians moved quickly into position; in a short space of time the horsemen were mounted and the foot soldiers had strapped on their weapons hoping to win one more glorious victory for their Great King.[5] The distance separating the two armies was not less than eight *stadia* – about 1.5km. Thus neither side could claim the advantage of surprise.

Herodotus suggests that the Greeks completed their battle order first. After summarizing the makeup of the Greek formation, he says that their line was equal in length to that of the Persians. According to Herodotus, this was done thanks to a thinning of the centre ranks and a beefing up of the wings.[6] In front of the first line Kallimachos conducted the ritual sacrifice which was deemed favourable,[7] and it is likely that the Polemarch subsequently gave the men a pep talk.[8] There may have followed a general roar of approval and battle-cries from the men, a common Greek tactic designed to keep up morale at the critical moments.[9] When the cries died down, a bugle call sounded from the ranks, and the men began to charge the Persians 'at a run'.[10] According to Herodotus, the Persians in the front line waited passively for the Greeks to hit them; Cornelius Nepos, however, asserts that it was the Persians who opened the action, attacking the Greek line with both cavalry and infantry. We believe that despite this contradiction, both writers are basically right about the start of the battle; in short, the Greeks may have attacked first (Herodotus), and the Persians would have counter-attacked immediately (Nepos).

To better understand the opening phase of the battle, especially the moves of the Persians as Nepos records them, we need to consider how their cavalry and infantry fought at the time of the Persian Wars. The Persians used their cavalry selectively as a striking force; the horsemen were tasked with punching holes in the enemy line which could then be widened by the attacking infantry.[11] Though we do not know where exactly the Persians placed their cavalry, we do know that the cavalry was a separate arm and not combined with the foot soldiery. This was the situation in the battle of Plataia, where Herodotus writes that the Persian cavalry was placed apart from the infantry.[12] Some scholars suggest that during the Persian Wars the Persians placed their cavalry in the centre, in front of the infantry, while others believe the cavalry operated simultaneously on the wings.[13] Kromayer, who backs the former view, says that the Persians and Saka who Herodotus says were in the centre were actually horsemen.[14] Other writers have followed suit, interpreting Herodotus to mean that Persian and Saka cavalry broke the Greek centre.[15]

There is some logic to this view. The Greeks generally gave the name Saka to the Scythian subjects of the Persians. All ancient sources agree that the Scythians were excellent horsemen; however, as foot soldiers they were considered quite inferior, as we gather from Herodotus' account of the battle of Plataia.[16] We know also that before a battle the Persians placed their best units in the centre along with the senior command.[17] The presence of the Saka in the Persian centre, then, argues for their being redoubtable warriors, that is, cavalrymen.[18] We conclude that at Marathon the Persian cavalry arrayed itself in front of the infantry and not at the wings, with the field free to hit the Greeks.

In his account of the battle of Plataia, Herodotus throws some light on Persian cavalry tactics of the time. The main tactic was to charge the enemy either en masse or unit by unit. Whichever the method used, the cavalry of the Persian Empire acted as a hammer, a fast-moving war machine pouring a rain of arrows and spears into the enemy.[19] Whenever the cavalry acted as a massed formation without gaps it would attack the enemy formation with arrows and spears and return to its own lines.[20] For this manoeuvre to be effective, the horsemen would ride in a curve so that their right arms would be able to shoot arrows or hurl spears. They would then ride back to their lines to replenish their projectiles, assess the situation and give the foot archers, who in the meantime had begun to move on the enemy, a chance to launch their own barrages.[21]

A Persian battlefield attack was therefore a ceaseless pounding by cavalry and infantry. The aim was to secure a position close enough to the enemy in order to strike him with arrows at close range. This is what occurred at the battle of Plataia in 479, where the Persians opened the action by a mass frontal assault by their cavalry against the Greek line, followed by an infantry charge.[22] The front-line Persian archers, once in position, would seek cover behind a wall of large wooden shields carried by soldiers called *gerrophoroi*.[23] These men were also combat soldiers, but instead of bows and arrows they carried the large shield in one hand and a spear or sword in the other.[24] Behind this wooden barrier the archers could shoot their volleys in safety. Once the arrows had been launched, the cavalry would make a fresh attack, and the alternation would continue until the enemy broke.

Even when behind the infantry, the Persian cavalrymen would continue to shoot their arrows at a high trajectory in order to impart more force to fall on the enemy.[25] The aim of the cavalry charge was to either break the enemy line or force the enemy to counter-attack.[26] In the former case, the enemy would be routed; in the latter, the Persians would hit the counter-attacking opponents with enough arrows to inflict considerable losses even before the lines could meet. If after that the enemy persisted in remaining on the field, then the attacks by cavalry and infantry would be renewed until the counter-attack was smashed. Once the first lines broke, panic would spread through the rest of the opposing force,[27] whereupon the Persian cavalry would pursue the fleeing enemy and complete its destruction.

When the Persian horsemen pursued a beaten foe from the field, they did not use their bows but struck at close quarters with large swords or long spears.[28] This would serve to further demoralize the enemy. The aim in this case would be to draw the enemy wings and rear echelons into the fight. These, not yet engaged, would be in the way of the retreating front-line men who then would be trapped and unable to proceed further, making them easy prey for the Persian cavalry. In the wake of the cavalry came the infantry, which now only occasionally used the bow, preferring to attack the enemy with swords. Though both the Persian cavalry and infantry fought separately in battle, they brilliantly coordinated their movements towards the battle's conclusion to break the enemy resistance. When it did break, horsemen and infantrymen together rushed into the pursuit.

Thus the tactics which the Persians adopted during an encounter differed greatly from the Greek tactics in the Archaic and Classical periods, which aimed at getting to the enemy at close quarters, man to man, as soon as possible. In confirmation, the ancient writers say that whereas the bow and arrow were the prime weapons of the Persians, the spear was the prime weapon of the Greeks.[29] The Persians fought at close quarters only when the battle was about to be decided and victory was in sight, when the aim became that of eliminating the enemy. Thus most Persian foot soldiers wore light defensive armament without shields and panoplies. The basic materials were wood and leather, which admittedly did not provide overmuch protection in a close fight. But their light equipment enabled them to move quickly and for longer distances than the heavily weighed-down hoplites. The Greeks, on the contrary, were prevented from pursuing the enemy for a long distance because of the weight of their panoply. The Persian aim, in short, was to inflict as many casualties on the enemy while minimizing their own.

The Persian cavalry would not charge the whole enemy line or any random part of it. It aimed at the wings that could be outflanked, or at weak spots that could be broken. Before a battle the Persians would have carefully examined which points in the enemy formation were most vulnerable to penetration. Such points could be gaps caused by defective deployment, but the Persian cavalry attacks could well punch holes in the enemy lines through the accurate use of arrows and spears while charging. The aim was to produce serious casualties that would reduce enemy morale and hopefully trigger wild flight. The cavalry could then charge through the holes in the enemy line and mop up remaining pockets of resistance.

At Marathon, however, as the Greeks completed their deployment in front of the Brexiza pass, the Persians realized that their cavalry could not attack the flanks of the Greek wings, as the left was in the Agrieliki foothills and the right was anchored at the sandy shore where horsemen could not operate. The Persians also must have noticed that the Greek wings were stronger than the centre, with soldiers who appeared to be more organized and better-armed. As the Greeks began their advance into the open plain, their wings must have appeared to the Persians as a moving wall of metal hoplite shields. The Greek centre, on the contrary, would have appeared weak and loosely strung out. The Persians would have seen that there were far fewer shields and spears in the centre than on the wings, concluding that the Greeks in that sector were not only fewer, but lighter armed. It probably did not surprise the Persians, as they knew that the Greeks habitually placed their best units on the right, and the second-best on the left, and therefore assumed that the troops in the centre would not be the most reliable.

The Greek troops in the centre might well have lacked adequate training, which may have been why gaps opened in the line and it appeared that they could not quite coordinate their forward movement with the wings.[30] It may even have occurred to the Persians that the apparent weakness of the Greek centre might have been deliberately planned by some Greek commander who was a supporter of Hippias and hence hoped for a Persian victory. Perhaps even the very soldiers in the centre were Hippias' men who had little stomach for fight. Yet the fact remained in Persian eyes that the Greek centre was weak, a potential Achilles heel. For the Persian cavalry it would have appeared as a gift on a platter; together with the intelligence gathered by scouts since the day of landing at Marathon, which indicated that the plain occupied by the Greeks was ideal for cavalry operations against them, it all but dictated a massed cavalry charge on the Greek centre. It would also suit Persian tactics, which according to Xenophon were based on the flank units pressing the opposing wings while the centre advanced on its front; the two wings would press forward simultaneously.[31] In this way the enemy would be encircled within a short time.[32] This was why the Persians placed their best units in the centre, in order to attack with the greatest force.

The Greeks had advanced a few dozen metres in the direction of the Persians when the order to attack sounded from the Persian lines. At once the Persian cavalry launched its counter-attack on the Greeks. As 1.5km or less separated the two armies, the Persian cavalry was free to acquire momentum over the open plain without unduly tiring the horses; the maximum force could thus be applied.[33] Before the Persian and Saka cavalry stretched the unobstructed plain at Valaria. The conditions could not be better. Hundreds of horsemen, in successive waves, hurled themselves at the Greek line. It took about three minutes for them to cover the distance;[34] when they reached the Greek line the Persians found that the Greeks in the centre, far from displaying a will to fight, were actually retreating before the Persian horse could reach them; only a few Greeks who could not get away in time dared to resist. These were easy meat for the Persians, who picked them off with arrows and spears at less than 100 metres distance.

The main objective of the cavalry was the fleeing mass of men that just moments before had been the Greek centre; the sight fired up the Persian attackers, filling them with confidence that they could easily seize the Greek rear. Indeed, their first strike had succeeded in effecting the desired breach. It would have appeared to the Persian cavalry that victory was already theirs, and so instead of halting the charge and leading the horses back to the lines, the cavalry pressed on with even greater impetus. The retreating Greeks must have appeared as cowards, and the chase took on an aspect of a hunt rather than a battle. The cavalry advanced in waves, followed at a few hundred metres distance by the fast-moving Persian infantry in the centre and wings. The infantry advanced along with the shield-bearers, the *gerrophoroi,* whose task was to set up the wooden shields as shelters behind which the archers could shoot their arrows. The attacking horsemen raised a great cloud of dust that would have hindered the infantry behind from seeing what was going on in front. The Persian and Saka cavalry were chasing the Athenians of the centre in the direction of the Mesogaia as hundreds of foot soldiers followed in the horses' wake. The archers aimed to hit the Greeks at short range and rout them.

The Persian foot soldiers were aware that the Greek wings would attempt either to close the gap opened by the retreat in the centre, where the cavalry was on the rampage, or defend themselves against the cavalry attacks as best they could. Either way, the Persians were confident that the Greeks would be immobilized in the plain and unnerved at the sight of the mass of cavalry bearing down upon them. The archers hoped to widen the breach in the Greek line by their own efforts and join in the general pursuit that would follow. Their arrows could cause serious injury or death at a distance of 170 metres, and in exceptional cases up to 200 metres.[35] Therefore the archers would have to advance little over a kilometre to be in a position to effectively hit the Greeks.

For days the Persian archers had been practising their tactics, and had come to be familiar with the ground they were to fight on. They knew in which direction they had to advance in the Marathon plain, and where to stop in order to employ their weaponry. They would have witnessed the cavalry's initial success before the cloud of dust raised by the horses, and must have been full of confidence themselves; their hail of arrows would certainly finish off the Greeks after the cavalry had done its work.

But it didn't work out that way …

B Phase II: the Persians are trapped and massacred at Brexiza

Without warning, through the dust, the Persian infantry in the advancing front line saw thousands of Greek hoplites running towards them a few dozen metres away. According to Herodotus, the Persians thought the Greeks had gone mad and, unprotected by either cavalry or archers, were hurtling to their own destruction.[36] A Greek attack at that point would have truly seemed inconceivable to the Persians. Their surprise would have been fully understandable, as logically the Greeks would have been madly trying to halt the Persian attack; instead, they were actually charging the two Persian wings without cover! However their surprise immediately turned to panic as the Persian archers realized that their weapons would now be useless; they may have managed to loose off a few shots before throwing down their bows and grabbing a sword or battle-axe. Within moments they were faced with the hitherto unthinkable task of fighting heavily-armed hoplites at close quarters. The *gerrophoroi* had not even time to set up their shield-walls before coming under a rain of Greek spears.[37]

The clash was not yet general all along the line. The Greeks in the centre were still retreating, pursued by the Persian cavalry and elite infantry units in the direction of Brexiza. The Persian foot soldiers in the centre were unaware that their compatriots on the wings had been stopped in their tracks. Reaching Brexiza, they found just the bodies of a few Greeks struck down by arrows or trampled by horses and pressed on. But the dust of the advance prevented the attackers from seeing what they saw just minutes later: instead of a craven mass of defeated Greeks, the scene that unfolded before them was that of a morass of their own men and horses milling about in confusion. Horses ran about riderless, while those horsemen still mounted desperately sought a way out of the trap they found themselves in. The front lines of the Persian infantry saw with horror that the cavalry had blundered into a muddy swamp that had thrown it into utter confusion.

How did that happen? The Persian and Saka cavalry had been charging full tilt through the wide gap that had opened up in the Greek centre and towards the Brexiza pass and the Mesogaia plain beyond. In their élan and enthusiasm, however, they had failed to notice that the solid ground they had been galloping over had become fragmented and was giving way to a sea of thick mud. But they were going too fast to be able to do anything about it; they were compelled to keep on chasing the fleeing Athenians beyond Brexiza even though their horses were getting stuck. The horsemen behind then blundered into the leading ones who were getting deeper into the mire. Many horsemen failed to stay mounted and toppled to the ground.[38] The main concern of the cavalrymen now was not to pursue the Greeks but to extricate themselves from the bog and return to the rear to reorganize. But this proved impossible, as the mass of oncoming cavalry prevented a turnaround.

The Persians had fallen into an extensive swamp that from a distance had not been distinguishable from the rest of the Marathon plain. The surface had appeared solid, but the sheer weight of horse made the ground give way. It was, in fact, the Lesser Marsh. Possibly the unstable ground had given way after the first ranks of Persian cavalry had gone through; if this was the case, then those leading ranks would have found themselves cut off from the others with no means of escape. Also, the rear ranks would now have become well and truly mired in the mud, with hundreds of horses – some riderless, some hurt – and riders in total disarray. Worse was to come. While the horsemen bogged down in the Lesser Marsh were trying to make some sense of their situation, the hundreds of infantrymen behind swarmed into the marsh, blocking the rearward avenue of escape for the cavalry. Neither could they go forward towards the Mesogaia plain beckoning just a kilometre away, as the marsh blocked that route as well.

The elite forces of the Persians had become trapped in a 'hidden' marsh far from their original line. They were in a position neither to attack the enemy nor to render any assistance to their own infantry in the plain. They had fallen into a trap of nature laid by men they had been relentlessly pursuing moments before. At about the same time, a few hundred metres to the north, the Persians on the wings came under strong attack from the spears of the Greek hoplites in their sectors.

The Persian and Saka cavalry, bogged down as they were in the Lesser Marsh, could not have known what was happening in the Marathon plain. Their sole thought was how to escape their predicament. But their situation worsened as the Greeks, who had been retreating precipitately, began to assemble in the marsh and hit the Persians at long distance with arrows, javelins, slingstones and rocks. The Persians – those, at least, who still carried bows – tried to strike back, but they were at a disadvantage, not only from being held up by the swamp but also from the sheer volume of projectiles being hurled at them. The Lesser Marsh offered no place they could take cover. The conflict continued for some time as the Persian horsemen, many of them wounded, sought an exit from the hellish swamp; then they saw a mass of Greeks materializing from various parts of the marsh and moving on them threateningly. These were men who had remained hidden in the marsh before the onset of the battle. Those Persians who could still ride and were not immobilized by the marsh tried to ride to the rear, but those who had fallen from their horses floundered about helplessly. The Greeks tried to pull horsemen from their mounts while throwing themselves fiercely on the unhorsed men on the ground.

Though the Persians found themselves in a critical situation at the Brexiza pass, the Greeks were not yet in a position to press any advantage as they had to confront the oncoming Persian infantry mass, as well as try to block any escape routes from the Lesser Marsh in the direction of the plain. The Greek battle plan was for the wings to advance at a steady pace on their fronts even when the Greek centre was being pushed back. The task of the wings was to drive back the Persians; they did not have to advance the full 1.5km separating them from the Persian lines, as the Persian infantry would already be in motion against them. In fact, only about half that distance separated the advancing lines;[39] the Greeks pushed on 'at a run' for some 150–200 metres when they came within range of the Persian arrows. The pace was quickened in order to surprise the Persians, whose vision would have been severely limited by the dust thrown up by the charging cavalry in the central sector. They probably did not become aware of the Greeks charging over the last 200 metres; the Greeks also must have not been able to see very well in the dust clouds, but they had the advantage of surprise and the poor visibility may well have reduced the expected casualty count.

The Greek advance at the wings aimed to surprise the Persian infantry in those sectors rather than attack the cavalry. The tactic worked. When the lines clashed the Greeks had the advantage of their long spears which picked off the enemy soldiers who were lightly armed with short swords which were virtually useless in this kind of combat. We would probably not be very far off the mark if we pictured the initial clash not quite as a pitched battle but as a massacre of the Persian front-line troops by the Greeks on the wings. This encounter, entailing heavy Persian losses, took place at Valaria, where the Tumulus of the Athenians stands. The actual clash was so severe that many Greek spears broke on the bodies of the Persians and had to be replaced by swords as combat weapons.

The rearmost ranks of the Persians saw the front line being overrun by the Greeks and must have wondered where their protectors, the cavalry, were. Men were falling wholesale. The ranks, overcome by panic, turned and fled, carrying with them those soldiers who had not yet joined the fight and had not known what was happening ahead. They appear to have been too panic-stricken to gather and re-form at their camp at Plasi, but surged on towards their ships at Schinias beach. Yet the main objective of the Greek charge was not the Persian flanks, which had just been beaten, but the main Persian cavalry and infantry force which had penetrated far behind the Greek lines in the centre. The swift Greek advance on the wings hopefully would give those wings the space to manoeuvre themselves into a unified formation that would attack the Persian centre from the rear. Instead of chasing the fleeing Persians, the Greeks duly carried out an about-face and moved quickly towards the Lesser Marsh about a kilometre away.[40]

There would have been some signal for this movement to begin – perhaps a bugle-call – for thousands of Greek troops to advance towards the Brexiza pass. We may imagine a gradual joining up of the two wings into a solid mass that appeared in the rear of the Persian centre like a moving wall of shields. Now the Persians were completely cut off from any access to the Marathon plain. At this time, the Persian cavalry bogged down in the Lesser Marsh was helpless, while those horsemen still on dry land were hemmed in by their own infantry. While the Greek hoplites at the Brexiza pass attacked, thousands of Athenian light-armed troops assaulted the Persian and Saka cavalry trapped in the marsh. Many horses in their panic trampled their own men. Any soldier trying to escape into the plain came up against other Greek troops in the rear, though some, fighting bravely, did manage to reach the sea and run to their ships farther up the coast. Surviving cavalrymen abandoned their horses and joined the fleeing mass of Persian infantry that had been overcome on the wings.

All this did not go unnoticed by the Athenian hoplites fighting by the beach; the right wing under Kallimachos launched a reckless charge on those Persians who had escaped the Lesser Marsh. His hoplites reached the first ships, where a sharp clash ensued. It was here that the Polemarch Kallimachos, Kynegeiros and the general Stesileos died heroically, along with other Athenian hoplites. These casualties, combined with the fact that the Greeks managed to seize just seven of the hundreds of Persian triremes, argues for an especially bloody phase of the battle. The Persians defending their ships and attempting to flee would have put up a ferocious resistance. Persian ship crews may also have joined the fighting. This phase is attributable to the excessive ardour of the Athenians; it is hardly likely that Miltiades would have planned it. Miltiades' objective was to neutralize and encircle the elite Persian and Saka units in the centre, not to pursue the already defeated foe to the ships. The risky and aggressive Athenian action, it must be said, in no way contributed to the victory; the hoplites acted individually and not as part of a phalanx, and were too few to have any real effect, and besides, the battle already had been won.[41]

While the Greeks and the Persians were desperately battling it out by the ships, the carnage at the Lesser Marsh and Brexiza continued. Thousands of light-armed and 'unarmed' Athenians, thetes and freedmen, including farmers from various parts of Attica but mainly Marathon and its environs, attacked the Persians with arrows, spears, javelins, slingstones, stones, farm implements and anything else they could get their hands on. Seeing the enemy faltering and disintegrating before their eyes, they took fresh courage and hit the Persians wherever they could be found on solid ground. The fight was long and hard, as the Persian and Saka cavalry resisted as best as they could; some, without horses, fought back with their bows and arrows. But despite their superior training and experience, they gradually succumbed as they ran out of arrows. The Persians trapped in the Lesser Marsh now came under murderous attack from Athenian and Plataian hoplites from the Marathon plain; the swamp filled with Persian bodies as the butchery lasted for some time until after the last Persian ships had sailed away.

The Persians left behind them at Marathon 6,400 dead. They would also have lost many to capture by the Greeks, though the surviving ancient sources mention nothing of this. A total of 192 Athenians fell at Marathon, plus an unknown number of Plataians and freedmen.[42]

Chapter 7

The Basis of the Battle Reconstruction

The first objective of the Greek strategic plan was to halt the progress of the Persians from Marathon to Athens, and then to entrap their elite cavalry and infantry units in the Lesser Marsh at the Brexiza pass. The main problem for the Athenian commanders was how to neutralize the cavalry – the most powerful arm that Datis had in the field – before it came into contact with the Greek hoplites in battle. Miltiades' solution was to separate the roles of the hoplites and the light-armed troops. The hoplites were tasked with driving the enemy back from the wings and then joining up behind the Persians to entrap them in the Greek rear.

But it was action of the light-armed troops that proved decisive, as they were the ones who drew the Persians on into the Brexiza pass 'towards the Mesogaia' to be massacred. It was their contribution that upset the balance of forces between the Greeks and the Persians; the unstoppable Persian cavalry and elite infantry in the centre were annihilated in a carefully-laid trap in the Lesser Marsh, where the Athenian arrows were 'literally dipped in Persian blood.' The phase in the Lesser Marsh is attested to by the south frieze of the Temple of Athene Nike and the mural of the battle of Marathon in the Poikile Stoa. It appears that after 490 the Athenians employed tactics similar to those of Marathon in other victorious battles.

Though the contribution of the light-armed troops, both thetes and freedmen, was noted by their contemporaries in the fifth century by being depicted in public works of art, later eras tended to erase any mention of their role. The victory was associated exclusively with the upper classes whose men served as hoplites in the Athenian army. Thus gradually the memory of the contribution of the light-armed troops to the victory of the Athenian demos in 490 faded and was eventually forgotten.

Introduction

Our reconstruction of how the battle of Marathon developed is based on the analysis of a wealth of literary, historical, archaeological, geographical and geological data. The main literary sources which we used are the narratives of Herodotus and Cornelius Nepos; while the former concentrates on how the Greek tactics developed during the battle, the latter says more about how the battle began. Our reconstruction includes Herodotus' account of the Athenians' initial pre-planned withdrawal in the centre, and pursuit by the Persians and Saka, the clashes on both wings where the Greeks prevailed, the joining up of the Greek wings and the ensuing flight of the Persians to the beach at Schinias. These tactics ensured the destruction of the Persians, some of whom managed to escape, only to be attacked by Athenian hoplites at the ships (at today's Aghios Panteleimon).

Nepos in his account gives us details of the commencement of the battle that Herodotus omits, such as the charge of the Persian cavalry and elite infantry against the Greek position, which we include in our reconstruction. Other sources on which we have drawn include ancient works of art such as the south frieze of the Temple of Athene Nike on the Acropolis of Athens, the mural of the battle in the Poikile Stoa (based on Pausanias' description, see Appendix II), the so-called 'Brescia Sarcophagus' and depictions on Attic pottery of the early fifth century. Both the frieze and the Poikile Stoa mural depict the entrapment of the Persians in a swamp, which we have shown to be the Lesser Marsh, and their massacre by the Greeks.

The main archaeological relics so far relating to the battle are the Tumulus of the Athenians and the Trophy (see Appendix III). We accept the claims of many scholars that the Shrine to Herakles stood at today's Valaria, near to the present ruins of the Byzantine church of Saints Theodore. Both the position of the tumulus and the presumed location of the shrine are useful data in themselves. The archaeological remains on the 206-metre spur on the north-east slope of Agrieliki are here, for the first time, cited as important evidence for the exact position of the Athenian and Plataian camp before the battle. It was from here that the Greeks descended to the plain of Marathon to confront the invaders. We also take into account geographical clues such as the probable position of the Marathon coastline at the time, the existence of swamps and the road towards Athens. The Brexiza pass, the Lesser Marsh and the location of the coastline all played important roles in the battle.

The prime Greek objective at Marathon was to stop the Persians from forcing the Brexiza pass. This was the theory first propounded by Finlay, to be elaborated more than a century later by Vanderpool and Koumanoudis. The idea that not only hoplites but also light-armed troops fought at Marathon on the Greek side, and that cavalry was actively involved on the Persian side, has been incorporated in various reconstructions of the battle. The biggest problem confronting the Greek commanders was how to handle the enemy cavalry; by the same token, the Persian infantry would have presented no serious problem to the Greek hoplites as long as the Persian cavalry could somehow be put out of action. Besides superior weaponry, the hoplites' phalanx tactics were far superior to those of the Persians in a close-quarters encounter. As long as the cavalry was neutralized, a Greek victory was a definite possibility.

Yet the way in which the Greeks did deal with the formidable Persian cavalry at Marathon remains an impenetrable mystery of the battle until the present day. Our reconstruction shows that Miltiades, who well knew how the Persians employed their cavalry as a striking force in the initial phase of a battle, worked out a plan to neutralize it through an ingenious use of the natural terrain – namely, the Lesser Marsh at the entrance to the narrow Brexiza pass.

1. The elimination of the Persian cavalry and role of the hoplites

One of the major gaps in Herodotus' account of the battle is how it got underway. His description of how the Greeks charged an inert Persian line strains credulity. Nepos, in his account, fills in the gap by describing the initial Persian moves; his narrative appears to be more realistic, and could have been based on some source, now lost, that was penned much closer in time to the battle. What adds credibility to Nepos' claim is also his reference that all Persian cavalrymen took part in the battle at Marathon but not all foot soldiers (Miltiades, 4–5). At the battle of Plataia something similar happened according to Herodotus, 9.66, as the entire

Persian cavalry fought there but many foot soldiers were held in reserve under general Artabanos. The aim of the Roman historian was not so much to replace Herodotus' story with his own, as he does not go into the tactics of both sides during the clash, as to fill out the general picture by adding more material; this argues in favour of its reliability.

We therefore believe that any account of the battle of Marathon must include the massed charge of the Persian cavalry and infantry against the Greek line as described by Nepos. Yet we must also explain how the Greeks managed to halt this charge and subsequently put in motion moves that would give them victory.[1] Most scholars agree that the Persians did indeed land their cavalry at Marathon; therefore, any reconstruction would have to include this in the Greek battle plan, even in the barely credible case that the cavalry might not have been used. In 490 the Greek commanders would have had to plan their tactics with the powerful Persian cavalry in mind, which meant knowing how it would be employed.[2]

The basic Greek military formation at the time was the hoplite phalanx; however, it had taken form through the practice of meeting other hoplite phalanges, rather than cavalry, in battle. Greek hoplites in the Archaic and early Classical periods had little experience in how to confront cavalry on the field. In the few cases we know in which hoplites were pitted against cavalry, the hoplites always came off the worse;[3] in 511 at Phaleron, a powerful Spartan force was trounced by 1,000 Thessalian horsemen;[4] in 479, during the battle of Plataia, a Theban cavalry force of less than 1,000 easily defeated a hoplite force four times its size from Megara and Phlious, killing 600 of them.[5] We must point out here that Greece's own best cavalry forces were, however, inferior in fighting quality to the Persian horse. We know that during Xerxes' expedition to Greece in 480, he was told that the cavalry of his Thessalian allies was Greece's best. He called for a contest between the Thessalian and Persian horse, which the latter won comfortably.[6] Before 490 one of the few occasions in which Greek hoplites fought a Persian cavalry force was at Malene in Mysia in 494, during the Ionian Revolt, when armies of the Aiolians and Ionians met Persian infantry in battle.[7] As the Persians delayed deploying their horse, the battle raged inconclusively; but when the cavalry did appear, it swept the Greek hoplites from the field.[8] Similar results could well have occurred in other clashes in Ionia at the time.[9]

By all indications, for a Greek army at the time of Marathon to handle a charge by a strong force of Persian cavalry would have been a difficult proposition, if not impossible. Some scholars, however, believe it could have been done if the Greek hoplite line held its ground behind its wall of shields, and, thus stationary, ward off the missiles being shot at it.[10] By this theory, the Persians would have been unable to break the Greek line and thus concede the initiative to the Greeks – on condition that the line remained solid, with no gaps opening up.[11] However, the Greeks would have had to display extraordinary coolness and fortitude to stand up to the sight of hundreds of horses bearing down on them; even if a few panic-stricken hoplites broke and ran, the effect on the rest of the army could well be disastrous.[12] A Persian cavalry charge depended heavily on the psychological effect it would have on a line of defenders.[13] It is, in fact, what happened later at Plataia, where desultory Persian cavalry attacks before the main encounter caused no small degree of panic and fear to the Greek hoplites.[14]

We have some idea of how a Greek army in the fifth century handled a Persian cavalry attack. For example, in 401, at the battle of Cunaxa, the Greek mercenaries of Cyrus the Younger, consisting of hoplites and light-armed peltasts, were frontally attacked by the powerful cavalry and chariots of Artaxerxes II. One might expect that the Greek hoplites would meet the charge by forming up behind their solid shield-wall; instead, they marched along, and when the enemy horses and chariots were about to close, the Greeks opened corridors in their ranks through which the horsemen charged and thus laid themselves open to relentless attacks from the flanks.[15] Xenophon, in his account of Cunaxa, claims that the 10,000 Greeks involved suffered only a single casualty.[16] Of course, as this successful neutralization of Artaxerxes' horsemen took place ninety years after the battle of Marathon, it is not much help in divining the Greek commanders' plans in the earlier battle. Moreover, in 401 the Greek hoplites were highly experienced fighting men, veterans of many battles, and above all professionals, something the men of 490 were not.[17]

Though Herodotus does not tell us how the Athenians handled the problem of the Persian cavalry at Marathon, he is rather more enlightening on how Pausanias handled it at Plataia in 479. The Spartan general had no idea how to repulse the Persian cavalry attacks before the main battle and in its initial phase;[18] if he had seen the solution to be a massed hoplite defence line behind a wall of shields, he would already have adopted that tactic. When the two sides finally formed up for the main clash, the best thing that Pausanias could come up with was to ask the Athenians to switch positions with his Spartans; the move placed the Athenians on the right, the place of honour, to the resentment of the Spartans.[19] Pausanias gave as his reason the fact that the Athenians' experience at Marathon made them better prepared to meet the Persians in battle than the Spartans were.[20] Shrimpton's view is that Pausanias made the change because of all the Persian force, only the cavalry seriously worried him.[21] Before the main clash at Plataia the Persian cavalry had been opposite the Greek right, occupied at first by the Spartans. The view appears plausible, as when Spartan infantry and Persian cavalry clashed at the start of the battle, Pausanias appealed to the Athenians to send their archers to help;[22] the conclusion is that the Spartans, though they boasted the best soldiers in Greece, were in no position to fend off the Persian cavalry alone.

Despite the overwhelming Greek victory at Plataia, the Persian cavalry managed to ride away from the field virtually unscathed, unlike the infantry, the great bulk of which was cut down. Though the Greek infantry carried the day, the Persian cavalry seriously harassed the Greek flanks, and provided protection for those Persians who were retreating.[23] Herodotus correctly pays tribute to the Persian horsemen, giving praise especially to the Saka, even though a week earlier the Persian cavalry commander, Masistius, had been killed in a skirmish.[24] Though the death of the Persian commander Mardonius during the battle also was a blow to the cavalry's morale, it suffered relatively lightly at Greek hands.[25] For the Greeks' part, they would have been relieved that the slaughter of the enemy infantry, by all appearances, put paid to the Persian expeditions to Greece, and in consequence there would be no more need to face the Persian cavalry.[26]

Unlike the cavalry, the Persian infantry did not pose a serious threat to the Greek hoplites. Herodotus cites Aristagoras, the tyrant of Miletos, who reportedly said in 499, echoing general sentiment, that the Greeks could beat any opponents who 'did not use either shield or spear', which held true for the bulk of the Persian foot soldiery.[27] Only a relative few Greek hoplites had fought Persian forces before 490, i.e. during the

Ionian Revolt. Yet the Greeks knew well enough the fighting qualities of the infantry, as it was equipped similarly to the Greek light-armed troops. From ancient literary and artistic sources, as well as what we see on Attic vases and other works, the Persian foot soldier had little or no metallic defensive weaponry; even his shield was made of wood. His prime weapon was the bow and short sword.[28] The Greeks also knew that the Persian infantry included men from the subject peoples of the empire whose fighting qualities were not equal to the master ethnic groups, the Persians and the Medes. The cavalrymen in particular came from the upper classes, were well-trained, and constituted the best fighters in the Great King's army.[29]

Not having experience of fighting cavalry, the Greek hoplites of the early Classical era had no training in the technique. There were psychological difficulties to overcome, such as maintaining the nerve to meet a massed cavalry charge. Thus Herodotus' admission that before the battle of Marathon the Greeks trembled before the Persians probably refers to their apprehensions about the cavalry.[30] Aischylos, who fought the Persians at Marathon and at Salamis ten years later, in his *Persians* credits the cavalry as the key to the Persians' victories and conquests.[31] Already thirty-five years old at the time of the battle, Aischylos would have been well aware of the danger posed by the Persian cavalry.[32]

Further attesting to the renown that the Persian cavalry enjoyed, it appears that at no point in the Persian Wars did the Greeks ever deploy their own cavalry against the Persians. We know that some Greek cities kept up respectable cavalry forces, such as Thebes since the Archaic era; however, when the Thebans joined in the defence against Xerxes in 480, they fought only with their infantry. When a year later they switched sides, they deployed a sizeable cavalry force at Plataia that gave the Greek defenders considerable trouble. Therefore, at the start of the fifth century the Greeks, even those who had cavalry forces, avoided using horsemen against the Persians, conceding them the superiority.[33]

It appears clear from the foregoing that the main problem of the Athenian commanders at Marathon was how to deal with the Persian cavalry; they would have had little idea of how to stop them with a wall of hoplites, much less defeat them. Yet one commander, Miltiades, did have experience of how the Persians fought, and would have had some notion of what to do.[34] He would have figured that once both armies had completed their movements into position, the Persians would employ their unvarying tactic of unleashing a cavalry charge on the opposing line. Their cavalry and infantry would alternate their thrusts against the Greeks, with a rain of arrows and spears; the moves would be designed to halt the Greek advance and deprive the Greeks of the battlefield initiative.

Faced with this unrelenting hail of projectiles from the cavalry and infantry, the Greeks at best would be surrounded, cowering behind their shields. After a succession of heavy blows, the first cracks would appear in the Greek line. So far, the Persians would strike at a distance, avoiding a close-quarters encounter in which the Greeks would have the advantage. But with the appearance of the first gaps in the Greek line, the Persian cavalry and infantry would pour through and complete the destruction of the Greek force.[35]

Miltiades well knew that the Persian cavalry needed to be dealt with before it could become a serious danger to the Greek army. Only then could the Persian infantry be encountered on more or less equal terms. Yet the Greek infantry was in no position to stop the cavalry by the conventional methods of the hoplite phalanx; a way had to be found to neutralize the cavalry's two advantages, speed and the ability to strike at long range with arrows and spears, and withdraw before the enemy could recover and strike back. If the cavalry somehow were to lose its manoeuvrability or ideally was immobilized, its striking force would be dramatically reduced. Then the Persians would be compelled to fight at close quarters, where the Greek tactics were superior.

The cavalry thus had to be prevented from coming into contact with the Greek hoplites, but the only way to accomplish this was to deviate from usual hoplite phalanx tactics and present the Persians with the unexpected. As we have seen, at Phaleron in 510 the Spartans may have erected an abatis, or protective rampart, around their position, against the Thessalian cavalry. Nepos' report on the Battle of Marathon suggests that the Athenians may have done the same at Marathon twenty years later. If the Athenians actually did so, they would have been able to temporarily halt the Persian cavalry, but it would not have made much difference, as the weight of the cavalry and infantry charge would have

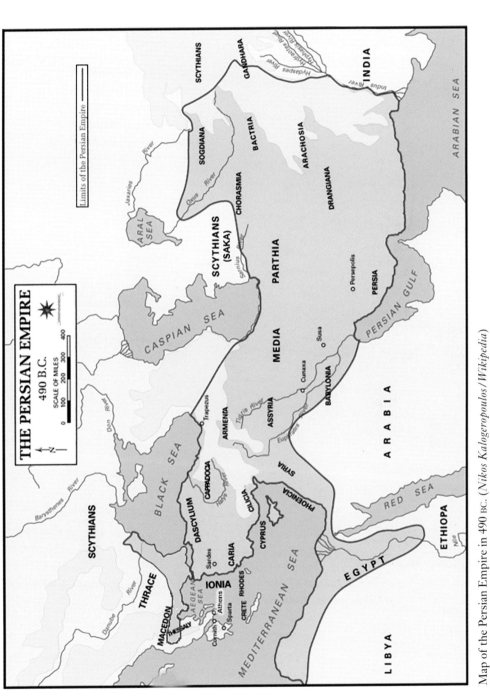

Map of the Persian Empire in 490 BC. (*Nikos Kalogeropoulos / Wikipedia*)

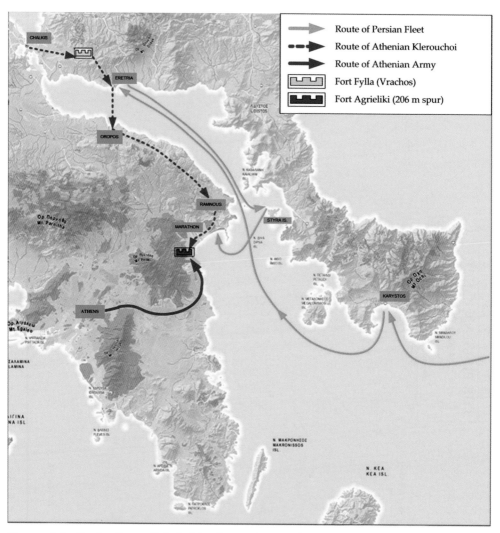

Course of the Persian fleet to Euboia-Marathon and route of the Athenian army towards Marathon. (*Design/credits: Nikos Kalogeropoulos/Assimakis Katsiaris*)

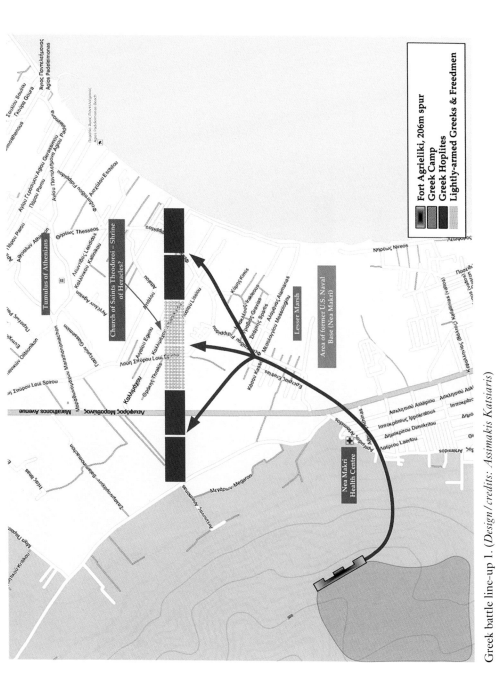

Greek battle line-up 1. *(Design / credits: Assimakis Katsiaris)*

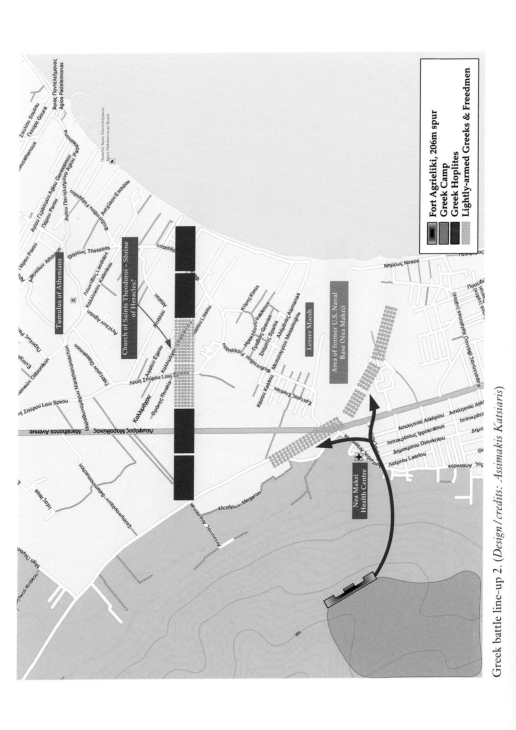

Greek battle line-up 2. (*Design/credits: .Assimakis Katsiaris*)

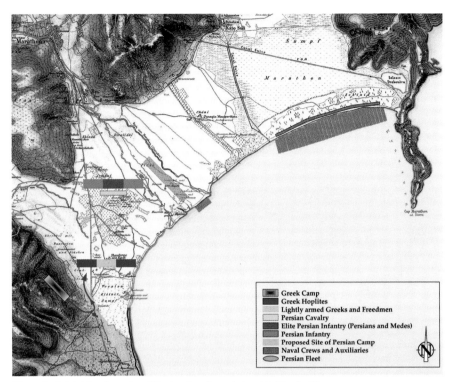

Phase 1: Initial battle order. (*Design / credits: Assimakis Katsiaris*)

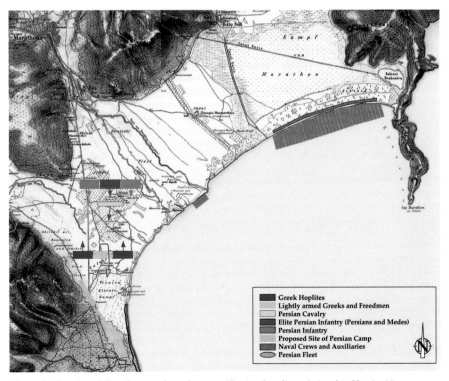

Phase 2: Greek and Persian armies advance. (*Design / credits: Assimakis Katsiaris*)

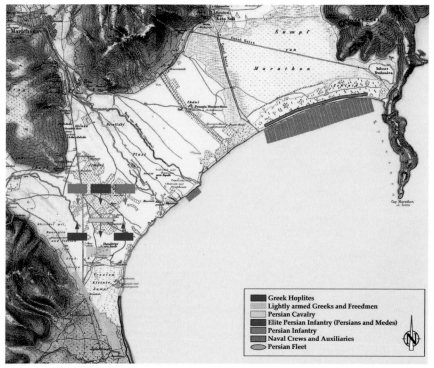

Phase 3: Greek centre retreats. (*Design/credits: Assimakis Katsiaris*)

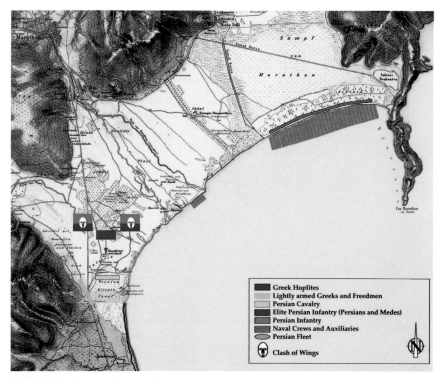

Phase 4: Persian cavalry reaches marsh and hoplite flanks engage Persians. (*Design/credits: Assimakis Katsiaris*)

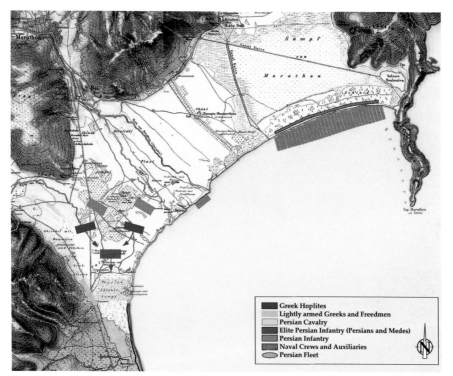

Phase 5: Persian cavalry pinned in marsh. Hoplite flanks start pincer move. (*Design/credits: Assimakis Katsiaris*)

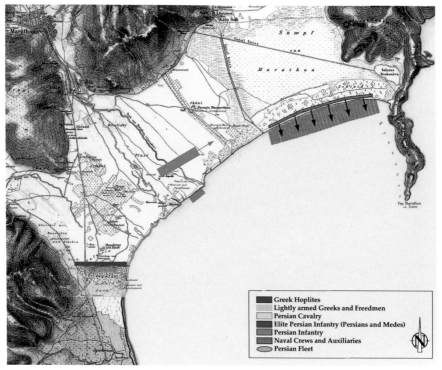

Phase 6: Persian centre entrapped. (*Design/credits: Assimakis Katsiaris*)

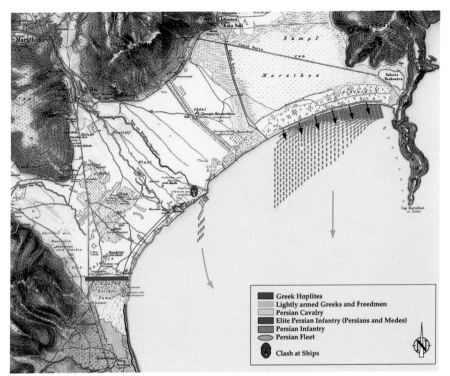

Phase 7: Persians retreat to ships and are attacked by Greeks. (*Design/credits: Assimakis Katsiaris*)

Aerial photograph of the area of the Lesser Marsh in the Brexiza pass next to the plain of Marathon.

outflanked any abatis.[36] Moreover, the Athenians in that position would have found it hard to manoeuvre into the close-quarters combat which they aimed at.

Thus the only solution for the Greeks was to deceive the Persian cavalry in the form of an ambush that would mask the Greeks' tactical weakness. Examples of such deception are rife in the annals of Greek warfare, going back to Homer's *Iliad* and *Odyssey*.[37] True, some authorities such as Demosthenes and Polybius condemned the practice of deception in warfare,[38] but it was widely used throughout the Classical era. It seems, in fact, to have been especially favoured by the Athenians.[39] Young Athenians undergoing their *ephebeia* training were given the role model of Melanthos (or Melanthios), a mythical hero who, according to legend, killed his opponent Xanthos in single combat by tricking him into turning his back.[40] In ancient Greece deception and trickery in warfare were identified with cunning, vigilance and cleverness. It is what a weaker party employs to defeat the stronger, to outwit him by the use of the mind.

We have here the ideal of the 'Odysseus ethos' that many ancient writers relate to stratagems and cunning in warfare.[41] This resourcefulness was represented in ancient Greece by the goddess Metis.[42] We know of a battle, possibly contemporary with Marathon, in which a Greek army of foot soldiers managed to eliminate a large cavalry force by resorting to trickery rather than traditional hoplite tactics. A few years before 480, in a war between the Thessalians and the Phokians, the Thessalians invaded Phokis with a large cavalry force.[43] The panic-stricken Phokians fled to the mountains while their army took up position at a pass leading to the city of Hyampolis, one of the Thessalians' prime objectives. To deal with the enemy cavalry the Phokians thought up the stratagem of digging a trench across the pass, filling it with empty earthenware jars and lining up behind it. The way the Thessalians operated showed that their horsemen were used to attacking a hoplite line-up, and at the same time the Phokians anticipated this tactic from the enemy cavalry.[44] The Phokian defenders saw the Thessalian cavalry bearing down on them, the horsemen confident of victory. But before the Thessalians could reach the Phokians their horses stumbled into the buried jars, throwing their riders who were then cut down by the counterattacking Phokians.[45] In this way, the Phokian foot soldiers were able to defeat the powerful

Thessalian cavalry by trickery and not hoplite tactics. A seer named Tellias is credited with thinking up this highly effective trick.[46]

At the time, as we have seen, Miltiades was quite influential at Athens. From what little we know of him from ancient literary sources, it emerges that he had successfully applied stratagems against his opponents on at least two occasions before 490. The first occurred when the Peisistratids appointed him governor of the Chersonese, where he secured absolute power. The murder of his brother Stesagoras, the previous governor, had showed that the local potentates were pretty much independent and only nominally subject to Athenian suzerainty.[47] Miltiades knew that he had to move quickly to eliminate this challenge to his authority. As soon as he arrived in the Chersonese he shut himself in his late brother's house as if in mourning; the local chiefs interpreted this as displaying a weak character, and showed up to offer condolences, but without taking any particular security measures. When they set foot in the house Miltiades had them arrested.[48]

During the Ionian Revolt, Miltiades employed another stratagem that helped the Athenians conquer Lemnos. The island's inhabitants had told the Athenians they would submit only if they could reach the island from Attica inside a day against northerly winds, something considered impossible. Miltiades, however, led Athenian ships from Elaious in the Chersonese, some 80km north of Lemnos,[49] to the island with the help of a northerly wind within a day. There he demanded the islanders' submission on the grounds that the Chersonese, as an Athenian possession, was in fact a part of Attica. The clever argument persuaded the tyrant of Hephaisteia, one of the two cities of Lemnos, to surrender his city peacefully to the Athenians.[50] Both stratagems were based on deception designed to fool the opponent by a false impression. They were typical of Miltiades' military and diplomatic talents that made use of persuasiveness, wisdom, careful judgement (*pronoia*), deception, alertness and a degree of recklessness.[51] In those years he was able to accumulate experience and become, like Odysseus, a resourceful *polytropos*.[52]

Miltiades' stratagem at Marathon, however, could be called the most celebrated of his military deceptions. His main aim was to neutralize the powerful Persian cavalry by luring it into a trap, something similar to the Phokian tactic at Hyampolis.[53] He planned to form the Greek line in such a way as to draw the cavalry into a position where it could be eliminated. In this case, nature had already provided a trap in the form of the Lesser Marsh dominating the entrance to the Brexiza pass, below the Greek camp on the north-east slope of Agrieliki. Miltiades would have gleaned information about the marsh from the locals and realized that it would seriously hamper the operations of the enemy cavalry and upset their tactics. This would give the Greeks the opportunity to take on the cavalrymen at close quarters. Once the cavalry was stopped, as Thucydides states, 'everything falls apart if one is hit where one is superior'.[54]

The Persian cavalry was committed to moving on the Brexiza pass. Miltiades' battle plan was to form up the Greeks in front of, not behind, the Lesser Marsh, and induce the Persian cavalry to penetrate to the Greek rear without, however, defeating the Greek army itself. Just as the Phokians at Hyampolis arrayed their forces to provoke a Thessalian attack, the Athenians would do the same at Marathon. Miltiades knew how the Persian and Saka cavalry operated, charging the enemy front line with a rain of arrows and spears. They would then return to their starting-point to prepare a fresh assault. The action would be repeated until the enemy broke or was destroyed. This was the practice when the enemy presented a solid line. But what would happen if the Persians cavalrymen discovered a large gap in the line at the start of their assault?

A credible answer is provided by William Tarn, a British historian and specialist in ancient military tactics. Tarn has analysed the probable thinking of a cavalry commander called upon to attack a line of heavily-armed foot soldiers. He bases his theories on the Hellenistic era, but they can be equally valid for the conditions of 490:

I have mentioned that there is one thing cavalry could not do, charge an unbroken spear-line; and I have also noticed the difficulty heavy infantry had in maintaining their line unbroken. Now if you will imagine yourself seated on a horse and watching an advancing line of spear-points, and if something happens to that line whereby the spear-points vanish from one bit of it, leaving a gap, you will realize that that gap must draw you irresistibly to it; that is the point you will certainly ride for. Over and over again, in Hellenistic literature, we get allusions to that gap.[55]

The gap theorized by Tarn, however, did not open in the Greek ranks at Marathon because of wrong moves or neglect; it was, on the contrary, handed to the Persian cavalry on a platter, plotted by Miltiades in cooperation with the Polemarch. The gap would be in the form of a deliberately weakened centre which would have orders to carry out a controlled withdrawal, drawing the Persian cavalry after it like a magnet. Miltiades also would have known that the cavalry would aim at driving through the enemy centre without the danger of encirclement, in order to strike in all directions; at the same time, the inferior-quality infantry at the wings would occupy the attention of the Greeks on their fronts to allow the cavalry to do its job. At Marathon the Persian horse, confident of victory, performed its duty admirably. Yet Miltiades had sprung a trap for it by opening up an avenue for attack and then closing it suddenly behind it.

One of the valuable aspects of Herodotus' narrative is that it supplies details of Greek battle tactics at Marathon. As we saw, he begins his description of the tactics by referring to the 'very weak' centre and the beefed-up wings. Herodotus says this was done deliberately in order to draw out the line to be as long as the Persian one, but not the reason why the Greeks did this. Probably it was to prevent the Persian cavalry from outflanking the wings. But the only way to realistically accomplish this would be to ensure that the Greek flanks were protected by some natural feature, and that could not be the case in any part of the Marathon plain where the Persian cavalry would make short work of the Greek wings. We therefore suppose that the length of the Greek line was determined not by the length of the Persian line but by the natural terrain features.

One might suppose that the Greeks lengthened their line by thinning out the centre. However, the Persian centre was made up of the best forces the empire had, and Miltiades certainly knew that. Common sense would have told him to strengthen that sector rather than weaken it, if necessary by transferring men from the wings that would have been protected from Persian attack anyway by the natural obstacles. There was a real danger that a battle depending on the strength of the wings and a weak centre could end in disaster, as many other Classical-era battles demonstrated. An army that could break the enemy centre was practically assured of victory.[56] If the Persians defeated the Greek centre they could turn to simultaneously attack both wings, helped by those men who had penetrated to the Greek rear. What would have been the morale of the Greeks on the flanks when they perceived that the enemy had overcome the centre?

The Greek centre, however, was weakened, and the attacking Persians and Saka quickly occupied the positions of the retreating Athenians. This has naturally led to the supposition that the centre was deliberately left fragile in order to allow the elite Persian units to rush on; if so, it would be the single recorded instance of such a planned tactic in ancient Greek history. The evidence is that the Greeks in the centre played a pivotal role in the execution of Miltiades' battle plan, the first move that would eventually grant victory to his side.

As soon as battle was joined, and the first Persians and Saka were galloping through the rift that had appeared in the Greek centre, both Greek wings began steadily but quickly advancing on the Persians opposite them. They were within sight of the Persian cavalry rushing forward with the mass of elite infantry behind them, but kept their attention steadily in front. In fact, they charged 'at a run' in order to surprise the Persians before they could employ their archers or take shelter behind their shields.[57] The strike had to be as strong as possible so that the enemy on the wings could be pushed back for some distance – far enough, in fact, to have enough room to about-face, join up into a single line, and advance towards the Brexiza pass, bottling up the cavalry and infantry in the Persian centre. Miltiades' objective was not the mass of second-rate infantry on the Persian wings; instead of pursuing them the Greek hoplites turned their attention to the elite enemy units in the centre that had penetrated to the Greek rear and were ripe for encirclement.

Many scholars believe that the Athenian and Plataian hoplites began their advance 'at a run' when they were about 200m from the enemy, which was the effective range of the Persian archers. The Persians on the wings would not have expected the Greek charge,[58] as dust from the advancing cavalry and elite Persian infantry in the centre would have covered the battlefield and reduced their visibility considerably.[59] The effect of the charge, and the heavy Persian casualties which ensued, must have entered the Athenian and Plataian collective consciousness, as soon

after the battle many Attic vases were painted with that scene on them –
indeed, some of the artists may have fought in the battle.[60]

It should occasion no surprise that the Persians on the two wings
fell back as soon as the Greeks hit them. But as we have seen, far from
pursuing them, the Greeks turned about to form a unified front,[61] closing
the route leading from Brexiza into the Marathon plain and blocking
the possibility of any Persian regrouping. These hoplites now advanced
towards Brexiza and the Lesser Marsh like an unbroken wall of metal.
They had no fear of attack from the rear, as the Persians they had attacked
were now in flight towards the ships, several kilometres away at Schinias.
The Persian and Saka cavalry and elite infantry, now cut off from the rest
of their army, were at the mercy of the Greeks. The role of eliminating
the bottled-up Persians now fell to the thousands of Athenian thetes and
freedmen who served as light-armed soldiers.

2. The light-armed troops in the centre

Most commentators on Marathon agree that the Greeks put into effect
a predetermined plan, rather than leave the outcome to chance.[62] They
assume that the orderly withdrawal of the Greek centre was part of that
plan, which was ultimately to entrap the Persians.[63] The main evidence
cited is the low Athenian casualty count of just 192 dead; if the Persians
had really smashed the centre of the Greek line, the reasoning goes,
then the Athenians' losses would have been in the thousands.[64] The
truth, however, is the opposite, as the Persians lost 6,400 men precisely
because the Greeks wiped out virtually all the force in the Persian centre.
Herodotus' description of the join-up of the Greek wings indicates that
the Athenians and Plataians acted according to a specific plan.

It is probable, then, that the Athenians in the centre acted as bait to
draw the Persians into the Lesser Marsh at Brexiza. This gives great
importance to the Greeks in the centre, who were called upon to carry
out a difficult and dangerous manoeuvre, that of a controlled withdrawal
at speed; if they were to delay even a little, not only their own lives but
also the whole outcome of the battle would be at stake.

The small Athenian loss count at Marathon suggests that the men
in the centre had been briefed about what they were to do, and not set

up like lambs for the slaughter; they must have been told in detail that their mission would not be a suicidal one but a formula for victory. There would have been a general briefing of the soldiers by the commanders about what Miltiades had in mind; moreover, the days of inaction before the battle would have given the commanders plenty of time to explain the tactics. We may take it as certain that the unusual manoeuvre of about-facing and bottling up would not have been possible without the men receiving detailed instructions beforehand. The task of the Greeks in the centre was, in fact, more difficult than that of those on the wings.

Herodotus' sole mention of the Greeks in the centre is a note on their formation; he says that they were fewer than those on the wings, though without specifying whether they were hoplites or light-armed troops.[65] There is strong evidence, however, that the Greek soldiers in the centre were not hoplites. A quick planned withdrawal would have been hard for hoplites to carry out, largely because of the weight of their shields, armour and weapons. Besides, their helmets would have limited their peripheral vision and made it hard to see what was going on around them.[66] Light-armed troops, on the other hand, were much less encumbered and therefore could move much more quickly. The Greek commanders would not have used hoplites in the centre but in the more important positions on the wings, where they could later be used to finish off the elite Persians who had penetrated to the rear of the centre.[67]

An implicit, *ex silentio,* indication from Herodotus that the men in the Greek centre were not hoplites is that he neglects to mention any who fell there, in contrast to those who fell in pursuit of the Persians and by the ships who receive special mention, a few of them by name. Those Greeks who perished in the centre, it seems, were not deemed equally worthy of mention, so therefore we may speculate that they were not hoplites but light-armed thetes and freedmen.[68] Thousands of such soldiers fought at Marathon in 490, but would it have made sense to place them in the centre without upsetting the traditional hoplite tactics of the time? We have seen that in ancient Greece light-armed troops were used to provide cover for an advancing hoplite phalanx, shooting arrows and slingstones at the enemy; to be effective at this, they had to form up either behind or alongside the hoplite phalanx in separate formations.

The first real indication we have that the Athenian hoplites were separate from the light-armed troops comes in 457, during a war between Athens on the one hand, and the Boiotians and Peloponnesians on the other. An Athenian army under Myronides had bottled up some 2,000 Corinthian hoplites on a farm near Megara. This farm had a wide moat around it and was also surrounded by hills, with only one way out. Myronides divided his hoplite and light-armed forces, placing the former to block the sole exit, while arranging the latter, mostly stone-throwers, around the periphery. These stone-throwers succeeded in killing almost all the Corinthian hoplites, handing the victory to Athens.[69]

Some years later, during the Peloponnesian War, there were several instances in which the Athenian hoplites and light-armed troops fought separately, indicating that the practice had by then become standard. The first such encounter took place in Akarnania in 426, where the Athenian general Demosthenes ranged his hoplites against a Peloponnesian and Ambrakiote force; at the same time he placed a force of light-armed Akarnanians alongside 400 Athenian hoplites separate from the phalanx, and hid both behind bushes. When the Peloponnesians and Ambrakiotes attacked the Athenian hoplite phalanx, the light-armed troops ambushed and trounced them.[70] Of course, these instances are no proof that the Athenians had employed similar tactics earlier in the Persian Wars, as some scholars suggest.[71] Some assert that in 490 hoplites and light-armed troops were mingled in battle, as they had been through the Archaic era.[72]

The few ancient sources we have at our disposal do not give us a clear picture of how the light-armed troops fought alongside the hoplites in the Persian Wars. Herodotus says only that in one instance they covered the hoplite flanks; in 479, during the battle of Plataia, the Greek commander, the Spartan Pausanias, appealed to the Athenians to send over bowmen to protect the Spartan flanks that were under attack from the Persian cavalry and in dire danger.[73] However, this could have been an emergency, and not indicative that archers were placed on the hoplite flanks; if this were the case there was no reason why Pausanias would have asked the Athenians to send bowmen as he could have easily covered the flanks with his own. Moreover, a few days earlier those same Athenian bowmen had taken part in a joint operation with their fellow-Athenian hoplites in which the Persian cavalry commander, Masistius, had been killed. Herodotus' account gives the impression that the Athenian archers fought alongside the hoplites in the phalanx.

Other ancient sources suggest that light-armed troops could have been mixed with hoplites in the Persian Wars. Aischylos, in his *Persians,* describes Athenian operations at Psyttaleia in 480, implying that archers and stone-throwers acted simultaneously with the hoplites.[74] Herodotus, in his description of the battle of Plataia, says that each Spartan hoplite had with him seven light-armed helots, who most likely fought with the hoplites and not separately.[75] As we have seen, many Attic vases of about 500 or a little later show archers in Scythian dress (but most likely Athenians) fighting alongside the hoplites. We conclude that in 490 at Marathon it was entirely possible for light-armed troops to be included in the Greek centre; their presence would in no way hamper the hoplite movements on the wings. Miltiades had many thousands of light-armed troops with which to man the centre, and some left over. He just needed a few hundred to serve as bait in the deliberately-thinned centre.[76]

When the Greek hoplites on the wings clashed with their opponents, a section of the light-armed troops stood in the centre. As the battle commenced, these men began to move forward into the Marathon plain; however, when they saw the Persian cavalry preparing to charge, they carried out an apparently hasty retreat towards the Brexiza pass, while the hoplites on the flanks quickened their step in the other direction. The Persian and Saka cavalry, seeing their adversaries retreating in the centre, spurred their horses in hot pursuit of what they thought was a beaten foe.

3. The trap at the Lesser Marsh

The Persians and Saka galloped into an empty space opened by the retreating Greek centre. According to Herodotus, this pursuit occurred 'to the Mesogaia', without giving details of what he meant.[77] Most modern scholars identify the *Mesogaia* with the area between present-day Nea Makri and Pallene, which today bears the name *Mesogeia*.[78] By this interpretation, the Greek centre retreated through the Brexiza pass towards the south, pursued by the Persians. But Herodotus' phrase must mean 'towards' rather than 'into' the *Mesogaia*, as it is unlikely that the Persian advance would have been stopped where this area begins, i.e.

modern day Nea Makri. Common sense rebels against the idea that the Persians got through the Brexiza pass and then somehow were repulsed by the re-formed Greeks, a most improbable development.[79]

The Greek centre was positioned directly in front of the Lesser Marsh, which lay in the path of the retreating light-armed troops. The retreat, as we have seen, had been well-prepared beforehand, with knowledge of the terrain. The manoeuvre of a feigned retreat was a difficult one to carry out, requiring knowledge of what the enemy might do, as well as good timing.[80] In morale terms, it deferred the display of valour until later in the battle. According to E. Mikroyannakis, valour is best displayed at a critical juncture when it is most required.[81] Thus a tactical withdrawal is no stain on a soldier's reputation. Valour consists of withdrawing and then resisting, not the other way round.[82] Those who fell back at Marathon knew that the chance to strike back at the enemy would soon come.[83] The idea finds an echo in Plato's *Laches*, a dialogue in which Socrates disputes the Athenian general Laches' assertion that a brave soldier stands his ground in the front line at all times; Socrates gives as an example the Scythians, who fought equally bravely in the retreat as in the advance. Likewise at Plataia, the Spartans initially fell back when the Persians attacked, only to counter-charge them in the end and win.[84]

While Miltiades' plan concentrated on the planned withdrawal of the men in the centre, the attack on the Persian wings was also carefully worked out. The aim here was not to eliminate the Persian forces on those fronts – something very hard to do given the sheer number of men – but drive them off the field of battle as far as possible. Then the hoplites would have had the job of halting the flight of the Persian cavalry and infantry from their repulse at the Lesser Marsh. Miltiades, as we have seen, was aware that the Persian wings consisted of inferior troops from the subject people,[85] and that one strong blow by the heavy-armed Greeks would be enough to send them flying; these were in contrast to the elite troops of the centre, who could be expected to fight the Greeks to the last and therefore required hard close-order combat to overcome. For this purpose, the hoplites had to bottle up the Persian elite forces in the marsh.

In marshy areas it is usual for the local people to mark out paths on solid ground to enable them to find their way. Pausanias claims that the Persians were unaware of these pathways.[86] The Greek plan could succeed assuming that some locals would have briefed the Athenians on how they could make their way through the paths if they had to retreat through the marsh; there would have been guides such as farmers and stockbreeders who regularly used the paths.

When the battle began, the light-armed troops withdrew from Valaria towards Brexiza, helped by locals who guided them through the maze of paths in the Lesser Marsh. Such patches of dry ground included what was later called the Island ('Nisi'), the area of the former US Naval base of Nea Makri and also where Marathonos Avenue runs today.

But was it possible that the Persians were ignorant of the presence of the Lesser Marsh and the risks it posed? One answer could come from Nepos, who writes that Datis sent in his Persian cavalry and infantry even though he knew the terrain was unsuitable for such a tactic.[87] But could such a description apply to the flat and dry Marathon plain? No, but it would certainly apply to the Lesser Marsh and Brexiza. We believe that this was meant by the ancient commentator on Plato (*Menexenos* 40c) who noted that the terrain of Marathon was not suited for cavalry operations.[88] If, then, it is true that the Persians, despite being aware of the risky nature of the ground, nevertheless attacked the Greeks, it could be put down to aggressive overconfidence or contempt of risk. It could be that the Persian cavalry, at the height of the charge and with adrenalin pumping, were too absorbed in chasing the retreating Greeks forgot where they were charging into. Yet this interpretation would not tally with what we know of the professionalism and experience of the cavalry commanders and the training and discipline of their men.

What appears more probable is that the Persians knew – possibly from Hippias – even before landing at Marathon that they would find a small marsh to the left of their planned route towards Athens through the Brexiza pass.[89] At the time, towards the end of summer, the marsh was believed to be mostly dry and thus present few problems. The Persians had total control of almost the whole Marathon plain within days after their landing,[90] and therefore could have been expected to send out scouting patrols as far as the Brexiza pass.[91] But the presence of the Greek camp on Agrieliki, and its control over the pass, would have deterred the scouting parties from going any further. The scouts would have noticed a few swampy spots near the sea, but to them, the area would have been mainly dry.

This information would have been passed on to the Persian commanders, who judged that the swamp in summer would not be very wet and hence suitable for operations. But they were under a delusion. The Lesser Marsh was created by water descending from the foothills of Pentelikon and being trapped in the Brexiza basin. Some of this water was able to flow to the sea through a narrow gully on the border of the swamp; however, a bigger outflow was prevented by a sandy ridge that had formed at the shoreline. The sandy ridge, known as the 'Island' ('Nisi'), extending roughly 100 by 150 metres, was thrown up by the northerly winds over the centuries. During winter the Lesser Marsh had plenty of water in its basin. However, by the end of summer a combination of hot temperatures and lack of rain meant that most of this water had gone; only a small amount fed into the Lesser Marsh from the mountain streams. There might have been a wet area by the sand near the so-called Island within the marsh,[92] but the surface of the rest of it would have been dry for weeks. This surface, however, was covered by a crust of salt blown in from the sea by the summer's north-easterly winds.[93] The hard crust prevented the growth of any vegetation,[94] thus giving the impression of solid barren land except for the spot near the Island, where there was some wetland vegetation.

Foreign travellers of the eighteenth and early nineteenth centuries visiting Marathon in summer had the exact same impression of the essential dryness of the Lesser Marsh.[95] It would have appeared so to the Persian mounted scouts in 490. Yet neither they nor the more recent visitors were aware of what the locals knew well: that in summer the apparent dry crust concealed a vast sea of mud – mixed with slime and rotting vegetation – left over from the water that had accumulated during winter.[96] The weight of a few mounted scouts would not have been enough to collapse this crust, and so the danger beneath would have remained undetected. Besides, as we have seen, the scouts would not have gone any farther in the marsh as the Athenians were just above them on Agrieliki.[97]

Today the Lesser Marsh has been largely drained except for a small area abutting the Marathon plain that is still swampy (its coordinates are: N38°06′13.80″, E23°58′15.40″). This spot is what we believe the retreating Greek light-armed troops lured the Persian cavalry into. The acquired momentum of a massed cavalry charge could not be easily stopped; each horse would tend to follow the other's tail, running from instinct rather than any command by the rider. The crust of salt began to crumble under the weight and pressure of the first few dozen mounted horses. Add a few hundred more horsemen, and the surface dissolved into a sea of muddy slime; the concave hollow of the horses' hooves would have stuck in the mud through suction,[98] and in their struggle to get free, many horses would have unseated their riders. Some horses broke their legs in the desperate struggle; others were overwhelmed and trampled by those behind. Within minutes, the charging force of Persians and Saka dissolved into chaos.

4. The clash

The roles of the combatants were now reversed: the elite Persian and Saka cavalry found themselves on the defensive inside the Lesser Marsh as the Athenian light-armed troops and freedmen hurled projectiles at them from outside. Thousands of these latter had been hiding in the Brexiza pass and the paths inside the Lesser Marsh, assembled in a number of separate groups, ready to strike. Miltiades might well have added a few hoplites that he could spare from the main encounter to come.[99] The muddy terrain, moreover, would have hindered a heavy-armed hoplite much more than a light-armed soldier,[100] and hence the latter were by far the more numerous in the Lesser Marsh area.

   The decisive phase in the battle in the marsh began when the light-armed troops began hurling javelins, arrows, slingstones and other projectiles at the Persian cavalry. This attack was sustained enough to cause considerable casualties among the unprotected Persians and their horses. Then the light-armed men moved in on the surviving Persians; the Brexiza pass was the scene of fierce hand-to-hand combat in the mud. Some Persian horsemen who were still on solid ground tried to turn round and retreat; but they had to run the narrow gauntlet between the marsh and Agrieliki, and besides, their way was now blocked by the oncoming mass of their own infantry that had been advancing in the cavalry's wake. When these infantrymen saw the Persian horse coming back they panicked; they joined a writhing, chaotic mass of Persians floundering under a hail of projectiles from the direction of the Lesser Marsh. At about that time, Greek hoplites suddenly appeared in the Persian rear and blocked off all possibility of withdrawal.

There followed an epic battle between the Greeks and the Persians where the Marathon plain meets the Brexiza pass. A possible echo of this clash has been immortalized in an epigram that was probably inscribed on the cenotaph to the warriors of Marathon at the *Demosion Sema* in Athens. According to Matthaiou, the line *herkos gar proparoithen*[101] suggests that Athenians, who during the battle found themselves 'in front of a defensive wall', suffered losses.[102] This wall is likely to be the rampart on the spur of Agrieliki; the Persian cavalry may not have been able to reach it during the battle, but were in a position to hit the Athenians who had formed up a few dozen metres below it. This interpretation of the phrase places the Greeks at the northern end of the Brexiza pass, where they would have sustained casualties while eliminating the entrapped Persians.

Another line in the same epigram might offer a further clue about where the decisive clash took place. Still according to Matthaiou, those Greeks who fell before the 'defensive wall' were at the 'edge of the richer plain' at the time.[103] It tallies with our reconstruction, which places the clash at the foot of Agrieliki and the southern end of the Marathon plain.[104] Other, less certain, clues could be contained in the following lines of the epigram,[105] *[pe]zoi te kai [?hippeis]* ('infantry and cavalry') (Line 1), *nesoi* ('to the island') (Line 2), and *valon* ('attacking') (Line 4). Clearly these lines refer to the Athenians possibly against cavalry as well as infantry. These clues have been a problem for specialists who could not, for example, reconcile the mention of an island with the battle of Marathon.[106] Yet we cannot rule out that the island referred to is the 'Island' at the sandy outer edge of the Lesser Marsh near the sea, and that it was called by that name in ancient times as well.[107] The aforementioned lines might well be connected with the spot where the Greeks and Persians clashed, and where the Athenian light-armed troops were in a position to strike at the floundering Persians.[108]

One of this book's basic premises is that Miltiades separated the roles of the hoplites and light-armed troops at Marathon.[109] That would explain why Herodotus says that the Greek charge at the wings took place without cover by archers.[110] According to the tactics of the time, hoplite charges were usually covered by archers and other light-armed troops; but at Marathon the light-armed had already taken up position in the rear centre around or at the Lesser Marsh, ready to hit the advancing Persian cavalry as soon as it appeared.

The predicament of the cavalry when it found itself bogged down and under a hail of projectiles could be connected with an epigram mentioning bows dedicated to the temple of Athene, possibly in Athens.[111] The epigram refers to the deadly effect that these bows had on the Persian horsemen, 'dipping the Persian riders in blood'. We know that Athenian bowmen scored some success against the Persian cavalry at Plataia in 479.[112] It is probable that the bows dedicated to the goddess Athene were indeed used in that battle. However, the Athene temple on the Acropolis in which they may have been dedicated was destroyed by Xerxes in 480; the new temple, the Parthenon, would not go up for four more decades.[113] We conclude that the phase of the battle that took place in the Lesser Marsh and the Brexiza pass was the origin of the Athenian archers' reputation as 'exterminators' of the Persian horsemen. Such was their prestige that eleven years later, at Plataia, Pausanias would implore the Athenians to send some archers to the Spartans to protect the Greek flank from Persian cavalry attacks.[114]

Besides archers and javelin-men, slingers and stone-throwers, a miscellany of light-armed combatants attacked the Persians trapped in Brexiza with anything they could get their hands on, such as farm implements, and even with their bare hands. While they were in action the Greek hoplites entered the fray with spears levelled. The phase of the battle that was depicted on the Poikile Stoa mural shows the slaughter of the Persians in a marsh that must have been the Lesser Marsh.[115] It may also have provided the dominant motif for the south frieze of the Temple of Athene Nike (see below). The dramatic scene possibly inspired Aristophanes to portray the Athenians as 'wasps' using their 'stings' (spears) to pierce the Persians who were milling about like 'trapped tuna fish'.[116] This Aristophanean reference probably applies to the hoplites at the edge of the Lesser Marsh who speared the Persians in their attempts to escape back to the plain.

We don't know how long it took the Greeks to finish off the Persians in the Lesser Marsh; Herodotus says the battle 'lasted a long time', but that was relative to previous Greek battles.[117] The length of the conflict could have been a result of the peculiar conditions at Brexiza and the marsh; ordinary hoplite encounters generally were brief. It would explain why Aristophanes wrote that the battle of Marathon lasted into the evening.[118]

There are, however, scholars who maintain that the Persians had removed their cavalry from Marathon before the battle, and that it took no part in it. They base their theory on three questions. First, even if the cavalry had been surprised by the quick Greek advance at the start of the battle, why did it not counter that advance? Second, why did the cavalry not cover the Persian infantry retreat at the wings? And third, how would it have been possible in the panic that overtook the Persians for the cavalry to board the ships fast enough for the ships to sail away practically unscathed?[119] These are logical questions, which can be adequately answered only if we theorize that the cavalry was indeed engaged, put out of action and ultimately destroyed. Thus it could neither attack the Greek rear nor cover the Persian retreat on the wings. And having been eliminated in the Lesser Marsh, it of course could not get on board the ships, which were able to make a quick getaway precisely because there were no horses to hold them up.

5. The south frieze of the Temple of Athene Nike

The phase of the battle in which the Greek light-armed troops fought the Persians at close quarters in the Lesser Marsh may be seen in a detail of the 'Brescia Sarcophagus' relief depicting the battle of Marathon.[120] In the left-hand corner of the scene a Greek soldier appears seizing a Persian horseman's head to unseat him. Such an action would not have been possible in the open plain of Marathon, but quite possible in a case where the horse was immobilized by some obstacle or unsuitable terrain. The soldier depicted is not carrying a shield – the prime weapon of the hoplite phalanx – like the other Greek soldiers in the scene. The artist may well have wanted to portray a light-armed soldier rather than a hoplite. Some scholars suggest that the Brescia relief could have been based on the Poikile Stoa mural;[121] therefore, the part which Pausanias said showed the Persians' effort to extricate themselves from the 'marsh' could be connected with the horseman on the relief being thrown from his mount by a light-armed Greek soldier.

There is, however, one major ancient work of art that could throw more light on the bitter fight in the Lesser Marsh. This is the south frieze of the Temple of Athene Nike on the Acropolis of Athens, a series of reliefs showing that the Persians did make extensive use of their cavalry during the Battle of Marathon.[122] The frieze is large enough – unlike the mere detail on the 'Brescia Sarcophagus' – to include several scenes from the critical phase, namely, the phase in which the Persian cavalry was employed and then eliminated by the Athenians. In the judgement of the American archaeologist and art historian Evelyn Harrison, the reliefs are not in the idealistic and heroic mode that was usual during the fifth century, but done rather more realistically. The depictions start from the right, where the Persian cavalry is seen bearing down on the Athenians, with some scenes in which the horsemen are pursuing foot soldiers.[123] This could well portray the initial withdrawal of the Greek centre as in our reconstruction.

The frieze goes on to depict the Persian horsemen being thrown from their mounts. One horse is shown buckling at the knees, throwing its rider who is also being pulled down by the arm by a Greek soldier.[124] The scene bears similarities to that on the 'Brescia Sarcophagus' which shows a Greek soldier hitting a Persian horseman on the head to bring him down. Another horse is shown rearing in panic, hurling its rider into the air.[125] Two other horsemen, still mounted, are battling Greek soldiers. Other Persians are depicted on foot, as presumably having lost their mounts; arguing for this interpretation is that they are shown without shields, unlike other Persian foot soldiers in the frieze. The fight appears to be fierce, with no quarter given; two light-armed Athenians are shown seizing Persians by the hair ready to slay them.[126]

These scenes show clearly that the Persian cavalrymen found themselves trapped in a situation they could not possibly have foreseen, as that is not the way they were habituated to fighting. They appear to be at a severe disadvantage, with none of the advantages their arm would normally have conferred, and being slaughtered by the Greeks to boot. Four dead soldiers, all Persians, are shown lying on the ground.

Some parts of the frieze show Persian horsemen, still mounted, trying to regain their previous positions; according to Harrison, the fact that these are facing from left to right, opposite to the initial direction of their charge, shows them in retreat. Greek hoplites are shown bodily trying to prevent this retreat. One horse, in its attempt to escape, is seen trampling a Persian on the ground, while another horse is attacking another Persian with its forelegs.[127] In their panic, the Persian horses are trampling their own men, both fallen and upright.

Harrison concludes on the basis of what is depicted on the south frieze that what prevented the Persian cavalry from completing its charge was not the resistance of the Greeks but the nature of the terrain.[128] In support of this thesis, Harrison cites the detail of the horse apparently buckling its forelegs and throwing its rider.[129] Comparing the stance of this horse with that of others depicted in ancient works of art, she concludes that this particular horse fell into a swamp, injuring its forelegs.[130] She also figures that it agrees with what was portrayed in the mural of the Battle of Marathon in the Poikile Stoa; the swamp in which the Persian horses seem to have fallen is quite likely the same as seen by Pausanias in the Stoa.[131] Pausanias, indeed, records that the Persians were shown jostling one another in their efforts to extricate themselves from the marsh, and the image on the south frieze showing the Persians being trampled by their own horses is not inconsistent with that.

Another feature of the south frieze on the Temple of Athene Nike that tends to back up Harrison's thesis is that the ground depicted in the marsh battle scene is uneven, with bumps and dips. The sculptor here apparently intended to portray a marsh; the Greeks are on the higher bits, while there is a dead Persian lying on what seems to be a mass of mud.[132] In another scene, believed to depict Kallimachos taking on a Persian horseman, the action takes place on flat ground, with none of the irregularities of the previous scene.[133] Whether or not the depiction is of Kallimachos, the flat land indicates that this particular encounter occurred on the Marathon plain and not in the marsh. Moreover, the reliefs on the other three sides of the Athene Nike frieze show uniformly flat ground. The conclusion is that the sculptor or sculptors employed the highest possible degree of realism in depicting that particular phase of the battle that took place in the marsh.[134]

Though Harrison does not distinguish between hoplites and light-armed soldiers on the south frieze, the frieze itself clearly does so. While the hoplites are shown carrying shields and wearing helmets, the light-armed troops are shown protected only by their cloaks and without helmets or other armour. Harrison notes an instance of a shieldless Athenian soldier trying to protect himself and a wounded comrade from Persian arrows by holding up a cloak.[135] The use of cloaks as protective gear by light-armed troops is typical of that category of soldier, as evidenced by the depictions on fifth century Attic vases.[136]

The basic scene on the south frieze is that of light-armed troops and hoplites fighting the Persians together;[137] however, it is the former who have the place of honour among those who unhorsed the Persians in the marsh, illustrated climactically by the two light-armed soldiers holding two kneeling Persians by the hair, apparently intending to kill them.[138] The Athenian hoplites, on the other hand, are shown as engaging with the still-mounted Persian cavalrymen, something quite realistic as it is more probable that a heavy-armed hoplite would have a better chance of overcoming a resisting rider on an immobilized horse than a light-armed man would.

The south frieze also shows two Persian infantrymen carrying shields; this would exclude them being unhorsed cavalrymen.[139] A Greek hoplite is in the act of attacking one of them. Those Persians were probably in the front line of the Persian centre who had charged along with the cavalry until reaching the Lesser Marsh, and confronting the Greek hoplites who came in from the wings to finish off the floundering centre.

Harrison concludes her study of the evidence on the south frieze of the Temple of Athene Nike, and its possible links to the mural of the battle of Marathon at the Poikile Stoa, with an appeal to researchers of the battle to give it serious attention.[140] Unfortunately, the appeal by and large has not been heeded.[141] This may be because the reliefs in question do not by themselves give a coherent picture of the battle of Marathon to a non-expert who has not studied the evidence. They also do not tally with Herodotus' narrative. On the surface, they portray a confused chaos of combat, with Persian cavalrymen, mounted or not, battling Athenian hoplites and light-armed troops; Herodotus mentions neither Persian cavalry nor light-armed Athenians in the battle. Neither is there any clear demarcation between friend and foe. Yet Harrison's ideas tally with our reconstruction, which gives the frieze an interpretative framework so far lacking.[142] Not only are the reliefs realistic; they also accurately portray the chaotic conditions of the bitter fight in the Lesser Marsh as we have imagined them.

It needs to be pointed out that Harrison believed the conflict portrayed in the south frieze of Athene Nike to have occurred in the Great Marsh of Marathon. She apparently concentrated more on interpreting the frieze itself than on assessing the historical and geographic factors. In accordance with other scholars she assumed that the Great Marsh was the scene of the crucial encounter 'in the marsh'. Yet in a way her own research disputed that assumption; the Persian cavalry stumbled into marshy ground while attacking the Greeks, not while they were retreating to the ships. Hence the marsh involved could only have been the Lesser Marsh. It is realistic to assume that before the battle the Greeks arrayed themselves in front of the Brexiza pass and hence drew the Persians on to their destruction in the adjacent Lesser Marsh.[143]

6. Marathon: a lesson in tactics

It is quite likely that Greek commanders at the time of the Persian Wars seriously considered the experiences of any previous battles, successful or not, they were engaged in.[144] We aver that the tactics adopted by the Athenians at Marathon served as a model for their future military successes, in which similar tactics were employed. The example nearest to 490 is the battle of Salamis ten years later, where Themistokles drew the Persians into a trap just as Miltiades had done at Marathon. This time the trap was laid at sea; when the Greek triremes backed water, the Persian ships attacked, confident that they would carry the day.[145] Thanks to a clever manoeuvre planned by Themistokles, the Greek vessels encircled those of the Persians and destroyed them.

It was a carbon copy of the tactic Miltiades had planned at Marathon, luring the Persians into an attack by means of a feigned retreat. At Salamis the Greek triremes played the part of the light-armed troops at Marathon; the equivalent of the Brexiza pass was the narrow channel between Salamis and the mainland, while the equivalent of the Lesser

Marsh was the irregular sea currents in the channel, which the Greek commanders knew and were able to make use of, preventing the Persian fleet from manoeuvring. An equivalent of the solid parts of the Lesser Marsh can be found in the islet of Psyttaleia, where Aristides had landed with a force of hoplites and light-armed troops to deal with any Persians who might land on it;[146] Athenian soldiers had occupied the solid bits of the Lesser Marsh to that purpose before the battle of Marathon. At Salamis Themistokles had faithfully copied the tactics of Miltiades at Marathon; as he himself had fought at Marathon, he would almost certainly have been familiar with Miltiades' plan.[147]

The Athenians seem to have applied the tactical lessons of Marathon in battles throughout the fifth century. They separated the tasks of the hoplites and light-armed troops, as we have seen, at Megara under Myronides in 457 and in Aitolia under Demosthenes in 426. In both cases, as both arms of the army cooperated, the separation worked well, surprising and eliminating the enemy. Myronides' tactics at Megara, in fact, bore striking similarities to Miltiades' tactics at Marathon as we have reconstructed them. Myronides trapped a sizeable number of Corinthian hoplites in a restricted space,[148] with Athenian hoplites blocking their sole avenue of escape, just as when the Greek wings at Marathon joined up to block the Persian retreat. In both battles it was the light-armed troops who delivered the most telling blows against the enemy, hurling projectiles from a safe distance; it could well have been a conscious application of the Marathon model. There may have been veterans of Marathon who fought at Megara in 457 who remembered what had happened a few decades earlier, that is, that victory was gained by the cooperation of hoplites and light-armed troops.[149]

Aelius Artistides reports that at Thermopylai in 480 even though the Greeks formed up in front of 'the Gates', they were defeated because in Aelius Aristides' view they did not apply the lessons of Marathon properly.[150] According to Aelius Aristides, at Thermopylai the Greeks tried to stop the Persian advance with a wall of hoplites; we know that during the battle the Greeks carried out a number of feigned retreats to draw the Persians farther into the Thermopylai pass, after which the Spartans about-faced and successfully fended off the attacks.[151] This is rather reminiscent of the Athenian planned withdrawal at Marathon, designed to lure the Persians and Saka into the Brexiza pass and Lesser Marsh. But things turned out rather differently at Thermopylai, which is why Aelius Aristides claims that the tactic failed. At Thermopylai the retreats were isolated efforts and not part of a wider tactical scheme; thus his claim that the Greeks at Thermopylai stayed and fought in their places is not quite literally correct.[152]

Other later battles echoed the tactics of Marathon, from Lake Kopais to Agincourt. The commanders in those encounters probably knew nothing of Marathon or its tactics, but the records show that they applied similar stratagems in difficult tactical situations where they were outnumbered and needed to deal with a strong enemy cavalry (see Appendix V). In modern times, one Greek general has mentioned Miltiades' specific method in battle; Major-General Haralambos Katsimitros commanded the Greek VIII Division during World War II (Greek-Italian War, 1940–41) and is credited with the first major Greek success against the Italian invasion in Epiros. In his memoirs he analyses the battle of Marathon in terms of our own reconstruction, describing how the Persian cavalry fell into a marsh after charging the Greek centre: 'The cavalry of Datis, the other Persian general, stumbled into the marsh because of poor reconnaissance and, sinking into the slime, was cut to pieces by the counter-attacking Greeks.'[153] Katsimitros' account has the air of a generally-accepted theory of what happened at Marathon rather than a radical new notion. Despite the fact that Katsimitros is not known to have written about ancient military tactics, he seems to have been the first to advance the theory of the marsh as crucial for the Greek victory.[154]

7. Glorification and a cover-up

Immediately after the battle of Marathon the Athenians made sure to commemorate their victory and their fallen. Even six-and-a-half centuries later Pausanias could record that the Athenians still rated that victory above all others in their history, filling them 'with the greatest pride'.[155] Thucydides writes that the Athenians credited the fallen at Marathon with 'especial valour', in apparent comparison with those killed in other battles.[156] The fallen of Marathon were indeed given special honours; their bodies were cremated, lending them the status of the mythical heroes of the *Iliad*.[157]

Games were instituted in their memory, both in Athens and at Marathon; the latter, begun shortly after the battle, were known as the 'Herakleian Games' and held at the tombs of the battle dead.[158] In the second century AD Pausanias reports that the fallen of Marathon were deemed 'heroes', as a worship of sorts had already grown up around them.[159]

It was during the 460s that Kimon, the son of Miltiades, built up the victory of Marathon into an issue of political importance. Imposing public monuments to the warriors went up, promoting Miltiades' contribution to the triumph. Kimon may well have been acting out of personal ambition, but his actions of course had a political dimension.[160] We know that he represented the Athenian large landowners;[161] some scholars have theorized that he glorified Marathon in order to promote the hoplites who came from the upper classes.[162] However, the victory at Salamis in 480 had been largely the work of the Athenian fleet oarsmen, who were mostly thetes. Kimon also could not ignore the contribution of the light-armed troops and freedmen at Marathon,[163] even if he had wanted to, as in the 460s many veterans were still alive. The action of the light-armed troops, in fact, was depicted on the Poikile Stoa mural of the Marathon battle, dating to c.461. One of those prominently displayed fighting in the front line, alongside hoplites such as Miltiades, Kallimachos, and Kynegeiros, was 'Echetlos' ('the man with the plough handle') or 'Echetlaios' ('the man with the plough') who is shown in peasant's attire fighting with his plough.[164] Pausanias' assertion that he saw the figure of this man killing Persians on the mural of the Poikile Stoa is strong evidence that the incident was a real one and not a figment of a later imagination. We thus presume that he was a person and not some divinity who helped the Athenians, as many recent scholars claim.[165] What Pausanias tells us about 'Echetlaios' gives us the picture of a brave fighter. He was portrayed as fighting with a farm implement that he turned into a crude, if effective, lethal weapon. The fact that he apparently vanished after the battle, and was found neither alive nor dead, places him in the missing-in-action category, perhaps the first such case in history. No sources which mention the Poikile Stoa painting say anything about active intervention in the battle by the deities shown.[166]

Pausanias' statement that the Athenians considered 'Echetlaios' a 'hero' does not necessarily mean that he was regarded as superhuman, as all the fallen warriors were given that honour. If he had been a local demigod, such as *Marathon*, also pictured in the Poikile Stoa, then the Athenians would have had to offer him a sacrifice before the battle; the gods, unlike mortals, wanted something in return before they would show favour to an army about to do battle. That according to Herodotus was how Pan is said to have asked the Athenians to honour him so that he could help them in the coming clash.[167] But as Pausanias claims that the Athenians did not even know the name of the warrior-farmer, the demigod theory falls down.

The evidence, then, points to 'Echetlaios' being an actual fighter and a heroic one at that. He seems to have been especially renowned for valour, and therefore the Athenians honoured him by portraying him fighting in the front line when his memory was still vivid in the minds of his comrades. 'Echetlaios' was very likely one of the poor peasants of Attica who joined the fray, fighting with the only weapon he had, which was a wooden plough-handle. Could his image have been used as a general symbol for all the Athenian farmers who fought at Marathon? Many years later, when the story of 'Echetlaios' was forgotten, those viewing the wall-painting may have seen him as just another light-armed soldier representing the rest of that category who fought at Marathon. That, however, does not seem to have been the intention of the artist who depicted 'Echetlaios'. Nevertheless, his presence in the mural was a clear signal that the generation that grew up after the battle recognized the contribution of the light-armed troops as well as the hoplites; hence the painting shows that the fight at the Lesser Marsh, involving soldiers of both categories, was of supreme significance.

The honours paid to the warriors of Marathon continued in later decades. The south frieze of the Temple of Athene Nike, sculpted in 427–424, shows light-armed soldiers battling the Persians alongside the hoplites. Thus by the later fifth century the role played by the light-armed troops was included in official depictions of the battle. Yet that does not appear to have applied to Athenian private as opposed to public life. The images on many Attic vases after about 490 appear to be Marathon-themed. However almost all the soldiers thus depicted are hoplites.[168] There were possible economic reasons for this apparent bias: clients who ordered expensive pottery tended to come from the better-off citizens who formed the hoplite class, and naturally wished to immortalize their own doings, notably repulsing the Persians on the wings.[169] The hoplites are portrayed bravely fighting man-to-man, with no sign of the light-armed troops who anyway were not present in that phase. The poorer soldiers who fought at the Lesser Marsh would not have had the means to order and purchase such expensive vessels in order to immortalize their own contribution. If any were thus fashioned, they would have been a good deal rarer than those with hoplite battles on them.[170]

The class aspect of the battle of Marathon, in which the hoplite was given all the glory, was brought out by Athenian writers in the first half of the fourth century, when all the veterans of the battle, and a good many of their direct descendants, had passed on.[171] At that time Athens and its democratic polity were in decline, and perhaps as a reaction to that, those writers built up an idealized version of the battle of Marathon along pro-aristocratic lines, attributing victory solely to the hoplites.[172] In this they were aided by the fact that neither Herodotus nor any other writer of the Classical period mentions the contribution of the thetes and freedmen at all.[173] We may put it down to plain indifference or a deliberate omission of any reference to any soldier other than hoplites in past battles.

Thus the Herodotean narrative was accepted as the 'official' account of the battle of Marathon from the Classical era onwards. The phase of the battle at the Lesser Marsh, which Herodotus does not mention, was ignored as a mere detail not worth considering.[174] The literary sources concentrate exclusively on the repulse of the Persian wings by the hoplites, the heroic sacrifice of Kallimachos during the pursuit, and the heroic death of Kynegeiros by the ships. These feats by the hoplites were undoubtedly immensely courageous; however, they were isolated phases of the battle that had no critical bearing on the outcome. Yet the feats of Kallimachos and Kynegeiros were highlighted simply because they were 'notable' Athenians.[175] The final narrative of the battle was shaped in Roman times, when the role of Miltiades was elevated over all others. It was an era of absolute monarchy which believed in the importance of a 'leader-saviour' who shaped the history of peoples. This idealized picture of Miltiades has persisted until our own time.[176]

Berthold, for one, has wondered why, if the Athenians had neutralized the Persian cavalry at Marathon and captured the horses, the feat did not pass into popular lore from which Herodotus would have included the fact in his history.[177] But Berthold probably was unaware that the feat was indeed immortalized on the south frieze of the Temple of Athene Nike on the Acropolis. Besides, though Herodotus fails to mention the Persian cavalry action, Cornelius Nepos provides a corrective by clearly describing this attack at the start of the battle, though he does not say how the Persians were defeated. What remains a mystery is why Athenian writers, especially those who composed panegyric speeches on the battle from the fourth century onwards, did not celebrate the defeat of the Persian cavalry. One might conclude that these writers were unwilling to acknowledge the truth; if they mentioned the destruction of the Persian cavalry in the Lesser Marsh, they would have had to mention also the light-armed troops and freedmen who made it possible.

The problem was not the blood shed at Marathon but the mud; the Athenian heroes must be stained with the blood of the Persians, not with the slime of a swamp! The victory at Marathon was attained by methods which the intellects of the fourth century, such as Plato, Xenophon and Demosthenes, would have considered quite irregular. These men dreamed of a return to a heroic age that idealized the virtues of the hoplite, and the upper classes to which they belonged, rather than the lower-order thetes.[178] Hanson notes that the Greeks of the Classical era (that is, the upper class), believed the hoplite phalanx to be the accepted structure for warfare.[179] We believe that the writers and orators of the fourth century consciously chose a narrative that exclusively promoted the image of the hoplites at the expense of the thetes and freedmen.[180] It is intriguing that of all the ancient writers, only Pausanias reported the contribution of Echetlaios who appeared in the Poikile Stoa mural. And yet that painting was the source of all the patriotic speeches made afterwards.

It was not only the uncomfortable fact that the lower orders played an important role in the battle that presented a problem for Athenian writers; there was also the fact that victory was attributable to an entrapment, or a deception.[181] Polybius, writing in the second century, claims that Greeks who lived before his time had contempt for military victories earned by deception rather than honest combat.[182] Of course, this bears no relation to today, where military victory is required to be attainable by any means possible – victory is all that matters, even if it is a result of devious cunning. But in Classical-era Greece the ideal of the brave warrior was still very strong; heroic Achilleus rather than crafty Odysseus was held up as a paradigm, even though the latter's ruses gave the Greeks victory at Troy. The Persian destruction at the Lesser Marsh, as we have seen, was the result of a huge trap that swallowed the cavalry – something the devious Odysseus might well have thought up.

Though the writers of the fourth century downgraded the part played by light-armed troops at Marathon, they did not fail to mention those soldiers who were their contemporaries. At the beginning of that century the Athenian army formed separate units of light-armed troops known as peltasts. These, under the command of Iphikrates, scored significant victories against Spartan hoplites. Iphikrates' tactics were based on trapping enemy hoplites in a position where the peltasts could make short work of them.[183] Thus Iphikrates could be said to have practised a deception of sorts, contrary to what Polybius said about the war ethic of the ancient Greeks. Yet Iphikrates and his peltasts became the heroes of the hour in Athens.[184]

In the first half of the fifth century, however, the hoplite phalanx was the standard battle formation. It formed the core and basis of tactics. Yet throughout the Peloponnesian War the light-armed contingents repeatedly displayed their tactical superiority over the hoplite phalanges. Their earlier achievements at Marathon in 490 and at Megara three decades later took place at a time when the hoplite phalanx was still the basic formation adopted by the Greek city-states. That could help explain why later writers tended to downplay or even ignore the importance of the light-armed troops. For example, the destruction of a Corinthian force by Athenian stone-throwers at Megara in 457 merited just a brief mention by Thucydides, while the ancient sources gave absolutely no credit to the light-armed men of Marathon.[185]

Chapter 8

Political and Social Consequences
of the Battle

The outcome of the battle of Marathon, and in particular the way it was won, had a direct and radical effect on political developments in Athens. The thetes acquired unprecedented political power, leading to the consolidation of the democratic polity. After the battle the demos gained self-confidence and flexed its muscle against the upper classes; all political offices were henceforth to be awarded by lot, while ostracism and the eisangelia became powerful weapons in the hands of the demos. The Assembly itself would now have the right to try archons.

The Athenian victory at Marathon constituted a landmark in history. Beyond its purely military value, it had unprecedented political and social consequences; the new self-confidence gained by the Athenians was transmuted into the classical civilization that became the basis of that of the West. A mere few years after the battle fundamental changes occurred in the Athenian political scene, changes directly attributable to the victory. The thetes as a class acquired important civil rights, helping establish the democratic polity as the dominant one for most of the fifth century.[1] It is generally accepted that this was the result of the reforms of Ephialtes in 461;[2] but there is evidence that the change took place thirty years earlier, and specifically between 490 and 487.[3] That the former date marks the start of the process is no accident.

Before 490 in Athens, full civil and political rights belonged only to the two upper classes, the five-hundred bushellers (*pentakosiomedimnoi*) and the knights (*hippeis*). The *zeugitai* also enjoyed some rights, but were not entitled to run for the office of the Nine Archons. The thetes, for their part, only had the right to vote in the Assembly.[4] However, the rights of the thetes increased sharply after the battle of Marathon, as evidenced by the passage of several radical measures. The first was the penalty of ostracism, which provided the citizenry with a means of exiling anyone suspected of working against the democratic polity. Though ostracism had been provided for in the reforms of Kleisthenes in 508/7, only two decades later, in 488/7, was it enforced for the first time.

The author of the *Athenian Constitution* directly connects this first application of ostracism with the battle of Marathon, attributing the former to the 'self-confidence' in the citizen body engendered by the latter.[5] There is evidence that in 488 some 'well-known' Athenian aristocrats were accused by the Assembly of harbouring pro-tyranny sentiments during the Persian expedition. The political atmosphere in Athens as a result would have been quite sour, and thus ostracism may have been a method of defusing a crisis.[6] What is important here, though, is not what motivated the Athenians to apply ostracism as a practice, but the fact that all the citizen body participated in this radical measure exclusively aimed at the upper classes. This is the strongest indication that the position of the thetes, who made up the majority of the citizenry, was dramatically strengthened after 490.[7] They had acquired an active role in protecting the democracy.

The record of ostracism shows that the great bulk of the Assembly was hostile to the idea of a tyranny. The first ostracisms carried out in the 480s were aimed at those whom the Assembly deemed supporters of Hippias.[8] Some of the *ostraka* (or potsherds used to cast votes) have the word 'traitor' scratched on them. Another bears a crude image of a Persian archer, while others call the aristocrat Kallias a 'Mede'.[9] These are convincing signs that the Assembly believed that during the Persian attack of 490 there were Athenian fifth-columnists in the city working for a restoration of Hippias. Ostracism votes were held each year in Athens from 488/7 to 482/1, and rather less often in later years.[10] Thus after the battle of Marathon the citizenry consolidated its newly-won power, not only to safeguard its own class interests but also to impose its will on the upper classes. The author of the *Athenian Constitution* makes it quite clear that this power was gained after the battle of Marathon and not that of Salamis.[11]

The same writer shows that it was not only ostracism that buttressed the power of the citizens immediately after Marathon, but also the decision of 487 to make all state offices available by lot.[12] Much later

Aristotle would praise this measure as a truly democratic one, as he believed elections tended to produce oligarchies.[13] The result was that the Nine Archons, though remaining nominally the chief Athenian state officials, essentially became powerless. Though the office of polemarch remained after Marathon, the men who occupied that post after 487 were mere figureheads in the army command; it would appear that the valour of Kallimachos at Marathon was not enough to offset the general decline of that essentially aristocratic office.[14]

The power of the old aristocratic families was drastically curtailed. Kleisthenes' democratic reforms of 508/7 had not been enough to clip the wings of the aristocrats who continued to hold high office in Athens. After 490 the only elected officials were the Ten Generals, elected in a body by the Assembly and not, as previously, individually by the members of their respective tribes. Even here, however, the electoral procedure was changed in order to thwart the influence of local clans. The decline in influence of the Nine Archons could not help but strengthen the Assembly.

The foregoing is well-known from our ancient literary sources. It seems, however, that right after the battle the Assembly assumed the right to try ex-archons, a right known as the *eisangelia*. The first known trial of this nature was held in Athens in 489, accusing and convicting Miltiades of a botched expedition against Paros.[15] Before that date we have no record of any such conviction of a former archon by the Assembly; only the Areopagus, made up of ex-archons (i.e. aristocrats, that is five-hundred-bushellers and knights), seems to have had the sole right to put ex-archons on trial. Kleisthenes' reforms appear not to have changed that privilege of the Areopagus. When in 493 Miltiades had been tried for tyrannical conduct as governor of the Chersonese of Thrace, and acquitted, the trial was almost certainly conducted in the Areopagus.[16]

Miltiades' second trial in 489, this time by the Assembly, shows clearly that judicial power had changed hands after the battle of Marathon. By its power of *eisangelia* the Assembly now had the right to try ex-archons accused of serious offences and even sentence them to death.[17] Those who convicted Miltiades were mostly thetes who employed their new weapon of the *eisangelia*.[18] The two innovations, ostracism and the *eisangelia*, played a basic role in Athenian politics in the 480s.

Before 490 any rising politician would have been advised to court the favours of the citizenry, but that was not necessary for success. But after that year it became a sheer necessity; otherwise, the politician risked not only his career but also himself, under threat of ostracism and the *eisangelia*. It explains the references of ancient writers to the sharp increase in the Assembly's powers at the expense of the upper classes. Plutarch writes that the battle of Marathon gave the Assembly 'such self-confidence as to turn against the aristocrats'.[19] Likewise, Aristophanes makes broadly the same point in his *Knights*, asserting that the citizenry had acquired a powerful voice with which to protect its interests – presumably against the upper classes.[20]

Two of the leading Athenian politicians of the 480s, Xanthippos and Themistokles, seem to have quickly adapted to the new order. They realized that after Marathon the thetes would play a decisive part in Athenian politics. Both men took on the role of 'protectors of the *Demos*', representing the thetes' interests.[21] As will be seen, Xanthippos was instrumental in eliminating Miltiades, the most visible representative, if not leader, of the aristocratic faction and prime opponent of the thetes. Themistokles, for his part, worked to build up a strong Athenian navy while he served as general in the years between 484 and 480. As Eponymous Archon in 493/2 he had tried to inaugurate a naval programme but with little success.[22] This time, thanks to the support of the politically-powerful thetes, Themistokles was able to implement his naval programme that would soon save Athens and its democracy from the Persian danger.

One indication of the major changes in Athenian society in those years was the inclusion of comedy into the Dionysiac festival at some time between 488 and 486. This was a new art form connected with the power of the citizens. Pseudo-Xenophon writes that comedy 'took aim at the rich and powerful and left the *demos* alone'.[23] Bowie includes comedy among the factors that strengthened the citizens against the aristocrats.[24] None of these early comedies survives, but a glance at their titles between 487 and 482 gives us a clue about a possible link to Marathon: *Persians* or *Assyrians*, *Paupers* and *Heroes*, penned by Chionides, the first known ancient comic playwright.[25]

After the battle there was one major political protagonist who refused to truckle to the *demos*, and that was Miltiades, who continued to be the traditional 'patrician-leader'.[26] It would appear that despite his intelligence and perception, he failed to understand the deep and abrupt political change the victory against the Persians had brought about, ironically, in large part through his own efforts. Some ancient sources imply that Miltiades tried to capitalize on his achievement by stressing his own contribution. The dedication of a monument to Pan on the Acropolis, in thanks for the deity's help in the battle, was his own initiative and not that of the Assembly.[27] In fact Miltiades is said to have petitioned the Assembly to grant him an olive wreath for his victory at Marathon; the petition was turned down, along with a pithy comment by one Sophanes, an Athenian citizen, to the effect that 'when Miltiades wins the battle against the Persians by himself, then he can get the honours as well'.[28]

The authenticity of this anecdote, provided by Plutarch, is not certain.[29] Yet it serves as an indication that after the battle Miltiades did not have the support of the Assembly; the esteemed general, far from enjoying the adulation of the citizens for his contribution to a great victory, was actually regarded with suspicion. Sophanes' comment, if it was made, was not in the spirit of ingratitude for Miltiades' accomplishment, but merely reflected the new state of affairs; all the Athenians had won at Marathon, citizens high and low, hoplites and light-armed troops together. The feeling was that all the people, and not some aristocratic hero on the model of the Homeric epics, had won the battle of Marathon![30]

Miltiades had been away from Athens for a long time[31] and quite likely had been unaware of the changes begun by the reforms of Kleisthenes. Until 493 he had been the absolute ruler of the Chersonese in Thrace; his regime had been an anachronistic version of a typical tyranny that the democratic regime in Athens had tolerated for purely economic reasons, such as exploiting resources in Thrace, controlling the Dardanelles and safeguarding grain shipments from the Black Sea region to Athens. Miltiades also seems to have played a key role in attaching Lemnos to the Athenian sphere of influence. But when Darius' expansionist policy detached the Chersonese from Athenian control, Miltiades was forced to return to Athens. The political situation he found there must have troubled him, especially after his trial in 493.

But the looming clash with Persia, with his own survival directly threatened, was to him more important than his distrust of the democratic polity that had emerged in Athens during his absence. He perceived that the democracy, in fact, offered him chances for political promotion that he would not have had under the tyrants. He acted on this assumption by submitting proposals to the Athenians and arguing for them in the Assembly. In 490 he canvassed for the position of general of his tribe, and won. Working in his favour were his rhetorical abilities in the Assembly giving the impression that he favoured the democratic polity, plus the fact that he harboured personal enmity towards Hippias and the Persians. Regardless of his real feelings about democracy, Miltiades acted within the new political framework. We have seen how this atypical alliance between Miltiades and the Athenian *Demos* led in September 490 to the Athenians', and the Greeks', greatest victory against the Persian Empire.

After Marathon, however, Miltiades believed he could act independently of the *Demos*. The dedication to Pan and his petition to be awarded an olive wreath could have been signs that he thought he could act on the political stage in the way he had been used to. The culmination of this stance was his demand to be given the Athenian navy and an expeditionary force for an attack on Paros.[32] However, the fact that he did not reveal this purpose to the Assembly might have led to the rejection of his demand;[33] on the contrary, it was approved, as no Athenian could doubt Miltiades' strategic genius in the wake of the victory at Marathon. Miltiades, moreover, touted the expedition as entailing economic benefits, an argument that could have won over the thetes.[34] The expedition took place in 489, on the pretext that the Parians had aided the Persians a year earlier.[35] But Paros was also one of the richest and most powerful of the Cyclades islands in the early Classical era.[36]

Herodotus writes that as soon as he arrived at Paros, Miltiades commenced the siege of its main town. He sent an ultimatum to the Parians demanding one hundred talents to break off the siege, but the Parians refused.[37] According to Cornelius Nepos, however, Miltiades attempted to negotiate with the Parians before beginning the siege; this claim appears plausible, and Miltiades would have been expected to try and treat with the Parians for a few days after his arrival.[38] But he appears to have subsequently hardened his attitude. Yannos Kouragios, a Greek archaeologist, recently discovered a large number of fragments of *kouros* statues during excavations on Despotiko, an islet near Paros; the statues had been used as building materials in the early Classical era or parts of a temple doorway.[39] Kouragios believes that those *kouroi,* though they had been sculpted just twenty or thirty years before, were not destroyed by any natural means such as an earthquake but deliberately, possibly in 489 by Miltiades and his Athenians.[40] The destruction probably served to intimidate the Parians after negotiations had failed.

But Paros did not capitulate, and Miltiades pressed his siege of the main town. Herodotus says the siege lasted twenty-eight days.[41] During that time Miltiades injured his leg trying to jump over the fence around the precincts of the temple of Demeter Thesmophoros that stood on a hill outside the town.[42] This may have been why he provisionally suspended operations at Paros; the reason also could have been the expiry of his year-long term as general in July 489. At the end of that month he probably returned to Athens, even though he could have maintained the siege of Paros until at least the end of summer.[43]

Miltiades' failure against Paros was the cause of his political and physical demise. It gave the *Demos* its first opportunity to flex its new-found muscle. It appears highly ironic that the first victim of the upgraded political power of the thetes after Marathon would have been the very man whose genius not only had saved Athens but also enabled them to acquire a decisive say in the city's politics. Miltiades' elimination occurred even before the implementation of ostracism.[44] As we have seen, in 493 he had been acquitted of the charge of ruling as a tyrant in the Chersonese after a trial by the Areopagus, where the judges were upper-class ex-archons like himself; however, in 489 the outcome of his trial by the Assembly on a charge of botching the operation at Paros was very different.[45] It is not clear when the Assembly acquired the right to try ex-archons; theoretically it may have had the right before 490 but had not so far used it. But after Marathon the Assembly's heightened power in this regard was not in doubt.

Miltiades' trial was especially tragic for himself, as he was gravely ill as a consequence of his leg wound. His condition deteriorated to such a degree that he could neither stand upright in court nor utter a word in his own defence.[46] His aristocratic friends no longer had the power to get him acquitted, and could only appeal to the Assembly not to condemn him to death, considering his past achievements such as the seizure of Lemnos and the more recent victory at Marathon. The Assembly nonetheless convicted him, but instead of the death penalty they imposed on him an enormous fine that he could not possibly pay.[47] He was then shut up in prison, where he died in agony from his wound a little later.[48]

The intensity of feeling against Miltiades on the part of the *Demos* is worthy of note; he had not, after all, been actually defeated at Paros and had returned with all his ships.[49] However, neither had he been able to take the island, and Athens had incurred considerable expense in the effort, yet the casualties were minimal. The callous, almost inhuman, way in which Miltiades was treated by his fellow citizens just months after his triumph at Marathon has never ceased to amaze later writers.[50] The general who by all accounts saved Athens from the greatest threat in its history was treated as if he were a traitor. It remains a source of astonishment how those citizens who fought as soldiers under Miltiades subsequently reviled him morally and politically and actually exterminated him. Twenty-three centuries later his fate intrigued Lord Byron enough for him to pen the following lines:

> *The tyrant of the Chersonese*
> *Was freedom's best and bravest friend.*
> *That tyrant was Miltiades,*
> *Oh! That the present hour would lend*
> *Another despot of the kind!*
> *Such chains as his were sure to bind.*[51]

Nepos, who could have been the influence behind this Byronic verse, may be close to the truth when he writes that the Athenians began to sour on Miltiades when they suspected he might be aiming for a tyranny over Athens along the lines of how he had governed the Chersonese. Thus the Assembly judged that he should 'suffer, even though innocent, than that the people fear him constantly'.[52] And this, just a year after the triumph of Marathon!

By moral criteria the Athenians' treatment of Miltiades was indeed appalling. But by political criteria Miltiades was simply a sacrificial victim whose glory and power had to be smashed in order to validate the new powers of the *Demos* over the old aristocratic order. To be sure,

Miltiades was also a victim of aristocratic clan rivalry, as we know that his chief accuser was Xanthippos of the Alkmaionid clan, which harboured enmity towards Miltiades' own clan of the Philaids.[53] Yet the outcome of the trial did not result in the rise of any prominent aristocratic family; in 487/6 the Assembly ostracized the Alkmaionid Megakles, and two years later, Xanthippos himself, despite the reference in the *Athenian Constitution* to the effect that Xanthippos was a 'protector of the *Demos*' and 'no friend of tyrants'.[54]

In 489, then, it was not Xanthippos personally who set in motion the *eisangelia* proceedings against the famous general; he was in fact the tool of the *Demos* itself, which in 485/4 turned against him and replaced his position as 'protector of the *Demos*' by Themistokles.[55] The citizenry had thus become the arbiter of the disputes among the Athenian aristocrats themselves, something unthinkable before 490. Themistokles was the master manipulator of this fact during the 480s, using ostracism to eliminate his political rivals.[56]

The conviction of Miltiades and the heavy fine imposed on him, just one year after Marathon, are a strong indication that the thetes had acquired considerable political power even before other signs of this power had manifested themselves, such as the downgrading of the office of the Nine Archons and ostracism. It was the thetes' performance at Marathon that earned them their new clout; the real reason why they turned on Miltiades later was that they were unwilling to allow him to reap the full glory of victory. They had fought as light-armed troops and did not want to see the aristocrat Miltiades getting all the credit, even though it was his strategic and tactical plans that had secured victory for Athens. He appears not to have been generally liked after the battle, despite the fact that the Assembly approved his expedition against Paros. His military abilities were in no doubt at all among the Athenians, yet what he represented and symbolized politically was by no means as popular.

The sudden post-Marathon social upheaval in Athens was the start of a brilliant period for that city. It marked the beginning of the era when the common folk would assume the helm of a city-state for the first time. The battle of Marathon in this respect was seminal, as it directly enabled the establishment of the democratic polity in Athens. The thetes acquired sweeping new powers they had not had before, at least not in practice;

rather than being granted these powers by the upper classes, the thetes earned them by fighting as light-armed troops at Marathon, especially when their big moment came in annihilating the enemy in the Lesser Marsh. [57]Aristotle would later note that when a certain social class takes the credit for winning a foreign war, that class inevitably acquires new political power.[58] If the hoplites alone had won at Marathon, it is doubtful whether the thetes would have attained their powers; in fact, the reverse might have happened, as the conservative aristocratic faction was vindicated. The thetes, moreover, were becoming more numerous, as several thousand freed slaves who also fought at Marathon added to their number.

The battle of Marathon immortalized the names of Kynegeiros and Kallimachos, and to this day Miltiades is given credit for the victory. The ancient literary sources are unanimous in giving him this credit. Yet it is too often overlooked that the man who laid the foundations for that victory, and who was no longer alive when it happened, was Kleisthenes. This great statesman, through his reforms of 508/7, had awakened and energized the potential of the entire Athenian citizenry at precisely the right time. Though Athenian society continued to be class-based after 507, the thousands of citizens of the lower thetes class realized that the democratic polity gave them access to the levers of power for the first time. More significant is that the democracy was able to mobilize the citizens in their hour of danger, and provide a body of determined citizen-soldiers prepared to fight and die for their city.[59]

Kleisthenes' reforms narrowly escaped being nipped in the bud by external foes that had ganged up against him. But in 507/6 all the Athenian citizens, who until then had had no say in public affairs, were mobilized to enable the newly-minted democracy to beat off its foes. Sixteen years later they were able to trounce the Persians at Marathon. Thanks to the recent administrative reforms in Athens, thousands of soldiers could be mobilized effectively; many of these men, who under a tyranny would have been excluded from the defence of the city, seem to have flocked to the ranks voluntarily. At the same time, the newly-aware citizens were in a position to defend their enhanced political status. The victory at Marathon not only confirmed this status but served as a springboard for new rights and privileges.

In 490 the thetes, Athens' largest social class, did the lion's share of eliminating the Persian invaders in the Marathon plain. As a result, they could not allow themselves to be pushed back into their previous political and social status, but used their power to make inroads into the privileges of the upper classes. It is worthy of note that to this day most scholars do not directly connect the victory at Marathon with the sweeping political changes in Athens after 490.[60] Moreover, the struggles of Athenian politics in the Classical era resulted in the downplaying of the role of the thetes in the battle; their contribution was hushed up by ancient writers, while memories of the battle faded and became distorted in the ensuing century, as the veterans passed away. Thus the victory at Marathon became identified exclusively with the hoplites, as all references to light-armed troops faded from history. Even though after 490 the thetes' political role was upgraded, the writers of the Classical era, who belonged entirely to the Athenian upper classes, ignored their contribution.

Their pen proved mightier than the sword.

Appendix I

After the Battle

According to Herodotus, 6.115, after the Persians left Marathon they sailed to Aigilia where they took the Eretrian captives. The fleet then circumnavigated Sounion with the aim of landing the troops at Phaleron who would seize Athens before the Greeks returned from Marathon. However, the Athenians anticipated this move of the invaders and soon after the battle most men hurried back to the city in order to prevent a new Persian landing. Frontinus, 2.9.8, records that Miltiades ordered the Greeks at Marathon to stop celebrating and return to Athens. This reference is realistic as the death of Kallimachos had left him supreme leader of the army; not only was Miltiades *commander of the day* but there was no replacement of the Polemarch. Plutarch, *Aristides*, 5.5, says that the Athenians returned to their city the day after the battle and only the men of the Antiochis tribe, under their general Aristides, remained at Marathon to guard the Persian prisoners and spoils. The Athenians took up defensive positions at a sanctuary of Herakles at Kynosarges overlooking Phaleron. When the Persian ships approached the coast, Datis realized the Athenians would have the upper hand in the fight as they could attack his men as they were disembarking. The Persians were also in the disadvantage as both cavalry and moral had been destroyed at Marathon. Datis ordered the fleet to leave for the Cyclades. Athens had been saved! The Spartans had promised the Athenians to send their military aid the first day after the full moon. Indeed, 2000 Spartans with an unknown number of helots arrived at Marathon, but too late to participate in the battle. The Spartans toured the battlefield and saw the dead Persians. They congratulated the Athenians on their victory and returned home. As the Persian fleet was sailing back to Asia it made a stop at Mykonos. There Datis discovered that the captain of a Phoenician ship had stolen a gilded statue of Apollo from his sanctuary at Delion in Boiotia. Datis took this statue to the temple of Apollo at Delos and asked the locals to return it back to its original sanctuary. Eventually, Datis and Artaphernes arrived at Sousa and delivered the captive Eretrians to Darius (Herodotus, 6.118-9). Nothing is known about the subsequent fate of the Persian commanders. Ktesias' claim in *Persika* (FGrH 688 F13.22) that Datis was killed at Marathon and the Athenians refused to give his body to the Persians is unlikely. Plato in *Menexenos*, 240b and *Laws*, 3.698c, states that Darius had threatened to behead Datis if he did not capture Eretria and Athens. However, there is no evidence that Datis died in this way.

Herodotus, 6.121, claims that after the end of the battle an unknown Athenian signalled to the Persians by deflecting the sun light on his shield. The signal was meant to be for the fleet as it was sailing away from Marathon. This odd event was considered so important by the Athenians that Herodotus dedicates to it a larger part of his work than the battle! It was supposedly the act of a follower of Hippias in the Greek camp who was betraying secrets to the enemy. The theory was that the Persians were about to sail to the Cyclades but after observing the signal changed course for Phaleron. However, such a signal could only make sense if they had pre-arranged it with their 'agent' in the Greek army. The message would have been for the Persians to disembark at Phaleron and attack unguarded Athens. But the Persians already knew that the Athenian army was at Marathon and that they could land unopposed at Phaleron. So why should they have waited for a signal to do the obvious? The story may have been an unfounded rumour invented/used by political opponents of the Alkmeonids to accuse them as collaborators of the Persians and Hippias. According to the *Athenian Constitution*, 22.5–6, in 487/6 the Athenians ostracized the Alkmeonid Megakles because he was 'friend of the tyrants'. Perhaps this is why Herodotus was so eager to exonerate the Alkmeonids of the accusation that they were behind the signal at Marathon.

Another story associated with the end of the battle of Marathon was the famous mission of the runner to Athens. Ancient writers record three different names for the runner: Thersippos, Eukles and Pheidippides (or Philippides). The last one was considered as the more likely by scholars since, as we saw, Herodotus recorded that a *hemerodromos* ('day-runner') with this name was sent by the Athenians to Sparta before the battle of Marathon. No source records what the mission of the runner was. He may have been carrying an order for the garrison at Athens to leave immediately for Phaleron and hold it against the Persians until the army returned from Marathon. According to Plutarch and Lucian, when the runner arrived in Athens he spoke the words 'Joy, we win!' and expired. If this story is authentic, the runner obviously left Marathon when the outcome of the battle was clear but the fighting was not yet over.

Appendix II

Herodotus and Ancient Literary Sources on the Battle of Marathon

The oldest extant narrative -and also the most detailed one- of the battle of Marathon is by Herodotus. What gives his work especial value is that in c 450, when he began to collect material, some veterans of the battle were still alive. The reference to Epizelos (6.114), for example, indicates that Herodotus did make use of personal accounts of the participants in the battle. He may well have recited parts of his history to an Athenian public before it took its final form and any errors or omissions would have been pointed out by surviving veterans or their kin. Herodotus may therefore have shaped his narrative in accordance with the real events of the battle. He also knew certain critical facts about the Greek battle plan at Marathon and could well have drawn information from the Athenian state archives. However, Herodotus' account of the battle, being relatively short, has many gaps.

Before Herodotus began writing his history, the Athenians officially commemorated their victory at Marathon by depicting the battle on one of the murals in the Poikile Stoa at the Agora. This was made in c. 461, less than 30 years after the battle, and would have included authentic details. According to Pausanias, 1.15.3, it depicted three main phases of the battle of Marathon as the Athenians perceived them not long afterwards: Phase 1, where the Athenians and Plataians clashed with the Persians at the start of the battle; Phase 2, where the Persians fell into a marsh and suffered great casualties; and Phase 3, where the Greeks attacked the Persians on the coast at the latter's ships. Pausanias and other ancient writers also mention several individual gods, demigods and men occupied special places in the painting.

Besides Herodotus and the mural in the Poikile Stoa there are other ancient literary sources which likely contain authentically historical elements on the battle of Marathon. Aristophanes makes several references to Marathon in his comedies that are absent from Herodotus. For example, *Knights*, line 781, records that the Athenians made extensive use of their swords during the battle. This has the ring of truth, as the ground combat between the Greeks and Persians was so intense that either the Greeks' spears would have remained stuck in their enemies' bodies or the shafts would have broken from heavy use. In such a case the fight would have been carried on with swords. The main reference to the battle that Aristophanes makes comes in the *Wasps*, lines 1071–90. Most authorities, judging by the details, agree that this passage reflects the battle. Most of what Aristophanes tells us here about Marathon was already recorded by Herodotus. They include the account that the Athenians stuck to their formation, fought hard and repelled the Persians thus thwarting the burning of their homes by the enemy. But Aristophanes includes a basic element which Herodotus omits: that the Athenians attacked with their spears the Persians who had become trapped in some spot and struggled with one another to escape. Aristophanes likens them to tuna fish flailing about, which suggests that they were trapped in some watery place. Jeffery, 1965, 44, notes that this sounds very like what Pausanias describes seeing in the Poikile Stoa mural, where the Persians are trapped in a 'marsh' and jostling one another to get out. Aristophanes also gives a more vivid impression of the ferocity of the battle, absent from Herodotus' account; the playwright very likely got his information from surviving veterans of the battle. In the *Acharnians*, staged in 425, when few veterans would have been still alive, the chorus is made up of elderly Marathon veterans. We presume that Aristophanes would have been in touch with such men so that he could freely use their representation in his play. Pausanias, 1.32.3, 7.15.7, 10.20.2, mentions the participation in the fight of freedmen of the Athenians. Plutarch, *Aristides*, 5, names Aristides as one of Athens' Ten Generals and other writers of the Roman period add details about Kallimachos and Kynegeiros' deeds missing from Herodotus.

It is clear that Herodotus did not tell all there was to tell about the battle and even in antiquity this raised questions. Plutarch, *Ethics*, 862D, in particular points out that one could get the impression from Herodotus' curt account that the battle of Marathon was little more than a skirmish between the Greeks and Persians, during which the latter were repulsed and got back onto their ships in an orderly manner. Plutarch may have drawn on the fourth-century historian Theopompos who in one of the few extant excerpts from his work avers that 'the battle of Marathon did not happen in the way that all [the Athenians] celebrated.' Theopompos may have been referring to the celebratory speeches delivered in Athens every year on the Marathon victory. None of those speeches has survived, though we get some idea of their content from references in ancient writers. The prevailing narrative was one of a huge number of Persian soldiers vanquished by the Athenians, with little mention of the stages of the battle and none at all of the Plataians. Anyone listening to such speeches would get the impression that the Athenian victory was easy and overwhelming. In this light, Herodotus' account would have been used to perpetuate the narrative and embellish it with whatever imaginary elements other writers and speakers might think up. Theopompos' point is that much of what was said about the battle in his time simply did not correspond to reality. What he likely meant is not that Marathon was a mere skirmish, but the opposite: a hard-fought battle in which the Athenians had a tough job overcoming the Persians. Theopompos' claim that the narrative of Marathon had become seriously distorted did not seem to impress later writers, who were attracted to the legendary aspects of the story as cultivated by the orators. Some of these added details border on the fantastic. Justin, 2.9, for one, writes that the Greeks 'fought with such valour as to make one think that on one side were men and on the other side a herd of beasts.' He avers that 11,000 Greeks took on 600,000 Persians, whom they utterly destroyed and captured or sunk their ships!

The criticism to which Herodotus' account on Marathon was subjected in antiquity did not deter scholars from the Renaissance to the eighteenth century from accepting it pretty much at face value. But in the nineteenth century, the narrative came under serious doubt from historians, literary scholars and archaeologists, who tried to reconstruct the battle and rejected certain elements of the story. New tests of proof were offered, such as the topography of Marathon, archaeological findings and common sense. Every scholar felt free to pick and choose whatever elements of Herodotus he saw fit and reject the rest. The result was an explosion of published theories about Marathon between 1890 and 1930. Some authors put forward various conjectures on the battle tactics involved bearing little relation to what the ancient author wrote. In 1891 the sole surviving full text of the *Athenian Constitution* (by either Aristotle or a pupil of his) was published, the doubts around Herodotus appeared to be justified, especially as he was shown to be wrong about the powers and duties of the Polemarch in 490 (*Athenian Constitution*, 22.2). Extrapolating from that, the whole work of Herodotus was deemed to be in error.

Since the 1950s, however, Herodotus has enjoyed something of a rehabilitation in contrast to the previous fashionable debunking. The turnaround was the result of archaeological discoveries and literary research that tended to confirm much of what Herodotus wrote. As regards Marathon, it was seen that reconstructions of the battle based on Herodotus' critics not only did not provide answers to key questions, but actually complicated them further. One point to be found in Herodotus' favour was the fact that he wrote his history a few decades after the battle, when memories were still fresh and exaggerated or mythical elements did not yet have a chance to insert themselves. Another realization was that Herodotus' story of the battle of Marathon was simply not a major part of his work which would explain its brevity. He most likely considered Datis' expedition of 490 as a mere continuation of the suppression of the Ionian Revolt, and hence having little to do with his main subject, which was the panhellenic attempt to thwart Xerxes conquest of Greece a decade later. Herodotus account contains no exaggeration of the Athenian achievement at Marathon and mentions the Plataians, who other Classical-era writers omit. Thus his reliability is greater than that of other ancient writers on the subject of Marathon. No attempt seems to have been made in antiquity to amend the account, and it was used by later historians to built their own narratives, even the critical ones. On this basis we can assess the claim of Nepos, *Miltiades*, 5, that it was the Persians who attacked the Greeks first, and not vice versa. This appears to be more credible than Herodotus' account of the Persians waiting passively for the Greek onslaught. But Nepos implies that the Greeks had already lined up in formation opposite the Persians; thus the first move could indeed have been made by the Greeks, provoking a Persian attack. Nepos' intention was not to contradict Herodotus but to provide a detail which the latter had omitted.

Today most researchers consider Herodotus' narrative on Marathon as objective, though it leaves out the fighting in the marsh as well as other elements included by later writers. Yet we should not reject anything of Herodotus in reconstructing the phases of the battle. Those who doubted him, far from approaching the truth, were led into various areas of fantasy. Lazenby, 15, commenting on the rejection of Herodotus, warned that 'we are cutting off the branch on which we sit.' Adds Krentz, 2010a, 16: 'We may decide that the branch is not very firm, or whittle away parts of it, but we should not fool ourselves into thinking that later writers provide anything sturdier to sit on.'

The Monuments of the Battle

According to Thucydides, 2.34.5, the Athenian dead at Marathon were buried in the place of honour where they had fallen. Pausanias, 1.32.3, who visited the site confirmed this report, writing that the tombs of the Athenians were there on the battlefield. Many other visitors during the eighteenth century and early nineteenth century, reported seeing a large earthen mound about twelve metres high and fifty metres in circumference in the southern part of the plain which the locals called *Soros* ('Mound'). It was the largest visible man-made object at Marathon, easily distinguishable at a large distance from the plain and the surrounding hills. Even though no-one was quite sure what was inside, most visitors were certain that it was the Athenians' mass grave, as it would be a fitting memorial to their heroism and sacrifice. In 1876 a moat was constructed around the monument and the excavated earth was used for the erection of a protective wall. These structures were financed by the last emperor of Brazil, Pedro II, and their only known illustration is a sketch published in the *London Illustrated News* in 1877 showing Alexandra, Princess of Wales visiting the monument. A few years later they were demolished by Schliemann who in 1883/4 did the first archaeological excavation of the Soros. Until then the mound had seen occasional acts of illicit diggings by antiquities smugglers. Schliemann failed to unearth any important finds and concluded that it was a prehistoric construction. However, a new excavation by Greek archaeologist, Valerios Stais, in 1890/1, brought to light many artefacts from the early Classical era showing that this monument covered the remains of the dead Athenians of the battle of Marathon. It is also likely that the tumulus marks where a key phase of the battle took place. This monument is known today as the Tumulus of the Athenians and is the most important structure associated with the battle.

Another monument that may be linked to the battle of Marathon is the so-called 'Tumulus of the Plataians' at Vranas, a much smaller mound than that of the Tumulus of the Athenians. In the late 1960s a Greek archaeologist Spyridon Marinatos, partly excavated it and uncovered eleven graves, nine burials and two cremations. All belonged to males, ten adults and one ten-year-old boy. Marinatos found that all the burials had been carried out in the same way, as each grave had its own provisional stele erected over it and the only ceramic offerings found date 500/490. These dead may have been Greek casualties of the battle of Marathon though not necessarily Plataians as Marinatos believed. The mound thus cannot be a reliable factor in reconstructing the battle until it is fully excavated and assessed.

The so-called 'Trophy of the Battle', a tall Ionic column erected about the middle of the fifth century in the northern part of the plain near the edge of the Great Marsh was excavated in 1965 by the American archaeologist Eugene Vanderpool. It's parts had been built in the walls of a medieval tower. Pausanias (1.32.5) saw it still standing on the Marathon plain in the late-second century AD. Many human bones have been discovered in the adjacent area, suggesting a hasty mass burial. It is likely that these belong to the 6,400 Persians who were killed during the battle of Marathon. Some researchers believe that both the 'Trophy' and the human bones are evidence of the fighting having occurred at the Great Marsh. However, as we saw, geological studies preclude this possibility since the marsh was a lagoon in 490 and no fighting could have taken place there. More importantly, the 'Trophy' stood about 5.5 kilometres distant from the Tumulus of the Athenians at Valaria, where the Greeks formed up for battle and most of the fighting took place. Thus neither were the Persians killed in this area nor is the column connected to the actual battlefield. It appears that the Greeks chose the area close to the Great Marsh as the burial ground for their foes as it was far away from Marathon's settlements and its soil was too poor to produce grain but soft enough to open the ditches in which according to Pausanias the dead Persians were placed.

It is likely that the Ionic column was not a typical war trophy marking the place the ancient Greeks erected their trophy, at the spot where the enemy began fleeing and thus the fighting turned ('trope') in their favour but the place where the 6,400 Persian dead were buried. Thus Lysias' reference in *Epitaphios*, 25, that at Marathon 'the Athenians raised a trophy on behalf of Greece over the Persians' would be literally and not just metaphorically accurate. Lysias cites a similar example in which the Athenians erected a trophy over dead enemies. In 403, when the Athenian democrats fought to oust the 'Thirty Tyrants' the Spartans send military aid to the latter. In a clash between the Athenian democrats and Spartans at Piraeus, according to Xenophon, *Hellenica*, 2.4.33, 'two [Spartan] polemarchs were killed, Chairon and Thibrakos, Lakrates an Olympic victor, and other Lakedaimonians.' The bodies of the Spartans were buried at the Kerameikos in the most prestigious spot before the gates of Athens. The city was still under Spartan occupation at the time. But shortly afterwards, when the Spartans left Athens and the Athenian democrats took over, Lysias tells us that 'the victors raised a trophy over their enemies, and witnesses to their valour are the tombs of the Lakedaimonians located near the monument [trophy].' It would thus appear that the Athenian democrats consciously adopted the practice of their forebears at Marathon. When Pausanias visited Marathon he was unable to locate the grave of the Persians as, he said, there was no visible mark on the surface of the ground, and he thus assumed that the Athenians had buried the Persians in mass graves without leaving anything to mark the site for a visitor. Pausanias, however, did not know that he had seen and described just such a mark, which was the 'Trophy'. It would seem that six centuries after 490 the monument's connection to the dead Persians had been forgotten.

Appendix IV

The Persian Cavalry at Marathon

One of the biggest problems in Herodotus' narrative is the absence of any reference to the action of the Persian cavalry during the battle of Marathon, even though according to him, the Persians chose Marathon exactly because the area was suitable for the deployment of their cavalry. This has led researchers to construct various imaginative theories about the fate of this force, based on the entry entitled 'Without Horsemen' in the tenth century AD lexicon of Souda:

> *The cavalrymen were away. When Datis invaded Attica, the Ionians climbed the trees and gave the Athenians the signal that the cavalry was away. Miltiades realized that, he attacked and won. From there comes the above-mentioned quote, which is used when someone breaks ranks.*

During the 1920s, British historian Arthur Munro came up with the idea that the Persian cavalry never disembarked at Marathon, since he considered that for tactical reasons the Persians had divided their force and were operating in different areas simultaneously. According to this theory, when Datis was in Euboia, he learnt that an Athenian army was on its way to aid Eretria. He decided therefore to lead a large contingent of his infantry to Marathon to prevent the Athenians from leaving Attica. The rest of the Persian infantry, together with the entire cavalry, remained at Euboia under Artaphernes' command. After concluding their operations at Karystos and Eretria, these forces would have been both transported by ship to Phaleron and disembarked in the rear of the Athenian army at Marathon. Thus, the latter would be trapped between two sections of the Persian army, and from Phaleron the Persians would have advanced and conquered unprotected Athens. Munro's theory, however, is unrealistic, since the Persians would not have divided their forces to risk operating simultaneously in two separate fronts far away from each other. More importantly, he added elements that are absent from ancient sources, and at the same time dismissed other elements in Herodotus' narrative.

In 1859 the German historian and archaeologist Ernst Curtius published a theory explaining the absence of the Persian cavalry from the battle, without however contradicting Herodotus' statement that the Persians chose to land at Marathon because of the advantages the area had for their cavalry. According to Curtius, the entire Persian army disembarked at Marathon, including the cavalry. When the Persian commanders realized that they could not lure the Athenians to fight them at Marathon before the arrival of the Spartans, they decided to attack Athens via Phaleron. The cavalry and part of the infantry undertook this mission, while most of the Persian infantry remained at Marathon to prevent the Greeks from withdrawing to Athens and defending the city from the new attack. Thus the Persian cavalrymen with the small force of infantry from Phaleron would have captured Athens, possibly with the aid of Hippias' followers who had remained in the city when the Athenians left for Marathon. The Greeks attacked the Persian infantry at Marathon, however, as soon as the cavalry sailed away.

This theory was accepted by many researchers of the battle of Marathon and was particularly popular with British historians until the 1960s. Some even embellished it with their own details. For example, in 1952 Gomme published a new version of this theory, according to which the Persians planned to send their entire army from Marathon to Phaleron, not just the cavalry and a small force of foot soldiers. During the night before the day of the battle, they started loading the horses on the ships. As dawn broke they were finishing this task and were about to start embarking their infantry. The Greeks, however, realized what the Persians were up to and charged the infantry that was waiting on the coast to get on the ships. A large contingent of Persian infantry was ordered to confront the Greeks. Since the Persian cavalry had already embarked, it could not take part in the battle and support the infantry lined up on the plain against the attacking Greeks. But they were soundly defeated and the survivors fled to the coast where the Greeks attacked them once again by their ships. Few of these Persians survived to sail away from the coast of Marathon with their cavalry.

The theory that the Persian cavalry withdrew from Marathon before the battle appears logical and is popular even today. Though first published in the mid-nineteenth century, it still appears in publications and television documentaries about the battle. However, what is not as well-known is that this theory has no real basis. Hammond states that no ancient source records the withdrawal of the Persian cavalry from Marathon to participate in any kind of expedition. Also, Whatley comments on the popularity of this theory during his time (early-twentieth century): 'What are mere theories tend to be regarded as established truths'.

The view that the Persians planned a surprise attack against Athens via Phaleron with their entire cavalry contingent and part of the infantry, leaving the rest of the army at Marathon, does not conform to the military strategy of the Persians at the time. Such a high-risk operation would contrast with the careful planning of their expedition. The embarkation of horses on ships at night would have been a hazardous and slow endeavour, and certainly noticed by the Greeks who could have attacked the Persians from an advantageous position, endangering the Persian troops and ships. The experienced Persian commanders would have known this. Their army was stronger than their opponents' and they had no reason to engage in risky endeavours not approved by Darius. It is unlikely that Datis would have taken the initiative of dividing his forces if this had not been in the plan that had his king's approval. If this were the case, then Datis would have sent his cavalry and part of the infantry straight to Phaleron from Marathon and would not have kept them idle at Marathon for days.

Even during the nineteenth century some scholars, for example Leake, Finlay and others, argued that the Persian cavalry was at Marathon on the day of the battle, but that it did not take part in the fighting. Since the 1960s this theory has become popular in academic circles. Most researchers believe that the charge 'at a run' ('dromaia ephodos') by the Greek hoplites surprised the mounted Persians, forcing them to retreat without a fight and embark on the ships during the battle. In Lazenby's words:

The most probable explanation for the absence of the cavalry from his account of the battle is that it actually played no part. The speed of the Greek advance would have precluded its usual hit-and-run tactics, which required a static target to be effective, and there was certainly no place for such cavalry in a hand-to-hand encounter.

However, this theory fails to give a rational explanation of how the charge of the Greek hoplites over a distance of eight stadia (about 1.5km) could have surprised the best cavalrymen and archers of the time. We should also take into account that the Persian cavalrymen would have been on high alert to begin battle immediately after the Greeks began lining up. The Persians thus had time to prepare and attack the Greeks, or at least to oppose their opening charge. Nevertheless, some researchers believe that the Persian cavalrymen were surprised by the attack of the Greek hoplites and did not fight, but may only have protected their defeated infantry as it was retreating to the ships. There is also the view that when the Persian cavalrymen realized their infantry had been defeated, they fled to their ships without even covering the retreat of their infantry.

The theory that the Persian cavalry could not fight because of the sudden attack of the Greek hoplite phalanx is problematic, since the cavalry could still have taken part in the fighting, even after the successful attack of the Greek hoplites against the infantry on both wings of the Persian line-up. If the Persian cavalrymen had been surprised in the beginning of the battle by the quick advance of the hoplites, they could fight – even if delayed – thus helping their infantry to win in the end. The fighting between the Greek hoplites and the Persian infantry took place on the plain of Marathon, and the level ground would thus have facilitated a Persian cavalry attack on the Greeks. This view is supported by an event dating only four years before the battle: in 494 during the battle of Malene, the Persian cavalry annihilated a Greek army even though the cavalry was late joining the battle that until then was fought between Greek and Persian infantry.

Our conclusion is that either the Persian cavalry was not at Marathon during the battle or that it was put out of action by the Greeks at the outset, before it could have any effect on the outcome. However, all evidence shows that the former theory should be dismissed. On the other hand, our research shows that the second case, the destruction of the Persian cavalry during the battle of Marathon, considered by few researchers including Kromayer, could be the correct one: the cavalry, before the battle, was at the centre of the Persian array, and it attacked the Greek centre. Shrimpton propounds a similar view, arguing that the references of Herodotus to Persians and Saka that broke the centre of the Greek line at the beginning of the battle were horsemen and not infantrymen. There is also an *ex silentio* clue that supports this view: Herodotus does not state that these Persian contingents were cavalry, but neither does he say that they were infantry. However, Shrimpton notes that in Herodotus' narrative of the battle of Plataia, wherever he records combined actions of Persian and Saka they refer exclusively to cavalry and not infantry. Shrimpton in his discussion of this evidence suggests that Saka infantrymen were not an elite force in Xerxes' army that invaded Greece in 480, and this would also be true a decade earlier. At Marathon, however, the Saka were placed in the centre of the Persian line, which was reserved only for elite forces. This indicates that they were cavalrymen and not infantry.

This view seems to be supported by Harrison who, as we have seen, argues that the south frieze of the Temple of Athene Nike records the clash between Greek infantry and Persian cavalry during the battle of Marathon. In this context, Harrison notes a detail of this work showing that before the clash, the Greeks had been pursued by the Persians. This clue is consistent with Herodotus' reference to the pursuing of the men in the Greek centre by the Persians and Saka at the beginning of the battle. Iranian historian Kaveh Farrokh also considers that the Persians and Saka who broke the Greek centre and pursued the Athenians in that sector were cavalrymen. However, their successful action failed to help their infantry on both wings who were overcome by the Greeks. Farrokh does not offer a view on what may have happened to the Persian cavalry that had broken through the centre of the Athenian line-up after the infantry's debacle on both wings.

As we have seen, many ancient sources clearly refer not only to the fact that the Persian cavalry was at Marathon on the day of the battle, but assert that it also fought there. Cornelius Nepos places the action of the Persian cavalry at the start of the fighting, recording its massive attack against the Greek line-up. Depictions on Attic vases as well as the frieze of the Temple of Athene Nike, and a Roman sarcophagus in Brescia, not only record the presence of the Persian cavalry at Marathon, but also the fierce clashes of Athenian infantrymen with mounted Persians during the battle. Moreover, archaeological finds seem to show that the Athenians had dedicated accessories and weapons of Persian cavalrymen as votive offerings to the sanctuaries of Olympia and the Athens Acropolis to thank the gods for their victory.

The active participation of the Persian cavalry in the battle of Marathon is closer to reality, since it would be consistent with the military tactics of the Persians during the Persian Wars of the early-fifth century. It is also clearly recorded in literary sources and art works of antiquity. The study of all the evidence at our disposal, with the aid of common sense, shows convincingly that Persian cavalry not only was at Marathon during the battle but it also fought in it. All reconstructions of the battle need to take this into account.

Marathon and Agincourt

History records many cases where an army in a defensive position managed to completely destroy a larger attacking opponent whose advantage was a powerful cavalry, after trapping this force in terrain where it could not manoeuvre, as the Athenians did during the battle of Marathon.

A well-known example is the 1415 battle of Agincourt. There the English had a small army consisting mainly of lightly-armed foot soldiers who were also archers. The French were more numerous and stronger, with a large force of knights who were heavily armed cavalrymen.

The English challenged the French knights who attacked them in a field covered in thick mud. There the horses of the French cavalry were immobilized and trapped with their riders, causing panic and chaos. Many English archers before the battle had hidden behind shrubs, unnoticed by the French. These archers hit the French knights with a hail of arrows, injuring their horses, which hurled their riders to the ground. Fierce hand-to-hand clashes took place in the mud. Two or three English foot soldiers rushed each French knight who had fallen from his horse and killed him on the spot by striking blows at close quarters on parts of his body not protected by armour and helmet. After eliminating the French cavalry the English attacked the French infantrymen, who were charging behind their knights. After worsting them also in the ensuing fight, they forced the survivors to retreat but refrained from pursuing them.

The similarities between the tactics employed by the Greeks at Marathon and those of the English at Agincourt are striking, especially in the matter of using the terrain to neutralize the enemy cavalry, which for the Greeks in 490, as for the English in 1415, was the greatest impediment. Another similarity is that the French, who were numerically stronger, were eager for battle and provoked the English to fight. On the contrary the English, being certain of imminent defeat, avoided a clash and remained behind roughly-built fortifications they had built on a hill above the plain. These fortifications prevented the French horsemen from attacking the English, who did not fall for the challenge of leaving their defensive positions and engaging in battle. At the same time, the French knights, all of them aristocrats, clearly underestimated the English army that consisted mainly of foot archers, considered socially inferior.

We believe that in Marathon in 490 a similar situation occurred. The Persian horsemen were aristocrats, while the lightly-armed Athenians belonged to the lowest social class. However, in the eyes of the Persian aristocrats even the wealthiest Athenians seemed far inferior to themselves, just as the French aristocrats looked down even on the English nobles facing them in the field.

The conflict at Agincourt began as soon as the English dared to move forward in front of their rough fortifications, causing the French cavalry to attack them. But the French knights became trapped in muddy ground in front of the English foot soldiers, who first struck them with arrows from a distance and then dispatched them in hand-to-hand combat. When the English infantrymen provoked the French knights to attack, they did so in the knowledge that they were leading them to entrapment.

Even the comparison of the losses of the armies involved in the battles of Marathon and Agincourt is of interest. The English had 112 dead, compared to about 7,000 dead Frenchmen, most of whom were knights. At Marathon the Athenians lost 192 men, compared to 6,400 Persians. Of the high-ranking officers who commanded the English at Agincourt, only two were killed: Edward, Duke of York, and Michael de la Pole, Earl of Suffolk. The former was the most senior officer of the English army, after King Henry V, and during the battle commanded its right wing. He was killed along with several other English when their right wing got involved in the heaviest fighting with the French. Something similar, as we have seen, happened during the battle of Marathon, where the Athenians lost only two commanders, Kallimachos and Stesileos. The former, like the Duke of York, was the head of the Athenian army and commanded the right wing of the Greeks. After the battle of Agincourt, the French dead were so numerous that the English buried them in large trenches. The same thing happened, according to Pausanias, with the thousands of dead Persians at Marathon two millennia before.

Another later battle that was fought in a similar way to Marathon and Agincourt was that of Kopais (also known as the battle of Boiotian Kifissos) in 1311. This encounter took place in Boiotia (Greece), between Catalan mercenaries and the Frankish knights of the Duchy of Athens and other Greek regions. The lightly-armed Catalan foot soldiers waited for the Frankish knights in one of the many marshes of Lake Kopais. The Frankish knights were aristocrats and scorned the Catalan mercenaries' low social status. Although the Franks were stronger, they were lured into a massive attack on the Catalans without having any idea of how inappropriate the terrain of the region was for cavalry operations. The Catalans, however, had previously built pathways inside the marsh to use as tactics required. The wetland vegetation there was quite tall, so the Frankish knights did not notice the marsh until it was too late. Their horses got stuck and became immobilized.

According to the Byzantine chronicler Gregoras, many horses collapsed with the knights in the marsh, while others were stuck so deep in the mud that they became as still as statues. The Frankish knights were attacked by the Catalans initially from afar with arrows and then slaughtered in the ensuing hand-to-hand fighting. The key element of victory for the Catalans was their clever use of the terrain to trap and annihilate the opponent's powerful cavalry.

It is worth pointing out that in the two examples we cite here, Agincourt and Kopais, the trap for the cavalry was set up by the invading forces who defended themselves even though they apparently did not know beforehand the natural environment in which they were to fight. But the defenders took full advantage of the characteristics of the environment. At Marathon the Athenians were fortunate enough to have with them men who lived in the area where the battle was to be fought and were familiar with the terrain. They also had the advantage of time, even a mere few days, to plan their battle tactics, taking into account the particular terrain that would determine the way in which the conflict would evolve.

It is of course unlikely that the English and the Catalans knew of Miltiades' battle plan and copied it. It seems, however, that in similar circumstances it is possible to apply the same tactics that can completely overturn the balance of forces in the battlefield, provided of course that the commander of an army is competent enough to plan and execute them.

Bibliography

Adler A., *Suidae lexicon*, Vol. I-IV, Leipzig, 1928–1935.

Aldenhoven F., *Itineraire descriptif de l' Attique et du Peloponnese avec cartes et plans topographiques*, Athenes 1841.

Ameling W., "Marathon, Herodes Atticus, and the Second Sophistic", *Marathon. The Day After, Symposium Proceedings, Delphi 2–4 July 2010*, 167–184, European Cultural Centre of Delphi, 2013.

Anderson G., *The Athenian Experiment. Building an Imagined Political Community in Ancient Attica, 508–490 B.C.*, Ann Arbor, The University of Michigan Press, 2006.

Anderson J.K., *Ancient Greek Horsemanship*, University of California Press, Berkley/Los Angeles California, 1961.

Anderson J.K., *Military Theory and Practice in the Age of Xenophon*, University of California Press, Berkeley/Los Angeles, California, 1970.

Armit M., "La date de l' alliance entre Athenes et Platees", AC 39 (1970), 414–426.

Arnush M., 'The Career of Peisistratos Son of Hippias', *Hesperia* 64 (1995), 135–162.

Avery H.C., 'Herodotus 6.111.2', *TAPA* 103 (1972), 15–17.

Bach N., *Anthologia graeca, sive, Delectus poesis elegiacae melicae bucolicae*, Hannover, 1838.

Badian E., 'Archons and Strategoi', *Antichthon* 5 (1971), 1–2.

Baitinger H., 'Waffen und Bewaffnung aus der Perserbeutte in Olympia', *AA*, (1999), 125–139.

Bakewell G., 'Written Lists of Military Personnel in Classical Athens', *The Politics of Orality: Orality and Literacy in the Ancient World VIII*, C. Cooper (ed), Brill, Boston/Leiden, 2007, 89–102.

Balcer J.M., 'The Persian Wars against Greece: A Reassessment', *Historia, Zeitschrift fur Alte Geschichte*, 38 (1989), 127–143.

Barrett A.A./Vickers M., 'The Oxford Brygos Cup Reconsidered', *JHS* 98 (1978), 17–24.

Barthelemy J.-J., *Maps, Plans, Views, and Coins Illustrative of the Travels of Anacharsis the Younger in Greece, During the Middle of the Fourth Century Before the Christian Era*, London, 1806.

Behr C.A., *Aelius Aristides, The Complete Works: Orations I-XVI, with an appendix containing the fragments and inscriptions*, Vol. I-II, Brill, Leiden, 1986.

Beloch J., *Griechische Gescτhichte*, Vol II: *Bis auf die Sophistische bewegung und den Peloponnesischen Krieg. 2*, Strassburg, 1916.

Bengtson H., *Griechische Geschichte: von den Anfängen bis in die römische Kaiserzeit*, 10th edition, C.H.Beck, Munchen 2009.

Benndorf O., *Das Heroon von Gjolbaschi-Trysa*, Jahrbuch der Kunsthistorischen Sammlungen des Allerhochsten Kaiserhauses XI, Vienna, 1890.

Bergk T., *Poetae Lyrici Graeci*, Vol III, Leipzig, 1882.

Berthold R.M., 'Which Way to Marathon?', *REA* 78/79 (1976/1977), 84–95.

Berve H., *Miltiades, Studien zur Geschichte des Mannes und seine Zeit*, Hermes Einzelschrift 2, Berlin, 1937.

Best J.G.P., *Thracian Peltasts and their Influence on Greek Warfare*, Wolters-Noordhoof, Groningen, 1969.

Bickford-Smith R.A.H., *Greece under King George*, Richard Bentley, London, 1893.

Bicknell P.J., 'The Command Structure and Generals of the Marathon Campaign', *AC* 39 (1970), 427–442.

Bicknell, 1972a: Bicknell P.J., *Studies in Athenian Politics and Geneology*, Historia Einzelschrift 19 Franz Steiner Verlag GMBH, Wiesbaden, 1972.

Bicknell, 1972b: Bicknell P.J., 'The Date of Miltiades' Parian Expedition', *AC* 41 (1972), 225–227.

Bigwood J.M., 'Ctesias as Historian of the Persian Wars', *Phoenix* 32 (1978), 19–41.

Blinkenberg C., *La Chronique du temple Lindien*, Copenhague, 1912.

Boardman J., 'The Frieze – Another View', Hockmann V./Krug A. (ed), *Festschrift fur F. Brommer*, Mainz am Rhein, 1977, 39–49.

Boedeker D., "Simonides on Plataea: Narrative Elegy, Mythodic History", ZPE 107 (1995), 217–229.

Boucher A., *La Bataille de la Marne de l' Antiquite, Marathon, après Herodote*, Nancy, 1920.

Bowie E., 'Marathon in Fifth-Century Epigram', *Μαραθών, Η Μάχη και ο Αρχαίος Δήμος*, Κ. Μπουραζέλης/Κ. Μεϊδάνη (ed), Ινστιτούτο του Βιβλίου-Α. Καρδαμίτσα, Αθήνα, 2010. 203–219.

Bowie E., 'Marathon, the 1500 Days After: Culture and Politics', *Marathon. The Day After, Symposium Proceedings, Delphi 2–4 July 2010*, Buraselis K. / Koulakiotis E. (ed), European Cultural Centre of Delphi, 2013, 59–74.

Bradeen D.W., 'The Trittyes in Cleisthenes' Reforms', *TAPA* 86 (1955), 22–30.

Bradeen D.W., 'The Athenian Casualty Lists', *CQ* 63 (1969), 145–159.

Brenne S., 'Portraits auf Ostraka', *AthMitt* 107 (1992), 161–185.

Briant P., *From Cyrus to Alexander: A History of the Persian Empire*, tr. Peter T. Daniels, Eisenbrauns, Winona Lake, Indiana, 2002 (*Histoire de l' empire perse. De Cyrus a Alexandre*, Paris, 1996).

British Museum: A Guide to Greek and Roman Life, 3rd edition, London, 1929.

Broneer O., 'Excavations on the North Slope of the Acropolis', *Hesperia* 4 (1935), 109–188.

Bugh G.R., *The Horsemen of Athens*, Princeton University Press, Princeton, New Jersey, 1988.

Burian P. / Shapiro A. (ed), *The Complete Aeschylus*, Vol II: *Persians and other Plays*, Oxford University Press, Oxford, 2009.

Burn A.R., *Persia and the Greeks: The Defence of the West, c.546–478 B.C.*, London, 1962 (Stanford University Press, 1984).

Burn A.R., 'Hammond on Marathon: a few notes', *JHS* 89 (1969), 118–120.

Burn A.R., 'Thermopylai Revisited and Some Topographical Notes on Marathon and Plataiai', Studies presented to F. Schachermeyr, Munchen, 1977, 89–105.

Busolt G., *Griechische Geschichte bis zur Schlacht bei Chaeronia*, Vol 2: *Die altere attische Geschichte und die Perserkriege*, 2nd edition., Gotha, 1895.

Byron Lord, *Don Juan, Cantos III, IV and V,* London, 1821.

Byron Lord, *Childe Harold* II, LXXXIX, *The Works of Lord Byron: Poetry*, II, E.H.Coleridge, 187, note to *Childe Harold* II, XII, London, 1899.

Cadoux T.J., 'The Athenian Archons from Kreon to Hypsichides', *JHS* 68 (1948), 70–123.

Camp J.M., *The Athenian Agora: Excavations in the Heart of Classical Athens*, Thames & Hudson, London, 1986.

Camp J.M., 'The 'Marathon Stone' in New York', *MMJ* 31 (1996), 5–10.

Carawan E.M., 'Eisangelia and Euthyna: the Trials of Miltiades, Themistocles and Cimon', *GRBS* 28 (1987), 167–208.

Cargill J., *Athenian Settlements of the Fourth Century B.C.*, Mnemosyne Suppl. 145, Brill, 1995.

Cartledge P., *Sparta and Lakonia: A Regional History, 1300–362* BC, 2nd edition Routledge, London, 2002.

Cary M., 'Cornelius Nepos on Marathon', *JHS* 40 (1920), 206–220.

Caspari B., 'Stray Notes on the Persian Wars', JHS 31 (1911), 100–109.

Casson, S., 'The Vita Miltiadis of Cornelius Nepos', *Klio* 14 (1915), 69–90.

Cawkwell G., *The Greek Wars. The Failure of Persia*, Oxford University Press, Oxford, 2005.

Chandler R., *Travels in Asia Minor and Greece*, Vol II, 3rd edition, London, 1817.

Christ M.R., 'Conscription of Hoplites in Classical Athens', *CQ* 51 (2001), 398–422.

Christ M.R., 'Draft Evasion Onstage and Offstage in Classical Athens', *CQ* 54 (2004), 33–57.

Command Decisions*: Battle of Marathon and Battle of Chalons*, A and E Television Networks, New York, 2004.

Cope E.M./Sandys J.E. (ed), *Aristotle: Rhetoric*, 3 Volume Set, Cambridge Library Collection, Cambridge, 2010.

Coulton J.J. (ed)/E. Sapouna Sakellaraki/Coulton J.J./Metzger I.R., *The Fort at Phylla, Vrachos: Excavations and Researches at a Late Archaic Fort in Central Euboea*, BSA Suppl. Vol., London, 2002.

Curtius E., *Griechische Geschichte*, II, *Bis zum Ende des Peloponnesischen Krieges*, 3rd edition., Berlin, 1869.

Curtius E. / Kaupert J.A., *Karten von Attika, Erlauternder Text*, von A. Milchhofer Heft III-VI, Berlin, 1889.

Curtius, 1898: Curtius E., Ελληνική Ιστορία, μετάφραση Σπυρίδωνος Λάμπρου, Αθήνα, 1898 (*Griechische Geschichte*, II, Berlin, 1861).

Davies J.K., *Athenian Propertied Families, 600–300 B.C.*, Oxford University Press, Oxford, 1971.

Day J.W., *The Glory of Athens. The Popular tradition as reflected in the Panathenaicus of Aelius Aristides*, Ares Publishers, Chicago, 1980.

Delbrück H., *Die Perserkriege und die Burgunderkriege*, Berlin, 1887.

Delbrück H., *History of the Art of War*, Vol I, tr. Walter, J. Renfroe, University of Nebraska Press, 1990 (*Geschichte der Kriegskunst*, I, Berlin, 1920).

Detienne M. / Vernant J.-P., *Cunning Intelligence in Greek Culture and Society*. Trans. Janet Lloyd. Chicago, University of Chicago Press, Chicago, 1991 (*Les Ruses de l' intelligence: la metis des grecs*, Paris, 1974).

Develin R., 'Miltiades and the Parian expedition', *AC* 46 (1977), 571–577.

Develin R., *Athenian Officials 684–321 BC*, Cambridge University Press, Cambridge, 1989.

Dillon M. / Garland L., *Ancient Greece: Social and Historical Documents from Archaic Times to the Death of Socrates*, 2nd edition, Routledge, London/New York, 2000.

Dindorf G. (ed), *Aelius Aristides ex recensione Guilielmi Dindorfii*, Vol III, Weidmann, Leipzig 1829.

Dindorf G. (ed), *Scholia Graeca in Aristophanem cum prolegomenis grammaticorum*, Paris 1833.
Dionysopoulos: Διονυσόπουλος Χ., *Η Μάχη του Μαραθώνα. Ιστορική και τοπογραφική προσέγγιση*, Καπόν, Αθήνα, 2012.
Dodwell E., *A Classical and Topographical Tour through Greece*, Vol II, London, 1819.
Doenges N.A., 'The Campaign and Battle of Marathon', *Historia* 47 (1998), 1–17.
Donlan W. / Thompson J., 'The Charge of Marathon, Again' *CW* 72 (1979), 419–420.
Dover K.J., 'Δέκατος Αυτός', *JHS* 80 (1960), 61–70.
Drew-Griffith M., 'The king and eye: the rule of the father in Greek tragedy', *PCPhS* 44 (1999), 20–84.
Drews R., *Early Riders, The beginnings of mounted warfare in Asia and Europe*, Routledge, New York/London, 2004.
Dubner F., *Anthologiae Palatinae. Epigrammatum Anthologia Palatia*, Vol. 1–2, Paris, 1872.
Ehrenberg V., *Aspects of the Ancient World*, Ayer Co, Oxford, 1946.
Eisler B., *Byron: Child of Passion, Fool of Fame*, Alfred A. Knopf, London, 1999.
Ekroth G., *The sacrificial rituals of Greek hero-cults in the Archaic to the early Hellenistic periods*, Kernos Suppl. 12, Liege, 2002.
Eliot C.W.J. / McGregor M.F., 'Kleisthenes: Eponymous Archon 525/4 B.C.', *Phoenix* 14 (1960), 27–35.
Enepekidis: Ενεπεκίδης Π.Κ., *Γράμματα προς τη Βιέννη 1824–1843, Από την αλληλογραφία του πρώτου Αυστρικού πρεσβευτή στην Αθήνα Αντόν Πρόκες φον Όστεν, Ωκεανίδα*, Αθήνα, 2007.
Erdmann E., 'Die sogennanten Marathonpfeilspitzen in Karlsruhe', *AA*, 1973, 30–58.
Erdmann E., *Nordosttor und Persische Belagerungsrampe in Alt-Paphos*, Universitatsverlag, Konstanz, 1977.
Eschenburg M., 'Topographische, Archaeologische und Militarishe Betrachtungen auf dem Schlachtfelde von Marathon', *Wochenschrift fur klassische Philologie* 4, 1887, n. 5–6, lines 152–156, 182–187.
Evans J.A.S., 'Note on Miltiades' capture of Lemnos', *CPh* 58 (1963), 168–170.
Evans J.A.S., 'Cavalry about the time of the Persian Wars: a speculative study', *CJ* 82 (1987), 97–106.
Evans J.A.S., 'Herodotus and the Battle of Marathon', *Historia* 42 (1993), 279–307.
Everson T., *Warfare in Ancient Greece, Arms and Armour from the Heroes of Homer to Alexander the Great*, Stroud, Sutton, 2004.
Farrokh K., *Shadows in the Desert: Ancient Persia at War*, Osprey, Oxford, 2007.
Ferrario S.B., *Historical Agency and the 'Great Man' in Classical Greece*, Cambridge University Press, Cambridge, 2014.
Figueira T.J., 'Xanthippos and the Prutaneis of the Naukraroi', *Historia* 35 (1986), 257–279.
Figueira T.J., *Excursion in Epichoric History: Aiginetan Essays*, Rowman&Littlefield Publishers, Maryland, 1993.
Figueira T.J., 'Khalkis and Marathon', *Μαραθών, Η Μάχη και ο Αρχαίος Δήμος*, Μπουραζέλης Κ. / Μεϊδάνη Κ. (ed), Ινστιτούτο του Βιβλίου-Α. Καρδαμίτσα, Αθήνα, 2010, 185–202.
Finlay G., 'On the Battle of Marathon', *Transactions of the Royal Society of Literature of the United Kingdom* 3 (1839), 363–395.
Finley M.I., *The Ancient Economy*, University of California, Berkeley, 1999.
Flaceliere R., *Daily Life in Greece at the Time of Pericles*, Macmillan, New York, 1965.
Fornara C.W., 'The Hoplite achievement at Psyttaleia', *JHS* 86 (1966), 51–54.

Fornara C.W., *The Athenian Board of Generals from 501 to 404*, Historia Einzelschrift 16, 1971.

Forrest G., 'Greece: The History of the Archaic Period', *The Oxford History of the Classical World*, Boardman/Griffin/Murray (ed), Oxford University Press, Oxford, 1993, 19–49.

Forsdyke E.J.,'Some arrow-heads from the Battlefield of Marathon', *Proceedings of the Society Antiquarian*, 32 (1919–1920), 146–157.

Forsdyke S., *Exile, Ostracism, and Democracy: The Politics of Expulsion in Ancient Greece*, Princeton University Press, New Jersey/Oxford, 2005.

Fotiou: Φωτίου Κ., *Η Τετράπολη του Μαραθώνα: συμβολή στην αναθεώρηση των δήμων και της μάχης*, Πανεπιστήμιο Αθηνών (Διδακτορική διατριβή), Αθήνα, 1982.

Fraser P.M./Matthews E. (ed), *The British Academy, A Lexicon of Greek Personal Names*, Vol II, *Attica*, Clarendon Press, Oxford, 1994.

Frazer F.G., *Pausanias's Description of Greece, Translated with a commentary*, Vol II, Macmillan, London, 1898.

Frost F.J., 'Themistocles' place in Athenian politics', *CSCA* 1 (1968), 105–125.

Gaebel R.E., *Cavalry Operations in the Ancient Greek World*, University of Oklahoma Press, Oklahoma 2002.

Galanakis G., 'Re-thinking Marathon: two memorabilia from the battle of Marathon at the Pitt-Rivers' http://web.prm.ox.ac.uk/rpr/index.php/object-biography-index/1-prmcollection/648-marathon-spearheads/

Gell W., *The Itinerary of Greece, Containing One Hundred Routes in Attica, Boeotia, Locris and Thessaly*, London, 1819.

Giannopoulos: Γιαννόπουλος Ν., 'Μαραθώνας (490 π.Χ.) Η Αθήνα συντρίβει την Περσική Υπεροψία', Στρατιωτική Ιστορία, Σειρά Μεγάλες Μάχες, 21 *Μαραθώνας (490 π.Χ.). Η Αθήνα συντρίβει την Περσική Υπεροψία*, Μπελέζος Δ./Γιαννόπουλος Ν./Κωτούλας Ι., Αθήνα, 2006, 20–55.

Glenn J., 'The Dream of Hippias', *Rivista di Studi Classici* 20 (1972), 5–7.

Goette H.R./Weber T.M., *Marathon, Siedlungskammer und Schlachtfeld-Sommerfrische und Olympische Wettkampftatte*, Verlag Philipp von Zabern, Mainz am Rhein, 2004.

Gomme A.W., *The Population of Ancient Athens in the Fifth and Fourth Centuries B.C.*, (Glasgow University Publications; XXVIII), Blackwell, Oxford, 1933.

Gomme A.W., 'Herodotus and Marathon', *Phoenix* 6 (1952), 77–83.

Graham A., 'Abdera and Teos', *JHS* 122 (1992), 44–73.

Grahay R., *La litterature oraculaire chez Herodote*, Paris. 1956.

Green P., *The Greco-Persian Wars*, University of California Press, Berkeley/Los Angeles California, 1996.

Greenhalgh F.A.L, *Early Greek Warfare*, Cambridge, 1973.

Grosso F., 'Gli Eretriesi deportati in Persia', *Riv. Ist.Cl.Torino* 36 (1958), 350–375.

Grundy G.B., *The Great Persian War and its Preliminaries; A Study of the Evidence, Literary and Topographical*, London, 1901.

Hagg T., 'Metiochus at Polycrates' Court', *Eranos* 83 (1985), 92–102.

Hall J.M., *Hellenicity: Between Ethnicity and Culture*, University of Oxford Press, 2002.

Hamel D., *Athenian Generals: Military authority in the Classical Period*, Mnemosyne, Bibliotheca Classica Batava: Supplementa 182, Brill, New York, 1998.

Hammond N.G.L., 'The Philaids and the Chersonese', *CQ* 6 (1956), 113–129.

Hammond N.G.L., *A History of Greece to 322 BC*, 2nd edition., Oxford, 1967.

Hammond N.G.L., 'The Campaign and the Battle of Marathon', *JHS* 88 (1968), 13–57.

Hammond N.G.L., *Studies in Greek History*, Oxford, 1973.

Hammond N.G.L., 'The Expedition of Datis and Artaphernes', *The Cambridge Ancient History, IV, Persia, Greece and the Western Mediterranean c. 525–479 B.C.* , Boardman J./Hammond N.G.L./Lewis, D.M./Ostwald M (ed), Cambridge University Press, Cambridge, 1988, 491–517.

Hammond, N.G.L., *The Macedonian State: The Origins, Institutions, and History*, Oxford, 1992.

Hansen M.H., *The Athenian Democracy in the Age of Demosthenes: Structure, Principles, and Ideology*, tr. Crook J.A., Blackwell, Oxford/Cambridge Mass., 1991.

Hanson V.D., *The Western way of War, Infantry Battle in Classical Greece*, Oxford University Press, Oxford, 1989.

Hanson V.D., *The Other Greeks: The Family Farm and the Agrarian Roots of Western Civilization*, 2nd edition, University of California Press, Berkeley/Los Angeles, 1995.

Hanson V.D., *Warfare and Agriculture in Classical Greece*, University of California Press, Berkeley/Los Angeles, California, 1998.

Hanson V.D., *The Wars of the Ancient Greeks*, Smithsonian History of Warfare, London, 2004.

Hanson V.D., 'The modern historiography of ancient warfare', *The Cambridge History of Greek and Roman Warfare*, Vol. I, *Greece, the Hellenistic World and the rise of Rome*, Sabin P., Van Wees H., Whitby M. (ed.), Cambridge University Press, Cambridge, 2007, 3–21.

Hanson V.D., *Hoplites War and Violence in Ancient Greece*, ed. van Wees Hans, Duckworth and the Classical Press of Wales, 2000, 'Hoplite Battle as Ancient Greek Warfare. When, Where, and Why', 201–232.

Harding P., *The Story of Athens, the fragments of the local chronicles of Attika*, Routledge, Oxford, 2008.

Harrison E.B., 'The South Frieze of the Nike Temple and the Marathon Painting in the Painted Stoa', *AJA* 76 (1972), 353–378.

Hart J., *Herodotus and Greek History*, Croom Helm, London, 1982.

Hauvette-Besnault A., *Herodote*, Paris, 1894.

Hignett C., *History of the Athenian Constitution to the End of the Fifth Century B.C.*, Oxford University Press, Oxford, 1952.

Hignett C., *Xerxes' Invasion of Greece*, Clarendon Press, Oxford, 1963.

History Channel (television network), Arts and Entertainment Network, and New Video Group, *Decisive Battles: Marathon*, New York: A and E Television Networks, 2004.

History of the Greek Nation: Ιστορία του Ελληνικού Έθνους, Αρχαϊκός Ελληνισμός, Συλλογικό έργο, Εκδοτική Αθηνών, Αθήναι, 1971.

Holoka J.P., 'Marathon and the Myth of the Same-Day March', *GRBS* 38 (1997), 329–253.

Holt P., 'Sex, Tyranny, and Hippias' Incest Dream' (Herodotos 6.107), *GRBS* 39 (1998), 221–241.

Hopper R.J., ' 'Plain', 'Shore', and 'Hill' in Early Athens', *BSA* 56 (1961), 189–219.

Hornblower S., 'Warfare in Ancient Literature, the paradox of war', *The Cambrige History of Greek and Roman Warfare*, Vol I, *Greece, the Hellenistic World and the Rise of Rome*, Sabin P. / Van Wees H. / Whitby M. (ed), Cambridge University Press, Cambridge, 2007, 22–53.

How W.W. / Wells J., *A Commentary on Herodotus, With Introduction and Appendixes*, Vol 2, Clarendon Press, Oxford, 1912.

How W.W., 'Cornelius Nepos on Marathon and Paros', *JHS* 39 (1919), 49–61.

How W.W., 'Arms, Tactics and Strategy in the Persian War', *JHS* 43 (1923), 117–132.

Humphreys S.C., *The Strangeness of Gods. Historical perspectives on the interpretation of Athenian religion*, Oxford University Press, Oxford, 2004.

Hunt P., *Slaves, Warfare, and Ideology in Greek Historians*, Cambridge University Press, Cambridge, 1998.

Hunt P., 'Arming Slaves and Helots in Classical Greece', *Arming Slaves: From Classical Times to the Modern Age*, Brown C.L. / Morgan P.D. (ed), University of Yale, 2006, 14–39.

Hunt P., 'Military Forces', *The Cambridge History of Greek and Roman Warfare*, Vol I: *Greece, the Hellenistic World and the Rise of Rome*, Sabin P. / Van Wees H. / Whitby M. (ed), Cambridge University Press, Cambridge, 2007, 108–146.

Hussey J.M. (ed) *The Journals and Letters of George Finlay*, Vol II, *Finlay-Leake and other Correspondence*, Porphyrogenitus, London, 1995.

Immerwahr H.R., *Form and Thought in Herodotus*, Philological Monographs, APA 23, Cleveland, Ohio, 1966.

Ivantchik A., 'Scythian' Archers on Archaic Attic Vases: Problems of Interpretation', *Ancient civilizations from Scythia to Siberia* 12 (2006), 197–271.

Jacoby F. (edy), *Die Fragmente der Griechisschen Historiker*, Brill, Leiden, 1923–1958.

Jacoby F., 'Patrios Nomos: state burial in Athens and the public cemetery in the Keramikos', *JHS* 64 (1944), 37–66.

Jacoby F., 'Some Athenian Epigrams from the Persian Wars', *Hesperia* 14 (1945), 157–211.

Jameson M.H., 'Seniority in the Strategia', *TAPA* 86 (1955), 63–87.

Jameson M.H., 'Sacrifice before Battle', *Hoplites: The Classical Greek Battle Experience*, V.D. Hanson (ed.), Routledge, London, 1991, 197–227.

Jeffery L.H., 'The Campaign between Athens and Aegina in the Years before Salamis', *AJPh* 83 (1962), 44–54.

Jeffery L.H., 'The Battle of Oinoe in the Stoa Poikile', *BSA* 60 (1965), 41–57.

Jung M., *Marathon und Plataia: Zwei Perserschlachten als 'Lieux de Memoire' im Antiken Griechenland*, Vandenhoeck/Ruprecht, Gottingen, 2006.

Jung M., 'Spartans at Marathon? On the origin and function of an Athenian legend', *Marathon. The Day After, Symposium Proceedings, Delphi 2–4 July 2010*, Buraselis K./Koulakiotis E. (ed), European Cultural Centre of Delphi, 2013, 15–37.

Kagan D., 'The origin and purpose of Ostrakism', *Hesperia* 30 (1961), 393–401.

Katsimitros: Κατσιμήτρος Χ., *Η Ήπειρος Προμαχούσα. Η Δράσις της VIII Μεραρχίας κατά τον Πόλεμον 1940–41*, Ηπειρωτική Εταιρεία Αθηνών, Βιβλιοθήκη Ηπειρωτικής Εταιρείας 61, Αθήνα 2007.

Keesling C.M., 'The Callimachus monument on the Athenian Acropolis (CEG 256) and the Athenian commemoration of the Persian Wars', *Archaic and Classical Greek Epigram*, Baumbach M./Petrovic A./Petrovic I. (ed), Cambridge University Press, Cambridge, 2010, 100–130.

Kluwe D., 'Das Marathonweihgeschenk in Delphi-eine Staatsweihung oder Privatweihung des Kimon' *WZjena* 14 (1965), 21–27.

Knoepfler D., 'La territoire d' Eretrie et l' organization politique de la cite (demoi, choroi, phylai)', *The Polis in an Urban Centre and as a Political Community, Symposium Aug., 29–31 1996*, Hansen M.H. (ed), Acts of the Copenhagen Polis Centre, Vol 4, Copenhagen, 1999, 352–449.

Kontorlis K.P., *The Battle of Marathon*, Athens, 1968.

Koulakiotis E., 'The memory of Marathon and Miltiades in late republican Rome', *Marathon. The Day After, Symposium Proceedings, Delphi 2–4 July 2010*, Buraselis K./Koulakiotis E. (ed), European Cultural Centre of Delphi, 2013, 151–166.

Koumanoudis: Κουμανούδης Σ., 'Μαραθώνι', Ανάλεκτα 11 (1978), 232–244.

Kouragios: Κουράγιος Γ., *Δεσποτικό. Το Ιερό του Απόλλωνα*, Επιμέλεια Κειμένων Νταϊφά Κ., Ίδρυμα Παύλου και Αλεξάνδρας Κανελλοπούλου, Αθήνα, 2012.

Kouragios Y. / Daifa K. / Ohnesorg A. / Papagianni K., 'The Sanctuary of Despotiko in the Cyclades. Excavations 2001–2012', *AA* 2012, 93–174.

Krentz P., 'Casualites in Hoplite Battles', *GRBS* 26 (1985), 13–20.

Krentz P., 'Deception in Archaic and Classical Greek Warfare', *War and Violence in Ancient Greece*, Van Wees H.(ed), Duckworth and the Classical Press of Wales, 2000, 167–200.

Krentz 2007a: Krentz P., 'War', *The Cambrige History of Greek and Roman Warfare*, Vol I, *Greece, the Hellenistic World and the Rise of Rome*, Sabin P. / Van Wees H. / Whitby M. (ed), Cambridge Univeristy Press, Cambridge, 2007, 147–185.

Krentz 2007b: Krentz P., 'The Oath of Marathon, not Plataia?', *Hesperia* 76 (2007), 731–742.

Krentz 2010a: Krentz P., *The Battle of Marathon*, The Yale Library of Military History, New Haven/London, 2010.

Krentz 2010b: Krentz P., 'A cup by Douris and the Battle of Marathon', *New Perspectives on Ancient Warfare, History of Warfare*, Vol. 59, Fagan G. / Trundle M. (ed.) Brill, Leiden/Boston, 2010, 183–204.

Kromayer J., *Drei Schlachten aus dem Griechisch-Romischen Altertum*, Abhandlungen der Philologische-Historischen Klasse der Sachsischen Akademie der Wissenschaften 34, 1921.

Kromayer J., *Antike Schlachtfelder, Bausteine zu Einer Antiken Kriegsgeschichte*, Vol IV, Berlin, 1924.

Labarbe J., *Loi Navale: La Loi navale de Themistocle*, Paris, 1957.

Lacey J., *The First Clash The Miraculous Greek Victory at Marathon – And Its Impact on Western Civilization*, Bantam Books, New York, 2011.

Lalonde G.V., 'IG I³ 1055B and the boundary of Melite and Kollytos', *Hesperia* 75 (2006), 83–119.

Lambert S.D., 'The Sacrificial Calendar of the Marathonian Tetrapolis: A Revised Text', *ZPE* 130 (2000), 43–70.

Lambert S.D., *Draft Paper on Sacrificial Calendar of Marathonian Tetrapolis for Proceedings of conference on 'Feasting and Polis Institutions'* , Utrecht 2014 [with cover note]) http://www.academia.edu/7191220/Draft_Paper_on_Sacrificial_Calendar_ of_Marathonian_Tetrapolis_for_Proceedings_of_conference_on_Feasting_and_ Polis_Institutions_Utrecht_2014_with_cover_note_

Lampros: Λάμπρος Σ., *Ιστορία της Ελλάδος μετ' εικόνων από των αρχαιοτάτων χρόνων μέχρι της βασιλείας του Όθωνος*, Α΄, Κάρολος Μπεκ, Αθήναι, 1886.

Lang M. L., *Ostraka, The Athenian Agora XXV*, ASCSA, Princeton, New Jersey, 1990.

Langdon M.K., *A Sanctuary of Zeus on Mount Hymettus*, Hesperia, Suppl. XVI, ASCSA, Princeton, New Jersey, 1976.

Langdon M.K., 'Some Attic Walls', *Studies in Attic Epigraphy, History and Topography, Presented to Eugene Vanderpool*, Hesperia, Suppl. XIX, ASCSA, Princeton, New Jersey, 1982, 95–97.

Lazenby J., *The Defence of Greece (490–479 B.C.)*, Aris and Phillips, Warminster, 1993.

Leake W.M., 'The Demi of Attica', *Transactions of the Royal Society of Literature*, Vol I, 173, London, 1829.

Leake W.M., *Travels in Northern Greece*, Vol II, London, 1835.

Leake W.M., *The Topography of Athens and the Demi*, Vol 2, *The Demi of Attica*, 2nd edition, London, 1841.

Lendon J.E., *Soldiers and Ghosts. A History of Battle in Classical Antiquity*, Yale University Press, New Haven/London, 2005.

Lewis D.M., 'Cleisthenes and Attica', *Historia* 12 (1963), 22–40.

Lewis D.M., 'Datis the Mede', *JHS* 100 (1980), 194–195.

Lewis D.M., 'Cleisthenes and Attica', *Athenian Democracy*, Rhodes P.J. (ed) (Edinburgh Readings on the Ancient World), Oxford University Press, Oxford, 2004, 287–309.

Liddell H.G. / Scott R. / Jones H.S. / McKenzie R., *A Greek-English Lexicon*, Oxford New Supplement, Oxford 1996.

Lolling N.G., 'Zur Topographie von Marathon', *AthMitt* 1 (1876), 67–94.

Loraux, J.N., *The Invention of Athens: The Funeral Oration and the Classical City*, translated by A. Sheridan, Cambridge, Massachusetts/London, 1986.

Macan R.W., *Herodotus. The Fourth, Fifth, and Sixth Books*, Vol. 1–2, Macmillan, London and New York, 1895.

Maier F.G. / Karageorgis V., *Paphos*, Nikosia, 1984.

Manfredi M., 'La cleruchia ateniese in Calcide, un problema storico e uno questione di critica testuale (Hdi. v, 77)', *SCO* 17 (1968), 199–212.

Manville P.B., *The Origins of Citizenship in Ancient Athens*, Princeton University Press, New Jersey, 1997.

Margoni: Μαργώνη Σ., *Έρευνα των Περιβαλλοντικών Διεργασιών Εξέλιξης των Υγροτόπων και της Πεδιάδας του Μαραθώνα κατά το Ολόκαινο με τη χρήση Γεωγραφικών Συστημάτων Πληροφοριών (G.I.S.)*, Διδακτορική Διατριβή που εκπονήθηκε στο Αριστοτέλειο Πανεπιστήμιο, Τμήμα Γεωλογίας, Τομέας Φυσικής και Περιβαλλοντικής Γεωγραφίας, Θεσσαλονίκη, 2006.

Margoni et al: Μαργώνη-Σ. Καπετάνιος Α., 'Διασταυρούμενες στρωματογραφίες: παλαιοπεριβάλλον και αρχαία πολιτισμικά κατάλοιπα στην πεδιάδα του Μαραθώνα' (In preparation) *Athens and Attica in Prehistory. Proceedings of the International Conference held at Athens, 27–31 May 2015* (ed. Papadimitriou N., Wright J.C., Sgouritsa N. & Fachard S.).

Marinatos S., *Thermopylae, An Historical and Archaeological Guide*, Athens, 1951.

Marinatos, 1972: Μαρινάτος Σ., 'Ανασκαφαί Μαραθώνος', ΠΑΕ (1972), 5–7.

Markle M.M., 'Jury Pay and Assembly Pay at Athens', *Athenian Democracy*, P.J. Rhodes (ed), Oxford University Press, Oxford, 2004, 95–131.

Matheson S. B., 'A farewell with Arms. Departing Warriors on Athenian Vases', *Periklean Athens and its Legacy*, Barringer J.M. / Hurwit J.M. (ed), University of Texas Press, Austin, 2005, 23–35.

Matthaiou, 1988: Ματθαίου Α., 'Νέος λίθος του μνημείου με τα επιγράμματα για τους Περσικούς πολέμους', *HOROS* 6 (1988), 118–122

Matthaiou A., 'Ἀθηναίοισι τεταγμένοισι εν τεμένεϊ Ἡρακλέος (Hdt. 6. 108.1)', *Herodotus and his World. Essays from a Conference in Memory of George Forrest*, Derow P./Parker R. (ed), Oxford University Press, Oxford/New York, 2003, 190–202.

Matthew C.A., "When Push Comes to Shove: What was the Othismos of Hoplite Combat?", Historia 58 (2009), 395–415.

Maurice F., 'The Campaign of Marathon', *JHS* 52 (1932), 13–24.

Mazarakis-Ainian A., 'A necropolis of the Geometric period at Marathon: the context', 703–716, *The Dark Ages Revisited: Acts of an International Symposium in Memory of*

William D.E. Coulson, University of Thessaly, 14–17 June 2007, Mazarakis-Ainian A. (ed), Edition of the University of Thessaly, Volos, 2011.

McCredie J.R., *Fortified Military Camps in Attica*, Hesperia Suppl. XI, ASCSA, Princeton, New Jersey, 1966.

McGregor M.F., 'The Pro-Persian Party at Athens from 510 to 480 B.C.', *Athenian Studies Presented to William Scott Ferguson*, Harvard University Press, Cambridge Massachutes, 1940, 71–95.

McLeod W., 'The Bowshot and Marathon', *JHS* 90 (1970), 197–198.

Mcneill R.L.B. l, 'Notes on the subject of the Ilissos temple friezes', *Periklean Athens and its Legacy*, Barringer J.M. / Hurwit J.M. (ed), University of Texas Press, Austin, 2005, 103–110.

McQueen E.I., *Herodotus, Book VI*, Bristol Classical Press (Duckworth), London, 2000.

Meidani K., 'Remarks on Miltiades' activities before and after Marathon', *Μαραθών, Η Μάχη και ο Αρχαίος Δήμος*, Μπουραζέλης Κ./Μεϊδάνη Κ. (ed), Ινστιτούτο του Βιβλίου-Α. Καρδαμίτσα, Αθήνα, 2010, 167–183.

Meiggs R./Lewis D.M., *A Selection of Greek Historical Inscriptions To the End of the Fifth Century BC*, Oxford University Press, Oxford, 1968 (updated edition, 1988).

Meissner B., 'War as a learning-process: the Persian Wars and the transformation of fifth century Greek warfare', *Μαραθών, Η Μάχη και ο Αρχαίος Δήμος, Μπουραζέλης Κ./Μεϊδάνη Κ.* (ed), Ινστιτούτο του Βιβλίου-Α. Καρδαμίτσα, Αθήνα, 2010, 275–296.

Meyer E., *Geschichte des Altertums*, III, Stuttgart, 1901.

Mikroyannakis: Μικρογιαννάκης Ε., 'Θεμιστοκλής και Δελφοί: Δύο γνώμονες', *Επιστημονική Επετηρίδα της Φιλοσοφικής Σχολής του Πανεπιστημίου Αθηνών*, Τομ. ΛΒ' (1998–2000), Αθήνα, 2000, 9–22.

Milchhöfer A., 'Marathon', E. Curtius/J.A. Kaupert (ed), *Karten von Attika: auf Verlassung des kaiserlich-Deutschen Archaologischen Institute*, Heft III, Berlin, 1889.

Milford W., *The History of Greece*, Vol II, 3rd edition, London, 1795.

Mommsen A., 'Zehn Eponymen: Die zehn Eponymen und die Reihenfolge der nach ihnen genannten Phylen Athens', *Philologus* 47 (1889), 449–489.

Moreno A., *Feeding the Democracy: the Athenian Grain Supply in the Fifth and the Fourth Centuries BC*, Oxford Classical Monographs, Oxford University Press, Oxford, 2007.

Morris S.P., *Daidalos and the Origins of Greek Art*, Princeton University Press, Princeton 1992.

Mosse C., 'Classes censitaires et participation politique', *Opus* VI-VIII (1987–1989), 165–174.

Mosse C., *Politique et Societe en Grece ancienne*, 1999.

Muller D., *Topographischer Bildkommentar zu den Historien Herodots: I Griechenland*, Tubingen, 1987.

Munro J.A., 'Some Observations on the Persian Wars', *JHS* 19 (1899), 185–197.

Munro J.A.R., 'Marathon', 229–267, *Cambridge Ancient History*, Vol IV, Bury J.B. / Cook S.A. / Adcock F.E. (ed), Cambridge University Press, Cambridge, 1926.

Nezis: Νέζης Ν., *Τα Βουνά της Αττικής*, Αθήνα, 1983.

Notopoulos J., 'The Slaves at the Battle of Marathon', *AJPh* 62 (1941), 352–354.

Ober J., 'Edward Clarke's Ancient Road to Marathon', *Hesperia* 5 (1982), 453–458.

Ober J., *Fortress Attica: Defence of the Athenian Land Frontier, 404–323 B.C.*, Brill, Leiden, 1985.

Ober J., 'Pottery and miscellaneous artifacts from fortified sites in Northern and Western Attica', *Hesperia* 56 (1987), 197–227.

Ober J., *The Athenian Revolution: Essays on Ancient Greek Democracy and Political Theory*, Princeton University Press, Princeton, New Jersey, 1996.

Ober J., 'I besieged that man: Democracy's Revolutionary Start', *Origins of Democracy in Ancient Greece*, Raaflaub K.A. / Ober J. / Wallace R.W. (ed), University of California Press, Berkeley/Los Angeles, California, 2007, 83–104.

Oberleitner W., *Das Heroon von Trysa : ein lykisches Fürstengrab des 4. Jahrhunderts v. Chr*, Sonderhefte der Antiken Welt; Zaberns Bildbände zue Archäologie, Issue 18, Zabern, Mainz, 1996.

Oikonomakou: Οικονομάκου Μ., 'Λαυρεωτική και Μαραθώνας: Νέες έρευνες', *Από τα Μεσόγεια στον Αργοσαρωνικό, Β΄ Εφορεία Προϊστορικών και Κλασικών Αρχαιοτήτων, Το έργο μιας δεκαετίας,* 1994–2003, *Πρακτικά Συνεδρίου, Αθήνα, 18–20 Δεκεμβρίου 2003, Βασιλοπούλου Β.* / *Κατσαρού-Τζεβελέκη Α.* (De.), Δήμος Μαρκοπούλου Μεσογαίας, 2009, 274–285.

Oliver J. H., 'Selected Greek Inscriptions', *Hesperia* 2 (1933), 480–494.

Onasoglou: Ωνάσογλου Α., 'Τα Ιερά της Τετραπόλεως του Μαραθώνα', Αρχαιολογία 39 (1991), 62–66.

Osbourne R., *Greece in the Making 1200–479 BC*, Routledge, London / New York, 1996.

Oswald, M., 'The Reform of the Athenian State by Cleisthenes', *The Cambridge Ancient History, IV, Persia, Greece and the Western Mediterranean c. 525–479 B.C.*, Cambridge University Press, 1988, 303–346.

Page D.H., *Epigrammata Graeca*, Clarendon, Oxford University Press, Oxford, 1975.

Page D.H (ed), *Further Greek Epigrams*, Cambridge University Press, Cambridge, 1981.

Palagia O., 'Interpretations of two Athenian friezes. The Temple on the Ilissos and the Temple of Athena Nike', *Periklean Athens and its Legacy*, Barringer J.M. / Hurwit J.M. (ed), University of Texas Press, Austin, 2005, 177–192.

Parke H.W., *Festivals of the Athenians*, (Aspects of Greek and Roman Life), Thames & Hudson, London, 1977.

Parker V., 'The Dates of the Messenian Wars', *Chiron* 21 (1991), 27–47.

Parker V., *Untersuchungen zum lelantischen Krieg und verwandten Problemen der fruhgriechischen Geschichte*, Historia Einzelschr. 109, Stuttgart, 1997.

Parthasarathy V.A., κ.α., *Chemistry of Spices*, CAB International, 2008.

Pavlopoulos K. / Karkanas P. / Triantaphyllou M. / Karymbalis E. / Tsourou T. / Palyvos N., 'Paleoenvironmental Evolution of the Coastal Plain of Marathon, Greece, during the Late Holocene: Deposition, Environment, Climate, and Sea Level Changes', *Journal of Coastal Research* 22 (2006), 424–438.

Petrakos, 1991: Πετράκος Β.Χ., *Ραμνούς*, Υπουργείο Πολιτισμού, Ταμείο Αρχαιολογικών Πόρων και Απαλλοτριώσεων, Αθήνα, 1991.

Petrakos, 1995: Πετράκος Β.Χ., *Ο Μαραθών. Αρχαιολογικός Οδηγός, Βιβλιοθήκη της εν Αθήναις Αρχαιολογικής Εταιρείας, αρ. 146, Αρχαίοι Τόποι και Μουσεία της Ελλάδος*, εκδόσεις της εν Αθήναις Αρχαιολογικής Εταιρείας, Αθήνα, 1995.

Pinney G.F., 'Achilles Lord of Scythia', *Ancient Greek Art and Iconography* (Wisconsin Studies in Classics), Moon W.G. (ed), University of Wisconsin Press, Madison, 1983, 127–146.

Plassart A., 'Les Archers d' Athenes', *REG* 26 (1913), 151–213.

Powell A., 'Mendacity and Sparta's Use of the Visual', *Classical Sparta: The Techniques Behind her Success*, Oklahoma University Press, Norman, 1989, 173–192.

Pownall F.A., *Lessons from the Past: The Moral Use of History in Fourth-Century Prose*, Ann Arbor, University of Michigan Press, 2004.

Pritchett W.K., 'New light on Plataiai', *AJA* 61, 1957, 9–28.

Pritchett W.K., *Marathon*, University of California Publications in Classical Archaeology 4. n. 2, Berkeley, 1960, 137–190.

Pritchett W.K., University of California Publications: *Classical Studies*, Vol. I: *Studies in Ancient Topography*, Berkeley, 1965.

Pritchett W.K., University of California Publications: *Classical Studies*, Vol. II: *Studies in Ancient Topography, Part II (Battlefields)* , Berkeley, 1969.

Pritchett W.K., *The Greek State at War*, Part I, University of California Press, Berkeley/ Los Angeles, California, 1971.

Pritchett W.K., *The Greek State at War*, Part II, University of California Press, Berkeley/ Los Angeles, California, 1974.

Pritchett W.K., *The Greek State at War*, Part III, University of California Press, Berkeley/Los Angeles, California, 1979.

Pritchett W.K., *Studies in Ancient Greek Topography IV, Passes*, University of California Publications, Classical Studies 28, Berkeley/Los Angeles, California, 1982.

Pritchett, 1985a: Pritchett W.K., *The Greek State at War*, Part IV, University of California Press, Berkeley/Los Angeles, California, 1985.

Pritchett, 1985b: Pritchett W.K., *Studies in Ancient Greek Topography V,* University of California Publications, Classical Studies 28, Berkeley/Los Angeles, California, 1985.

Pritchett W.K., *The Greek State at War*, Part V, University of California Press, Berkeley/ Los Angeles, California, 1991.

Pritchett W.K., *Pausanias Periegetes II, Αρχαία Ελλάς*, Monographs of Ancient Greek History and Archaeology Vol 7, J.C.Gieben, Amsterdam, 1999.

Psilobikos: Ψιλοβίκος Α., *Φυσικές και ανθρωπογενείς διεργασίες στην πεδιάδα του Μαραθώνα κατά το Ολόκαινο*, Θεσσαλονίκη, 2004.

Raaflaub K.A., ΄Einleitung und Bilanz: Kleisthenes, Ephialtes und die Begrundung der Demokratie΄, *Demokratia: Der Weg zur Demokratie bei den Griechen*, Kinzl K.H. (ed), Wege der Forschung Bd. 657, Darmstadt, 1995, 1–54.

Raaflaub K.A., *The Discovery of Freedom in Ancient Greece*, University of Chicago Press, Chicago, 2004.

Raaflaub K.A., ΄Herodotus, Marathon, and the Historian's choice΄, *Μαραθών, Η Μάχη και ο Αρχαίος Δήμος*, Μπουραζέλης Κ./Μεϊδάνη Κ. (ed), Ινστιτούτο του Βιβλίου-Α. Καρδαμίτσα, Αθήνα, 2010, 221–235.

Raubitschek A.E., ΄Two monuments erected after the victory of Marathon΄, *AJA* 44 (1940), 55–59.

Raubitschek A.E., ΄Das Datislied΄, *Charites Studien zur Alterumswissenschaft*, Schauenberg K. (ed), Bonn, 1957, 234–242.

Rausch M., ΄Miltiades, Athen und die "Rhamnusier auf Lemnos" (IG I3 522Bis)΄, *Klio* 81 (1999), 7–17.

Rawlings L., ΄Alternative Agonies – Hoplite Martial and Combat Experiences Beyond the Phalanx΄, *War and Violence in Ancient Greece*, Van Wees H. (ed), Duckworth and the Classical Press of Wales, 2000, 233–260.

Rhodes P.J., *A Commentary on the Aristotelian Athenaion Politeia*, Clarendon Press, Oxford, 1981.

Rhodes P.J., ΄Herodotean Chronology Revisited΄, *Herodotus and his World. Essays from a Conference in Memory of George Forrest*, Derow P. / Parker R. (ed), Oxford University Press, Oxford/New York, 2003, 58–72.

Ridley R.T.,΄The Hoplite as citizen: Athenian Military Institutions in their social context΄, *AntClass* 48 (1979), 508–548.

Robert J.-L., ΄Bulletin épigraphique΄, *REG* 80 (1967), 453–573.

Ross L., *Αναμνήσεις και Ανταποκρίσεις από την Ελλάδα*, μετάφραση Σπήλιου Α. Πρόλογος-Επιμέλεια Βουρνά Τ., Αφοί Τολίδη, Αθήνα, 1976 (Erinnerungen und Mittheilungen aus Griechenland, Berlin 1863).

Rutishauser B., *Athens and the Cyclades: Economic Strategies 540–314 BC*, Oxford University Press, Oxford, 2012.

Sargent R.L., 'The Use of Slaves by the Athenians in Warfare I: in Warfare by Land', *CPh* 22 (1927), 201–12.

Schachermeyr F., 'Marathon und die Persische Politik', *HZ* 172 (1952), 1–35.

Schefold K., *Die Bildnisse der antiken*, Dichter, Redner und Denker, Basel, 1997.

Scott L., *Historical Commentary on Herodotus, Book 6*, Brill, Mnemosyne Suppl. 268, Leiden/Boston, 2005.

Sealey 1976a: Sealey R., *A History of the Greek City States, ca 700–338 B.C.*, University of California Press, Berkeley, California, 1976.

Sealey 1976 b: Sealey R., 'The Pit and the Well: the Persian Heralds of 491 B.C.', *CJ* 72 (1976), 13–20.

Sears M.A., *Athens, Thrace, and the Shaping of Athenian Leadership*, Cambridge University Press, Cambridge, 2013.

Sekunda N., *Marathon 490 BC*, T*he First Persian Invasion of Greece*, Osprey Publishing Ltd, London, 2002.

Seni et al.: Σένη Α. / Καψιμάλης Β. / Παυλόπουλος Κ., 'Προσδιορισμός των πρόσφατων μεταβολών στην παράκτια πεδιάδα του Μαραθώνα Αττικής, με χρήση Συστημάτων Γεωγραφικών Πληροφοριών', Πρακτικά 7ου Πανελληνίου Γεωγραφικού Συνεδρίου, Vol 1, 2004. 478–485.

Sfikas: Σφήκας Ι.Α., *Θαλάσσιες Υδροδυναμικές Διεργασίες με χρήση μαθηματικών μεθόδων και Γεωλογικά Χαρακτηριστικά του Πυθμένα της Παράκτιας Ζώνης του Κόλπου του Μαραθώνα*, Διπλωματική Εργασία στο Διατμητικό Μεταπτυχιακό Πρόγραμμα Σπουδών 'Ναυτική και Θαλάσσια Τεχνολογία και Επιστήμη', Εθνικό Μετσόβιο Πολυτεχνείο, Σχολή Ναυπηγών Μηχανολόγων Μηχανικών, Ιούνιος, 2011.

Sfyroeras P., 'The Battle of Marathon: Poetry, Ideology, Politics', *Marathon. The Day After, Symposium Proceedings, Delphi 2–4 July 2010*, Buraselis K./Koulakiotis E. (ed), European Cultural Centre of Delphi, 2013, 75–94.

Shapiro H.A., 'The Marathonian Bull on the Athenian Akropolis', *AJA* 92 (1988), 373–382.

Shear T.L., 'The Persian destruction of Athens. Evidence from Agora deposits', *Hesperia* 62 (1993), 383–482.

Shimron B., *Politics and Beliefs in Herodotus*, Historia Einzelschriften. 58, Franz Steiner, Stuttgart, 1989.

Shrimpton G., 'The Persian Cavalry at Marathon', *Phoenix* 34 (1980), 20–37.

Snodgrass A.M., *Early Greek Armour from the End of the Bronze Age to 600 B.C.*, Edinburgh University Press, Edinburgh, 1964.

Snodgrass A.M., *Arms and Armour of the Greeks*, Cornell University Press, London, 1967.

Sotiriadis, 1927a: Sotiriadis G., 'The New Discoveries at Marathon', *The Classical Weekly*, Jan. 10, 1927, 83–84.

Sotiriadis, 1927b: Σωτηριάδης Γ., 'Η Τετράπολις του Μαραθώνος και το Ηράκλειον του Ηροδότου', *Επιστημονική Επετηρίδα της Φιλοσοφικής Σχολής του Πανεπιστημίου της Θεσσαλονίκης*, Έτος Α' (1927), 118–150.

Sotiriadis, 1932: Σωτηριάδης Γ., 'Ανασκαφαί Μαραθώνος', ΠΑΕ (1932), 28–43.

Sotiriadis, 1934: Σωτηριάδης Γ., 'Ανασκαφή Μαραθώνος', ΠΑΕ (1934), 29–38.

Sotiriadis, 1935: Σωτηριάδης Γ., 'Έρευναι και Ανασκαφαί εν Μαραθώνι', ΠΑΕ (1935), 84–158.

Spyropoulos: Σπυρόπουλος Γ., Οι Στήλες των Πεσόντων στη Μάχη του Μαραθώνα από την Έπαυλη του Ηρώδη Αττικού στην Εύα Κυνουρίας, Ινστιτούτο του Βιβλίου-Α. Καρδαμίτσα, Αθήνα, 2009.

Stais: Στάης Β.,'Ανασκαφαί τύμβων εν Αττική. Ο τύμβος των Μαραθωνομάχων', ΑΔ 6 (1890), 65–71, 123–132.

Stathakopoulos: Σταθακόπουλος Γ., 'Οι Δύο Κόσμοι: Η περσική αυτοκρατορία και οι ελληνικές πόλεις στις παραμονές της μάχης του Μαραθώνα', Η Μάχη του Μαραθώνα, Ιστορία και Θρύλος, Ίδρυμα της Βουλής των Ελλήνων για τον Κοινοβουλευτισμό και τη Δημοκρατία, Αθήνα, 2010, 11–45.

Steinhauer, 2009a: Σταϊνχάουερ Γ., Ο Μαραθών και το Αρχαιολογικό Μουσείο, Κοινωφελές Ίδρυμα Ιωάννη Σ. Λάτση/Τράπεζα EFG Eurobank Ergasias A.E., Αθήνα, 2009.

Steinhauer, 2009b: Σταϊνχάουερ Γ., 'Οδικό δίκτυο της Αττικής', Αττικής Οδοί, Αρχαίοι Δρόμοι της Αττικής, ed Μ. Κορρές, 34–73, Μέλισσα, Αθήνα, 2009.

Steinhauer, 2010a: Σταϊνχάουερ Γ., 'Η Μάχη', Η Μάχη του Μαραθώνα, Ιστορία και Θρύλος, Ίδρυμα της Βουλής των Ελλήνων για τον Κοινοβουλευτισμό και τη Δημοκρατία, Αθήνα, 2010, 50–72.

Steinhauer, 2010b: Σταϊνχάουερ Γ., 'Προβλήματα Διεξαγωγής της Μάχης του Μαραθώνα', 2.500 έτη από την ιστορική μάχη του Μαραθώνα, Πολεμικό Μουσείο, Γενικό Επιτελείο Στρατού, Διεύθυνση Ιστορίας Στρατού, Αθήνα, 2010, 8–13.

Stockton D., The Classical Athenian Democracy, Clarendon Press, Oxford, 1990.

Storey I.C., Eupolis, Poet of Old Comedy, Oxford University Press, Oxford, 2003.

Syntomoros: Συντομόρος Γ., Εισαγωγή, Μετάφραση, Σχόλια, Ηροδότου, Βιβλίο Στ΄-Ερατώ, Ζήτρος, Αρχαίοι Συγγραφείς 79, Θεσσαλονίκη, 2006.

Tadlock S.K., Poor in Life, Naked in Battle: Athenian Thetes as Psiloi in the Classical Age, MA Thesis, North Carolina State University, Raleigh North Carolina, 2012.

Tarn W., Hellenistic Military and Naval Developments, Cambridge University Press, Cambridge, 1930.

Themelis: Θέμελης Π., 'Μαραθών: Πρόσφατα Ευρήματα και η Μάχη', ΑΔ 29 (1974), Μέρος Α΄ Μελέται, 226–244.

Theocharaki: Θεοχαράκη Ε., ΑΔ 38 (1983), Χρονικά Β΄1, 61.

Toher M., 'On 'Thucydides' Blunder': 2.34.5', Hermes 127 (1999), 497–501.

Tountopoulos: Τουντόπουλος Β., 'Αποστολή στο Αγριελίκι', Speleo News, Τεύχος 6, Ιούνιος 2005: http://www.actiongr.com/speleonews/t06.htm

Traill J.S., The Political Organization of Attica, Hesperia Suppl. 14, ASCSA, Princeton, New Jersey, 1975.

Travlos J., Pictorial Dictionary of Ancient Athens, Praeger, New York, 1971.

Travlos J., Bildlexicon zur Topographie des antiken Attika, Tubingen, 1988.

Trevor-Hodge A., 'Marathon: The Persians' Voyage', TAPA 105 (1975), 155–177.

Tsirigoti-Drakotou: Τσιριγώτη Δρακωτού, 2010a: Τσιριγώτη-Δρακωτού Ι., 'Μαραθών: Η κατοίκηση της περιοχής κατά τους κλασικούς χρόνους', Η Μάχη και ο Αρχαίος Δήμος, Μπουραζέλης Κ./Μεϊδάνη Κ. (ed), Ινστιτούτο του Βιβλίου-Α. Καρδαμίτσα, Αθήνα, 2010, 51–62.

Tuplin 2010a: Tuplin C., 'Marathon. In search of a Persian dimension', Μαραθών, Η Μάχη και ο Αρχαίος Δήμος, Μπουραζέλης Κ./Μεϊδάνη Κ. (ed), Ινστιτούτο του Βιβλίου-Α. Καρδαμίτσα, Αθήνα, 2010, 251–274.

Tuplin, 2010b: Tuplin C., 'All the King's horse: In Search of Achaemenid Persian Cavalry', *New Perspectives on Ancient Warfare*, History of Warfare, Vol 59, Fagan G./ Trundle M. (ed), Brill, Leiden/Boston, 2010, 100–182.

Typaldos: Τυπάλδος Ι.Α., 'Η εν Μαραθώνι Μάχη', Παρνασσός, Τόμος Η' (1884) 207–224, 253–272 and 341–355.

Van der Veer J.A.G., 'The Battle of Marathon. A topographical survey', *Mnemosyne* 34 (1982), 290–321.

Van Wees H., 'The Myth of the Middle-Class Army: Military and Social Status in Ancient Athens', *War as a Cultural and Social Force; Essays on Warfare in Antiquity*, Bekker T. / Nielsen / Hannestad L. (ed), Det Kongelige Danske Videnskabernes Selskab, 2001, 45–71.

Van Wees H., 'War and Society', *The Cambridge History of Greek and Roman Warfare*, Vol I, *Greece, the Hellenistic World and the Rise of Rome*, Sabin P. / Van Wees H. / Whitby M. (ed), Cambridge Univeristy Press, Cambridge, 2007, 273–299.

Van Wees H., *Greek Warfare: Myths and Realities*, Duckworth, London, 2011.

Vanderpool E., 'An Archaic Inscribed Stele from Marathon', *Hesperia* 11 (1942), 329–337.

Vanderpool E., 'Ostraka from the Athenian Agora', *Hesperia* 8 (1949), 408–409.

Vanderpool, 1966a: Vanderpool E., 'The Deme of Marathon and the Herakleion', *AJA* 70 (1966), 319–323.

Vanderpool, 1966b: Vanderpool E., 'A monument of the battle of Marathon', *Hesperia* 35 (1966), 93–106.

Vanderpoool E., 'Regulations for the Herakleian Games at Marathon', *Studies Presented to Sterling Dow on his Eightieth Birthday*, GRBS Monograph 10, Durham, NC, 1984, 295–296.

Varouha-Chrystodoulopoulou: Βαρουχά-Χριστοδουλοπούλου Ε., ΑΕ (1953–1954), Μέρος ΙΙΙ, 321–349.

Vidal-Naquet P., 'La tradition de l'hoplite athenien', *Problemes de la guerre en Grece ancienne*, Vernant J.-P. (ed), Paris, 1968, 161–181.

Vidal-Naquet P., *The Black Hunter, Forms of Thought and Forms of Society in the Greek World*, tr. A. Szegedy-Maszak, London, 1986 (*Le chasseur noir, formes de pensée et formes de société dans le monde grec*, Paris, 1983).

Vigneron P., *Le chevel dans l' antiquite Greco-romaine*, Vol I, Nancy, 1968.

Vos M.F., *Scythian Archers in Archaic Attic Vase-Painting*, J.B.Wolters, Groningen, 1963.

Wade-Gery H.T., 'Miltiades', *JHS* 71 (1951), 212–221.

Wade-Gery H.T., *Essays in Greek History*, Oxford, 1958.

Walker K.G., *Archaic Eretria: A Political and Social History from the Earliest Times to 490 BC*, Routledge, London, 2004.

Wallace W.P., 'The Demes of Eretria', *Hesperia* 16 (1947), 115–146.

Wallace W.P., 'Kleomenes, Marathon, the Helots, and Arkadia', *JHS* 74 (1954), 32–35.

Wallinga H.T., *Ships and Sea Power before the Great Persian War: the Ancestry of the Ancient Trireme*, Leiden, 1993.

Waters K.H., *Herodotos, the Historian: His Problems, Methods, and Originality*, University of Oklahoma, 1985.

Weber T.M., 'Where was the Ancient Deme of Marathon', Μαραθών, Η Μάχη και ο Αρχαίος Δήμος, Μπουραζέλης Κ./Μεϊδάνη Κ. (ed), Ινστιτούτο του Βιβλίου-Α. Καρδαμίτσα, Αθήνα, 2010, 63–71.

Welwei K.W., *Unfreie im Antiken Kriegsdiens*, Vol. I, Wiesbaden, 1974.

Whatley N., 'On the Possibility of Reconstructing Marathon and Other Ancient Battles' *JHS* 84 (1964), 119–139.

Wheeler E.L., *Stratagem and the Vocabulary of Military Trickery*, Mnemosyne Suppl. 108, E.J. Brill, Leiden 1988.

Wheeler E.L., 'The General as Hoplite', *Hoplites: The Greek Battle Experience*, Hanson V.D. (ed), Routledge, London, 1991, 121–170.

Wheeler E.L., 'Land Battles', *The Cambridge History of Greek and Roman Warfare*, Vol I, *Greece, the Hellenistic World and the Rise of Rome*, Sabin P. / Van Wees H. / Whitby M. (ed), , Cambridge Univeristy Press, Cambridge, 2007, 186–224.

Whitehead D., 'The Archaic Athenian ΖΕΥΓΙΤΑΙ', *CQ* 31 (1981), 282–286.

Whitley J., "The Monuments That Stood before Marathon: Tomb Cult and Hero Cult in Archaic Attica", AJA 98 (1994), 213–230.

Wrede W., *Attika*, Deutsches Archäologisches Institut, Athen, Deutsches Archäologisches, 1934.

Wycherley R.E., 'The Painted Stoa', *Phoenix* 7 (1953), 20–35.

Wycherley R.E., *The Stones of Athens*, Princeton University Press, Princeton, New Jersey, 1978.

Zahrnt M., 'Marathon, the Century After', *Marathon. The Day After, Symposium Proceedings, Delphi 2–4 July 2010*, Buraselis K./Koulakiotis E. (ed), European Cultural Centre of Delphi, 2013, 139–150.

Journals

Arethusa, Baltimore (Md.): Johns Hopkins University Press.

Chiron – Mitteilungen der Kommission für Alte Geschichte und Epigraphik des Deutschen Archäologischen Instituts. München: Beck.

Eranos – Acta Philologica Suecana. Oslo: Scandinavian University Press.

Hermes – Zeitschrift für Klassische Philologie. Stuttgart: Steiner.

Hesperia – The Journal of the American School of Classical Studies at Athens. Princeton (N.J.): American School of Classical Studies at Athens.

Historia – Zeitschrift für Alte Geschichte. Stuttgart: Steiner.

Horos – Ὅρος: Ἕνα Ἀρχαιογνωστικό Περιοδικό. Ἀθήνα: Ἑλληνική Ἐπιγραφική Ἑταιρεία. Andromeda Books.

Kernos – Revue Internationale et Pluridisciplinaire de Religion Grecque Antique. Liège; Athènes: Centre international d'étude de la religion grecque antique.

Klio – Beiträge zur Alten Geschichte. Berlin: Akademie Verl.

Mnemosyne – Bibliotheca Classica Batava. Leiden: Brill.

Opus – Rivista Internazionale per la Storia Economica e Sociale dell'Antichità. Firenze: All'Insegna del Giglio.

Philologus – Zeitschrift für Antike Literatur und ihre Rezeption. Berlin: Akademie Verl.

Phoenix – Journal of the Classical Association of Canada. Toronto (Ont.): University of Toronto Press.

Wzjena, Wissenschaftliche Zeitschrift der Friedrich-Schiller-Univ. Jena, Gesellsch.- & sprachwiss. Reihe.

Notes

Chapter 1

1. The sole exception to this rule was the annihilation of the expeditionary force that Darius had sent to Karia in 495 during the Ionian Revolt. Herodotus, 5.121. However, this failure was reversed the following year, when a new Persian expeditionary force seized Karia.
2. The title borne by every monarch of the Persian Empire.
3. For Darius' expedition against Scythia, see Herodotus, 4.1–142. Darius decided against prolonging the operations in Scythia and ordered his army to withdraw while it was still in formation and good condition. That way he was able to save the greater part of his force. If Napoleon and Hitler had studied Herodotus' report on the expedition to Scythia, they might well have avoided the destruction of their own armies in that same area more than two millennia later.
4. Herodotus 5.1–2.
5. Aischylos, *The Persians*, lines 860–863.
6. According to Lazenby, 17, at the start of the fifth century the Persian Empire was the largest in the world.
7. Krentz, 2010a, 2.
8. On the number of Athenian citizens and the population of Attica generally in 490, we provide an analysis below.
9. Maurice, 14.
10. Hammond, 1968, 35.
11. Herodotus, 4.84, 7.38–39, 7.108.
12. In Herodotus' extended description (7. 61–95) of the units of Xerxes' army that invaded Greece in 480, there is an account of the variety of costume and equipment of the various peoples recruited by the Persians.
13. Herodotus, 6.48.2. On his description of the ships of the Persian fleet, see Evans, 1993, 298.
14. Herodotus, 6.95.2. According to Hodge, 163, the horse transports (*hippagoga*) of the Athenians during the Peloponnesian War were old triremes from which the two last rows of rowing benches had been removed to make room for the horses. That was not the case with Darius' horse transports in 490, as Herodotus' text makes clear that they were built that same year specifically to carry the Persian cavalry's horses and were not converted triremes. Dionysopoulos, 73–74, asserts that the Persian *hippagoga* of 490 were a specific type of trireme rowed by sixty men and capable of carrying thirty horses along with their riders and orderlies.
15. Herodotus, 6.95.2.
16. How and Wells, 103; Evans, 1993, 298; Scott, 341. According to the last-named, in Herodotus' day the term 'trireme' was used exclusively for warships. However, Dionysopoulos, 74–75, considers that the 600 triremes mentioned by Herodotus would have included troop and horse transports as well.

17. For example, he reports that the Persian fleet that blockaded Miletos in 494 during the Ionian Revolt and then took part in the sea battle of Lade also consisted of 600 vessels (Herodotus, 6.9.1).

18. Plato, *Menexenos*, 240a.

19. Cornelius Nepos, *Miltiades*, 4.

20. Evans, 1993, 293, wrongly states that Diodorus Siculus, 11.3.9, reported that the Persian fleet that sailed against Greece included 850 horse transports. Diodorus, however, stated that those ships he described were used by Xerxes in his invasion of Greece a decade later.

21. Hammond, 1968, 32–33.

22. Balcer, 130.

23. Wallinga, 137–138; Dionysopoulos, 70–71. Scott, 482, accepts that the whole Persian fleet totalled 600 vessels of various types.

24. Herodotus, 7.89–95.

25. Herodotus, 6.98.1.

26. According to Wallinga, 137–138, n. 22, all the Persian ships in 490 were of 'Levantine' provenance, as the whole fleet assembled at the Aleian Plain in the area of present-day Adana. The majority of ships and their crews indeed appear to have come from that region, especially Phoenicia. But Herodotus writes that the Persian fleet included Ionians and Aiolians. Thus some scholars consider that besides Phoenicians, the crews included Ionians, Aiolians and Hellespontians (Dionysopoulos, 71).

27. Wallinga, 137–138, n. 22, rules out the possibility that the Persians would have employed ships from the Greek cities of Asia Minor for use against Greece just a few years after snuffing out the Ionian Revolt. Yet Herodotus expressly mentions the presence of crews from Ionia and Aiolis who probably would have manned their own triremes. The Persians also recruited men from the Cyclades islands and Karystos, which they had just seized, to use in the fight against other Greeks.

28. Herodotus, 6.133.1.

29. Herodotus, 6.99.1.

30. Medes: Herodotus, 6.109; Persians and Saka: Herodotus, 6.113.1; Ionians and Aiolians: Herodotus, 6.98.1; Phoenicians: Herodotus, 6.118.1; Cycladians: Herodotus, 6.99.1 and 6.133.1 (Paros). Herodotus writes that when the Persians overran the Cyclades they forced the inhabitants to serve in their expeditionary force. He does not specify if they were inducted into the army or the navy, though the latter is more likely. Persian weapons such as helmets, arrowheads and bronze quiver fragments have been found at Olympia. To judge from an inscription found on one helmet reading: 'Athenians took this from the Medes', it was very likely an Athenian dedication to Zeus for the victory at Marathon, see Baitinger, 125–139; and Tuplin, 2010a, 252. These weapons may well have been Athenian booty from Marathon. The helmet with the inscription was of a type used by Assyrians in the Persian army. An indication that there were Assyrians in the Persian army comes from the 480s when the comic playwright Chionides penned a play called *The Assyrians* that according to Bowie, 2013, 70, could be connected with the battle of Marathon. Herodotus, 9.27.5, reports that the Athenians on the eve of the battle of Plataia in 479 told the army commander Pausanias that the Persian forces at Marathon had included forty-six nationalities. Aelius Aristides, *To Plato: In Defence of the Four*, 199, repeats the assertion. Yet that figure appears excessive, and probably refers to the total number of subject peoples of the Persian Empire in

490. Lykourgos, *Against Leocrates*, 109, is also wrong when he describes the Persian expeditionary force as having men 'from all Asia'.

31. Herodotus' reference on the battle of Plataia (9.68) indicates that the Persians constituted the most reliable and battle-worthy component of the army. Despite their defeat the Persians fought bravely and with great self-sacrifice, unlike the subject peoples whose soldiers retreated before clashing with the Greeks.

32. Herodotus, 7.64.2.

33. According to Scott, 390, four or five Scythian tribes were subject to Darius, living in a wide region between the Caspian Sea and the Pamir.

34. See Shrimpton, 29–30, for references to ancient literary sources.

35. Thucydides, 6.59.4; Diodorus, 11.6.3; Plutarch, *Theseus*, 35.5; Pausanias, 1.17.6. Diodorus asserts that at the start of the battle of Thermopylai in 480 Xerxes placed in his front line Medians who had lost fathers or brothers at Marathon, intimating that the Persian army at Marathon consisted mainly of Medes. We know, however, that the Classical Greeks identified the Medes with the Persians. The reason is that most Persian armies that first conquered the Ionian Greeks of Asia Minor were led by generals of Mede origin (see Herodotus, 1.156, 162, and Scott, 337). That gave rise to the common Greek misconception that Medes and Persians were two different names for the same people.

36. Datis the 'Mede': Herodotus, 6.94; Diodorus, 10.27.1. Some modern scholars accept that Datis was a Mede (see Evans, 1993, 281, and Krentz, 2010a, 90). According to Pseudo-Plutarch, *Ethics*, 305b, and Souda, 'Hippias', Datis was the satrap of Media when he took command of the 490 expedition. Strabo, 9.1.22, calls Datis a 'Persian'. On that basis some modern scholars speculate that Datis was not a Mede in origin but the Persian governor of Media (Sekunda, 15–16).

37. Sekunda, *op. cit.* Datis may have been in command of the Persian fleet at Lade in 494 (see Burn, 1962 (1984), 210–211, and Lewis, 1980, 195).

38. Munro, 1899, 185–186.

39. Herodotus, 6.95.1.

40. Sekunda, 20.

41. Ampelius, 15.9.

42. Pseudo-Simonides' epigram in honour of the Athenians who fought at Marathon that was supposedly in the Poikile Stoa at Athens said that the Athenians 'killed 90,000 Persians [Medes]'. Bergk, 449–450 and Hammond, 1968, 33, believe that the verb 'killed' (*ektinan*), was a spelling mistake, and that the original would have read 'confronted' (*eklinan*). The mistake would have intruded in some copying of the original, and emerged in subsequent copies. Souda, 'Hippias', repeats Pseudo-Simonides and raises the Persian number of killed or confronted to 200,000.

43. Nepos, *Miltiades*, 4.

44. Pseudo-Plutarch, *Ethics*, 305b; Pausanias, 4.25.5; Souda, 'Hippias'. Pausanias writes that 300,000 Persians 'were worsted' at Marathon – i.e., killed or otherwise eliminated. This is excessive, and the author probably meant they were simply defeated.

45. Plato, *Menexenos*, 240a; Lysias, *Epitaphios*, 21; Justin, 2.9. According to Behr, 434, n. 144, there was a scholion in a lost work by Aelius Aristides that puts the number of Persians at Marathon at 500,000, a number apparently copied from Plato and Lysias.

46. Aelius Aristides, *Panathenaic*, 101.

47. 'Sinking the city': Aelius Aristides, *op. cit.* Himerios, 6.200, probably copies Aelius Aristides in asserting that the high figures given for the Persian force were probably the result of the ancient authors' uncertainty about the actual figure. Isocrates in his *Panegyric,* 86, says the Persians numbered 'many tens of thousands', Pseudo-Demosthenes, *Against Neaira,* 94, that the expeditionary force was 'big', and Plutarch, *Ethics,* 862D, that the number of Persians killed at Marathon was so great as to be impossible to count.
48. Milford, 96.
49. Leake, 1829, 184–185.
50. Leake, 1829, 185: 30,000 men; 188: 26,000 infantry and 6,000 cavalry (totalling 32,000 combat-ready troops). On the total number of active and auxiliary Persians, see Leake, 1829, 187.
51. Finlay, 373, used the same method of calculation of the Persian force that Leake had: on the basis of the 600 triremes mentioned by Herodotus and their carrying capacity, which gives the figure of 24,000 Persian fighting men in 490.
52. See Hanson, 2007, 7–8.
53. Delbrück, 1887, 161.
54. Delbrück, 1920, (1990), 72.
55. Sotiriadis, 1932, 38, n. 1.
56. Herodotus, 6.117.1.
57. We will see that the overwhelming majority of the Persians who fell at Marathon were combat soldiers, as most of the auxiliaries and ship crews managed to escape.
58. Delbrück, 1920, (1990), 72.
59. Munro, 1926, 234, is probably the first scholar during the twentieth century who estimated the battle-ready Persian troops at Marathon at about 25,000 men. After him, only few authorities give a larger number than 30,000; the authors of the *History of the Greek Nation, Vol II,* 1971, 301, estimate 44.000–55,000 front line Persian troops at Marathon;Van der Veer, 309, 40,000–42,000; Dionysopoulos, 206, 40,000 (38,000 infantry and 2,000 cavalry); Kontorlis, 10, 30,000 (25,000 infantry and 5,000 cavalry).
60. Hammond, 1968, 32, opted for a figure of 30,000. On p. 33, he estimates the total number in the Persian force at more than 80,000.
61. Berthold, 92, n. 53.
62. Scott, 611.
63. Hignett, 1963, 71, reaches this conclusion on the basis that the 6,400 Persian dead in the battle were mainly in the central formations which were almost annihilated by the Greeks. Thus the Persians in the centre amounted to one-third of their combat force of some 20,000 men. Sealey, 1976a, 188, comes to the same conclusion.
64. Lazenby, 46. The same number of Persian combat soldiers was earlier suggested by Maurice, 18.
65. According to Herodotus, 7.184.2, in 480 every trireme in Xerxes' fleet carried thirty combat soldiers. However, the vast bulk of Xerxes' force marched to Greece overland. Therefore, the numbers on board bear no relation to the situation in 490, when the Persians used every available space on their ships to ferry the expeditionary force over the sea. Herodotus, 6.15.1, reports that every trireme from Chios that took part in the 494 battle of Lade carried forty soldiers; the assumption is that a similar arrangement applied in 480 (see Lazenby, 46). A century and a half before Lazenby, Finlay, 373, had proposed the same number of 24,000 combat soldiers on the basis of Herodotus' number of 600 triremes. Lazenby, however, does not quote

Finlay or mention him in the bibliography, hence he must have arrived at the same conclusion independently.

66. See Van der Veer, 309, n. 78. He estimates that each of the 600 Persian triremes carried about seventy combat soldiers, nearly double the forty estimated by others. There could have been a reduction in the number of rowers in each ship to save space for the soldiers (Evans, 1993, 298, n. 87). Wallinga, 137–144, places the number on board at between 60–170, but concludes (p. 138) that every trireme was rowed by 60 men. Wallinga finds agreement in Dionysopoulos, 70–71, who speculates that every transport vessel in the Persian fleet could carry 100 soldiers, and every combat trireme about 40. That could also apply to the horse transports, as we know that the Athenian horse transport in the Peloponnesian War was rowed by 60 men (Wallinga, 171). Hodge, 166, notes that if the Persians had removed two rows of oars from their triremes each ship could carry 60–120 soldiers. Of course, that burden would seriously reduce the speed of the fleet, making it vulnerable to the Athenian fleet. We believe that Datis kept some ships at full rower strength to guard the slower vessels against raids by Athenian ships in the Aegean. As Herodotus, 7.184, says, each Persian ship in Xerxes' fleet had a crew of 200, it is doubtful whether in 490 the Persians had converted all their ships into transports with a mere 60 rowers each. It is also possible that the Persian rowers served as light-armed fighting men, as we know that like the Athenian rowers they were free men and not slaves. In that case, the number of Persian combat-ready troops would rise dramatically. Leake, 1829, 186, asserts that the Persian rowers were also light-armed, some of them archers. When, as will be seen, the Athenians continued the fight by the ships at Marathon, it may be that they confronted ship crews.

67. Hodge, 165.
68. Sekunda, 25.
69. Sekunda, *op. cit.* .
70. See Lazenby, 23, based on Herodotus, 7.81. The smallest unit of the Persian army consisted of ten men, the next largest of 100 men, and so on.
71. For example, Doenges, 5–6, suggests just 12,000–15,000 Persian combat troops at Marathon, Zahrnt, 140, 15,000 infantry. Steinhauer, 2010b, 9, n. 2, estimates that the Persians were no more than two or three times the number of Athenians and Plataians, numbered at 10,000 men, as otherwise the Persians could have encircled the Greeks. Yet this argument supposes that the Greeks numbered just 10,000 which, as we will see, was not the case.
72. Xenophon, *Hipparchikos*, 7.2.
73. Sotiriadis, 1932, 38, n. 1, assumes that the Persians knew the Spartans would help the Athenians and rebuts the figure of 10,000–11,000 Persian fighting men at Marathon estimated by Boucher but considered too low by Sotiriadis, who suggests that the Persians thought they would be fighting a combined Athenian and Eretrian force. Hammond used that argument to rebut estimates by Meyer, 306, of under 20,000 and Hignett, 1963, 71, of 20,000.
74. Strabo, 10.1.10. It is clear that this geographer refers to Eretria before 490, but does not precisely say when – probably not long before the battle of Marathon.
75. As will be seen, in all the Greek cities except Sparta the number of light-armed troops exceeded the number of citizens recruited as hoplites.
76. An analysis of what we know of the number of men fielded by both cities is set out below.
77. Cawkwell, 88, 116, n. 4, notes that in 338 Philip II of Macedon attacked the Athenians and their allies with more than 30,000 infantry and no less than 2,000

cavalry. He figures that Datis and Artaphernes would have had a similar number of soldiers in 490, though he wrongly names Mardonius as the Persian general who attacked Greece in that year. Dionysopoulos, 73, opines that Cawkwell does not accurately state the number of Persians but sets a logical limit.

78. Leake, 1829, 186: 7.000; 188: 6.000.

79. Curtius, 1898, 285, n. 1, writes that the Persian cavalry in the campaign numbered 10,000. But he simply admits to following Nepos and does not supply his own estimate.

80. Kontorlis, 10. Dionysopoulos, 75, 206, speculates that the Persian force had available some 3,000 horse, of which 1,000 was a reserve.

81. Sekunda, 25.

82. Munro, 1926, 234

83. Berthold, 92, n. 53.

84. Lazenby 46, concludes that the Persian cavalry would not have exceeded 1,000 horse. Sealey, 1976a, 188, estimates the number at about 800. Krentz, 2010a, 93, agrees on the 800 horse but puts the number of horsemen rather lower as he believes that each cavalryman would have had more than one mount. Hammond, 1968, 44, puts the Persian cavalry figure at 1,000 at the least. In a later work (1988), Hammond reckons the number at 1,200. Finally, Zahnt, 140, puts the cavalry at 'several hundred horsemen'.

85. Evans, 1993, 299: 'not more than 200 horsemen'; Doenges, 5: 'fewer than 200 horsemen'. Tuplin, 2010a, 269, says the number 'will not have exceeded the low hundreds'.

86. Drews, 140. 194, n. 4.

87. Herodotus, 6.48.2 and 6.95.

88. Drews, 194, n 4. Almost a century before, Curtius, 1898, 307, had come to a similar conclusion, doubting Finlay (p. 373) who believed that the Persians had only a small cavalry force at Marathon and hence avoided involving it in the battle.

89. Herodotus, 5.63.3, and *The Constitution of the Athenians*, 19.5. Those horsemen were Thessalians under the command of their king Kineas, an ally of Hippias.

90. Herodotus, 5.105.

91. Herodotus, 6.94.2.

92. Mardonius' expedition, even though it didn't accomplish all of its aims, such as punishing Athens and Eretria as Darius had wished (see Herodotus, 6.43–44), cannot be considered a failure, as Herodotus, 6.45, says. During his campaign Mardonius subjugated important Greek city-states such as Thasos, Abdera and the whole kingdom of Macedon. It appears that the wider area of Macedon was incorporated into the Persian empire, something that Megabazus had failed to accomplish a few years before even though he had also conquered Macedon (see Herodotus, 7.108 and the comment by Lazenby, 45). Mardonius had even managed to overcome the Brygians, a Thracian tribe that had offered strong resistance to the Persians.

93. This is apparent from Herodotus, 7.9 *et seq.*

94. Herodotus, 6.45.1.

95. Scott, 484. For example, though Megabazus had annexed Thrace to the Persian empire, a year after taking command of the Persian forces in the area he was replaced by Otanes.

96. Herodotus, 6.94.2. names the second commander as Artaphrenes, while later sources alter the spelling to Artaphernes, which has prevailed in the Greek.

Ampelius, 15.9, wrongly names him as Tissaphernes; Souda, 'Hippias' calls him Artabazus or Antiphernes. Scott, 339, believes that the first spelling is probably wrong, but the other two are alternative renditions in Greek.

97. Plato, *Menexenos*, 240a; Plato, *Laws*, 3.698c; Pseudo-Demosthenes, *Against Neaira*, 94; Diodorus, 11.2.2.

98. Herodotus, 6.94.2; Plutarch, *Ethics*, 829A.

99. Scott, 339, observes that Herodotus (6.94.2) refers to Artaphernes only at the start of the expedition and at the return of the army to Susa (6.119.1). Otherwise Herodotus makes no further mention of him.

100. Ktesias, *Persika* FGrH 688 F13.22, asserts that Datis returned from the Pontus to take command of the Persian expeditionary force that would fight at Marathon. According to Scott, 338, Herodotus and other ancient Greek writers referred to the wider Black Sea region as the Pontus. Thus it is possible Ktesias here is referring to Datis' actions in Scythia and not some other operation in the Pontus before 490. This may show that Datis participated in Darius' expedition in 513. If that were the case, then Datis would have been in Darius' service for many years. Scott, 340, thinks that Artaphernes, as a relation of the Great King, may have been at Marathon as his representative. In such a case Artaphernes would have had no operational responsibilities; they would have been the exclusive province of Datis.

101. Lewis, 1980, 194–195. For a connection between the text on the clay tablet and Datis, see also Sekunda, 15–16 and Tuplin, 2010a, 253.

102. Herodotus, 7.88.1.

103. Ancient literary sources attribute to Datis specific diplomatic initiatives that will be analysed below. Herodotus records his appeal to the inhabitants of Delos to return to their island when the Persian fleet first sailed to the Cyclades. Datis also personally delivered to Delos a statue of Apollo which some Phoenician captain of a Persian trireme had stolen from the shrine at Delion in Boiotia, so that it could be returned there. Diodorus records the ultimatum Datis sent to the Athenians on the eve of the battle of Marathon, couched in 'diplomatic' language.

104. Herodotus, 6.94.2.

105. Herodotus, 7.74.2.

106. On the Athenian diplomatic mission to Sardis in 507/6, see Herodotus, 5.73.2–3.

107. It must be stressed that Herodotus is the only writer who lived close to the time of the Persian Wars and who mentions the offer of 'earth and water' to the Great King. There is no such mention in the few sources that have come down to us from the Persian empire. Krentz, 2010a, 38–39, records some of the interpretations about this act, from an acknowledgement of the dominance of the Great King over the people making the offer to complete subjugation and annexing of the territory to the empire. A people giving 'earth and water' to Darius were accepting him as a suzerain, not an ally. This entailed obligations such as paying tax and contributing to his expeditions with contingents. Tuplin, 2010a, 261, arrives at the same conclusion as Krentz, but adds the interesting observation that the offering of 'earth and water' was a surrendering to the Great King of all the productive capacity of the people and allowing him to exploit it at will. According to Balcer, 130, earth and water were symbols of the prevailing Persian Zoroastrian religion. Perhaps the delivery of this symbolic right was accompanied by some religious ritual.

108. Krentz, 2010a, 39.

109. The Athenians' refusal to accept the actions of their envoys who gave 'earth and water' to Darius could be explained by the fact that they meanwhile had beaten their foes in Greece and no longer needed Persian help. Tuplin, 2010a, 260, says that the Athenian envoys who met Artaphernes at Sardis in 507/6 agreed to offer 'earth and water' but in the end didn't do so. But Herodotus states flatly that they did.
110. Herodotus, 5.96.2.
111. Herodotus, 5.97.3, 5.99.1. On the military force that Athens sent to help the rebellious Ionians in 498, see Krentz, 2010a, 73.
112. On the burning of Sardis by the Greeks, see Herodotus, 5.100–102.1, who reports that Artaphernes the Elder held on to the citadel of Sardis while commanding a strong force.
113. Many modern scholars believe that in 498 Darius already considered the Athenians his subjects, as in 507 they had offered him 'earth and water'. (Krentz, 2010a, 37–39). Thus when the Athenians sent military aid to the Ionians they were considered to have rebelled against Darius (see Zahrnt, 140). Herodotus may have consciously masked the fact that at the time the Athenians were technically subjects of Darius.
114. Artaphernes the Elder may not have taken part in the 490 campaign, either because he was too old or because Darius wanted to keep him at Sardis
115. Pausanias, 1.32.7.
116. Herodotus, 7.74.2. On this basis Krentz, 2010a, 90, avers that Artaphernes the Younger would not have been very young in 490. Sekunda, 17, McQueen, 180, and Tuplin, 2010a, 264, n. 54, wrongly conflate Artaphernes the Younger and the grandson Artaphernes as the same person. The latter opines that Artaphernes was younger than Datis, but there is no confirmation from any ancient source.
117. Herodotus, 6.102, 107–108; Thucydides, 6.59.4. Hippias had been born about 570, and by 490 would have been about eighty years old (see Scott, 358).
118. For example, Demaratos, a deposed king of Sparta, accompanied Xerxes' expedition to Greece in 480 and was his adviser.
119. We conclude this from Herodotus, 6.107, where it seems that Hippias gave orders to the Persian soldiers landing at Marathon. Also, according to Scott, 358, Herodotus' phrasing indicates that Hippias actually ordered rather than advised the Persians.
120. See Scott, 358; Tuplin, 2010a, 259, n. 40.
121. Scott, *op. cit.*
122. Herodotus, 6.94.2: 'To them the Persian king gave the orders and sent them to subjugate Athens and Eretria, and to bring the citizens of those cities before him as slaves'. Herodotus also asserts (6.102) that the Athenians 'had the impression that the Persians would move against them, just as they did with the Eretrians'. That is, to depopulate the city.
123. Herodotus, 6.109.3.
124. Plato, *Menexenos*, 240b, and *Laws*, 3.698c, alleges that Darius' aim from the outset was to depopulate Athens as well as Eretria. Aristophanes, *Wasps,* lines 1075–90, describes the Persian attack on Athens in a passage which most scholars believe refers to the 490 campaign; in line 1079 he says the Persians intended to burn Athens. Also, a line in one of the three inscriptions in IG 503/4 which honours the Athenian fallen in the Persian Wars, says that the Athenians gave battle and 'prevented [the Persians] from burning the city'. Many researchers regard this as a reference to the battle of Marathon, and consider that the three inscriptions honour the Athenian dead. These quotes record what the Athenians feared might

happen to them, and shed no light on what the Persians actually intended to do if they seized Athens in 490.

125. Herodotus, 6.95.2.
126. The expedition against Naxos in 499 had the approval of Darius and two of its commanders, Artaphernes Senior and the admiral Megabates, were his close associates. However, it was the result of co-operation between Persian officials and Aristagoras, the tyrant of Miletos, and therefore not exclusively a Persian operation.
127. Herodotus, 6.48–49, 6.94. Rhodes, 2003, 60–62, deems that Darius dispatched his heralds to the Greek cities to demand submission at the start of Mardonius' campaign. However, from the citation of events in Herodotus' narrative, the dispatch of the Persian heralds to the Greek city-states should date after Mardonius' campaign in 492 but before the start of Datis', most possibly in 491.
128. The first to record this view was Herodotus, 6.94.1, who mentions that Darius' main aim through the 490 campaign was to conquer the Greeks who had not offered him '*earth and water*'. According to Plutarch, *Aristides*, 5.1, on the pretext of his campaign against Greece the Persian monarch sought to conquer the whole of Greece. Scott, 337, considers that while Herodotus was compiling material for his history in the mid-fifth century, he received this piece of information by an Athenian source, as the idea that in 490, Athens defended the whole of Greece against the Persian empire, was Athenian propaganda. Nonetheless, it seems that the Athenians had already formed this view since 490. Simonides of Keos in his famous epigram about the battle at Marathon, dating shortly after, praises the Athenians who fought there against the Persian invader on behalf of '*all the Greeks*'. See Lycourgos, *Against Leocrates*, 109. A verse of the epigram on 'Kallimachos' Monument' at the Acropolis of Athens – a monument dated shortly after the battle – may read '*to Marathon – for the salvation of the Greeks*'. Petrakos, 1995, 48–49. According to Keesling, 126, if this interpretation is correct, the Athenians considered their victory in 490 of Panhellenic importance. Furthermore, a verse in another epigram honouring the Athenian fighters who were killed in the battle of Marathon and dating a few years after 490 (IG I3 503/504, Lapis A II) is interpreted by many scholars as the Athenians at Marathon having saved Greece from slavery to the Persians, see Tuplin, 2010a, 258, n. 36. These epigrams dismiss the view of Zahrnt, 150, that there is no evidence showing that the Athenians claimed in the fifth century that their victory at Marathon had saved all Greeks. Plato, *Menexenos*, 239d, mentions that even before the battle at Marathon the Persians had started the conquest of Europe, while in *Laws*, 3.698b, he deems that the Persian campaign of 490 may have aimed at conquering also other peoples who inhabited Europe, apart from the Greeks. Plato's view is repeated by Aelius Aristides, *To Plato: In Defence of the Four*, 280–281, who mentions that the Athenians at Marathon not only defended the freedom of the Greeks, but also that of all peoples of Europe. Lysias, *Epitaphios*, 21, claims that the real target of Darius in 490 was to conquer all nations of Europe starting with the Greeks. This is the oldest source recording that the Athenians at Marathon not only defended the freedom of the Greeks but that of all inhabitants of Europe. Aelius Aristides, *Panathenaic*, 95, claims with the exaggeration of an orator, that Darius' aim, after conquering Greece, was the conquest of the entire Earth!
129. Sealey, 1976b, 17.

130. According to Herodotus, 6.49.1, 'many [Greeks] of mainland Greece and all the islanders gave 'earth and water' to Darius'. Herodotus mentions later on that other islanders – most certainly the Aiginites – also gave *'earth and water'* to Darius. Herodotus refers to two distinct 'categories' of islanders: the first probably include the inhabitants of eastern Aegean islands, all of which submitted to the Persians while the second those who inhabited islands closer to mainland Greece – like the Cyclades – include some who refused to submit. As we will see, the Persians attacked Naxos, while the inhabitants of Delos evacuated the island before the Persians arrived there, events showing that the inhabitants of these two islands refused to submit to Darius.

131. Herodotus, 6. 47.

132. Herodotus, 7.133.1, records that when the Athenians and Spartans threw Darius' heralds down the *barathron* and the pit respectively, they shouted to them that they would find there *'earth and water'* to take to their king. Although the authorities of these two Greek cities may have agreed between them in advance to execute the Persian heralds, it is hardly believable that they used the same ironic phrase in both Sparta and Athens, as Herodotus narrates.

133. Most scholars agree that the *barathron* in Athens was located in the area of the *deme* of Keriadai, west of Pnyka. Lalonde, 115–116.

134. There are scholars who deem that the executions of the heralds in the two Greek cities in 491 were not related. Thus Sealey, 1976b, 18–20, suggests that the Athenians executed the Persian heralds due to the public outcry against them; not so much because they were furious at their demand for *'earth and water'*, but because they found out that their mortal enemies, the Aeginites, had accepted it. According to Sealey, 1976b, 16–18 the execution of the Persian heralds in Sparta must have been arranged by king Kleomenes I, in order to commit in this way all Spartans to his policy against the Persian Empire. Herodotus, 7.133.1, points out that Xerxes didn't dispatch heralds to Athens and Sparta to demand *'earth and water'* before the start of his own campaign against Greece in 481. It seems that for many years, the Persians avoided sending heralds to both cities: In 479 Mardonius, who was the commander of the Persian force in Greece at time, again asked Athens to surrender. The ultimatum was taken to the Athenians, not by some Persian herald, but by Alexander I, king of Macedonia, who was a Persian subject but on good terms with the Athenians, see Herodotus, 8.143.3 and Lycurgus, *Against Leocrates*, 71.

135. Pausanias, 3.12.7.

136. Plutarch, *Themistokles*, 6.2. Aelius Aristides, *Panathenaic*, 99. Aelius Aristides refers to the interpreter as 'a colonist of the Athenians', insinuating that he was from Ionia. During antiquity, the Ionian cities of Asia Minor were considered colonies of Athens, see Herodotus, 7. 95.1. A scholiast of Aelius Aristides (Dindorf, 1829, 3, 125) records that the interpreter was from Samos and called Mys.

137. According to Plutarch, and Aelius Aristides, Themistokles proposed arresting the interpreter and bringing him to trial. These authors date the event in 481, that is, in the context of Xerxes' campaign against Greece. Thus, some modern scholars (e.g. Hignett, 1963, 87) consider that the execution of the heralds belongs to events of that campaign and not 490. This is incorrect, as Herodotus, expressly states that Xerxes didn't send heralds to Athens and Sparta demanding *'earth and water'* before the launch of his own campaign against Greece. Moreover, Pausanias, 3.12.7, makes it clear that the Persian heralds executed in Sparta and Athens had been dispatched by Darius. Themistokles may have been responsible for the arrest of the interpreter

in 491; he was already influential in Athens at the time, having been elected a year earlier Eponymous Archon, see below. It is worth pointing out that the verdict of the Athenian court on the conviction of the interpreter is timeless and identical to the indictment issued after World War II against citizens of European countries which had been conquered by the Germans and who collaborated with them as interpreters. Just as their ancient 'colleague', most of them pleaded at their trials that they 'were just doing their job'.

138. Plutarch, *Themistokles*, 6.2.
139. According to Herodotus 7.133–137 and Pausanias, 3.12.7, the executions of the Persian heralds in Athens and Sparta enraged Talthybius, their mythical hero. Herodotus states that he does not know what sort of evil befell the Athenians for killing the Persian heralds but rejects the idea that it was the destruction of Athens by Xerxes in 480. However, Pausanias believes that Talthybios' curse affected just one Athenian: Miltiades, who according to him was to blame for their death. As we shall see, Miltiades had an unjust and painful end.
140. Herodotus, 6.73.
141. Herodotus, 6.49.2, 6.50, 6.61.1 The specific military operation against Aegina is an episode of the continuous conflict between this island and Athens during the 490s and 480s. Herodotus, records certain events that according to Rhodes, 2003, 61, and Krentz, 2007b, 738, n. 20, took place before the battle at Marathon and after Aegina had submitted to Darius, dating either to 493/492 – and before Mardonius' expedition – or 492/491. Cf. Immerwahr, 212, n. 65; Jeffery, 1962, 44–55; Figueira, 1993, 35–60, who claim that some of these events must date a few years after the battle at Marathon.
142. Herodotus, 6.49.2.
143. Despite its defeat at Marathon, Datis' army could have spent the winter of 490/489 in Aegina and repeat the campaign against Athens the following spring. But this never happened as the Athenians held the hostages from Aegina, so their fellow citizens didn't co-operate with the Persians. See Figueira, 1993, 126.
144. Although in 491 the Greeks fell into this clever trap of Persian diplomacy, they soon realised their error. Thus, a decade later, in 481, when Xerxes asked the Greeks to submit, those who decided to fight him didn't move directly against their fellow Greeks who had submitted but at the congress held at the Isthmos swore to punish them severely, after having first beaten the Persians. Herodotus, 7.132.2 and Diodorus 11.3.3. Lazenby, 29–30, presents examples of the Persians successfully using diplomacy in the context of '*diplomatic warfare*' with a view to reducing the power of their adversaries, even before they had dispatched a military force against them.
145. Aelius Aristides, *Panathenaic*, 100. Plutarch, *Ethics*, 829A, also refers to cuffs brought along by Datis and Artaphernes in 490 to bind all Athenians on orders of Darius. Himerios, 6.200, mentions only that Datis carried schackles with him for the Athenians. It is unclear if these bindings were for hands or feet.
146. Herodotus, 6.119.
147. Herodotus, 6.95.1. Mardonius' troops had also assembled in Kilikia, in 492 and this is where his campaign against Greece started, see Herodotus, 6.43. Herodotus, 6.95.1, records that the Persian expeditionary force and its two commanders departed from Darius and arrived at the Aleian plain. It is likely that the troops were inspected by Darius himself in his capital – Sousa – and that he supervised the last stage of the expedition's preparation. However, Scott, 340, considers

that the Persians had already encamped at the Aleian plain in the autumn of 491, awaiting the arrival of the fleet the following spring. The Aleian plain is located in Kilikia, modern day Adana of southeastern Turkey. The distance between Sousa and the Aleian Plain is 1,700 km and Scott supposes that it would have taken the Persian troops two months or more to cover this distance.

148. Lazenby, 29–31, analyzes the important advantages that the Persians had during the Median Wars against the Greeks: excellent spying techniques, excellent diplomacy and meticulous organisation of their campaigns.

149. See above, the case of Aigina. According to Krentz, 2007b, 738–739 and 2010a, 99, just before the battle at Marathon, Athens had fought with Thebes. This theory is not based on strong evidence but cannot be ruled out either. Before Krentz, Raaflaub, 2004, 117, had argued that Thebes may have defeated Athens in a war not recorded in known literary sources. However, he dates this imaginary war at the end of sixth century, not 490.

150. Herodotus, 6.95.2.

151. The likely operation against Rhodes in the context of the campaign of 490 is analyzed by several scholars: Hammond, 1968, 44. Scott, 334–335. Sekunda, 29–30. Krentz, 2010a, 94–95.

152. The *Lindos Chronicle* is attributed to the local historian Eudemos and all known extracts have survived in an inscription dating in 99. See Blinkenberg, 18, 22–24.

153. Aischylos, *The Persians*, line 891, mentions Rhodes as Darius' domain without clarifying when he conquered it. Sekunda, 30, postulates that the Persians besieged Lindos in 490 and not at the end of the Ionian Revolt in 493 as older scholars considered, for example Burn, 1962 (1984), 210–211 and 218.

154. The sailing of the Persian fleet towards Samos and then the Cyclades was the usual sea route for any ancient fleet between Asia Minor and the southern mainland Greece. It is likely that contingents of ships of the Persian fleet sailing from various ports of Asia Minor may have joined the rest of the fleet at Samos.

155. For Samos as the main naval base of the Athenians in the fifth century, see Cargill, 7–8. In later periods the island was an important naval base of the Ptolemies and the Byzantine Empire.

156. After the execution of its tyrant, Polycrates, by the Persians in 522. Herodotus. 3.125.

157. Herodotus, 6.13–14.

158. Herodotus, 6.25

159. Herodotus, 6.95.2.

160. Herodotus, 5.30–34.

161. Herodotus, 6.96. Herodotus makes it clear that the Persians took captives at Naxos. We know that the Persians after the conquest of Eretria seized many of its inhabitants; ancient literary sources record details about their subsequent fate (see below), but don't make the slightest mention about the Naxian captives. The Persians may have left them on a friendly island – such as Paros – and returned to Asia with them after their defeat at Marathon. However, it is also possible that they sent them straight to Asia, even before they had sailed away from the Cyclades. Herodotus, 6.98.1, after mentioning that Datis and his fleet departed from Rheneia, notes that he '*took with him Ionian and Aeolians*', insinuating that the ships carrying Ionian and Aiolian forces sailed separately from the rest of the Persian fleet which they eventually joined at Rheneia. As we have seen, though, Datis had probably sailed away from Samos with all forces available. Thus, the Ionians and Aeolians

may have carried the captive Naxians away to Asia Minor on their own ships and – after completing this brief mission – returned to the Cyclades where they once again joined the rest of the Persian fleet.

162. Plutarch, *Ethics*, 869 A-C, accuses Herodotus of concealing the fact that the Naxians managed to drive the Persians away from Naxos after they had burned their city. Although Plutarch's reference is not realistic, it could be an indication that in 490 the Naxians may have resisted the Persian onslaught. See Krentz, 2010a, 96.

163. Not only did the Naxians not participate in the Ionian Revolt, but the fact that its leader was Aristagoras, the same person who had attacked them in 499, would have deterred them from giving any assistance to the Ionian rebels. Walker, 261 and 285, n. 23, erroneously postulates that the Naxians dispatched five or six warships to support the Ionian Revolt. He mentions also (Walker, 271, 273), that Aristagoras asked Naxos to support the Ionian Revolts and that her citizens dispatched military aid along with that of Eretria. Walker then goes on to claim that Herodotus concealed Naxos inhabitants' participation in the Ionian Revolt. Nevertheless, these theories, as well as the accusation levelled against Herodotus, are groundless; not only there is no evidence showing that Naxos sided with the Ionian Revolt, but it is certain that its leader, Aristagoras, would have not dared set foot on the island to ask for the inhabitants' help just a few months after he had besieged the place. As we shall see, the ships that, according to Walker, Naxos sent to support the Ionian Revolt were in fact those, according to Hellanikos, Ephoros and Plutarch, whose crews seceded from the Persian fleet and joined the Greeks shortly before the Battle of Salamis (see below). Walkers' erroneous postulations are repeated by other scholars, for example, Rutishauser, 75.

164. The fact that in 480, a decade after its occupation by the Persians, Naxos was forced to contribute to Xerxes just four triremes according to Herodotus (8.46.3), or five according to Ephoros (FGrH 70 F187), or six according to Hellanikos (FGrH 323a F28) is an indication of the sharp decrease in its population. Herodotus records that the crews of all four triremes from Naxos seceded from the Persian fleet and joined the Greeks shortly before the battle of Salamis. According to Plutarch, *Ethics*, 869 A-C, the crews of the triremes from Naxos fought bravely at Salamis. Diodorus, 5.52.3, makes the same claim, adding that the crews of the triremes from Naxos were the first to secede from the Persians and join the Greek fleet. These references by the ancient authors demonstrate that the Naxians kept the spirit of resistance even after the Persian conquest of 490.

165. Herodotus, 6.96.

166. Herodotus, 6.97. McQueen, 182, erroneously deems that Herodotus records 'incense weighing 300 talents' instead of 'valued at'. McQueen assumes that Herodotus is referring to the 'talent' of Aegina, weighing roughly 26 kgs, and thus postulates that the Persians burnt at Apollo's temple over 7.5 tons of incense! According to Herodotus, 3.97.5, throughout the Persian Empire incense was produced only in the part of Arabia controlled by the Persians, and whose inhabitants were obliged to pay Darius a submission tax of 1000 talents of incense annually. Herodotus probably refers here to the weight and not the value of the incense. Therefore, Datis couldn't have burnt at Apollo's temple in Delos nearly one third of the annual quantity of incense that the Great King received from Arabia. Consequently, Herodotus' reference is to 300 talents 'worth' of incense burnt at Apollo's temple.

167. How and Wells, 103. Delos was of great importance to the Ionians, as the birthplace of Apollo, their protector god. Thucydides, 3.104, mentions that it was Peisistratus who gave prominence to Delos and the local temple of Apollo by making it the political centre of the Ionians. Thus, Hippias may have requested from Darius that the Persians behaved respectfully on Delos due to his personal relationship with the island. Scott, 343–344.

168. Datis not only offered incense to Apollo's temple at Delos but also a gold necklace. Several inscriptions at Delos after 490 record this item. Krentz, 2010a, 189, n. 17.

169. Herodotus, 6.99.1. These hostages would have been members of the most prominent families of the Cyclades' islands.

170. Herodotus, *op.cit.* Scott, 350.

171. Herodotus, 6.133.1.

172. Herodotus, 6.49.1. Aelius Aristides, *Panathenaic*, 102, stresses how fast the Persians conquered the Aegean islands. However, according to Scott, 343, it is likely that the islands had already submitted to Darius and '*if so, Datis would be confirming Persian suzerainty rather than imposing it*'.

173. Aischylos, *Persians*, lines 884–886.

174. According to Scott, 349, and Krentz, 2010a, 97, Datis may have divided his forces in the Cyclades and thus been able to send divisions of his fleet to operate simultaneously on different islands. However, we consider that this could have happened on smaller islands, but not at Naxos against which the entire Persian army and fleet would have operated.

175. Krentz, 2010a, 97.

176. Scott, 344.

177. Herodotus, 6.99.2.

178. Karystos' resistance in 490 implies that it had refused to give '*earth and water*' to Darius a year earlier. However, in his communication with the inhabitants, Datis did not demand their surrender but practical support as if they had already submitted to the Persians.

179. Maurice, 19, analyses the advantages the Persians gained from occupying Karystos.

180. Herodotus, 6.100.1. Scott, 603, wrongly mentions that Herodotus records that the Athenians refused to send aid to the Eretrians, but put at their disposal their 4.000 *klerouchoi*.

181. Herodotus, *op. cit.*

182. Herodotus, 5.77.2. After the defeat of the Chalkidians in 506, the Athenians occupied and distributed territory of Chalkis to their landless countrymen, by ballot who thus became *klerouchoi*, i.e. *landowners by the ballot*.

183. In the years between 506 and 490, several Athenian *klerouchoi* who had initially taken land in Chalkis would have died. Their sons or other relatives would have then inherited their land. Therefore, the initial number of 4.000 *klerouchoi* would have been the same in 490. See Figueira, 2010, 193–194.

184. Raaflaub, 2004, 117, considers that at the end of the sixth century, the Thebans 'released' Chalkis from Athenian rule. In addition, Krentz, 2007b, 738–739 and 2010a, 99, deems that shortly before the battle at Marathon, the Thebans invaded and expelled the 4.000 Athenian *klerouchoi* from Chalkis. According to this theory, Krentz claims that in the summer of 490, before the Persians attacked Eretria, the *klerouchoi* were already in Athens, having been forced to abandon their lands in Euboia. For this reason, the Athenian authorities could dispatch them quickly and co-ordinated to Eretria. No ancient literary source, however, mentions a war

between Athens and Thebes in 506–490. Raaflaub and Krentz made their case based on a Theban inscription of the early Classical period, which supposedly records the 'liberation' of Chalkis from the Thebans.

185. In 490 Chalkis had lost most of its fertile land that the Athenians and perhaps the Eretrians had occupied. The city itself may have been under Athenian rule, if Diodorus (10.24.3) is true about the Athenians conquering Chalkis after the defeat of its army. Walker, 247–252, makes a deduction that in the war and the victory of Athens against Chalkis in 507, Eretria had sided with Athens.

186. Herodotus, 5.99.1. The Eretrians sent an army and five triremes to the Ionian rebels in return for the aid Miletos had made to Eretria during one of its wars with Chalkis. The Eretrians helped the Ionians on their own initiative, not because of the Athenians. Furthermore, they remained in Ionia and kept on fighting on the side of the Ionians against the Persian Empire, even after the withdrawal of the Athenian force.

187. Plato, *Menexenos*, 240b. Plato's view concerning the military might of Eretria about 490 is supported by Strabo, 10.1.10, who records that a short time before, at the local festival of *Amaryntheia* – in honour of Artemis – the procession of Eretrians from Amarynthos, a suburb of Eretria, towards the city consisted of 3.000 hoplites, 300 cavalrymen, and 60 chariots.

188. Herodotus, 6.100.2.

189. Herodotus, *op. cit.* The fact that Eretria was eventually betrayed by two aristocrats, reveals that an organised network may have been at work within the framework of the ruling class of the city for its subjugation to the Persian Empire. Their contact with the enemy may have been Goggylos, a fellow countryman who lived in exile in Persia. According to Xenophon, *Hellenika*, 3.1.6, Goggylos was an important citizen of Eretria, who was exiled because he was the only one having supported the Persians. To reward him for his philo-Persian stance, the Great King gave to him the revenues from certain cities of Aeolis. Although Xenophon does not mention when and on what pretext Goggylos supported the Persians or which Persian king rewarded him, it is clear in his text that this happened before 490 and the destruction of Eretria by the Persians. The beneficiary of Goggylos was most likely Darius. We may note that a Goggylos from Eretria is mentioned by Thucydides, 1.128.6, as a contact between Xerxes and Pausanias in 477–476. The rarity of the name and his birthplace make it almost certain that he is the same as the namesake who was favoured by Darius. Avery, 17, claims that the exiled Goggylos may have participated in the 490 campaign as an advisor of Datis as Hippias the deposed tyrant of Athens. He also postulates that Goggylos may have had contacts with aristocrats in Eretria, propping up the philo-Persian party of Eretria that eventually betrayed the city to the Persians. If this scholar is right, then Darius conceding the revenues of the cities in Aeolis to Goggylos might have been his reward for the role he played in the Persian conquest of his city, rather than for his philo-Persian stance before 490. Krentz, 2010a, 100, is of the opinion that the two traitors from Eretria may have been Goggylos' relatives; an opinion for which there is no evidence whatsoever. About a century after Goggylos was exiled from Eretria, Xenophon, records meeting his descendants in Asia Minor.

190. Herodotus, 6.100.3. We deem that the philo-Athenian Aischines didn't act on his own initiative but on behalf of the Eretrian authorities.

191. This interpretation is based on Herodotus' text. Notwithstanding this, it is also possible that this move by the eminent Eretrians was made because they decided at

the eleventh hour to negotiate with the Persians for the peaceful surrender of their city. These negotiations would not have been possible if they had the Athenian force in Eretria; for this reason they asked for its withdrawal. Nevertheless, even if negotiations between the Eretrians and Persians did take place, they were fruitless. Walker, 280, regards Aischines as pro-Persian, one of the influential Eretrians quick to betray his city to the invaders. According to Walker that was the real reason why the Athenian *klerouchoi* were notified of the need to leave Eretria by Aischines. However, Herodotus' text does not support Walker's view, nor can something like that be inferred from another literary source. Concerning the departure of the Athenians from Eretria – upon Aischines' exhortation – some scholars consider that Herodotus embedded the official Athenian view that Eretrians were solely responsible for this move. See How and Wells, 105. Scott, 353. Walker, 279–281. Scott, deems that in this way the Athenians tried to cover up their own responsibilities for not dispatching a general as head of their force and for withdrawing it from Eretria. Moreover, this scholar also accuses the Athenians of '*of having failed to offer Eretria even moral support, much less tangible help*'. Conversely, Walker, claims that the Athenian force was significant and could have helped in its defence when it was besieged by the Persians, if Aischines had not sent it away from the city. However, we deem this view is incorrect for when an ancient Greek city dispatched troops to aid another in war, they were expected to fight in the battlefield not behind the walls of the allied city. In case a city decided to defend itself in this way, its allies had no obligation to fight for it. See How, 1919, 53–54. The odds are that Athenian *klerouchoi* would have left Eretria on their own initiative, even if they had not been notified by Aischines, as soon as they found out that its inhabitants would defend themselves in their city. The dispatch of 4,000 men from the Athenians to the Eretrians was significant for the backdrop of that era. Some days later, Sparta sent half that number of men to aid the Athenians at Marathon. Herodotus, 6.120.

192. Herodotus, 6.101.
193. Most scholars postulate that the Athenian *klerouchoi* of Chalkis fought the Persians at Marathon within the divisions of their respective tribes in the Athenian army. See for example, Macan, 1895, 1, 355. Scott, 352. Figueira, 2010, 201.
194. Herodotus, *op. cit.*
195. Wallace, 1947, 130–133, who locates all three shores mentioned by Herodotus in the Gulf of Aliverion.
196. Scott, 354–355. Tuplin, 2010a, 265, n. 59. According to Muller 426–427, and Knoepfler, 373, 379, Tamynai must be identified with Temenos, an area close to Eretria. Choireas and Aigilia must have been areas in Amarynthos, close by to the city of Eretria. Aigilia was a coast of Euboia, not to be confused with the islet of the same name in the region of Styra, where the Persians took the Eretrian captives after the occupation of their city. See Scott, 355. The name Aigilia, 'goat area', was an ordinary name for small islands and islets in ancient Greece.
197. Herodotus, 6.100. Gaebel, 71, suggests that the Persian cavalry must have been used during the siege of Eretria in order to seclude the city, cutting off its supplies, and protect Persian foot soldiers from surprise attacks by the besieged. Wallace, 1947, 132, n. 42, rejects the view of Maurice, 17, that the region of Eretria didn't lend itself to cavalry operations and that the Persians disembarked there only the high-ranking officers' horses and not their entire cavalry force. Wallace postulates that the Persians disembarked all their horses and this happened on a coast close to

the foot of Mount Kotylaion in a field that their cavalry could use. As this scholar mentions, the territory of Eretria is appropriate for cavalry operations, something demonstrated by the fact that at the end of the Archaic period the Eretrians had significant cavalry, see Strabo, 10.1.10. Aristotle, *Politics*, 1289b38-39, referring to a war between Eretria and Chalkis during the Archaic period, mentions that both cities possessed cavalry forces.

198. Little is known about the Persian city siege tactics in 490. A few decades earlier, during Cyrus' reign, the Persians besieged and conquered the Ionian cities of Teos and Phocaia by constructing embankments in front of their walls and thus forcing their way up the city walls. Herodotus 1.162.2 and 1.168. See Lazenby, 31. During Miletos' siege in 494, at the end of the Ionian Revolt, the Persians attacked the city in another way: they caused rifts in its walls by making burrows in their foundations and by using other battering techniques. Herodotus, 6.18. Excavations at Paphos uncovered outside the ancient city the remains of a mound that rose as high as its walls. It seems to have been constructed by the Persians during the siege of the Cypriot city in 499/498 during the Ionian Revolt. The Persian soldiers must have stepped on this mound in order to reach up to their enemies at the walls of Paphos and in this way enter the city and conquer it. Erdmann, 1977. Even more impressive in the same excavation is the discovery of a pile of 450 round stones outside the walls of Paphos. Those may have been collected by the Persians with the intention of using them as catapult projectiles. Older literary sources date the use of catapults to the fourth century and onward. However, this discovery in Paphos may show that the specific technology was developed a century earlier than experts believed. Maier and Karageorgis, 198–200. Pritchett, 1991, 43. The available evidence indicates that in 490 the Persians had the most cutting-edge battering techniques applied in the Near East since the time of the Assyrians, see Lendon, 160. Sekunda, 27, points out that the Persians in their campaign to Greece in 490 didn't bring along with them battering machines, without quoting any evidence to bear out this view. Notwithstanding this, it needs to be pointed out that in 480 the Persians besieged and conquered the Acropolis of Athens in a very short time, just a few days or even one day! Herodotus, 8.53.1. Throughout the centuries that the Acropolis was the stronghold of Athens, the Persian conquest was the quickest. In other cases when the Athenian Acropolis was besieged, its garrison didn't surrender unless it was short of food. This shows that the Persians during the time of Greco-Persian Wars were highly experienced in laying siege and conquering fortified places.

199. Krentz, 2010a, 100. For the names of the traitors, see Herodotus, 6.101 and Pausanias, 7.10.2. Plutarch, *Ethics*, 510B, claims that Darius gave land to the two traitors as a reward; but he may have been drawn that conclusion from the name of one of the traitors: 'Philagros', i.e. 'lover of fields'.

200. Herodotus, *op. cit.* The excavations of the Swiss Archaeological School of Athens in Eretria seem to confirm Herodotus' claim that the Persians desecrated and burned the temples: the biggest Archaic temple of the city, *Apollo Daphneforos*, was burned down in c. 490. In the place of devastated Eretria, a new city was erected in the mid-fifth century by the inhabitants of Styra; so it is hard to trace the extent of the damage in 490, see Balcer. 130, n. 16. Therefore, it is uncertain if the Persians burned the entire city or only its temples, as recorded by Herodotus. In 479, when Mardonius occupied Athens, he demolished nearly all public and private buildings

alike, see Shear, 416. The Persians may have done the same in Eretria upon occupying it, a decade earlier as Strabo (10.1.10) claims.

201. Plato, *Menexenos*, 240b–c and Aelius Aristides, *To Plato: In Defence of the Four*, 169.

202. Plato, *op. cit.* Aelius Aristides, *Panathenaic*, 102. Philostratos, *Apollonius*, 1.23. Himerios, 6.210–212, all mention that the Persians applied this technique in order to capture all Eretrians. This way of capturing the inhabitants of a region is similar to a fisherman casting his net to catch fish. It had already been successfully applied by the Persians in Chios, Lesbos and Tenedos during the suppression of the Ionian Revolt. Herodotus, 6.31.1–2. It seems to have been common practice for the Persian army: thus it was also applied in Eretria. Plato, who recorded in *Menexenos* this action in Eretria, in *Laws*, 3.698d, points out that he is not certain if the Persians applied the specific method there in order to capture the entire population of Eretria. Strabo, 10.1.10, wrongly ascribes to Herodotus the reference of this action of the Persians at Eretria. Ancient authors sometimes made wrong quotations, too! Evidently, Strabo mixed up Herodotus' quotation about Chios, Tenedos and Lesbos at the end of the Ionian Revolt with the quotation in Eretria in 490, which is by Plato. Both Sekunda, 33, and Scott, 356, point out Strabo's error.

203. Nowadays the name of the islet is *Styra* or *Large Island* and its size is 1.7km².

204. A period of approximately ten days elapsed between the disembarkation of the Persians at Marathon and the battle. See a detailed presentation below.

205. According to Philostratos, *Apollonius*, 1.24, the Persians took with them 780 Eretrians, men, women, children to Asia. Of these, only 400 men and 10 women, survived the passage to Sousa. The exact numbers cited by Philostratos exude a sensation of a pitifully realistic situation. But this was recorded seven centuries after the event described and there is no other known source referring to the Eretrian captives closer to 490. Grosso, 350, and Bigwood, 24, n. 21, presume that Philostratos may have taken this evidence from the *Persika* of Ktesias dating to the Classical period, most of which is now lost. This assumption is not based on strong evidence, though. The number of captive Eretrians Philostratos quotes could not be historically precise for Eretria's circumstances during the early Classical period. Not only was Eretria Euboia's largest city at the time, but also one of the most significant in Greece. Its population must therefore have been tens of thousands of people, even allowing for the fact that some of those may have left the city for the mountains prior to the Persian siege. Philostratos mentions that most Eretrians were not captured by the Persians as they sought refuge in Kaphireas and the mountains of Euboia. Contrary to what Philostratos presumed, something like that doesn't seem to have happened as Herodotus, 6.100.2, specifically mentions that some Eretrians considered leaving but eventually decided to stay and fight the Persians behind the walls of their city. Thus Eretria does not seem to have witnessed the massive exodus of its inhabitants to the mountains, as Naxos. Besides, according to Plato, *Laws*, 3.698d, Datis claimed that his men captured the Eretrians who were outside the city too, something that Philostratos accepts. The Persians must have killed many of Eretria's inhabitants upon occupying the city but also captured many of those alive, especially women and children, in order to exhibit them like trophies to Darius. We postulate, therefore, that the Persians captured a lot more people than the 780 Eretrians cited by Philostratos. We therefore agree with Graham, 72, who concludes that Philostratos' record is erroneous and considers that most Eretrians were captured by the Persians.

206. Herodotus, 6.119.4. The ancient historian mentions that in his time – about half a century after the events he describes – the Eretrians still lived there and spoke Greek. He gives meticulous information about the natural environment of the region in which the Eretrians settled, explaining that there were reserves of carbohydrates on the surface. Herodotus must have known these details having himself visited Arderikka – near Sousa – and having met the descendants of Eretrian captives. At the same time, he may have been informed of details on the siege and the conquest of Eretria by the Persians; e.g. the names of the two traitors. Philostratos, *Apollonius*, 1.24, records that the exiled Eretrians had short life expectancy as the water they drank was contaminated by tar. How and Wells, 114, identify Arderikka with Kir-Ab, 35 miles from Sousa.
207. Some Eretrians seem to have survived the calamity of 490. Herodotus, 8.1.2 mentions, that a decade later, during Xerxes' invasion of Greece in 480, Eretrians manned seven triremes of the Greek fleet. These crews could have been seafarers and merchants who in 490 happened to be away from Eretria, only to return after the devastation of the city. In 479, the Eretrians – along with the inhabitants of Styra – fielded at Plataia 600 hoplites, see Herodotus, 9.28.5. As we have seen, shortly before 490 the Eretrians had 3,000 hoplites by themselves, proof of the magnitude of destruction inflicted upon them by Datis' men.
208. Dionysopoulos, 79–98, concludes that Eretria was occupied by the Persians on the 27th or 28th August 490.
209. Scott, 619, points out that the fact the Persians took the captive Eretrians to Aigilia islet shows their certainty that they would occupy Athens in a brief time. If the Persians expected that their operation against Athens would be time consuming, they wouldn't have taken the Eretrian captives to a barren islet but would rather have kept them in Euboia and in due time sent them to Asia.
210. Plato, *Menexenos*, 240c and *Laws*, 3.698d.
211. Aristophanes, *Wasps*, lines 1075–1090, records details that many scholars regard as connected to the battle of Marathon. There he mentions the rage and ire the Athenians felt due to the Persian attack.
212. According to Scott, 357, after the fall of Eretria, the Persian stay there for rest and restructuring of the army must have been longer than just the one day that Xerxes offered his troops after the battle of Thermopylai in 480. Scott's view about the Persians staying in Eretria three to four days seems reasonable.
213. During antiquity these two coasts were the most appropriate to disembark troops in great numbers at Attica. This is also revealed by the fact that the Persians disembarked at Marathon and after their defeat there, attempted to do the same at Phaleron. Before the construction of a war harbour in Pireaus in the 480s, the Athenians used the shore of Phaleron to take their warships on land.
214. Concerning the distance from Athens, we use the Agora as a landmark. In antiquity the point in the city used for measuring distances was The Altar of the Twelve Gods, in the entrance of the Agora, built in 522/521, see Herodotus, 2.7.1. Concerning Phaleron, the most appropriate shore for disembarking a military force was that extending today between the Phaleron Delta and the Trokadero area; while respectively for Marathon it was its northern shore, Schinias.
215. Herodotus, 5.63.3, and *The Constitution of the Athenians*, 29.5
216. Herodotus, 1.62.1–63.2.
217. For the location and borders of Marathon during antiquity see Strabo, 9.1.22. Frazer, 431. According to Plutarch, *Theseus*, 32.4, (from Dichaiarchos) the name

originates from 'Marathon', a hero from Arkadia, but Pausanias, 1.15.3 and 1.32.4, considers him the local eponymous hero. Petrakos, 1995, 1–2, believes it more likely that the name originates from the plant marathos (fennel) which is found in the area and quotes a verse from Hermippos, a fifth century comic play writer. The name *Marathon* (for the plant) is one of the oldest in the Greek language as it is found in Linear B′ as *ma-ra-tu-wo*. Parthasarathy, 227.

218. The length of Kynosoura is 2,300 metres and its width 400 metres. Goette and Weber, 27. This name is recorded by Hsychios 'Kynosoura', i.e. 'tail of dog' because of its distinctive shape.

219. See Krentz, 2010a, 116. This little bay appears on nineteenth century maps of Marathon. According to Sfikas, 5, the Schinias shore is separated from the rest of the Marathon shore by the estuaries of the river Charadros.

220. The name Schinias may have its origin in the word *shoinous*, the ancient Greek word for thicket or brush of rushes. Dionysopoulos, 2012, 144 and n. 484. The Great Marsh is close to Schinias and covered in rushes, which may have given to the shore its name.

221. Trevor-Hodge, 159 and 161.

222. Pavlopoulos et al., 435: '... hence the apparent coastal stability of the area from the Classical times onwards'.

223. Krentz, 2010a, 116, with reference to the latest available geological research.

224. The landscape at Marathon inspired Lord Byron to write these verses describing the environment of the area: '*The Mountains Look on Marathon and Marathon Looks on the Sea*'. (Lord Byron, *Don Juan, Canto the Third* – LXXXVI, 'The Isles of Greece', lines 11–12). According to Eisler, 251, one of the most recent biographers of Byron, these verses are the most widely known work of the famous English poet. This is one of the many pieces of evidence proving the timelessness of Marathon in Western civilization.

225. An ancient scholiast of Plato's, *Menexenos*, mentions Marathon as 'kathygro', i.e. full of water. In addition, Soudas, 'Marathon', notes that Kallimachos, poet of the Hellenistic period, characterizes Marathon as 'ennotios', which he also interprets as 'kathygros'.

226. The name 'Brexiza' or 'Vrexiza' may derive from the Greek verb, $\beta\rho\acute{\epsilon}\chi\omega$, i.e. *to water*, and is probably associated with the water-generated environment of the Lesser Marsh. On maps of Marathon designed by travellers who visited the area in the eighteenth and early-nineteenth centuries, the marsh of Brexiza is recorded as the 'Lesser Marsh'. That was a conventional name given to the marsh to distinguish it from the Great Marsh in the northern part of the Marathon plain. Nonetheless, this marsh at Brexiza may have been known as 'Lesser', in antiquity as well, as an ancient scholion to Aelius Aristides, *Panathenaic*, records that 'there is a small marsh next to Marathon' (Dindorf, 1829, 3, 134). Both names: 'Lesser' or 'Brexiza' are used nowadays about this specific marsh.

227. For the results of geological studies of the Great Marsh, see Krentz, 2010a, 116–117 and Dionysopoulos, 144–150.

228. In recent years geological probes have been carried out at Marathon that throw light on how and when the Lesser Marsh could have been formed. Based on the evidence gleaned, both marshes began to be formed under similar circumstances sometime during the third millennium. According to one group of geologists that examined the soil at Marathon, 'the seaside swamp that filled the area between Brexiza and Nea Makri was formed between 2460 and 2310 BC'. See Psilobikos. As

its extent was much smaller than that of the Great Marsh, the Lesser one may have assumed its final form earlier. Besides, the latter was not subject to the process of transformation from sea inlet to lagoon, as the Great Marsh was, as it was entirely composed of fresh water. Significant scientific facts about the Lesser Marsh – based on drilling implemented there by a team of geologists – were announced by Margoni and Kapetanios (Margoni, *et al.*) during the conference, 'The Prehistory of Athens and Attica', held by the American School of Classical Studies at Athens and co-sponsored by the Hellenic Ministry of Culture, the University of Athens, and the Museum of Cycladic Art, Athens, 27–31 May 2015. Their findings confirmed that the Lesser Marsh was created many centuries before 490. As we shall see, this marsh played an important role in the battle of Marathon.

229. The drainage of the Lesser Marsh commenced in 1933 and was funded by the Rockefeller Foundation. Krentz, 2010a, 114.

230. Diodorus, 4.57. Plutarch, *Theseus*, 14. Strabo, 8.7.1. Herodian, 3.1.92. According to Strabo, Xouthos was the founder of the Tetrapolis: he settled all four cities at Marathon. Xouthos' son was Ionas, the primogenitor of the Ionians; therefore, Marathon was their birthplace. However, Philochoros, *FGH* 328. 74, regards a Titan, Titinios, as Marathon's first settler; Titinios had refused to fight against the gods during the Titanomachy and thus escaped their fate of being cast in Tartarus. According to the administrative system introduced by Kleisthenes in 508–507, the citizen residents of Probalinthos were integrated into the Pandionis tribe, while those of the other three settlements of the Tetrapolis belong to the Aiantis tribe. Nonetheless, despite this administrative separation, the Probalinthians remained members of the Marathon Tetrapolis throughout antiquity. In fact, a fourth century inscription record a Probalinthian as *demarch* ('mayor') of the Marathonians. *SEG* XLVIII, 129.

231. Stephanos Byzantios, *Ethnika*, 'Tetrapolis of Attica': 'Tetrapolis formerly called Hyttenia'.

232. There are in total four published inscriptions connecting this specific shrine with the Tetrapolis showing its importance for this political institution. See Lambert, 2014, 8–11. The shrines and the deities of Marathon that are directly related to the battle are presented in a later chapter. Only a few extracts are known from the *Tetrapolis* by Philochoros *(FGH* 328.73–75) that deals with the mythological traditions of the Tetrapolis of Marathon.

233. The position of the shrine of Dionysos at Marathon may be identified with that of 'Pyrgos', in the centre of the Marathon plain, as two of the inscriptions referring to Dionysos and his shrine at Marathon were found there. Onasoglou, 65.

234. Lambert, 2000, 67, estimates that during the fourth century the total number of citizens of all four *demes* of Tetrapolis at Marathon would have been 1,100–1,320 people. A century earlier, at the time of the battle, this number would have been even smaller.

235. Lambert, 2000, 66, n. 23.

236. The inscription of the 'Calendar of Sacrifices of the Tetrapolis', (IG II^2 1358) refers to this office. The title of 'Dimarchos of Marathonians' exists even today and is considered as one of the most prestigious in Greek local administration.

237. According to Leake, 1841, 2, 78, ancient authors used the name *Marathon* to describe the whole territory of the Tetrapolis; not just the settlement by the same name and the plain. In the Roman period, the *deme* (city) of Marathon remained the largest settlement while some of the smaller ones, like Oinoe and Probalinthos,

had been abandoned. Therefore, the use of the name Marathon for the entire area – not just for the namesake city – was unquestionable in the sources.

238. Traill, 111–112.
239. In the early-nineteenth century, several foreign travellers and scholars believed that the ancient *deme* of Marathon was located in the same place as the modern town. However, this identification was not supported by evidence, and was quickly turned down by later scholars. See Van der Veer, 293.
240. Vranas as the location of the ancient *deme* of Marathon was particularly popular with archaeologists and scholars during the nineteenth/early-twentieth century. See Van der Veer, *op. cit.* Leake, 1841, 2, 102, records that after a big flood in the beginning of the 1800s, foundations of ancient houses and vases were revealed in an area that may have been Plasi. At the end of that century, Eschenburg, 33–39, noticed a large number of pottery shreds on the surface at Plasi, leading him to believe that this was the site of the ancient *deme* of Marathon. This theory was later supported by Pritchett, 1969, 1–11, and Themelis, 233, based on archaeological finds in the area. Apart from Plasi and Vranas, some scholars have suggested possible locations of the ancient city of Marathon at different spots. Sotiriadis, 1932, 35, considered it was at the foothills of northeastern Agrieliki while Fotiou, 179, in the Stamata valley of Pentelikon. These theories had little or no acceptance by other scholars.
241. Themelis, 233–234.
242. Themelis, *op. cit.*
243. This theory appears to be supported by the fact that an ancient shrine excavated in Plasi was destroyed and abandoned at the end of the Archaic period, see Themelis 234, who also suggests that the inhabitants of the *deme* of Marathon moved away from Plasi to another area for security reasons and founded there a new settlement.
244. Tsirigoti-Drakotou, 53, records that the excavations of 2006 at Plasi uncovered architectural remains and vases of the Classical period. Weber, 63–71, assumes that the findings are evidence that the *deme* of Marathon of the Classical era was in Plasi. In addition, he postulates that parts of burial monuments of the Classical times discovered by archaeologists in the ruins of a Byzantine tower and other buildings in the Pyrgos region – near Plasi – may originate from the cemetery of the *deme* of Marathon, further evidence showing that its settlement was probably in this area. In 2014–2018, the Department of Archaeology of Athens University excavated at Plasi, at the site of the Archaic shrine, and brought to light finds that re-enforce the idea that the centre of the ancient *deme* of Marathon before the Classical period was located there.
245. Ptolemy, 3.14.21 (see Fotiou, 101).
246. Petrakos, 1995, 55.
247. The name *Ninoe* is a modern-day corruption of the ancient name 'Oinoe'. In a cemetery excavated at Ninoe, with burials from the geometric to the Classical era, a tombstone was found bearing the name of a resident of the *deme* of Oinoe. Theocharaki, 61.
248. Marinatos, 1972, 7. Themelis, 242.
249. Oikonomakou, 273–274.
250. Frazer, 440, describes the walls and believes that they belonged to the Acropolis of Trikorynthos. McCredie, 41, gives a detailed description of the walls of Trikorynthos pointing out that they may belong to the Mycenaean period.
251. Oikonomakou, *op. cit.*

252. Leake, 1841, 2, 102, argued that the name *Valaria* was a corruption of Probalinthos, but this was accepted by no other scholar. Probalinthos may have included the northern part of modern-day Nea Makri (Xylokeriza).
253. IG. II² 7292. The tombstone was donated by the Greek government to New York College in 1923. Some years later the college donated it to the N.Y. Metropolitan Museum of Arts and today it is on display in its permanent exhibitions with inv. no. L.1994.82. See Camp, 1996, 5.
254. According to Strabo, 9.1.22, Probalinthos was located between Myrrinounda and Marathon; in that point of his text, the ancient geographer records the settlements near the coast of Attica. Myrrinounda is modern-day Nea Makri and this reference shows that Probalinthos was south of the *deme* of Marathon. See Leake, 1841, 2, 87–88, for the method Strabo used for recording in his work the location of settlements.
255. Pindaros, *Olympionikos*, 13.110, calls Marathon 'Lipara', i.e. fertile. Furthermore, Aristophanes, *Birds*, lines 245–246, talks about Marathon's 'lovely meadow'. Chandler, 184, ascertains that when he visited Marathon in 1765 its plain was really fertile and produced a type of grain of spectacular size.
256. Marathon and nearby Ramnous possessed 8% of the cultivated land of Attica. Moreno, 37, n. 2. In the Classical era Marathon's products may not have been exported outside Attica and its basic market was Athens as the export of grain from Attica was forbidden in antiquity.
257. Leake 1841, 2, 84–85, records that during his visit to Marathon in 1802, he saw no fruit-bearing trees in the plain and concluded that these trees must have been few and far between at the time of the battle.
258. Nunnus, *Dionysiaka*, 47, 18, makes a passing reference to the existence of vineyards at Marathon.
259. The 'Calendar of Sacrifices of the Tetrapolis' mentions the existence of an *Eleusinion*, a shrine of Demeter and Kore, goddesses of the grain harvest, which Lambert, 2000, 52, postulates must have been in the area of the Tetrapolis. Lambert deems that the remains of the Eleusinion at Marathon need to be sought in the Koukounari location, where excavations by American archaeologists at the end of the nineteenth century unearthed the inscription of the 'Calendar of Sacrifices of the Tetrapolis'.
260. It seems that the cultivation of grapevines on a large scale at Marathon only began in the mid-nineteenth century by the Soutsos family, who had land next to the Great Marsh. Later in the century the property passed on to the Skouze family who produced there the famous 'Clos Marathon', one of the best Greek white wines. In the late nineteenth century, this wine was exported to Paris exclusively for the clients of the Grand Hotel. See Bickford-Smith, 61–62.
261. For references by ancient literary and epigraphic sources to Marathon's stock breeding during antiquity, see Ameling, 175.
262. Plutarch, *Theseus*, 14.1, records that Theseus after capturing the bull at Marathon sacrificed it to Apollo, whereas according to Pausanias, 1.27.9–10, he took it to the Acropolis of Athens where he sacrificed it to Athene. Pausanias also records that he saw at the Athens' Acropolis a votive offering of the *deme* of Marathon relating to the sacrifice of the specific bull there. He does not describe this object and Shapiro, 373–382, postulates that it must have been a bronze statue of a bull. A different interpretation of the myth is recorded by Steinhauer, 2009a, 82, who considers that

the bull of Marathon may have symbolized the cascading waters of the Charadros river that flooded a large part of the plain of Marathon.

263. IG I³ 503/4, Lapis C. This particular epigram is associated with other three epigrams, all of which are likely to honour the fallen Athenians of the battle of Marathon. Matthaiou, 2003, 200, has published evidence in support of this theory and furthermore claims that certain references in the epigrams of geographical points belong to Marathon. In this context, the 'fertile plain' referred to in the verse of one of the epigrams is likely to be that of Marathon. Cf. Bowie, 2010, 208–209, who deems that this particular epigram honours Fayllos, an athlete from Kroton, who fought on the Greek side with his own trireme at the battle of Salamis. According to Bowie, the plain of the epigram is that of Kroton, Fayllos' city. As we shall see, however, Matthaiou's view that the epigrams concern exclusively the battle of Marathon is more likely and so is his identification of the plain in the epigram with that of Marathon.

264. Schachermeyr, 18, records that the Persians must have got their water from wells close to the shore of Schinias. In antiquity, though, there must have been potable water throughout the Marathon plain, even during summer. According to Van der Veer, 308, the Persians got water from farms dispersed in the plain, which were abandoned by their owners when the Persians disembarked at Marathon. Aristophanes, *Frogs*, lines 1296–1298, mentions the existence of wells at Marathon.

265. The Persians probably used their ships to transfer supplies from Euboia to Marathon. Nevertheless, local products of Marathon may have covered a big part of their needs in foodstuff, at least in the beginning of their campaign against Athens.

266. Herodotus, 6.107.1–2, expressly mentions that Hippias led the Persians to Marathon and took the Eretrian captives to Aigilia. Then he directed the Persian fleet to the coast of Marathon, where the ships should anchor. After the Persian troops disembarked, Hippias made arrangements for their temporary camping at Marathon.

267. For Peisistratos' disembarkation at Marathon in 546, see Herodotus, 1.62.1–1.63.2.

268. Herodotus, 1.61.2–3.

269. During the late Archaic era, Eretria possessed a significant cavalry force, see Strabo, 10.1.10.

270. See Herodotus, 1.62.1, about the support of the residents of Marathon to Peisistratos, when he returned to Athens after his second exile. According to him, Peisistratos' supporters rushed to Marathon to join his forces. Hopper, 198, postulates that Marathon was one of the regions of Attica that constituted a base for Peisistratos' political power. In addition, Bicknell, 1972a, 32–33, cites evidence that Marathonians were ardent supporters of the Peisistratids. Cf. Lewis, 2004, 289–290, who argues that there is no evidence to prove that they supported the tyrant more than other Athenians.

271. As we have seen, when the Persians conquered the Cyclades they most likely recruited locals in their fleet. However, it is ambivalent if they could trust them as navigators.

272. Evans, 1993, 282, notes that it is quite uncertain what Herodotus (6.102) meant by the verb 'enippeusin' about Marathon and the use of cavalry. It may apply to a region appropriate for the cavalry to operate in, or appropriate to support it by providing the right pasture and plentiful water for the horses. Typaldos, 213, and Dionysopoulos, 203–204, postulate that through this verb Herodotus wanted

to show that Marathon was the most appropriate place for the cavalry to move through but not to fight
273. Kratinos 506 K-A.
274. On this scholion of *Menexenos* 240c, see Petrakos, 1995, 6.
275. Leake, 1841, 2, 209–210.
276. Theophrastos, *Enquiry into Plants*, 9.13.1, lists Marathon in the areas of Greece known for their marshes. In addition, some ancient scholia of Aristophanes refer to Marathon as a marshy region (Dindorf, 1833, 216, 309).
277. Herodotus, 5.63.4.
278. For Hippias as an expert on cavalry and its tactics, see Evans. 1993, 283. Even the Peisistratids' names reveal a close relationship to horsemanship: Hippias, Hipparchos and Thessalos. Concerning that last name, we may note that during the Archaic period, Thessaly was the region in Greece mainly identified with the cavalry.
279. Whatley, 138, thoroughly analyses this theory and refutes the arguments of its adherents by presenting the many advantages Marathon had as an appropriate area for the Persian landing. We have included in our book several of Whatley's points.
280. Most scholars believe that Athens in 490 was a walled city, even though no traces of a wall have been found from that time.
281. The Spartans would send their men to help the Athenians on condition that they would fight the Persians in the battlefield and not behind the walls of Athens. As we have seen, the same must have happened with the Athenian *klerouchoi*, who were sent to join the Eretrians but may have left upon finding out that they would fight behind the walls of their city.
282. Aelius Aristides, *Panathenaic*, 106.
283. Pseudo-Plutarch, *Ethics*, 305B.
284. Pseudo-Demosthenes, *Against Neaira*, 94. Plutarch, *Aristides*, 5.1.
285. Themelis, 234, in his report about the small shrine of the Archaic period unearthed in Plasi at Marathon, which was abandoned shortly after 500, suggests that it may have been destroyed by the Persians in 490. In addition, Pritchett, 1969, 8, claims that Datis' troops devastated the *demes* of Marathon and Trikorynthos, without however presenting evidence to back up his theory.
286. Van der Veer, 308, n. 72.
287. Most scholars accept that the Athenian *klerouchoi* of Chalkis joined the main body of the Athenian army and fought at the battle of Marathon. Their argument is that after the *klerouchoi* left Eretria they didn't return to their farms at Chalkis but dared disembark at Attica in grave danger from the Persian Navy. These scholars conclude that the *klerouchoi* acted in this way in order to join their fellow citizens from Athens and with them fight the invader. Furthermore, Herodotus expressly mentions that Aischines of Eretria 'gave them (the *klerouchoi*) *the go-ahead to depart for their country*'. Herodotus goes on to record the safe disembarkment of the *klerouchoi* at Oropos. However, there are a few scholars who suggest that the *klerouchoi* remained there and didn't go on to fight the Persians. For example, Bicknell, 1972a, 53, claims that the Athenians were forced to clash with the Persians at Marathon because the *klerouchoi* were Hippias' supporters and upon leaving Eretria were ready to join the Persians. This scholar believes that while the Athenian army was encamped at Marathon, the *klerouchoi* remained at Oropos awaiting Datis' army. Based on this kind of logic, we are quite impressed that Bicknell didn't accuse the Athenian *klerouchoi* of Chalkis of abandoning the

Eretrians on their own initiative! Bicknell's view is completely unfounded: if the Athenian authorities had the slightest suspicion that the *klerouchoi* would backstab them and co-operate with the Persian, they would not order them to go with the Eretrians. It is also doubtful if the *klerouchoi* would have obeyed such an order. More importantly, if the Athenian *klerouchoi* didn't want to clash with the Persians, they would not jeopardize their lives to sail from Eretria to Oropos abandoning their property in Chalkis. It should also be pointed out that their land in Euboia had not been granted by Hippias but by the Athenian democracy. Therefore, the majority of *klerouchoi* would be its ardent supporters, as the preservation of their property was inextricably linked with democracy not tyranny. Dionysopoulos, 66–67, is another scholar who postulates that the *klerouchoi* remained at Oropos though without disputing their patriotism. He bases his view on the fact that Herodotus does not mention what the *klerouchoi* did upon disembarking at Oropos and believes that these men remained there to guard the area against a likely Persian attack. Although the Athenians had had control of Oropos since 506, after their victory against the Boiotians, the area didn't yet have the strategic importance for the Athenians as it did later on during the fifth century. See Macan, 1895, 1, 356. Therefore, dispatching 4.000 men to protect it would have been unjustified in 490. The fort of Ramnous, the most powerful Athenian fortification in northeastern Attica, was first constructed at the end of fifth century, showing that the region gained strategic importance for the Athenians at that time. However, even if we accept the view that the *klerouchoi* had been initially ordered to remain at Oropos by the Athenian authorities, it is reasonable to assume that they would then have been ordered to rush either to the spot where the Persians would disembark or to Athens. The Athenian army desperately needed reinforcements and it would not have let 4.000 of its combatant men to sit idle at Oropos when the fate of the city was hanging in the balance a few kilometres away to the south.

288. In antiquity, the route between Oropos and Athens headed south towards Marathon through Ramnous. Pausanias, 1.33.2, mentions a road connecting Oropos to Marathon.

289. Aischylos, *Seven Against Thebes*, 38–68, describes the dispatch of Theban soldiers to spy on the moves of the troops of Polynikes and his allies as they approached Thebes with a view to besieging it. These men notified by messenger the king of the city, Eteocles, of all their enemy's moves. Similarly, the *klerouchoi* must have used runners for their communication with Athens. However, for the transmission of simple messages they may have used 'phryctories', i.e. communication towers that transmitted fire signals. In 490 the Athenians are likely to have had phryctories on the hills and mountain tops to communicate fast between the city of Athens and the regions of Attica. These would have been manned by small groups of men who would have observed the coasts for an enemy attack or disembarkation and would have been the first to relay to Athens the news of the Persian disembarkation at Marathon.

290. Finlay, 378–379, was the first to publish the theory that the Athenian *klerouchoi* had already started preparations to defend Marathon against the Persians, before the main body of the Athenian army arrived there.

291. The conscripts from Tetrapolis, if they had not already left for Athens, would have joined the Athenian *klerouchoi* at Marathon; perhaps together with those from Ramnous. The distance between Ramnous and Marathon is about 11km and the former is situated on the road starting from Oropos and going past Marathon.

Parts of this ancient road have been excavated by archaeologists in the Tetrapolis and Ramnous regions. Steinhauer, 2009b, 51. The men of Ramnous, though few at the time of the battle of Marathon, were no strangers to war. During the excavation of the temple of Nemesis in Ramnous, part of a Corinthian helmet of the late-Archaic period was recovered inscribed with the phrase 'the Ramnousians took this – as war booty – from the Lemnians'. see Rausch,7–17. This happened when the Athenians, together with Miltiades – who was then governor of the Chersonese in Thrace – conquered Lemnos some time between 499–496. The dedication of this helmet shows that in 490 the residents of Ramnous had recent military experience and had already fought side by side with Miltiades. These same men most probably fought with him once again, this time in their own 'neighborhood' at Marathon. Besides, the erection of the splendid marble temple of Nemesis at Ramnous in the place of the small porous temple of the later Archaic era – which must have been destroyed by the Persians – may also have shown the role of Nemesis in the Battle of Marathon. The Archaic temple of Nemesis at Ramnous appears to have been destroyed by the Persians in 480/79. see Petrakos, 1991, 20. However, we cannot rule out the possibility of its destruction having occurred a decade earlier, during the few days when the Persians were at Marathon. Green, 31, postulates that as soon as the Persians disembarked at Marathon, they took precautionary steps in the region and on the way to Ramnous as well. We deem that this may have happened so that the invaders could safeguard their rear against an Athenian attack. For that reason they may have sent some of their cavalrymen to Ramnous, where they destroyed the Archaic temple of Nemesis. Scott, 619, also considers that Datis may have attacked Ramnous and Oropos before the battle at Marathon. The Persians had brought with them to Marathon a piece of marble from Paros with the intention of making a trophy of their 'imminent victory' with the Athenians. This piece of marble fell into the hands of the Athenians after the Battle of Marathon, and from it the statue of Nemesis was sculptured. This is in tune with the punishment of the invaders for committing hybris towards the goddess. Pausanias, 1.33.2–3, notes that this hybris could have been setting her temple on fire, not punishment for campaigning against Athens, and this reference is more in line with a destruction in 490 than 480/79.

292. Herodotus, 6.103.1. Isocrates, *Panegyric*, 87, also mentions that the Athenians rushed to Marathon 'to aid those on the border of Athens', without adding something new in connection to Herodotus' reference.
293. Berthold, 85, claims that this refers to the inhabitants of Marathon.
294. In his narrative of the battle of Marathon, Herodotus frequently uses the verb 'εβοήθεον' and its derivatives to describe the support Athens sent to Eretria (6.100.1); the military aid Athens asked from Sparta straight after the destruction of Eretria by the Persians (6.106.2); the aid of the Plataians to Athens (6.108.1, 6) and the speedy return of the Athenian army to Athens after the Battle of Marathon (6.116.1). See Berthold, 85, n. 6. In all these cases, Herodotus describes the reinforcement of another noteworthy force that had been put together, ready to be used in military operations. This also applies to the last case, as the Athenians on departing for Marathon would have left a garrison in Athens which they rushed to join with after the battle.
295. Herodotus 6.101.1, records that the Persians first ensured the control of the coasts at Eretria with their fleet and then disembarked their cavalry there. Disembarking cavalry during a military operation was no easy task, even in the modern era, and

Maurice, 17, presents the problems arising when disembarking horses at a shore without harbour facilities during a military campaign.

296. Munro, 1899, 194–195. Grundy, 181–182. How and Wells, 358–359.

297. Whatley, 138.

298. Berthold, 92, postulates that right after completing the disembarkation at Schinias, Datis sent cavalry to reconnaissance the southern part of the plain of Marathon. Similarly, Whatley, 138, does not rule out the possibility of the Persians having sent reconnaissance teams to several points in the Marathon region. These are logical assumptions as the Persians possessed highly-skilled horsemen who were capable of accomplishing speedily such missions. Before the battle at Thermopylai, a Persian horseman on a reconnaissance mission of the Greek camp gave a thorough account to Xerxes about the Spartans who were there. Herodotus, 7.208.2–3.

299. Whatley, 138. 'There is no Thermopylae between Athens and Marathon.' However, as we shall see, not only were there 'gates' at Marathon, but they were also at the most strategic spot on the way from Marathon to Athens.

300. Evans 1993, 292, claims that this specific theory by Whatley overturned older scholars' views that the Persians should have had placed under their immediate control the passages between Marathon and Mesogaia, in order to reach Athens soon after their disembarkation. He contradicts himself, though, as he postulates that the Persians should have occupied Probalinthos, which he locates within the Brexiza pass, so that they could safely cross it. Therefore, Evans in fact disagrees with Whatley and claims, as the older scholars did, that the Persians were at a disadvantage over the Greeks at Marathon, because they failed to control the region's passages to Athens.

301. For Datis' ultimatum to the Athenians following the capture of Eretria, see Plato, *Laws*, 3.698d and Diodorus, 10.27.

302. Most scholars postulate that in 490, not only were Hippias' supporters in Athens few but also had no essential political power. McGregor, 71–95. However, this seems to be contradicted by the fact that in 496, just six years before the battle at Marathon, their presumed leader, Hipparchos, son of Charmos, was elected Eponymous Archon, the highest official of the Athenian Democracy. It is ironic that Hipparchos – who may have been a grandson of Hippias – bore the same name as Hippias' brother who was assassinated by Harmodios and Aristogeiton, later proclaimed as the 'founding heroes' of the newly-established Democracy in Athens. See Stockton, 38. Arnush, 154–155. For Hipparchos as leader of the philotyrants, see *The Constitution of the Athenians*, 22.4.

303. Badian, 11, was the first scholar to point out that Hipparchos must have fought at the battle of Marathon, and many have accepted this theory. Badian's main argument is that Hipparchos lived in Athens at the time of the battle and up until 488/487. Therefore, Badian deems that if Hipparchos had refused to join the Athenian army at Marathon, his fellow countrymen would have punished him in 490, or he would have left Athens then and not in 488/487.

304. Stockton, 38, analyses the importance of Hipparchos' election to the highest office of the Athenian Democracy as an attempt by the Athenians to use Hippias' relatives to negotiate with or placate Darius when they realized that the end of the Ionian Revolt was imminent. Nonetheless, even if the Athenians had tried in the mid-490s to follow a policy of appeasement with the Peisistratids and Darius, this ended the day the Persian envoys arrived in Athens and demanded 'earth and water'.

305. See Evans 1993, 282 and Hart, 92, about Hippias' unrealistic planning to re-establish his rule in Athens with the supposed aid of his supporters in Athens. It is worth pointing out that one of the aristocrats who benefited from Hippias' tyranny, but later advanced his interests through the democratic regime, was Kleisthenes himself, the so-called 'Father of Democracy'. In 525/524, Hippias appointed Kleisthenes as Eponymous Archon and the following year, Miltiades, the same person who thirty-four years later confronted him and his Persian allies at Marathon, as one of the Ten Generals of the Athenian Democracy. On the evidence of Kleisthenes and Miltiades holding the office of Eponymous Archon under Hippias, see Eliot and McGregor, 27–35; Dillon and Garland, 108–109.
306. Herodotus, 6.107.3. Souda, 'Hippias' (I).
307. Within the same context is the story that Herodotus, 6.107.1–2, cites about Hippias dreaming the night before the disembarkation of the Persians at Marathon that he had intercourse with his mother! According to Herodotus, the interpretation Hippias gave for his dream was that he would be re-instated as tyrant in Athens and die there at an old age (at the time, Hippias was already 80 years old). His interpretation of course proved wrong. We consider also wrong the view of Grahay, 255–256, that Hippias' dream of having intercourse with his mother meant that he would soon die. Herodotus mentions nothing about his death. Furthermore, according to Plutarch, *Julius Caesar*, 32.6, the night before Julius Caesar crossed the Rubicon he also dreamt that he had intercourse with his mother; his attempt to seize power was highly successful and he died five years later.
308. Glenn, 5–7. Drew-Griffith, 121–122. Holt, 221–241, present various theories linking Hippias losing his tooth at Marathon with his dream. We deem that 'the lost tooth event' may symbolize the refutation of Hippias' conviction that he would restore his power in Athens in 490. It may also be linked to the dream he had the night before the Persian disembarkation at Marathon that he was having intercourse with his mother. Hippias' mother symbolizes Attica and Hippias interpreted the sexual act with her as a sign of him ruling Athens and thus securing the future of his own family there. However, at the end Hippias didn't leave his sperm (family) in Attica but just a tooth, out of which life cannot be pro-created.

Chapter 2
1. Aelius Aristides, *Panathenaic*, 104–105.
2. Herodotus, 6.102.
3. Herodotus, 6.105–106.
4. A similar event that occurred in Athens more than a century later could shed light on what may happened in the city in 490, a few days before the Persians disembarked at Marathon. One evening in 339, the news arrived in Athens of Philip II of Macedonia leading his troops against the city. Throughout the night the Athenians were given notice by bugle-calls and fire signals to participate in an emergency assembly at dawn to decide measures against Philip. Demosthenes, *On the Crown*, 169.
5. According to the author of *The Constitution of the Athenians*, 7.3, the thetes acquired the right to participate in the Assembly in accordance with Solon's legislation (early-sixth century). Herodotus, 5.97, clearly shows that by 490, the Athenian Assembly decided upon all public matters. See Manville, 196.
6. According to Plato, *Laws*, 3.698c, as soon as the Athenians were notified of the advent of the Persian danger they set aside their differences and decided to unite in solidarity.

7. Herodotus, 6.109.5, records that there was a discussion between Miltiades and the Polemarch Kallimachos in the Athenian camp at Marathon a few days before the battle. Miltiades' words reveal that within the few days the two opposing armies were encamped at Marathon, there was a real risk of the Athenians surrendering to the Persians and accepting the restoration of Hippias' tyranny without a fight. Based on this report some scholars make the assumption that Hippias' supporters must have acted in favour of the Persians behind the scenes and the Athenians were eventually forced to clash with the Persians to pre-empt negative consequences. Evans, 1993, 287, n. 37, refers to the fear that would have been instilled in the Athenians that some fellow countrymen were about to betray them to the Persians, as this happened at Eretria. Nonetheless, no ancient source specifically records any evidence showing that fifth-columnists were active in Athens in 490. However, as we discuss below, after the battle of Marathon, many Athenians may have suspected that some fellow citizens were ready to betray them just before or during the battle. In this context, even the notorious story of the reflection of the shield as the Persians were leaving Marathon (Herodotus, 6.121), regarded by the Athenians as definite proof of treachery by the supporters of Hippias, may have only been a rumour by the political rivals of the Alkmaionidai to use against them.

8. Herodotus, 6.105.1. In most manuscripts of Herodotus' work, the name of the runner is *Pheidippides* and few have it as *Philippides*. The latter is mainly found in literary sources of the Roman era. Both names appear in modern bibliography but Pheidippides is more popular. Scott, 605, points out that Herodotus' reference that the generals dispatched the messenger belongs to his own time, not 490, when the commander-in-chief of the Athenian army was the Polemarch.

9. Plato *Menexenos*, 240c, and *Laws*, 3.698d-e, notes that the Athenians sent requests for military assistance throughout Greece, but no city came to their aid except Sparta, the army of which arrived at Marathon one day after the battle. Although Plato places the dispatch of these messages after the fall of Eretria, it is certain that Athens had requested Spartan help before the Persians launched their attack against Eretria and this had been accepted. Plato points out that the rest of the Greeks didn't help the Athenians – the contribution of the Plataians is not mentioned – due to the fear instilled in them by the Persian might. Besides, as we have seen, Herodotus recorded that many Greek cities had given 'earth and water' to Darius even before Datis› campaign had started, something that would rule out any help to Athens by these cities.

10. Cf. McQueen, 192, who suggests that the Spartan magistrates to whom Pheidippides made his plea were the two kings or the Gerousia. Jung, 2013, 20–21, n. 18, argues that the use by Herodotus of the term 'Archons', which was unknown in Sparta, suggests that he may have copied the story of the messenger to Sparta from an oral tradition of Athens.

11. Herodotus, 6. 106.

12. Herodotus 6.108, also mentions this event without however specifying when it took place. Thucydides, 3.68.5, places it about 519 and during Hippias' tyranny; some scholars accept this dating, for example, Frost, 292 and Dionysopoulos, 51. Cf. Macan 1895, 1, 363, and Armit, 416–426, who date the dispatch of Athenian help to Plataia in 509, while Shrimpton 1984, 294–304 and G. Anderson 2006, 259, n. 11, date it in 506.

13. In 507 Kleomenes invaded Athens with few troops and occupied the Acropolis in an attempt to install Isagoras in power in Athens. But the Athenians besieged

Kleomenes and forced him to leave Attica. The following year, he put together an army of Spartans and Peloponnesian allies with the aim of invading Attica once again. Nonetheless, Kleomenes had to abandon the expedition when many Peloponnesian allies and Demaratus, the other king of Sparta, left him and returned home. Between 505–501, Kleomenes planned to restore Hippias tyranny by launching one more invasion against Athens. However, this time the campaign didn't even start as the Corinthians refused to take part and convinced most other Peloponnesians allies of Sparta to follow suit.

14. Herodotus, 6.106.3–107.1.
15. See Pritchett, 1971, 116–117.
16. Curtius, 1869, 24. Pritchett, 1971, 116–124. McQueen, 192–193. Cf. Krentz, 2010a, 109, considers that the Spartans were not so much attached to the dictates of their religion as ancient authors claim. However, other scholars who accept the Spartans' obsession with their religion are probably right. We see for example, at the start of the battle of Plataia in 479 while the Persians had started attacking the Spartans and killing many of them with their arrows, Pausanias, the Spartan commander, avoided taking any preventive measures and kept on sacrificing animals in a desperate attempt to get a favourable omen before sending the signal to his men to give battle. Herodotus, 9.61–62.
17. Plato, *Laws*, 3.692d, 3.698d–e. Aelius Aristides, *To Plato: In Defence of the Four*, 169. Aelius Aristides, records both versions about the refusal of the Spartans to send immediately troops to help the Athenians. Plutarch, *Ethics*, 861E–F, claims that the Spartans had carried out many campaigns at the start of the month before the full moon and that Herodotus falsely tells that they delayed their aid to Athens using this excuse. Plutarch goes on and states that the Spartans went to Marathon as soon as the Athenians called them. According to him, they were eager to fight at Marathon, but they arrived there only to find out that the battle was already over. Alas! They were not responsible for this. However, Plutarch's version is unrealistic, openly biased against Herodotus and is mentioned by no other ancient author.
18. One day delay: Plato, *Laws*, 3.698e and *Menexenos*, 240c. Aelius Aristides, *Panathenaic*, 160. Three days: Isocrates, *Panegyric*, 87. Herodotus, 6.120, also writes that it took the Spartans just three days to reach Attica on a fast track. He does not clarify in his narrative, though, how many days after the battle they arrived at Marathon. We conjecture from the fact that the dead Persians were still unburied that this must have happened within a short period after the battle.
19. Plato, *Laws*, 3.698e. Plato's version of the events relating to the battle of Marathon in *Menexenos* and *Laws* differs in several points to that of Herodotus. Therefore, scholars consider that Plato consciously produced a historical record different to that of the ancient historian. Most modern scholars accept that he did this to make fun of the eulogies that orators delivered during festivals praising the city of Athens and eliciting information mainly from Herodotus. Pownall, 49–50. In any case, it is certain that Plato didn't have his own reliable sources to delve into and use authentic evidence about the battle. Apart from the battle at Marathon, Plato erroneously records other events of Athenian history.
20. See Wallace, 1954, 32–35. Sekunda, 37. Cartledge, 132–133. Krentz, 2010a, 109–110. These scholars postulate that Plato's report is correct and claim that the real reason why the Spartans could not send immediately troops to the Athenians was a revolt by the helots. Cf. Parker, 1991, 43, who cites strong evidence discrediting this theory.

21. This would apply to other Greek cities as well, with the exception of Sparta. The Athenian army of 490 was not professional and didn't include foreign mercenaries, such as Thessalian cavalry or Thracian peltasts, who only a few years before the battle of Marathon had offered their services to Athens (see below). Many scholars draw parallels between the Athenian army of 490 and a National Guard.
22. Ridley, 516.
23. In antiquity the absence of group military discipline was a general phenomenon in the armies of Greek cities – with the notable exception of the Spartan army – and not just of Athens, see Pritchett, 1974, 232–245 and Hornblower, 32.
24. Ridley, 513. According to Vidal-Naquet, 1983 (1986), 85, the Athenians did not rule their city as warriors but marched to war as citizens.
25. About Greek armies in the Classical period as 'cities' and how this was connected to lack of team discipline for Greek soldiers at the time, see Hornblower, 28–39.
26. Hornblower, 36, and Ridley, 514, regard discipline as an individual characteristic of each soldier in the military forces of Greek city-states.
27. During the Classical period, the Athenian generals had the right to punish their soldiers for discipline offences but refrained from doing so; instead they would rather chastise them with words. See van Wees, 2011, 109–110.
28. See Hanson, 1989, 158–159 and Wheeler, 1991, 121–170. Marathon, as we shall see, is a typical example of this: despite the Greek triumph and the small number of Athenians killed there, among them were Polemarch Kallimachos, who was the commander-in-chief of the army and Stesileos, one of the Athenian generals. Contrary to the Greeks, the Persian generals during a battle commanded their troops from the rear. They only fought in the first line if there was no other option, as Mardonius did at Plataia in 479.
29. The term 'hoplite phalanx' is a modern term and therefore unknown to ancient authors. Wheeler, 2007, 192.
30. For the introduction of the hoplite phalanx in Greece and its development in the Archaic and Classical times, see Snodgrass, 1967, 84.
31. For the weapons of the hoplite, see Snodgrass, *op. cit.* J. Anderson, 1970, 13–42.
32. Krentz, 2010b, 193.
33. Hunt, 2007, 113. Van Wees, 2011, 167–168.
34. This action is recorded in ancient literary sources as 'othismos'. Herodotus, 7.225.1. Thucydides, 4.96.2. See Matthew, 2009, 395–415. Van Wees, 2011, 188–191. makes a realistic representation of the way a hoplite phalanx clashed with an adversary. At the start of the battle, some hoplites probably used their shields to push and try throwing down their foes. Several modern scholars deem that *othismos* was not a team effort by all men in the front line, as older scholars thought, but rather a slow, gradual move involving hoplites one-by-one in the front line. In this context, Krentz, 2010a, 55–56, rejects the similarity of othismos with rugby which some American and British scholars apply.
35. Wheeler, 2007, 212. Krentz, 1985, 20. Hanson, 1989, 70.
36. Burn, 1962 (1984), 51.
37. According to Krentz, 1985, 20, in most battles among Greek city-states although casualties were twofold or threefold between the winning and defeated sides, those of the winners rarely outnumbered one fifth of the men who had fought at the battle. Wheeler 2007, 212–213, estimates that in battles of ancient Greece, those killed on the side of the winners came up to approximately 5% of the total force, and 14% for the defeated side. These casualties are not unlike those of armies in modern wars.

38. Today the prevailing image of the instruction of a hoplite in ancient Greece is that of a Spartan. In fact, the Spartans were the only Greeks who were subjected to continuous and rigorous military training, focusing on getting and staying in perfect shape. Aristotle *Politics*, 1338b9-19, succinctly points out – in an exaggerated way – that physical fitness made the Spartans look like wild beasts! Conversely, the Athenians worked out in the gymnasium. Opinions differ among modern scholars concerning hoplites' instruction in combat tactics; that is, if it was done and to what extent. Although no relevant reports have been preserved in literary sources, we can presume that hoplites were trained in essential tactics of the hoplite phalanx. Hoplites didn't perform complex manoeuvres, even the parade was an unknown procedure to them. However, they must have had some basic training in order to be able to march in a synchronized step within the ranks of the phalanx, to hold the shield in the right way, to wield a spear and a sword etc, see J. Anderson, 1970, 87. Ridley, 530. Wheeler, 2007, 208.
39. Hanson, 1989, 101.
40. According to Diodorus, the word hoplite derives from '*oplon*' ('weapon') which means 'shield', 15.44.3, but the word applied also to the entire equipment of the hoplite. See Wheeler, 2007, 195. Krentz, 2007a, 150, n. 10, claims that this reference by Diodorus is an implication that the shield was the distinct characteristic the hoplite had in contrast to the light-armed soldiers.
41. In a famous poem, Archilochos boasts about being a 'ripsaspis' invoking in this way the morals of his time. The Spartans turned away Archilochos on his arrival at their city due to this poem.
42. About the technical inspection of hoplites in Athens by officials, see J. Anderson, 1970, 59.
43. Hanson, 1989, 94, postulates that some men in the hoplite phalanx neither had the full equipment of a hoplite nor was the one they had made entirely of metal. Besides, in several works of art of the Classical period, hoplites are depicted naked, bearing only a shield and wearing a helmet. This way, though, it was an idealistic depiction of the hoplite as armour was in reality absolutely essential for hoplites in battle.
44. Christ, 2004, 38. In ancient literary sources, there are references to men with disabilities who fought in the hoplite phalanx. These cases were however very few and exceptions to the rule.
45. Wheeler, 2007, 207.
46. Hanson, 1989, 163–172.
47. Mosse, 1999, 227.
48. See Aristophanes, *Acharneans*, line 279. A tradition still applicable in our time as many who possess weapons place them on the mantelpiece at their home.
49. Meiggs and Lewis, 26–27.
50. Aristophanes, *Peace*, lines 1224 and 1251, records that a cuirass cost 1,000 drachmai, while a helmet 100 drachmai. These prices are over the top and probably a comic exaggeration. Other ancient references show that the arms of a hoplite in the Classical period cost between 75–100 drachms, see Hunt, 2007, 116.
51. In the fifth century, the rowers of the Athenian fleet earned three obols a day, i.e. a half drachma, see Scott, 443. This was likely the highest wage that a thetes could earn for his services to the Athenian state. We may also note that he received this income only during the summer months when the Athenian navy was in operation.

52. Herodotus, 7.144. This money was not eventually given to the Athenian citizens, but on Themistokles' proposal, which was approved by the Assembly and became law, funded the building of a powerful military navy.
53. Mosse, 1987/1989, 165–174.
54. *The Constitution of the Athenians*, 7. 2–4. 63.
55. According to Moreno, 325, in Classical Athens a medimnos (bushel) of wheat weighed 32.96 kg and barley 27.47 kg.
56. J. Anderson, 1961, 136, quotes prices horses were sold in Athens during the Classical period: for example, Xenophon sold a horse for the immense sum of 1000 drachmai. This was obviously one of the priciest horses in Athens. All the same, even an ordinary horse could be sold at 300 drachmai, a considerable sum of money in the Classical period. Apart from purchasing a war horse, the cost of maintenance was also high as it had to be fed, have its own facilities (stable) and a servant to look after it. This servant would also need his own horse to accompany his master to war. A horse consumed as much grain as six adult men on a daily basis. Therefore, a *zeugite* could not afford a horse as he had an annual production of grain to feed for a year at least 12 people (see below). According to Anderson, the less prosperous Athenian knights spent as much as half of their income on the maintenance of their war horse.
57. Cf. Whitehead, 282 and 285–286, who deems that the word '*zeugitai*' refers to the fact that each hoplite in the phalanx was 'tied' to his nearby fellow soldier. So, the rows of lined-up men reminded of pairs of oxen ploughing in the same line, being 'ypo ton zygon', i.e, in the same row. According to Whitehead, then, the rows in the hoplite phalanx were identified with the yokes of oxen and as most hoplites belonged to the lowest class who could put hoplites in the field (see below) they got the name '*zeugitai*'. It is interesting to note that even in modern Greece the rows of lined-up soldiers are called *zygoi*.
58. Van Wees, 2007, 276. As we have seen, a medimnos in Athens corresponded to 32.96kg of wheat. Consequently, a farmer had to produce at least 6.5 tons of grain in order to belong to the class of the *zeugitai*. In antiquity this produce met the nutritional needs of 12 people.
59. Hanson 1995, 188–189, considers that Athenian farmers possessing 4–6 hectares (40 to 60 acres of land) were able to purchase the equipment of a hoplite. Cf. Van Wees, 2007, 276, who argues that pieces of land this size could produce at most 100 medimnoi, resulting in their proprietors belonging to the class of thetes rather than that of *zeugitai*.
60. Vidal-Naquet, 1983 (1986), 89, wrongly characterizes the hoplite army of Athens as '*an army of small holders*'. As we have seen, most Athenian small land-owners were thetes and at the time of the battle of Marathon served in the Athenian army as light-armed soldiers, not hoplites.
61. Finley, 39–41. Tadlock, 33.
62. Finley, *op. cit.* For the distinction between poor ('*ptochoi*') and *penes*, see Markle, 100–101 and Tadlock, 34, quoting Aristophanes, Ploutos, lines 537–554, where the poor was destitute but the *penes* could cover his basic financial needs from his employment.
63. Labarbe, 172.
64. During the Archaic era, Athens was divided into 48 naukrariai, each obliged to offer two horsemen to Athens. Polux, 8.108.
65. When Hippias needed the support of cavalry to confront the Spartans in 511, he employed Thessalian horsemen as mercenaries. Herodotus, 5.63.3. The cities of

southern Greece started using their cavalry in an orderly and systematic way in battles only during the Peloponnesian War, see Gaebel, 91–109.

66. Evans, 1987, 98–99. Lendon, 44, notes that during the fifth century, well known *pentakosiomedimnoi* Athenians, such as Kimon and Pericles, participated in campaigns as hoplites.

67. Mosse, 1999, 227, n. 274, highlights the absence of cavalry from the Athenian army during the Greco-Persian Wars, postulating that this was due to the cavalry being a secondary weapon for the Athenians. We should point out, though, that no other Greek city-state lined up horsemen in any battle against the Persians, see below.

68. Stockton, 15, n. 16 and Evans, 1993, 284, wrongly call *zeugitai* the entire 9,000 hoplites that fought at the battle of Marathon.

69. Ober, 2007, 97. A thetes could acquire the equipment of a hoplite either through an inheritance bequeathed by an affluent relative or as spoils from a battle in which he fought as a light-armed soldier or through the financial support of friends. Socrates seems to have belonged to the latter category. Although he was a thetes, whose entire property – house and furniture – was not worth more than 500 drachmai, he fought three times in the ranks of the Athenian army as a hoplite. See van Wees, 2011, 55.

70. Cf. Van Wees 2001, 45–71 and 2011, 56, who claims that half the Athenian hoplites were thetes. The evidence he presents is contradictory, as he claims on the one hand that only the members of the upper classes could afford a hoplite's equipment, and on the other that a thetes would spend his meagre income on this equipment.

71. This would apply to most other city-states, as well – with the exception of Sparta whose case was idiosyncratic.

72. At the end of the fifth century, a spear in Athens cost between 1 drachma and 4 obols or 2 drachmai and 4 obols, sums affordable by most thetes. J. Anderson, 1961, 138.

73. Some scholars believe that during the fifth century the thetes had no experience in using their weapons as there is no evidence that Athens saw to their training. However, they do not take into consideration that many thetes, especially those living outside the city, made frequent use of their bows, spears or slings in peacetime, getting in this way accustomed to the use of their weapons. Additionally, Xenophon mentions hunting as a way to practice warfare. Vidal-Naquet, 1983 (1986),128, n. 72.

74. Slingers made their weapons themselves and many of their missiles were made of stone. Even lead sling bullets were at minimal cost. The view of some scholars, for example, Tadlock, 48, that the sling was the most difficult weapon to handle is erroneous as many thetes would have played with slings as children.

75. See Pritchett, 1991, 1–67. Xenophon does not even mention stone throwers as category of troops in a Greek army, indicating that this specialty had the least military value, according to the ideas of the members of the ruling classes at the time.

76. Krentz, 2010a, 59–60 and Van Wees, 2011, 196. During the battles between armies of the Greek city-states, opposing light-armed soldiers fought amongst themselves before the clash between the opposing hoplite phalanges. See Wheeler, 2007, 203–204. However, they played an important role at the end of the battle also, when the cohesion of a phalanx broke down. That is when the defeated hoplites dealt with the co-ordinated blows of the spears and the swords of the opposing hoplites and simultaneously the sling shots, arrows and stones from their light-

armed opponents. At the same time light-armed soldiers carried out raids in hostile territory, where they destroyed agricultural property. This action of the light-armed is regarded by some modern researchers of ancient Greek war tactics as important enough for the outcome of those conflicts as the battles between hoplites. See for example, Hanson, 1998, 19–25.

77. Greenhalgh, 79.
78. Van der Veer, 299–300. Van Wees, 2011, 196.
79. Herodotus, 9.60.3.
80. The Athenian generals may have found Pausanias' request to get their light-armed men to protect the Spartans – the most renowned hoplites in Greece – amusing. Still, the Spartan commander was right to ask for the Athenian archers' aid. A few days before the battle at Plataia, this force, along with a division of 300 Athenian hoplites, had saved many Megarian hoplites from the Persian cavalry. Additionally, an Athenian archer played a decisive role, before the battle of Plataia, in the killing of Masistios, commander of the Persian cavalry and high-ranking officer of Mardonius. During an assault of the Persian cavalry, Masistios fell off his horse when the hapless animal was hit with an arrow shot by an Athenian archer. This gave the opportunity to the Athenian hoplites to slay Masistios as he lay on the ground. Herodotus, 9.21–22.
81. Herodotus, 5.78.1.
82. See Manville, 200 and Ober, 2007, 97.
83. For example, in most fifth century tragedies, the hoplites gain all the glory, while light-armed soldiers' actions are underrated. Hanson, 1989, 44.
84. Van Wees 1997, 153–178, has collected many references from ancient sources showing that light-armed Greek soldiers fought in the phalanx since at least the seventh century.
85. Thucydides, 1.106.2–8.
86. Thucydides, 3.107–108.
87. Thucydides, 4.94.1
88. Thucydides, 4. 36–40.
89. At the start of fourth century, peltasts fighting for Athens under general Iphikrates, won great victories against the hoplite phalanges of the Peloponnesian city-states.
90. Herodotus, 6. 112.
91. How, 1923, 121. Van der Veer, 300. Dionysopoulos, 44.
92. As we will see in detail below.
93. Van Wees, 2011, 61. Herodotus 8.25, claims that after the battle of Thermopylai in 480, the Persians who visited the battlefield were under the impression that the corpses of helots they saw there were some of the 300 Spartans who were killed in the battle. Still, he mentions nothing about the actions of these men at Thermopylai and how they died. According to Herodotus 9.29.2, at the battle of Plataia, the Greek army consisted of the same number of hoplites as that of light-armed men. In the skirmishes that preceded the battle, Herodotus records the activity of Athenian archers. Additionally, he makes a passing reference to light-armed helots, who served alongside the Spartan hoplites. Although the ancient historian insinuates that these men took part in the battle, too, he does not mention them during the battle in the slightest, contrary to his analytical presentation of the actions of the hoplites.
94. Aischylos, *Persians*, line 460.
95. Herodotus, 8.95. See, also Plutarch, *Aristides*, 9.2.

96. Pausanias, 1.32.3, 7.15.7, 10.20.2. According to Pausanias these slaves were set free by the Athenians before the battle at Marathon; thus, it would be preferable to refer to them as former slaves or freedmen, instead of slaves.

97. Most scholars accept Pausanias' evidence about the conscription of former slaves of Athenians in their army who then fought at Marathon, see Hunt. 1998, 27, n. 5. So the contribution of the former slaves at the battle of Marathon assigns to it a symbolic and universal significance as the first battle in history for the freedom of Man; those with newly acquired liberty fought beside the Athenians striving to protect it at the battlefield. Pausanias, 1.32.3, mentions that he visited the common grave of the (former) slaves and Plataians at Marathon. He may have noticed at that spot a stele referring to these men who fought and died at Marathon and used this as his main source of information. However, he may also have had other sources of information that are lost today.

98. Pausanias, 7.15.7.

99. Thucydides, 2.43.4

100. Notopoulos, 353–354, postulates that the freedmen who fought at the Marathon became Athenian citizens after the battle. We may note that a few years before the battle of Marathon, in 508, Kleisthenes had granted Athenian citizenship to foreigners who were former slaves. Aristotle, *Politics*, 1275b. This may have set a precedent that simplified the procedure in 490.

101. Sargent, 210.

102. Sargent, 210–211.

103. Dionysopoulos, 49, discusses in detail this aspect of slavery in Athens at the time of the battle of Marathon.

104. In 490, the Athenian Assembly may have copied the older example set by Kleisthenes who conferred citizenship on former slaves.

105. Welwei, 28, claims that for the first time in Greece slaves were freed and fought with their – former – masters in 494 during a war between Argos and Sparta. Cf. Dionysopoulos 49–51, who presents evidence against this theory; he also argues that the Athenians set free and then conscripted slaves for the first time in 490 and not during the war against Aegina as other scholars believe based on a reference by Pausanias.

106. Aristophanes *Frogs*, lines 33–34, 190–191, 687–689, refers to the conscription of ex-slaves who served in the Athenian triremes before the battle of Arginousai (406); he mentions that these slaves were set free and then acquired Athenian citizenship, actions he applauds. Sargent, 209, and Pritchett, 1985a, 146–147, state that in 338 the Athenians conscripted slaves, who subsequently fought with them at the battle of Chaironeia against Philip II of Macedonia. This is not correct and neither is Pritchett's view that after this battle the Athenians buried the slaves that were killed at Chaironeia in their Public Cemetary (*Demosion Sema*). Also, Vidal-Naquet, 1983 (1986), 94 and Dionysopoulos, 49, wrongly state that the Athenians conscripted slaves immediately after their defeat at Chaironeia. At the time, the politician Hyperides, *Fragmenta* 28, had put a proposal to the Athenians to set their slaves free so that they would reinforce their city walls defences against Philip II. However, his proposal was rejected and the Athenians signed an armistice.

107. Pausanias, 7.15.7.

108. Plato, *Protagoras*, 319c.

109. *The Constitution of the Athenians*, 28.2. Aelius Aristides, *To Plato: In Defence of the Four*, 173–174.

110. See below, for other measures proposed by Miltiades for the defence of Athens against the Persians. Miltiades may have submitted the proposal of freeing and conscripting the slaves but we should note that in Pausanias' time – the second century AD – Miltiades was seen as the supreme commander of the Athenian army with absolute powers. Therefore, each initiative and measure the Athenians took to counter the Persian menace was accredited by authors of the Roman era to Miltiades. Nevertheless, Sears 247–249, presents convincing evidence that may point to Miltiades as the initiator of this measure. He records that a high percentage of Athenian slaves in 490 were from Thrace. As we shall see, Miltiades was governor of the Chersonese in Thrace and thus knew from first hand about the military value of the locals. He may therefore had proposed that they be set free and conscripted in the Athenian army as he knew well how they could be used in battle.

111. There is plenty of evidence in ancient literary sources about hoplites using personal slaves on a campaign, with most famous Thucydides' references to Potidea (428), Delion (424) and Sicily (416). See Pritchett, 1971, 49–51. Hanson, 1989, 99. Van Wees, 2011, 68–71.

112. Krentz, 2007a, 152.

113. There were exceptions, though; in 401 Xenophon's *hypaspistes* defected, taking with him his master's shield. Xenophon, *Anabasis*, 4.2.20.

114. Pausanias, 1.32.3 and 7.15.7. Notopoulos 353–354, postulates that the freedmen were slain while fighting in the first line, as the Persians didn't reach the Athenian camp during the battle of Marathon and therefore could not have inflicted casualties upon the slaves who would – presumably – be there to carry out their duties as aides. Cf. Burn 1962 (1984), 250, and Ridley, 510, who deem that the freedmen were killed by the Persians inside the Athenian camp. This, however, is wrong.

115. Hunt, 1998, 27, believes that the former slaves fought at Marathon in the hoplite phalanx. He erroneously points out that Herodotus records that only hoplites participated in the battle, something which the ancient historian in fact does not do. Labarbe, 170, and Vidal-Naquet, 1983 (1986), 91, also postulate that the freedmen fought at Marathon as hoplites along with the Athenians and were positioned in the centre of the Greek line-up. According to Vidal-Naquet, these men had carried the weapons of their masters at Marathon were then freed and 'armed as hoplites at the last minute to reinforce the centre of the Athenian line'. This leads us to ask the obvious question: what weapons did the Athenians use if they had – presumably – handed over theirs to their former slaves? As we will see, some of the former slaves did in fact fight in the centre of the Athenian line-up, but as light armed and not hoplites. Dionysopoulos, 48, and n. 90, also considers that the Athenians equipped their slaves like hoplites and positioned them in the phalanx.

116. Evans, 1993, 293, n. 65, also considers that the former slaves fought at Marathon as archers. This may be true for some of them, especially any who had previous experience in the weapon, like the Scythians. The correct handling of the bow, as well as the spear, was the result of training, which the majority of slaves in 490 lacked. On the other hand, neither using the sling nor throwing stones required any special training. For this reason, Xenophon, *Cyropaedia*, 7.4.15, calls the sling *'the weapon of the slaves'*, recording in this way the Greeks' perception of this weapon. Lazenby, 64, Doenges, 12. Sears, 247–248, consider that the ex-slaves at Marathon were positioned on the edges of the hoplite phalanx and covered it as light-armed men.

117. Van Wees, 2011, 180 and 297, n. 45: 'Actually, the Athenians went so far as to mobilize their slaves for this battle, so there was surely a levy of all available manpower to meet the threat, as one would expect, including poor citizens who fought with any weapons they could lay their hands on.' He presents his view to contradict Hunt, 1998, 26–28, who claims that in 490 the Athenians conscripted their ex-slaves in their army, but not their fellow citizens who were thetes. According to Van Wees, the Athenians conscripted both. Lacey, 129, repeated Van Wees' argument about the participation of light-armed men in the Athenian army at Marathon.
118. We analyse below, the way Athenian citizens were conscripted during the Classical period to participate in a military campaign.
119. Herodotus, 6.108.1. It is clear that by using the word *pandemei*, Herodotus refers to conscription of Plataian citizens from all classes.
120. Vidal-Naquet, 1983 (1986), 92, deems that through his reforms, Kleisthenes *'integrated and activated all sources of power'* of Athenian society. The same scholar, however, records that at the Battle of Marathon, the Athenians had exclusively hoplites who, as he claims, comprised a third of the military power of the city. He then expresses his puzzlement about the fact that the Athenian authorities didn't mobilize all citizens, but only one third, despite the mortal danger threatening Athens in 490. Although Vidal-Naquet could tell the flat contradiction, he didn't go on to examine it. If he had done so, he might have come to the conclusion that the Athenians did in fact mobilize the remaining citizens who were the majority and fought the Persians as light-armed soldiers.
121. For example, Dionysopoulos, 44 and 49.
122. Van der Veer, 299–300. Van Wees, 2011, 196.
123. Giannopoulos, 34. Also as we have seen, Bicknell, 1972a, 53, believes the 4,000 Athenian *klerouchoi* of Chalkis were followers of Hippias.
124. Most scholars accept that the Athenian assembly acquired the right to decide on matters dealing with war following Kleisthenes' reforms, see for example, Manville, 196 and G. Anderson, 2006, 55–56. As we have seen, it is widely accepted that by the time of the battle of Marathon, the thetes participated in it and had the right to vote on its proposals.
125. *The Constitution of the Athenians*, 22.4.
126. According to Plutarch, *Aristides*, 7.6, for an *ostrakophoria* to be valid there had to be a count of 6,000 *ostraka* (potsherds used to cast votes).
127. Hunt, 1998, 26–28.
128. Aristotle, *Politics*, 1306a20–37.
129. Aristotle, *Politics*, 1304a20–31.
130. Evidently, Hunt means that should former slaves have become Athenian citizens and fought at the battle of Marathon, they would belong to the class of thetes.
131. Hunt, 1998, 27.
132. See below for an analytical presentation of all evidence showing that the thetes gained power after 490.
133. According to Van Wees, 2011, 175, there are 750 Attic vases dating between 525/500 which depict archers, usually along with hoplites.
134. See Hunt, 2007, 122, who characterises them as 'mercenaries from Scythia'. Additionally, Vos, 61–88, believes that depictions of Scythians disappear from Attic vases shortly after 500 because they stopped coming to Athens to be employed as mercenaries, owing to the Persian penetration in the Balkans that cut off the route between southern Greece and Scythia.

135. See for example Ivantchik, 200, n. 9. According to Van Wees, 2004, 170, these depictions show that Greek archers had adopted the characteristics of the attire as well as the bow of the Scythians. However, this scholar – in a later publication, 2011, 175 – sets forth the view that at the end of the Archaic period, there may have been some Scythian archers in Athens. Pinney, 130, postulates that there were no Scythian mercenaries in Athens at the time. See Krentz, 2010b, 186.
136. Pinney, *op. cit.*, Krentz, *op. cit.*, Ivantchik, *op. cit.*
137. Krentz, 2010b, 202.
138. Krentz, 2010b, 203–204. This refers to the 'attack on the run' of the Greeks against the Persian wings; a tactic analysed below.
139. According to Aristotle, *Politics*, 1290b39–1291b30, the members of higher classes – whom he calls 'gnorimoi' – were not part of the *Demos* (people), but only those who worked to earn a living or those on a low income. Aristotle refers here exclusively to thetes. That *Demos* represented the thetes, can be seen in Aristophanes, *Knights*, lines 47–50 where Kleon as *Paflagon* manipulates *Demos*, his patron. The political power of Kleon derived mainly from the thetes, so here they are identified with the *Demos*.
140. Aristophanes, *Knights*, lines 781–785.
141. Krentz, 2010a, 151, also claims that this specific reference by Aristophanes shows that light-armed soldiers Athenians fought at Marathon.
142. The members of the upper classes who served in the Athenian fleet during the battle of Salamis, didn't row and were either commanding officers of triremes or hoplites who fought as marines.
143. For example, on the south frieze of the temple of Athene Nike on the Acropolis of Athens. The relationship between the iconography of this artwork and the battle at Marathon, as well as the role of the light-armed soldiers depicted there, is thoroughly analysed in a later chapter.
144. For details of the Tumulus of the Athenians or 'Soros' and its importance as the mass grave of the Athenian dead of the battle of Marathon, see Appendix III. The British traveller, Sir William Gell, who visited Greece in 1804–1806 and 1811, was the first to publish a reference about the finds of bronze arrowheads in the earth of this monument. It is unclear if he found arrowheads or just heard about such findings, see Krentz, 2010a,127. Foreign travellers who found bronze arrowheads at the Tumulus of the Athenians, include Leake, 1829, 172 and 1841, 2, 100, and the Austrian diplomat, Prokesch Von Osten. For the latter, see Enepekidis, 177. The British admiral Brock is alleged to have made an illegal excavation of an ancient tomb at Marathon in 1830, which could have been the Tumulus of the Athenians, where he recovered ten iron arrowheads and took them home to Britain, see below. Evidence that bronze arrowheads were found in the soil of the Tumulus of the Athenians may be found in a document that the Greek Minister of Education in 1835, Iakovos Rizos Neroulos, addressed to the Regional Department of Attica. In it Neroulos writes that foreign travellers made illegal excavations with the help of locals at the Tumulus of the Athenians, aiming at finding 'arrowheads of the Battle of Marathon'. The minister requested measures be taken to end this practice. Therefore, foreign travellers at Marathon searched for arrowheads at the Tumulus of the Athenians and obviously knew that such artefacts were to be found there. If no arrowheads had been found at the monument, neither the travellers would have searched for them, nor Neroulos would have taken the trouble to put in black and white this specific document. As we have seen, Leake recorded in two of his

publications in 1829 and 1841 that he himself had found bronze arrowheads in the earth of the Tumulus of the Athenians, ('I found many brazen heads of arrows') but in a publication in between, in 1835, he writes that 'I have heard that arrow heads of bronze have also been found here, but we searched for them without success.' His first publication, where he records that he had found bronze arrowheads appears to be true. This occurs in the context of Leake's lecture at the Royal Society of Literature that he delivered in 1828 and was published in the Society's journal the following year. At the time, Greece was not yet officially an independent state and Leake would have no problem mentioning in public that during his trips there under the Ottomans, he found antiquities at historical sites he visited and smuggled them to Britain. However, in 1830 Greece became independent and four years later passed the first law against the looting of antiquities on its territory. At the same time the smuggling of antiquities outside Greece was being condemned by prominent people. Apparently, Leake didn't wish to become known as a looter/smuggler of antiquities since he retained contacts with Greece even after independence. Therefore, we postulate that he 'corrected' his second reference to bronze arrowheads found at Marathon since this appeared in a book published in 1835. However, his 1829 lecture was re-published in a book in 1841 and the initial text was inserted unaltered, even the matter in question. So, this would explain why Leake claimed in 1829 and 1841 that he found bronze arrowheads at Marathon but in a publication in 1835, he assured his readers that he had found none.

145. Leake, 1829, 172 and 1841, 2, 100.
146. Galanakis, 2011.
147. In 1919, Forsdyke claimed the same about a collection of 41 bronze arrowheads in Karlsruhe supposedly from the battlefield of Marathon. See E. Forsdyke, 1919–1920, 147 and 152–153. Erdmann, also rejected a link of these arrowheads with the battle of Marathon. See Erdmann, 1973,58 and Krentz, 2010a, 128.
148. British Museum Catalogue, 1864, 0220.83.
149. E. Forsdyke, 1919–1920, 147.
150. We use here the term 'type' to describe the metal – bronze and iron – arrowheads in the British Museum that may have been found in the region of Marathon. This categorization serves to help the reader distinguish them in relation to the photographs cited.
151. E. Forsdyke, 1919–1920, 146.
152. Sekunda, 60, published a photograph of this particular arrowhead referring to it as '*spear*'. This wrong identification has been copied by Goette and Weber, 8, fig. 5 as well as Steinhauer, 2009a, 108.
153. According to E Forsdyke, 1919–1920, 147, this is what Brock's daughter told the curators of the British Museum when she sold her father's arrowheads to the museum in 1906.
154. Persian arrowheads at the Athens' Acropolis, see Broneer, 113–117. For such finds at Thermopylai, see Marinatos, 1951, 61–65, and Plate 21.
155. Baitinger, 128–131.
156. Broneer, 116, Plate 5.
157. Leake deems that the bronze 'triangular shaped' arrowheads he found at Marathon ('first type' in our book; it includes 13 of the 14 arrowheads of the Strangford collection and all of Meyrick's arrowheads in the British Museum) were 'Persian', a view adopted by later scholars, see Bronner, 114–115. Snodgrass, 1964, 151 and 153–155. 1967, 99. Thus, these arrowheads were considered Persian in the past

purely because of the prevailing view that only the Persians had archers at the battle of Marathon. Nonetheless, some scholars in the early-twentieth century characterized arrowheads probably found at Marathon as 'Greek'. Casson, 77, n. 1, and E. Forsdyke, 1919–1920, 147, identified the arrowheads presumably found at Marathon as Greek, and consider them evidence that the Athenians had archers during the battle. It is worth noting that a few years ago these arrowheads exhibited in the British Museum had a label with the description 'Persian arrowheads from Marathon'. Nowadays the same arrrowheads are described in the museum's inventory as 'Archaic Greek (late)-Classical Greek (early)', with reference to Galanakis, 2011.

158. See below, for the proposed dating of the Fylla fort.
159. Coulton et al. 114–115.
160. Coulton et al. 112, 114–115, 85–87, Plate 6.1, fig. SF 15, sketch of arrowhead and fig. 6.2, photograph of arrowhead.
161. Coulton et al. 112.
162. This theory is corroborated by other findings in the room the arrowhead was found and some distinctive features of the room. For example, most pottery finds date to the later Archaic period. Coulton et al. 63–65. Evidence points to 'Room 2' being inhabited in 490 and used by the Athenian *klerouchoi* of Chalkis. These are the same men who as we have seen after departing from Eretria went to Marathon where they joined the ranks of the Athenian army. Though most scholars accept that the fort was abandoned by the Athenian *klerouchoi* in 490, they disagree on when and why it was constructed. The archaeologists who excavated it believe that it was erected after 506 for the protection of Athenian *klerouchoi* against locals of Chalkis, see Coulton et al., 113–115. Cf. Figueira, 2010, 196–197, considers that the fort at Fylla was erected by the Athenians to defend the *klerouchoi* in case the Persians campaigned in Euboia. If this happened the *klerouchoi* could have used Fylla and other fortifications in the wider area to fight the Persians in Euboia and thus delay their assault against Athens. According to Figueira, the facilities of the fort in Fylla must have been constructed not in 506 but 493 when a Persian attack against Athens became imminent.
163. The *Decree of Themistokles* mentions that in 480 archers served on Athenian triremes. Although many scholars question the validity of this specific epigraphic source.
164. In a guidebook for an exhibition at the British Museum in 1929 there is a reference about some of the lead sling bullets in the museum's collection which were found at Marathon (*The British Museum Guide to the Exhibition Illustrating Greek and Roman Life*, London 1929, 101). Dodwell, 160, notes that at the beginning of the nineteenth century lead sling bullets were found in the Marathon plain. When Dodwell visited the area in 1806, the trade of 'souvenir' weapons from the battle was still non-existent. Thus, those lead bullets may have indeed been found at Marathon and be connected to the battle. The sling has been a traditional weapon for the Greeks since the time of Homer. Therefore, the possibility of the Greeks having used slingers in the battles against the Persians is highly likely. The fact that Herodotus does not mention Greek slingers during the battles with the Persians, or that slingers are scarcely depicted in artworks of the period, is no proof that this specialty of light-armed soldiers didn't exist during the Greco-Persian Wars. As we have seen, references in ancient sources to light-armed men in the early Classical period are quite rare.

165. The oldest reference to 'Persian slingers' belongs to Xenophon and dates to the fourth century, see Pritchett, 1991, 54.

166. Archaeologists who excavated the fort at Fylla found a number of small round stones in one room that they think were selected by slingers to be used as missiles. Coulton et al. 85, 112.

167. According to some scholars, for example Berthold, 86, n. 16, the number of 4,000 Athenian *klerouchoi* in Euboia in 490 is an exaggeration and should be rejected. Aelian, *Varia Historia*, 6.1, who gives a number of 2,000 Athenian *klerouchoi* in Euboia, is considered more plausible, see for example Manfredi, 211. Should we therefore accept the number Herodotus cites or that of Aelian who lived more than seven centuries after the battle of Marathon? The evidence points to the former; despite the omissions and the uncertainties in his narrative, Herodotus remains the most reliable literary source we have about the battle of Marathon (see Appendix II). Besides, Herodotus records the number of 4,000 Athenian *klerouchoi* twice in his text (5.77.2 and 6.100.1) which reduces the chance of error. Quite the reverse is true about Aelian's works as they include many inaccuracies. We should also bear in mind that Aelian may have mixed up the number of Athenian *klerouchoi* of 490 with one of a later Athenian klerouchia founded in Euboia during the mid-fifth century. see Parker, 1997, 164–165. Thus, most scholars accept the number of *klerouchoi* recorded by Herodotus.

168. See below for the number of 9,000 Athenian hoplites at the battle of Marathon.

169. Hammond, 1968, 34, n. 98, accepts that the 4,000 *klerouchoi* of Chalkis were hoplites. However, he is also puzzled by the fact that if his view is correct, these men would have made up approximately half of the total force of Athenian hoplites that fought at Marathon. Nonetheless, the problem which concerned Hammond in fact does not exist as most Athenian *klerouchoi* of Chalkis in 490 served in the Athenian army as light-armed soldiers. Figueira, 2010, 200, infers that the 4,000 *klerouchoi* were highly unlikely to have been hoplites.

170. See Figueira, 2010, 194. During the late-sixth and fifth centuries, Athenians of a higher social class than that of thetes could take part in the founding of an (Athenian) colony but not a klerouchia.

171. An inscription of c. 500 records the obligations of *klerouchoi* at Salamis to the Athenian state and reveals that some were conscripted in the army as hoplites. see Athens Epigraphic Museum 6798+6798α+6815+12936, 13500. Hansen, 45, mentions two cases, known from literary or epigraphic sources, where social mobility allowed thetes to become members of higher classes.

172. According to Dionysopoulos, 66, Athens did not aim to build up the number of her hoplites through the institution of clerouchia.

173. Herodotus, 8.1.2.

174. The view that the 'Chalkidians' who manned these triremes were Athenian *klerouchoi* is recorded by many scholars, see for example, Scott, 352, and Figueira, 2010, 201–202. Their arguments are convincing, contrary to those presented by other scholars who propose that these were indigenous residents of Chalkis.

175. Krentz, 2010a, 102 and 105–106, accepts that the number of 9,000 or 10,000 Athenians who according to ancient literary sources campaigned at Marathon concerns only hoplites. Nevertheless, he assumes that the Athenian expeditionary force that fought there was much larger thanks to the participation of light-armed soldiers. Krentz, 2010a, 211–212, estimates that between 16,000–22,000 Athenians fought at Marathon, which means he has included 7,000 to 12,000 light-armed

men. As a matter of fact Krentz also records references by other scholars with estimates of the number of light-armed Athenians in the battle of Marathon. For example, Leake, 1841, 2, 222, claims that there were 10,000, that is, one light-armed soldier for each hoplite. He based his estimate on Herodotus' reference that at the battle of Plataia, for each hoplite in the Greek expeditionary force there was one light-armed soldier. Leake assumes that the same would also have applied at Marathon. Beloch, 2.1.21, postulates that the Athenians had 6,000 to 7,000 light-armed men at Marathon, while Munro 1899, 189, deems that the entire Athenian army that fought in 490 consisted of 15,000 men, with a few thousand light-armed soldiers – 'thetes and former slaves' – among them. Apart from the scholars Krentz refers to, there are others who have deemed that the Athenian army that marched to Marathon included in its ranks not only hoplites but also light-armed soldiers. The first scholar to advocate that the Athenians had such soldiers at Marathon was Mitford, 97–98, in the late-eighteenth century, who estimated the total Greek force between 28,000 and 30,000 men, with the hoplites and light-armed men split in half. Finlay, 382, deemed that the Greeks at Marathon could not have been fewer than 20,000 men, of which 11,000 were light-armed soldiers. Sotiriadis, 1927b, 132, claims that the number of Athenians at Marathon was 18,000 men; 9,000 hoplites and as many light-armed soldiers. Lampros 1886, 387, mentions that Athenians had a total of 20,000 men at Marathon; 9,000 of these were hoplites, quite as many were freed slaves and the remaining 2,000 light-armed Athenians. Van Wees 2011, 180, considers that in the Athenian expeditionary force of 490, there were also 'poor citizens' fighting with any weapon at their disposal, without mentioning an estimate of how many they might have been. Other scholars 'suspect' the presence of light-armed soldiers at the battle of Marathon without delving into it any further. Whatley, 133–134, sets forth the general view that in any conflict during the Greco-Persian Wars, the Greeks had light-armed soldiers who played in battle a secondary role in relation to hoplites. Berthold, 86, n. 17, also notes the possibility of some 'highly skilled' light-armed Athenians fighting in the battle at Marathon, a view shared with Lacey, 129.

176. Sargent, 209–210, was the first to point out that Herodotus deliberately avoided any reference to the freedmen fighting in the battle of Marathon and attributed this to his intention to glorify the hoplites to the detriment of the historical truth. These omissions by Herodotus, according to Hunt, 1998, 42–43, prove the ancient Greeks' prejudice against their slaves, even when the latter fought for their masters' freedom. However, we should not forget that members of the higher social classes of Athens also held in contempt the thetes, their low class follow citizens, who fought alongside them as light-armed soldiers for the protection of their city.

177. *The Constitution of the Athenians*, 22.3.

178. Nepos, Miltiades, 5: '9,000 men'. Pausanias, 'no more than 9,000' (10.20.2) and 'less than 10,000' (4.25.5). Pseudo-Plutarch, *Ethics*, 305B: '9,000 men'. Souda 'Hippias': '9,000 men'. Justin, 2.9, and Libanios, 32 '10,000 men'.

179. Herodotus, 9.28. Pritchett, 1957, 24, quotes evidence showing that the number of Greek hoplites – and as a consequence those of Athens – recorded by Herodotus in the battle of Plataia in 479 must be correct. Still, Athenian light-armed men (archers) also fought in Plataia. Labarbe, 190–191 and Vidal-Naquet, 1983 (1986), 102, n. 52, state that only the Athenians had no light-armed soldiers at Plataia. However, Herodotus expressly mentions that for each Greek hoplite in Plataia there was one light-armed soldier and does not exempt the Athenians! As a matter

of fact, Herodotus, as we have seen, records in detail the Athenian archers' actions at Plataia, something he rarely does for any light-armed Greek soldiers in his narrative of the battles of the Greco-Persian Wars. Krentz, 2010a, 102, considers that the Athenians had at Plataia 8,000 light-armed soldiers, a number which equalled their hoplites.

180. One of these may have been Aischylos, who fought as a hoplite at the battle of Marathon, but a decade later served in the Athenian fleet at the battle of Salamis. Aischylos is unlikely to have served as a rower on a trireme at Salamis but as a (marine) hoplite. For Aischylos' war record, see Burian and Shapiro, 11, n. 16.

181. Many scholars believe that this was the total number of men in the Athenian expeditionary force at Marathon. How, 1923, 121; Van der Veer, 300; Dionysopoulos, 44 and 49, claim that the Greek forces at Marathon consisted entirely of hoplites; they had neither cavalry nor light-armed soldiers and quote Herodotus, 6.112, in support of this view. Nevertheless, in this reference Herodotus makes it clear that the Greek hoplites were not backed up by cavalry nor by archers throughout the entire battle, but in one of its phases, when they attacked the infantry on either flank of the Persian line-up.

182. Nepos, *Miltiades*, 5.

183. Pausanias, 10.20.2.

184. Pausanias 'no more than 9,000' (10.20.2) and 'less than 10,000' (4.25.5).

185. Herodotus, 5.97.2, mentions that in 499/8 there were 30,000 Athenian citizens. In 483, the Athenians who were entitled to get a share in the silver found in Lavrio were as many as 40,000. This number however also included males of the age of 16–18, who were too young to have political rights. However, the majority of the 40,000 men were citizens in 490; Labarbe, 210, puts their number at 34,448.

186. Pausanias, 10.20.2. Dionysopoulos, 64, n. 153, argues that at this point Pausanias refers both to the 'very young' (*neotatoi*) and 'elderly' (*presbytatoi*) Athenian soldiers.

187. We discuss below, how Athenians were conscripted in their army in 490, and reveal ways that these men could have avoided doing so and fighting at Marathon.

188. Aristophanes, *Peace*, lines 1181–1186, mentions a farmer who found out at the last moment that he had been conscripted for an expedition. As a result, he left for the campaign without the necessary foodstuff for its first three days as he had no time to purchase them!

189. Hunt 2006, 21, mentions that at the battle of Marathon, the Athenians conscripted 300 slaves, without providing references for this number. Dionysopoulos, 64, taking for granted that the total number of men in the Athenian army at Marathon was 9,000, estimates the hoplites at 8,612, based on Labarbe's estimate of the citizen population in 490. Thus, he comes to the conclusion that the slaves who were conscripted were 388. However, in his reasoning he arbitrarily counts in a significant percentage (25%) of citizens who should be conscripted as hoplites but never were. Hammond, 1992, 147–150, postulates that in the so-called 'Tomb of the Plataians' at Marathon (see Appendix III) had been buried freedmen who fought and died in the battle of Marathon. The number of these dead is 10 male adults, leading Hammond to the conclusion that in 490 the Athenians conscripted in total 400 freedmen as hoplites. Nonetheless, these estimates are based on a series of unsubstantiated assumptions. The number of conscripted freedmen that these scholars suggest is not only erroneous, but also very small; the Athenian authorities would not have the taken the trouble to embark upon such a complex procedure

190. Herodotus, 6.132.
191. During the battle of Marathon, the Athenians seized seven Persian ships. Herodotus, 6.115. These were probably triremes and would have been added to their war fleet.
192. These two categories of conscripts existed in 457 (Thucydides, 1.105.4) and this may be true a few years earlier during the battle of Marathon. Dionysopoulos, 63, states that 'elderly' were 50–59 year old soldiers, and that the choice not to dispatch men older than 40 years old in military expeditions belongs chronologically to the fourth century. The 'elderly' may therefore have been soldiers between 40–59 years old. In 490, due to the deadly menace that threatened Athens, men up to the age of 59 years old may have been sent to Marathon, without ruling out the possibility of even older men joining the Athenian expeditionary force as volunteers. Still, most young soldiers aged between 18 and 20 doing their compulsory military service in 490, known as 'ephebeia' – if this already existed at the time, see below – may not have fought at Marathon. Van Wees, 2011, 94, postulates that the 'very young' didn't take part in campaigns; but whenever there was a military crisis they stayed back in Athens as a guard. Ridley, 533, postulates that Thucydides' reference shows that at the start of the Peloponnesian War the 'very young' carried out duties as guards in the city and at various Attican forts; so, they constituted a separate corps from the rest of the Athenian troops. In 490 one of these soldiers was 20-year-old Kimon, son of Miltiades. No source mentions that he fought at Marathon and he and his peers must have stayed on to guard Athens in 490, along with the 'elderly'.
193. In 424, during the Peloponnesian War, the Athenians lined up 7,000 hoplites at the battle of Delion and 'a lot more' than 10,000 light-armed soldiers. Thucydides, 4.93.3–4.94.1. The population of Attica was greater in 424 than what it was at the time of the battle of Marathon, but most thetes during the Peloponnesian War served in the navy.
194. Van Wees, 2011, 65 and 241–243.
195. Milford, 97.
196. Finlay, 382.
197. Krentz, 2010a, 101. This estimate is based on Herodotus' reference that at the battle of Plataia there was one light-armed soldier for each Greek hoplite.
198. Lampros, 387. Sotiriadis, 1927b, 112. For the other estimates, see Krentz, 2010a, 211–212.
199. Milford, 97, was the first to record this view. See also Leake 1829, 189, who deems that this happened because ancient authors recorded only the number of Athenian hoplites who fought at the battle of Marathon and not that of their light-armed soldiers. The reason for this was that they wished to present the smallest number of Greeks having defeated the almighty Persians in 490.
200. Herodotus, 6.108.1.
201. Nepos, Miltiades, 5. Justin, 2.9. Scholion on Aristophanes, *Knights*, line 781. Souda, 'Hippias' (II).
202. Herodotus, 9.28.6.
203. Krentz, 2010a, 101. Dionysopoulos, 41–42, believes that the Greeks didn't have light-armed men at the battle of Marathon and hypothesizes that the Plataians lined up 1,000 hoplites there. Cf. Van der Veer, 309, estimates the total number of Plataians in the battle of Marathon at 600 hoplites.

204. The problem about the total number of men in the Persian fleet of 490 stems from the fact that we are uncertain about the number of triremes it had and how many of these were fully manned. As we have seen, Wallinga suggests a total of 42,000. Hammond, 1988, 504, of 90,000 and Van der Veer, 309, 178,000–180,000.

205. See below about the possibility of Persian crews having fought in the battle of Marathon when the Athenians attacked their ships on the coast.

206. As we have seen, in 546 Peisistratos seized power in Athens for the last time, with the aid of many mercenaries he had hired. In 511 Hippias hired 1,000 Thessalian horsemen who fought against the Spartans who had tried to overthrow him.

207. Best, 6.

208. Best, 7.

209. Best, 7, n. 26, considers that the conquest of the Thracian coast by the Persians in 492 was the reason why Athenians stopped hiring as mercenaries peltasts from this region.

210. It is likely that in 490 alongside their former slaves the Athenians conscripted also the metics (foreign residents) who lived in Athens. However, those metics in 490 were few compared to the large number residing in the city some decades later. Gomme 1933, 47, estimates that in 431 as many as 25,000 metics lived in Athens.

211. Pausanias, 10.20.2.

212. Aelius Aristides, *Panathenaic*, 105. There is a scholion on Aelius Aristides, *To Plato: In Defence of the Four* (Dindorf, 1829, 3, 542), which records that when the Athenian youth left for Marathon the elderly along with the women stood guard at the walls of Athens.

213. Plutarch, *Aristides*, 5.4.

214. Herodotus, 6.21.2.

215. The Athenians vented their anger on Phrynichos by imposing on him a huge fine of 1,000 drachmai as punishment. At the same time they prohibited the use of the topic 'the capture of Miletos by the Persians' in any other play.

216. Hammond, 1968, 44.

217. Our only source – earlier than the Roman era – about the mobilization of the Athenians during the Greco-Persian Wars, is the so called 'Themistocles' decree', recorded in an inscription of the third century. However, several scholars question whether the text of this specific inscription includes authentic historical evidence from the time of Greco-Persian Wars.

218. Bakewell, 90–91.

219. Christ, 2001, 398–422, makes an analytical presentation of the known evidence about the conscription of Athenian hoplites and horsemen during the Classical period.

220. The Athenian tribes' names – belonging to mythical heroes of Athens – were chosen by the Delphi Oracle out of a list of 100 names.

221. Traill, 75–76.

222. During antiquity the Athenians belonged for administrative purposes to the *deme* of Attica which their predecessors came from, and not the one where they were born in or lived in, if these were different to the former.

223. Something which is ascertained by Herodotus, 6.111.1, with his description of the Athenian line-up at Marathon.

224. Thucydides, 2.34. Vidal-Naquet, 1983 (1986), 89.

225. Bicknell, 1972a, 20–21 and n. 67, postulates that the Athenian hoplite phalanx in 490 numbered about 9,000 men divided in 10 tribes; each tribe consisted of three *trittyes* with 300 men each. Herodotus mentions an Athenian *lochos* having 300 men

during the battle of Plataia. It seems therefore that in the Athenian army, the *trittya* and *lochos* were terms applied for the same divisional unit.

226. Vidal-Naquet, 1983 (1986), 98–99.

227. Rawlings, 357–358.

228. For example, Socrates took part in three military campaigns: against Potidaia, in Amphipolis and at the battle of Delion; Socrates was 46 when he fought as a hoplite at the last battle.

229. About the role of a general in the Athenian army, see below.

230. The generals had certain commitments regarding the selection of their fellow citizens for a military expedition; for example, they could not choose each year the same men. Some generals however didn't always comply with this procedure and we have the testimony of a citizen who protests because he had been selected to go on campaigns two years in a row while other citizens had never been mobilized. Ancient sources also record generals getting bribes from wealthy men who didn't want to go to an overseas campaign, as well as generals who – out of fear or ambition – avoided conscripting citizens who exerted political influence. Christ, 2001, 400–403. The names of the men selected for a campaign were written on wooden boards at the base of the statue of the Eponymous Hero of each tribe on the Monument of Eponymous Heroes at the Athens Agora. *Demes* of Attica outside Athens were notified by heralds about the men who had been selected for a campaign.

231. For differences between 'general' mobilization and 'list recruitment' see Van Wees, 2001, 45–71 and Krentz, 2010a, 211.

232. Thucydides, 4.94.1.

233. See Hansen, 45. Cf. Bradeen, 1969, 153–154, and other scholars who consider that the thetes were registered in the *lexiarchike grammateia*. Hanson 1998, 23–25, assumes that in Athens of the Classical period there was a distinction between light-armed soldiers with an expertise in a particular weapon, such as archers, peltasts, spear users and sling users and non-experts or 'unarmed' ones, who fought in battles with their agricultural tools or threw stones at the enemy. If this is true, it is possible that some light-armed Athenian soldiers of the former category could have been included in the *lexiarchike grammateia*.

234. During these campaigns light-armed Athenian soldiers also built the temporary camps and carried out patrolling and guarding duties. Hanson, 1998, 23–25.

235. Thucydides, 4.94.1.

236. Krentz, 2010a, 106: 'Sometimes, however, the Athenians declared a campaign that welcomed all volunteers, whether they were fully equipped or not. Marathon was surely one such campaign.'

237. As we have seen, the thetes participated in the Assembly as a result of Solon's legislation.

238. Oswald, 334, believes that thetes were not conscripted in the Athenian army in 490, in accordance with the view that only hoplites fought at the battle of Marathon. Nevertheless, he stresses that the thetes 'could make their influence felt in voting for the army commanders', without pointing out the contradiction in this statement.

239. This way a foreigner could be deterred from impersonating an Athenian citizen. Solon's legislation gave thetes the right to become jurors. *The Constitution of the Athenians*, 7.3.

240. Some parametres of this procedure, such as compensation for the owners of slaves who had been freed and their subsequent naturalization as Athenian citizens, must have concerned the authorities after the battle.

241. Though the earliest known references to *ephebeia* date to the fourth century, Ridley, 531–534, Matheson, 34, n. 9, Hornblower, 35–36, believe that the institution existed in Athens during the fifth century and Flaceliere, 249, suggests as early as 490. Scholars do not agree if thetes who fought in campaigns as light-armed soldiers or as rowers in the navy participated in *ephebeia*. Rhodes, 1981, 503, and Manville, 10, n. 34, consider that during the fourth century only those who would become hoplites took part. Cf. Vidal-Naquet 1983 (1986), 97, who believes that thetes were included. According to the author of the *Constitution of the Athenians*, 42.3, the Athenians in *ephebeia* trained as hoplites, archers, slingers and spear users, something that appears to support the idea of thetes' participation.
242. For the wars the Athenians fought in 507/506–492, see Krentz, 2010a, 40–65.
243. Manville, 200 and Ober, 2007, 97.
244. For Athenian mobilization before Kleisthenes' reforms, see Bakewell, 91.
245. Raaflaub, 1995, 1–54.
246. Christ, 2001, 408–409.
247. According to Thucydides, 4.94.1, there was a general mobilization in fifth century Athens for the campaign against Boiotia in 424. His description makes it clear that the Athenian troops that invaded Boiotia at the time consisted – apart from hoplites – of thousands of light-armed Athenians.
248. Hammond, 1968, 44.
249. During the Classical era, only the Spartan army imposed uniformity in the dress code of its men. They all had long hair and wore a uniform scarlet cloak. Furthermore, everyone's shield, from those of the two kings to the least important hoplite, used the insignia the capital Lambda ('Λ') for 'Lakedaimoniai'. Xenophon, *The Constitution of the Lacedaemonians*, 11.3. Quite the reverse was true for the Athenians, who wore whatever they wished and decorated their shields as each one liked. For example, Alkibiades had on his shield Eros, a symbol of his conquests in this field but irrelevant to war. Additionally, he and other wealthy Athenians wore extravagant gilded armours. Ridley, 520 and Van Wees, 2011, 52–54
250. Based on ancient sources, Christ, 2001, 408–409, concludes that during the Classical era mobilized Athenians mustered at the Agora, Pnyx, or the area of Apollo Lykeion.
251. Lysias, *For Mantitheos*, 14, mentions that men of a *deme* of Attica outside Athens mustered and left altogether to take part in a military campaign.
252. Plutarch, *Aristides*, 5.4.
253. Herodotus, 6.116.
254. According to the author of the *Constitution of the Athenians*, 22.2, the institution of Ten Generals was founded in 501/0, see Rhodes, 1981, 264–266, and Manville, 203–204. Cf. G. Anderson, 2006, 258, n. 3, who believes that it was part of the reforms of Kleisthenes of 508/7.
255. *The Constitution of the Athenians*, 3.2. and 22.2.
256. Herodotus, 6.109.2.
257. *The Constitution of the Athenians*, 22.2. Apart from the author of the *Constitution of the Athenians*, Pausanias 1.15.3 also records that Kallimachos had been elected by the Athenians in 490. It is rather odd that Thucydides 1.20.3, who recorded Herodotus' inaccuracies – 6.57.5 and 9.53.2 – concerning the military organisation of Sparta, failed to point out this specific error of Herodotus on an Athenian issue. Today the reference by the author of the *Constitution of the Athenians* is generally accepted over that of Herodotus on the administration of the Athenian army in 490.

258. Herodotus, 6.111.1. This reference shows that Herodotus accepts that the Polemarch was in fact the head of the Athenian army at the battle of Marathon, even though he doesn't expressly state this in his narrative.

259. Nonetheless, the office of Polemarch in Athens was in existence well into the Classical period. Scholars who consider that it was abolished after the battle of Marathon are wrong. For example, Hamel, 7, 9, claims that after Kallimachos no other Polemarch is mentioned by name in ancient sources. However, in the fourth century, Pseudo-Demosthenes, *Against Neaira*, 40, records a certain Aitis as Polemarch.

260. Bradeen, 1955, 26; Hammond, 1968, 49–50; Scott, 358; G. Anderson, 2006, 258, n. 3, postulate that between 507 and 501, each Athenian tribe elected its own general but from 501/500 and afterwards, the Ten Generals were elected from the Assembly, one for each tribe. Cf. Fornara,1971, 5–6 and 10, who argues that the institution of Ten Generals did not exist before 501/0 and from that year until the battle of Marathon each tribe elected its own general.

261. Fornara, 1971, 6.

262. Fornara, 1971, 3–4, n. 11.

263. Fornara,1971, 10 and Scott, 380–381.

264. Herodotus, 6.110.

265. Most scholars accept Herodotus' record regarding the daily alternation of generals in the overall command of the army, as well as the fact that this procedure had to do with the operational responsibility of the whole Athenian army.

266. As Ridley, 517, puts it bluntly: 'It is unlikely that the Athenians were so stupid as to elect men to lead them in battle whom they regarded as incompetent.'

267. Curtius, 1898, 298, points out that Athenian magistrates of 490/89 took on their duties on 27th July 490. Scott, 615, dates this event the previous day. About the most likely date of the battle of Marathon a few weeks later – either on September 11 or 12 – see below.

268. As we have seen, perhaps in the mid-490s, when the Ionian Revolt was going badly for the Greeks, the Athenians may have sought to placate Darius through Hippias or his relatives. This may explain the election of Hipparchos, a likely grandson of Hippias, as Eponymous Archon in 496/5 and the possible permission to some of the exiled members of Hippias' family to return to Athens, see Arnush, 155.

269. For Miltiades before Marathon, see Berve, 1937; Wade-Gery, 1951, 212–221; Meidani, 167–176.

270. The Chersonese of Thrace had been under Athenian rule ever since Peisistratus' first tyranny in c. 560. Miltiades Senior was dispatched to the area by Peisistratus as its first Athenian governor. After Miltiades Senior's death, his nephew Sistagoras was appointed governor and, following his assassination, his step-brother Miltiades Junior succeeded him. Miltiades was dispatched by Hippias to Chersonese before 517/6 and ruled it until 493, when the Persians forced him to flee to Athens. Hammond, 1956, 113–129.

271. Miltiades in Darius' expedition against Scythia. Herodotus, 4.137–138, and Nepos, Miltiades, 3.1–6. The Scythians' attack against Chersonese: Herodotus, 6.40. See Meidani, 169–171.

272. About the important role Miltiades played in the conquest of Lemnos by the Athenians, see Herodotus, 6.140. Nepos, *Miltiades*, 2. Diodorus, 10.19.6. Past scholars believed that Miltiades conquered Lemnos shortly after coming to power in the Chersonese, around the time of Darius' Scythian campaign, in 513. See Hammond, 1956, 129. Evans, 1963, 168, assumes that Miltiades occupied the island

either before 511/0 or after 496, the latter date being more probable. Most modern scholars date Lemnos' occupation by Miltiades some time during the Ionian Revolt. According to Meidani, 171–173, the Athenian troops that participated in Lemnos' occupation along with Miltiades might have been the same that had reinforced the Ionians against Darius and had left Ionia after burning down Sardis.

273. Miltiades backed the Scythians' proposal to the Ionian tyrants who were allies of Darius, to demolish the bridge constructed by the Persians over the Istros River so that the Great King and his army would be trapped and vanquished in the mainland of Scythia. However, this proposal was not accepted by the Greek tyrants who had been assigned by Darius to guard the bridge. Herodotus, 4.137.

274. Nepos, *Miltiades*, 3.6.

275. Herodotus 6.41. Miltiades fled the Chersonese and took with him his family and all his belongings with five triremes. While these ships were sailing along the northern Aegean they were pursued by the Phoenician fleet for a considerable distance up to Imbros. During this pursuit, the Phoeniceans seized a trireme that was commanded by Metiochos, Miltiades' eldest son, whom they captured and handed over to Darius. His enmity for Miltiades notwithstanding, the Great King not only showed respect to his son but also offered him a house and married him to a Persian aristocrat with whom he had children who were considered Persians. These were great honours the Great King seldom granted to a foreigner residing in his empire. See Briant, 350. Darius showed mercy to defeated foes on other occasions, too; as we have seen, this happened with the Eretrian captives who appeared before him at Sousa. Regarding Metiochos though, Darius not only treated him with leniency, unbecoming towards an enemy's son, but also granted him special honours which are more in line with a generous reward. Within this context, Krentz, 2010a, 80–82, assumes that Metiochos may have gone to the Persians of his own free will. Therefore, years later the story of the alleged captivity by the Phoenecians may have been contrived aiming at the Philaed clan concealing the dissidence of the eldest son of Miltiades to the Persian court. If this assumption is correct, Metiochos may have found himself – along with other Athenian friends of Darius – in Hippias' entourage during the 490 Persian campaign against Athens. Though it may seem incredible, it is possible that one of Miltiades' opponents on the battlefield of Marathon may have been his first-born son! There is no evidence whatsoever on this, however, as nothing is recorded about Metiochos' later life after his marriage with the Persian lady. Oddly enough, during the Hellenistic period, an unknown author has Metiochos as the protagonist in his novel *Metiochos and Parthenope* whose topic is the supposed love affair between Metiochos and Parthenope, daughter of Polycrates, tyrant of Samos. See Hagg, 92–102. According to the plot in the novel, Metiochos left the Chersonese because his step-mother Hegesipyle, daughter of Oloros, king of Thrace, Miltiades' wife and Kimon's mother (Herodotus, 6.39) tried to poison him. Thus, there might have been some rumour about conflicts in Miltiades' family that inspired the author of this novel. Miltiades' first wife and Metiochos' mother might have been a daughter of Hippias (Davies, 302). If this is true, then the reason why Metiochos chose to go to Darius may have had to do with his grandfather's presence at his court. So, the honours bestowed by Darius upon him may have derived from his kinship with Hippias whom, as we have seen, the Great King held in high esteem.

276. Herodotus, 6.104.2. Miltiades, as former Eponymous Archon, was a member of the Areios Pagos. According to Carawan, 193 and Meidani, 173, Miltiades trial in 493 was held by this institution.

277. Herodotus, 6.132. According to the author of *The Constitution of the Athenians*, 18.1, Miltiades was a political leader of the ruling classes of Athens. Therefore, his *good reputation* must have circulated among high class members, not so much the lower classes.
278. Lewis, 1963, 24–25, argues that the Philaed clan originated from Brauron. However, this region belonged to the Aigeis and not the Oineis tribe. It seems that Miltiades had registered in the *deme* of Lakiades, which belonged to the Oineis, and not Brauron. We also know that Kimon, Miltiades' son, was a member of Oineis. In ancient Athens each young man registered in his father's tribe.
279. Lewis, 1963, 26–27. G. Anderson, 2006, 37–38.
280. *The Constitution of the Athenians*, 28.2.
281. Shimron, 63. Lazenby, 37.
282. Shimron, 63, claims that the image of Miltiades by Herodotus before the battle of Marathon: 'This is not exactly the image of a great warrior or a great saviour'.
283. Herodotus, 6.39.
284. Herodotus, 6.140. Nepos, *Miltiades*, 2, wrongly records that Miltiades captured peacefully the whole island and not only Hephaisteia.
285. As we shall see, after the victory at Marathon, Miltiades didn't act with his typical prudence, which had kept him out of harm's way for so long. The failure of the Paros expedition in 489 led to his conviction and indirectly to his death. It is no coincidence that even the charge on which he was convicted in Athens in 489 was fraud.
286. Even though Herodotus 6.39 and 6.103.3, records that the Peisistratids behaved as though they had nothing to do with Kimon's assassination, the evidence he quotes show them as the culprits. This would have been a common secret in Athens, which everybody – including Miltiades – would have known. According to Scott, 360, Kimon was assassinated between 527/525, when he decided to stay in Athens permanently, having returned from exile to which he had been sent by Peisistratos. Wade-Jery, 1958, 152, deems that Kimon had returned to Athens in 532. His high position in Athenian society, his victories at three successive Olympic Games and his leadership qualities may have been seen as a threat to Hippias' power, who had just become tyrant of Athens after Peisistratos' death. That is probably why he decided to murder Kimon. However, in 525/524 Hippias appointed Miltiades as Eponymous Archon in Athens and a few years later, the tyrant even lent him his personal trireme so that he could travel to the Chersonese in luxury. Herodotus, 6.39. It is likely, as we have seen, that Miltiades' first wife and Metiochos' mother – whose name is unknown to us – was Hippias' relative or even his daughter. These moves indicate that the tyrant wished to be on good terms with the Philaids and in particular Miltiades. Within this context, the shrewd and intelligent Miltiades would have been careful to hide his personal feelings towards the tyrant who had murdered his father and avoid having the latter's end. So, during his stay in Athens – which was under Hippias' rule – Miltiades would have pretended to have been a friend of the tyrant. Nonetheless, Kimon's assassination and the fact that he was unable to seek revenge would have haunted Miltiades. In this context we should note that Miltiades didn't name his first son – probably born during Hippias' tyranny – after his own father. Miltiades may have avoided naming him after his father – therefore not conforming to the strong custom of name giving in ancient Greece – not to provoke the omnipotent Hippias. But his second born son was given the name of his grandfather, perhaps because he was born in c 510, when

Hippias was no longer in power, and it would have been safe for Miltiades to name his newly born son, *Kimon*, thus honouring his murdered father.

287. Sekunda, 12, postulates that Miltiades fought at Marathon because he had no other choice; not an unreasonable view. It needs to be noted, however, that even scholars who consider Miltiades' actions at Marathon to have been self-serving, do not underestimate the decisive role he played in securing victory on the battlefield against the Persians and thus saving Greece.

288. Jameson, 1955, 63–87 and Pritchett, 1960, 148, speculate that Miltiades' moves in relation to the battle of Marathon show a leader, who, though not institutionally commander-in-chief of the army, took the initiative on important matters and gave sound advice to his colleagues and the commander of the army which was accepted by them.

289. Fornara, 1971, 12–19, postulates that on no occasion during the Median Wars did the Athenian Assembly grant extraordinary powers to any of the Ten Generals. The fact that some of them stood out, for example Themistokles at the battles of Artemision and Salamis in 480, or Xanthippos in the operations of the Athenian fleet at Mykale and Sestos in 479, was thanks to the leadership qualities these specific generals possessed, and not because they had greater powers than their peers. Fornara argues that the same also applies to Miltiades and his actions at Marathon and Athens in 490.

290. On the view in Roman times that Miltiades was supreme commander of the Greeks at Marathon, see Jung, 2006.

291. Herodotus, 6.103.1.

292. Macan, 1895, 1, 358. How and Wells, 1912, 357.

293. Dover, 70. Scott, 359. Scott assumes that Herodotus wanted to set Miltiades apart from the other Athenian generals because of the pivotal role he was going to play in the battle and that is the reason why he refers to him as 'the tenth' of the generals.

294. According to a scholion on Aelius Aristides, *Panathenaic* (Dindorf, 1829, 3, 131–132), 'the generals were ten, and each day one succeeded the other as commander of the army; the day the Persians disembarked at Marathon, Miltiades was the commander'. If Miltiades had daily command of the Athenian troops on the day the Persians disembarked at Marathon and the Athenians departed from the city, then ten days had to go by till the next time Miltiades commanded the army again. As we shall see, Herodotus records that the Battle of Marathon indeed took place on the day Miltiades once again had overall command of the army. Leake, 1829, 175–176, and Finlay, 384.

295. Herodotus, 6.110. and Plutarch, *Ethics*, 628E.

296. Herodotus, 6.109.2.

297. For Aphidnai as birthplace of Harmodius, see Plutarch, *Ethics*, 628E.

298. IG I² 609.

299. Morris, 292–293, and Keesling, 119–121, consider the statue to be of Nike but most other scholars agree that it is Iris.

300. According to Keesling, 115 and n. 38, his votive offering may show that before the battle of Marathon, Kallimachos made an offering not only to Artemis Agrotera (see below) but also Athene. Keesling postulates that Kallimachos' votive offering was in fact a monument of the Athenians at the Acropolis to honour their victory at Marathon.

301. In 480, the Peisistratids – Hippias' relatives – who accompanied Xerxes in his campaign against Greece were ordered by the Persian king to make a sacrifice

on the Acropolis that he had just occupied. Herodotus, 8.54–55. It is likely that the Peisistratids may have pointed out to the Persians the significance of the Kallimachos' monument-votive offering and the invaders destroyed it.

302. Raubitschek, 1940, 56.

303. See below about Kimon's likely contribution in promoting and blazoning Miltiades' role in the battle of Marathon at Kallimachos' expense.

304. Cf. Harrison, 353, who claims that the central figure in the southern frieze of Athene Nike at the Acropolis of Athens may be Kallimachos. The temple of Athene Nike was erected between 427/4 and if Harrison's theory is correct, then Kallimachos would still have been – along with Miltiades – the main protagonist of the battle of Marathon at least until the late-fifth century.

305. Herodotus, 6.114.

306. Both in the Berlin Staatliche Museen (inv. nos. 1906 and 3274).

307. Bicknell's 1970, 432, view has been adopted by several scholars. The rarity of the name is confirmed by the fact that Fraser and Matthews record in *The British Academy, A Lexicon of Greek Personal Names, Vol II, Attica,* only the above-mentioned references to this name in the later Archaic-early Classical periods.

308. Plutarch, *Aristides*, 5.1. Aelius Aristides, *To Plato, In Defence of the Four*, 173.

309. Hammond, 1968, 55–56 and Bicknell, 1972a, 53, accept the idea that Aristides was the general of Antiochis tribe at Marathon. Cf. Fornara 1971, 41–42, rejects Plutarch's references and does not include Aristides in his record of Athenian generals of 490/89.

310. For ancient literary sources recording Aristides' election as Eponymous Archon in 489/8, see Cadoux, 117.

311. According to Plutarch, *Aristides*, 5.2, Aristides was one of the generals at Marathon who was in favour of Miltiades' plan for the Athenians to fight the Persians. He was also the one who convinced this group of generals to concede their daily overall command of the army to Miltiades. Plutarch also records that Aristides and his men of the Antiochis tribe, fought courageously in the centre of the Athenian line-up. After the end of the battle they didn't return to Athens with the rest of the army to confront the Persians at Phaleron but remained at Marathon guarding the captives and booty.

312. Pritchett, 1960, 145, is one of the many scholars who have erroneously recorded that Plutarch referred to Themistokles as the general of the Leontis tribe at Marathon.

313. Themistokles was born c. 528; but due to a misunderstanding by Justin, 2.9, there is a general impression that he was very young at the time of the battle of Marathon. As a matter of fact, he was about 38 and had already been Eponymous Archon. This means that he was one of the most prominent Athenian politicians in 490.

314. Dionysios of Halikarnassos, 6.34, mentions that in 493/2, Themistokles was Eponymous Archon, something accepted by most scholars today.

315. Themistokles was for ancient authors one of the most popular historical personalities; whereas ancient references to Aristides are fewer.

316. Plutarch, *Themistokles*, 3.3–4.

317. The generals that the Athenians elected to confront Xerxes may be connected to those at Marathon a decade earlier. We can deduce that the Athenians would choose generals highly experienced in winning wars against the Persians. In all likelihood, any generals of the battle of Marathon who were still alive at the time must have been the first choice again for election to this office. According to Herodotus, 9.28.6, and Plutarch, *Aristides*, 11.1, Aristides was the Athenian general

in the battle of Plataia in 479. The same occurred with Arimnestos, the general in command of the Plataians (see below). Within this context, Themistokles as well as Xanthippos who – as we know – were generals of Athens during Xerxes' campaign, are likely to have been generals at Marathon in 490.

318. Herodotus, 6.136.
319. *The Constitution of the Athenians*, 28.2
320. Pausanias, 9.4.2. For Arimnestos at the battle of Plataia, see also Herodotus, 9.72. Plutarch, *Aristides*, 11.5. In 479, Arimnestos closely co-operated with Aristides before the battle of Plataia, designating several details for operations of the imminent clash with the Persians. See Plutarch, ibid. Their good relationship at Plataia may stem from the fact that they knew each other and had also successfully cooperated a decade earlier at Marathon under equally hard circumstances.
321. For example, Munro, 1926, 246.
322. Pausanias, 9.4.2.
323. Aristophanes, *Acharnians*, 569. Aristophanes, *Peace*, 1172. Thucydides, 8.92.4. There was one taxiarch for each Athenian tribe, see *The Constitution of the Athenians*, 61.3.
324. Vidal-Naquet, 1983 (1986), 89.
325. *The Constitution of the Athenians*, 61.3.
326. Herodotus, 9.21.3.
327. Krentz 2007b, 731–742, postulates that the 'Oath of the Athenians' recorded in the 'Inscription of Acharnae' was taken at Marathon in 490, not at Plataia in 479, as most scholars believe. If his opinion is correct, this specific source records the existence of the rank of taxiarchos in the Athenian army at Marathon. Develin, 1989, 4, considers that in 501 the rank of taxiarchos existed in the Athenian army. Cf. Scott, 381, deems that the Athenians introduced this rank after 490, as a result of the experience they acquired during the battle of Marathon.

Chapter 3

1. The shrine was located on a low hill, on the left side of Ilissos river, overlooking the area of the temple of Olympian Zeus. Travlos, 1971, 112–113.
2. Xenophon, *Anabasis*, 3.2.12.
3. Miltiades: Aelian, *Varia Historia*, 2.25. Kallimachos: Scholion Aristophanes, *Knights*, line 660.
4. Hammond, 1968, 41 and 1988, 507.
5. Plutarch, *Ethics*, 862C.
6. *The Constitution of the Athenians*, 58.1. Polux, 7.91.7.
7. Herodotus, 6.117.1.
8. Xenophon, *Anabasis*, 3.2.12. Plutarch, *Ethics*, 862 B-C. In the fourth century AD, Himerios, 6.195–198, claimed that the Persian dead at Marathon were so many that the Athenians didn't fulfil their pledge to Artemis Agrotera, even though they had kept up the annual sacrifice to her for centuries. This is an exaggeration, which is in tune with his rhetorical style.
9. Aristophanes, *Knights*, 660–662. Xenophon, *Anabasis*, 3.1.12. Aristophanes states that 1.000 goats were destined for the sacrifice to Artemis Agrotera; it is obvious, though, that he has doubled the animals to be sacrificed to make a comic juxtaposition. Therefore, according to Aristophanes the real number of animals to be sacrificed to the deity was 500. This was a standing sacrifice by the Athenians through to the Roman period, see Plutarch *Ethics*, 862B-C and Aelian, *Varia*

Historia, 2.25. Aelian records that in his time, the Athenians sacrificed to Artemis Agrotera 300 goats.

10. Krentz, 2010a, 156 and 192, n. 23.
11. Parke, 55. Dionysopoulos, 89.
12. Plutarch, *Camillus*, 19.
13. Hammond, 1968, 44.
14. Parke, *op. cit.*
15. Based on Plutarch, *Ethics*, 350E. Hammond, 1968, 44; Parke, 55; Rhodes, 1981, 650.
16. Krentz, 2010a, 156.
17. Krentz, *op. cit.*
18. Parke, *op. cit.*
19. Travlos, 1971, 112–113.
20. We have estimated this time period to two weeks on the basis of the following facts: The Persian expeditionary force conquered Karystos very quickly, where it remained for two-three days at most. Then the Persians must have taken at least two days for their fleet to sail to the coast of Eretria and to disembark there all forces that would operate against the city of Eretria, whose siege lasted six days. After the fall of Eretria, the Persian army remained there for a few days, perhaps three or four. Finally, the move of the Persian fleet from the coast of Eretria to Marathon would have taken up a few hours. Therefore, we consider that a fortnight must have passed between the surrender of Karystos and the Persian disembarkation at Marathon. Scott, 333–334 and Dionysopoulos, 98, make similar estimates of the time that elapsed in-between these two events.
21. Aristotle, *Rhetoric*, 3.10.7; Nepos, *Miltiades*, 4.5; Justin, 2.9; Polemon, 2.5; Scholion Demosthenes, *On the False Embassy*, 303. See Hammond, 1968, 34.
22. Justin, 2.9; Polemon, 2.5; Aelius Aristides *To Plato, In Defence of the Four*, 175.
23. Souda, 'Hippias' (II).
24. Demosthenes and Scholion Demosthenes, *On the False Embassy*, 303; Aristotle, *Rhetoric*, 3.10.7. Modern scholars postulate that in fourth century Athens there was an inscription recording measures that Miltiades proposed to the Athenian Assembly in 490 against the Persian invasion. These were voted by the Athenians and turned into law, known as *Decree of Miltiades*. Ancient authors used extracts from its text to show the decisive role Miltiades played in the defence of Athens in 490.
25. Aristotle, *Rhetoric*, 3.10.7. At this point Aristotle refers to the politician Kephisodotos, who in the fourth century urged the Athenians to launch an immediate military campaign to Euboia. In this context, Kephisodotos refered to the decree bearing the name of Miltiades, in which the general is recorded as having urged the Athenians to leave their city immediately for a campaign, without taking any supplies with them, as they would replenish them upon arriving there. In Miltiades' case this incitement was about the campaign at Marathon, not Euboia. Based on this specific extract from Aristotle, most scholars in the past accepted that Miltiades urged the Athenians to depart straight away for Marathon 'after having taken foodstuff with them' ('ἐπισιτισαμένους'), see for example, Lazenby, 52 and Sekunda, 36. However, Cope and Sandys, 113, two of the best researchers of Aristotle, are certain that the participle should have been in the future tense: 'ἐπισιτισομένους', i.e. 'where they would take foodstuff from') and that the Aristotelian text we have with 'ἐπισιτισαμένους' has been wrongly copied from

older manuscripts. Their point of view makes sense as it is in tune with Miltiades' haste – something that Aristotle wants to stress at this point – that the Athenian troops had to depart for Marathon at once.

26. During the Classical period an Athenian soldier on campaign had to replenish his own supplies. At the start he had to have with him supplies for three days. Aristophanes, *Acharnians*, line 197 and *Peace,* lines 311–312; Thucydides, 1.48.2. See Christ, 2001, 403, n. 24. Thereafter he replenished it by either making purchases from traders who followed the army or from friendly local farmers. While in enemy territory, he usually got supplies by looting farmhouses. After the soldiers procured supplies, personal slaves prepared the rations of the wealthy, whereas the poorer ones prepared their own. With the exception of Sparta, no Greek city during the fifth century had a central service in charge of rationing or central cooking facilities for its army on a campaign. Van Wees, 2011, 104–106.

27. Ancient Greek troops on the march placed the supply carts in the middle of the column for security reasons, thus limiting considerably its speed. Ridley, 515. Thus, they could only cover a distance of 30km per day at most, taking into account also that ancient Greeks used oxen – very slow animals – to pull the four-wheel carts laden with supplies. In consequence, the Athenians would not have been able to reach Marathon on the same day the Persian disembarkation started, if they took along with them their supply carts.

28. As we have seen, during the Classical era, Sparta was the only Greek city-state to have a public system to provide supplies for troops on a campaign. However, it is logical to assume that any other Greek city facing a crisis threatening its very existence, as Athens in 490, would have done its best to provide its defenders with supplies.

29. In 490, the Athenian authorities may have organised a network to supply their troops at Marathon similarly to what the Greeks did in 479 for their men at Plataia. In both cases, the Greeks had no access to the nearby plains that were under Persian control and had to rely exclusively on supplies coming from the rear.

30. Aristophanes, *Wasps*, line 1081.

31. Many scholars believe that *Wasps*, lines 1075–1090, refer to events of the battle of Marathon.

32. Isocrates, *Panegyric*, 87.

33. Polemon, 2.5.

34. Polemon, *op. cit.*

35. As we will see, the Persians, in order to advance from Marathon to Athens would have used exclusively the passage through Brexiza and not those of Pentelikon.

36. As we have seen, the Brexiza pass is likely to have come under the control of the 4,000 *klerouchoi* from Euboia, possibly in tandem with conscripts from the Tetrapolis and the wider area of northeastern Attica. However, it was only by the timely arrival of the main body of the Athenian army that the complete control of this strategic point was secured by the Greeks.

37. How and Wells, 358, state that Miltiades was: '*the true author both of the strategy and of the tactics which won Marathon*'.

38. Xenophon, *Cyropaedia*, 6.3.2–4, points out that the ideal array for Greek troops on the march was the horsemen at the head, supply carts-pack animals in the middle and foot soldiers at the end. In this way, when coming across a narrow pass, the foot soldiers would proceed in two files placing between them the supplies in order to protect them. During the Peloponnesian War, most Greek troops on the march adopted the square formation: light-armed men and supply carts were placed in

the middle of the column while the hoplites surrounded them from all sides, see Krentz, 2007a, 159. It is unknown if any of these marching tactics were already in use by Greek armies in 490.

39. Aristophanes, *Acharnians*, lines 1136–1137.
40. Van Wees, 2011, 104 and 279, n. 10.
41. Pack animals covered longer distances than carts pulled by oxen. According to Krentz, 2007a, 152–153, oxen could cover a 15–32km distance daily; donkeys and mules more than twice that distance, between 40–80 km.
42. Herodotus 7.75.1, records that Thracian troops campaigning in Greece with Xerxes in 480 were armed with 'small daggers'. According to Best, 7–8, this weapon must have been the 'machaira', i.e. *long knife*, which was quite popular in Thrace and southern Greece. This would have been a favourite weapon for men who didn't have the means to purchase hoplite weapons.
43. The leather cap of the poor was made out of dog hide and for that reason was known as 'kyne', see Aristophanes, *Birds*, line 1203.
44. For the *gylion*, see Aristophanes, *Acharnians*, lines 1099–1101, and *Peace*, lines 527–529.
45. Van Wees, 2011, 104. *Opson* was mainly fish, but it could also have been meat, olives or some other food but not bread or other food made of cereal. Aristophanes, *Peace*, lines, 529 and 1129, records that the Athenians on campaigns usually carried with them cheese and onions. This of course was true for most of them who had limited means.
46. The average Athenian of the Classical period had to have a daily intake of 3.000 calories, equivalent to the consumption of about one kg of food. Krentz, 2010a, 107. Thus, each Athenian soldier leaving for Marathon would have with him three kgs of food for the first three days of the campaign.
47. Wine is omnipresent in ancient sources about the supplies of Greek armies on campaign.
48. According to Matheson, 25–26, many images on Attic vases show a woman, perhaps a relative, or even the mother, of an Athenian hoplite making a sacrifice, before leaving his house for a campaign. Sometimes the hoplite is depicted receiving his helmet by an elderly female, probably his mother. There are also depictions on vases of the hoplite examining the bowels of a sacrificed animal just before his departure, see Krentz, 2007a, 156–157.
49. Miltiades was born c 554/553. Wade-Gery, 1951, 168–199. Meidani, 167.
50. Here we follow most researchers of the battle, who deem that in 490 the ten Athenian generals were elected by citizens of their individual tribes, not the Athenian Assembly in total, something that began in 487.
51. The Athenian soldiers always marched within the ranks of their respective tribes and lined up in the same way. Only in the temporary camps did each Athenian lodge wherever he wanted and not necessarily with men of his own tribe, see below
52. Berthold, 84.
53. Matthaiou, 2003, 202, n. 38.
54. On this route, see Leake, 1841, 2, 79–80; Frazer, 441–442; Ober, 1982, 453–458, and 1985, 182–183. Dionysopoulos, 32–34. It is likely that in modern times the footpaths of Pentelikon followed similar routes as the ancient ones.
55. Frazer, 441. According to Ober, 1985, 183, the second path after Stamata headed northeast towards Amygdalesa, went past north of Koukounari and reached Loukas. Then, going past Oinoe reached modern-day Marathon.
56. Frazer, 442; Milchhöfer, 41 and 56; Dionysopoulos, 32–33.

57. Ober, 1985, 182, gives a description of this path, pointing out that it was 'no military road'.

58. Finlay, 368, states that the route from Athens to Marathon through Pentelikon – he means the path between Kifissia and Vranas – is 22 miles; whereas the one through Mesogaia is 26 miles. Sotiriadis, 1927b, 133, n. 1, quotes the same distances and stresses that the difference is negligible and that the Mesogaia route would have been more convenient for the Athenian army to march to Marathon than that of Pentelikon. He also hypothesizes that the Athenians would not opt to go to Marathon by way of Pentelikon, even though this was shorter in length compared to the one through Mesogaia, as they would not have saved time.

59. Finlay, 367–368.

60. Finlay, 379.

61. Finlay, *op. cit.* Matthaiou, 2003, 202, n. 18, agrees with the view that in 490 the Athenians reached Marathon following the Pallini route. According to Steinhauer, 2009b, 49–50, the temple of Athene Pallenis, where Peisistratos beat his rivals in 546, might have been on the point of departure of three ancient roads: one of which headed to Marathon. Finlay, 368, even uses mythology to back his view regarding the route the Athenians used to reach Marathon in 490. According to the myth of the Herakleides, when the Athenians slew Eurystheus at Marathon, they buried his body there but took his head to Gargytos in Mesogaia. This means that Athenians returned to their city through Pallini, which is next to Gargytos, instead of Pentelikon.

62. See Frazer, 442; Berthold, 85; Green, 32. This argument stands to reason from Finlay's stance, too; although he does not expressly record it. Cf. Dionysopoulos, 32–37, who argues that the Persians would not have been able to start their advance right after their disembarkation at Marathon. He also postulates that the Athenians would fear being attacked by the Persian navy if they took the way beside the coast. The essential question which remains unanswered in Dionysopoulos' theory is why the Athenians would risk leaving the main entrance to the city – the Pallini route – unguarded for the invader to get in. As Berthold and Green emphasise, if the Brexiza pass was not under the control of the Athenians, the Persians could have occupied it even before completing their disembarkment of the entire troops at the shore of Marathon. A small cavalry force would have been adequate to accomplish this mission. In 1895, both Busolt 586, and Macan, 1895, 2, 241, accepted that the Persians would have used the southern pass and the coastal route from Marathon to reach Athens, not the Pentelikon paths.

63. Finlay, 367. During this period guides used to take foreign visitors from Athens to Marathon through the route of Kifissia and Stamata.

64. Ober, 1982, 453–458.

65. Ober postulates that this road was built in the first half of the fourth century and was one of the best examples of road construction in Attica during antiquity. However, Pritchett, 1985b, 150, n. 14, is convinced that this road is not ancient, as details of its construction and the fact that its gradient was only 3%, despite the mountainous environment, indicated that it was built in modern times. Pritchett was an expert in ancient Greek roads.

66. Curtius 1898, 301, emphasizes that *the southerly road* is the central route between Marathon and Athens, while Typaldos records that the most appropriate route between Athens and Marathon was the coastal road and not the mountainous route through Pentelikon.

67. Frazer, 441–442.

68. Meyer, 329; Kromayer, 1921, 13–14; Sotiriadis, 1927b, 133–134.
69. Themelis, 236; Berthold, 85; Steinhauer, 2009b, 48–49.
70. Berthold, *op. cit.* Mesogaia in antiquity possessed 26% of cultivated land in Attica. Moreno, 37, n. 2.
71. Hammond, 1968, 34; Doenges, 7; Dionysopoulos, 32–37.
72. Hammond, 1967, 216, n. 2.
73. Hammond, 1968, 37, n. 107.
74. Burn, 1962 (1984), 242–243; Berthold, 84–85
75. Green, 32.
76. Hammond, 1988, 507.
77. Finlay, 367–368; Frazer, 441–442.
78. The Athenians' defence on the mountainous part of Pentelikon could have been carried out by dispersed teams of men, who would have attacked the Persians in unpredictable ways, using any means available: setting traps; hurling stones; even setting on fire the Pentelikon forest while the Persian troops were inside.
79. According to Burn, 1962 (1984), 242, the path from Kifissia to Marathon could only have been used by messengers. Additionally, Berthold, 90, n. 48, deems that the specific path could only have been used by small groups of soldiers.
80. According to Frazer, 432, at the end of the nineteenth century the greatest width of the Lesser Marsh was 'half a mile'.
81. See above for the available scientific – geological – evidence on these topics.
82. Sotiriadis, who did archaeological research at Marathon before the Lesser Marsh was dried up, records that on the 34–34.5 km of the Athens-Marathon Road the width of the Brexiza pass was 100–200 m. Sotiriadis, 1927a, 83.
83. Berthold, 92, estimates that it took the Athenian army 9–10 hours to reach Marathon. Scott's, 607, estimate is roughly 8–10 hrs.
84. First recorded by Finlay, 377–380, and followed by many later scholars. Cf. Munro, 1926, 241–243, and Steinhauer, 2010a, 60, who consider that the Persians didn't pursue their advance to Athens because only part of their troops disembarked at Marathon and this was a diversional operation with the aim of keeping the Athenians there. As we shall see, this theory is not realistic and should be rejected.
85. Nepos, *Miltiades*, 5; Aelius Aristides, *Panathenaic*, 106; Pausanias, 1.32.7; Pseudo-Plutarch, *Ethics*, 305B.
86. Nepos, *op. cit.*
87. Pausanias, 1.32.7.
88. We can be certain that Pausanias had visited Marathon, see Macan, 1895, 2, 226, who underscores that Pausanias' visit to Marathon is beyond the shadow of a doubt. As a matter of fact, the ancient author himself saw the evidence he recorded in this area, as he expressly mentions that he was not able to find a sign on the ground indicating the spot of the mass burial of the Persians who had been slain in the battle.
89. For stone quarries at Drakonera, next to the Great Marsh, see Tsirigoti-Drakotou, 2010, 56.
90. Leake, 1841, 2, 96, saw at the foot of Drakonera a crevice, which he deemed was what Pausanias had seen and imagined as a manger of the Persian horses. Based on this flimsy evidence, Leake thought he had found the area where the Persians had encamped. Frazer, 432, argues that Pausanias probably heard tall stories by locals about the location of the Persian camp.
91. Pausanias, 1.32.7.
92. See above for evidence on the formation of the Great Marsh during antiquity.

93. Hammond 1968, 42 and Dionysopoulos, 171–173, present evidence that Schinias was the best shore for the Persian ships to anchor.
94. Hammond, 1968, 42.
95. Herodotus, 6.115.
96. Pausanias 1.14.5.
97. Whatley, 138.
98. As we have seen, in 490 the *deme* of Marathon would have been either at Plasi or Vranas. The Persians most likely gained control of both areas soon after they disembarked at Schinias.
99. Evans, 1993, 292.
100. Finlay, 378–379, was the first to record the theory that the Athenian *klerouchoi* of Chalkis occupied places at Agrieliki before the Athenian troops arrived there.
101. Vanderpool, 1966b, 103 and Kontorlis, 20–23, postulate that the Persians moved their front-line troops from Schinias to a camp they constructed in the Marathon plain. Most scholars, though, deem that the Persian troops encamped at Schinias or next to the Great Marsh and remained there up to the day of the battle.
102. As we shall see, these tactics were used by the Persians with great success against a foe before a battle. Herodotus presents in great detail how the Persians applied them in 479, before the battle of Plataia.
103. Polyainos, 2.30.3, records how Klearchos, tyrant of Herakleia, exterminated his co-patriots that were his enemies by forcing them to camp in marshland during summer. If the Persians had encamped nearby the Great Marsh at the end of the summer of 490, many of them would have had the end of Klearchos' adversaries.
104. Kontorlis, 20–23, places the camp in the same area.
105. Seni et al. 482–483.
106. Pritchett, 1960, 156–157.
107. For characteristics of the Persian temporary camps, see Pritchett, 1974, 139–140, and Krentz, 2007a, 163. According to Xenophon, *Cyropaedia*, 3.3.26–27, the Persians built a moat around each temporary camp for fear of a nocturnal surprise attack by the enemy.
108. Herodotus, 9.15.2, 9.65.1, 9.70 and 9.98. In his first reference, Herodotus writes that the Persians felled the trees of a forest and with the wood barricaded their temporary camp in Boiotia.
109. Schinias is close to the Great Marsh but the environmental conditions must have been bearable for the crews of the Persian ships, as they would have stayed next to the sea and not the marsh.
110. As we have seen, the coastline at Aghios Panteleimon and Valaria in 490 was more or less where it is today. The anchorage on that spot probably existed then and may have been used by the Persians.
111. Grundy, 187, postulates that part of the Persian fleet had anchored southwest of Schinias, away from the rest of the ships and close to where the combat Persian troops had encamped in the Marathon plain.
112. The Athenians and Plataians had encamped together in the same place; for this reason, their settlement is characterised as 'Greek camp'. However, the Athenians made up the great majority of men encamped there and did most of its construction, so it could also be referred to as 'Athenian camp'.
113. Herodotus, 6.108.
114. Herodotus, 6.116.

115. Herodotus, 6.111.1. Herodotus uses the verb *tasso* in connection with a military force exclusively when it is lined up to give battle: 1.80.2, 1.80.4, 1.191.2, 1.191.4, 6.108, and 6.113.1.

116. Herodotus' work is full of digressions and his narrative about the battle of Marathon is no exception. Hammond, 1988, 493, notes the many problems caused to researchers of the battle by these digressions.

117. Berthold, 91 and Scott, 608. A shrine in Attica of the Archaic/Classical era, like that of Herakles at Marathon, was an enclosed part of land with an altar and perhaps a small temple in the centre. Wycherley, 1978, 175.

118. See for example, Finlay, 383. Berthold, 91. Scott, 374. Hammond 1961, 262–263. Scott, *op. cit.*, postulates that the shrine was erected by Peisistratos, as the tyrant had adopted Herakles as his personal deity, and the Athenians by camping there wished to deal a political blow to Hippias and his followers. But this is unlikely, as only practical matters would have designated the choice of location for the camp. It was probably a coincidence that the shrine of Herakles happened to be in the Greek camp site. Of course, after their victory, the Athenians may have used the fact that they encamped or lined up on spots dedicated to Herakles as proof of the hero being on their side and not Hippias'.

119. Nepos, *Miltiades*, 5.

120. Nepos, *op. cit.* How, 1919, 51, points out the errors in Nepos' narrative regarding the battle at Marathon, but accepts as plausible his reference that the Athenians made use of mountainous positions to protect themselves from the Persians. Delbrück, 1920 (1990), 73, considers realistic Nepos' details about the battle of Marathon.

121. Aelius Aristides, *Panathenaic*, 106.

122. Benndorf, 23, Pl. 13, A 10.

123. Harrison, 364.

124. Aischines, *Against Ktesiphon*, 186.

125. Aelius Aristides, *To Plato: In Defence of the Four*, 174.

126. Nepos, *Miltiades*, 6.

127. Harrison, 364.

128. Pseudo-Demosthenes, *Against Neaira*, 94.

129. Oberleitner, 56–61.

130. The Athenians officially commemorated their victory at Marathon by depicting the battle on one of the wall paintings in the centre of the Poikile Stoa at the Agora that had as their subjects Athenian victories in historical and mythical battles. Neither this work nor any copy of it has survived, and therefore what we know of the battle derives entirely from ancient writers, and especially Pausanias who saw it during the second century AD. The Poikile Stoa was built in the 460s and sponsored by Peisianax, a politician who served as Eponymous Archon. As Peisianax acted in the name of Athens' *Demos*, the wall paintings have a distinctly public character designed to present the official Athenian narrative of the events they portrayed. It was the last public building in Athens bearing the name of its sponsor and would therefore have been erected before 462/461, when it became illegal to give the name of an individual to a public building. For the mural of the battle of Marathon in Poekile Stoa, see Wycherley, 1953, 27–29 and 1972, 78. Hammond 1968, 26. Petrakos 1995, 35.

131. The depiction of the specific scene at the Heroön of Trysa may have referred to some local event of Lykia – either mythological or historical – not necessarily the

battle of Marathon. Nonetheless, the source of inspiration may have been the mural of the Marathon battle at the Poekile Stoa.

132. In many modern literary works on the battle of Marathon the Athenian camp is placed on a highland/elevated position and not in the Marathon plain. It is interesting that this parameter is usually accepted as a fact without any need of explanation. Additionally, in modern artistic reconstructions of the battle of Marathon the Athenian camp is depicted usually in a hill next to the plain.

133. Hammond, 1968, 34, n. 96.

134. Polybius, 6.42, records that the Greeks during a campaign built their temporary camps in places that offered strong defence by nature. He emphasises that for this reason the Greeks adapted their camps to the natural environment. Quite the reverse was true for the Persians who erected artificial fortifications for their temporary camps; thus, their camps all looked alike. From the evidence Polybius quotes, he implies that the Greeks encamped on highlands whereas the Persians on lowlands. Thucydides, 4.4–5, gives ample details on the way that in 425 the Athenians occupied a highland position at Pylos and built a defensive wall. He notes that the Athenians left unfortified any spots which were naturally impenetrable. It is generally accepted by archaeologists and scholars alike that the ancient Greeks opted to erect their temporary campaign camps on highlands. See McCredie, 96–97. J. Anderson, 1970, 62–66. Pritchett, 1974, 133–146. Krentz, 2007a, 162–167.

135. Plutarch, *Aristides*, 11.6–7.

136. Herodotus, 9.20–21. See Kromayer, 1921, 12–13.

137. Plutarch would have known from first hand the characteristics of the natural environment where the Greeks had encamped in 479 at Plataia as he was from Boiotia.

138. Pausanias, 9.4.2.

139. A few modern scholars like Pritchett, 1960, 138–140. Burn, 1962 (1984), 242–243, and Berthold, 89, agree that the Athenians followed the Pallini route to reach Marathon, but that they built their camp at Vranas. Lolling, 88, states that the shrine of Herakles was in Avlonas at Marathon, where there is an ancient terrace surrounding some facilities, which the locals called 'Yard of the Old Woman'. These ruins, though, proved to have belonged to a farmstead of Herodes Atticus, dating to the second century AD. They have no association whatsoever to the shrine of Herakles and the Athenian camp of the battle of Marathon. Many scholars point out that Avlona needs to be ruled out as the Greek camp›s position in 490; not only because its architectural remains are much later than the battle, but also because it is located behind mount Kotroni. The Athenians would not have been able to observe the Persians' moves on the shore and the plain if they had encamped there.

140. Caspari, 102–103. How and Wells, 109. Lampros, 1886, 388, marks on a map 'Shrine of Herakles' at Saint George. Ross, 1863 (1976), 201, claims to have seen ancient marble architectural remains at this monastery during the 1830s.

141. These include Leake, Ross, Milchhöfer, Kromayer and others, see Berthold, 88, n. 26. Some of the scholars who accepted this identification deemed that there was a possible link between Herakles and Saint Demetrios. They assumed, thus, that the inhabitants of the region selected for this reason to built a church dedicated to Saint Demetrios on the remains of the shrine of Herakles. Similarly, Caspari, 102–103, deemed that Saint George in Vranas could have been erected on the site of the shrine of Herakles at Marathon as the inhabitants might have related the specific saint to Herakles. Interestingly, enough, in the southern and the southeastern part

of the Marathon plain, within the wider area where the battle was fought, all the Byzantine and post-Byzantine churches are dedicated to military saints: Saint Demetrios at Agrieliki, Saints Theodore at Valaria and Saint George's monastery at Vranas. As we shall see, the church of Saints Theodore was erected within the battlefield of 490. It is uncertain if the dedication of these churches to military saints has to do with the memory of the battle surviving in the Byzantine period or is simply a coincidence.

142. Sotiriadis, 1932, 42–43.
143. Pritchett, 1965, 89, and Vanderpool, 1966a, 322. Pritchett argues that the terraced enclosure found by Sotiriadis had been erected in modern times by farmers who cleared their land from stones. Vanderpool reached a similar conclusion.
144. Marathon Archaeological Museum cat. no. 19.
145. Sotiriadis, 1935, 90. Vanderpool, 1966a, 319–321.
146. Sotiriadis, *op. cit.*
147. Sotiriadis, *op. cit.*
148. For example, 'The Calendar of Sacrifices of the Tetrapolis' (IG II² 1358) contains a reference to the shrine (*Hellotion*) and the expensive sacrifices that were conducted there.
149. A scholion to Pindaros, *Olympionikos*, 13.56, locates the *Hellotion* in the 'Marsh of Marathon'. Other scholia to Pindaros refer to this marsh as 'close to Marathon' or 'towards Marathon'. See Hammond, 1968, 24–25.
150. Whether the *deme* of Marathon was located at Plasi, Vranas, or extending to both areas, the so-called 'Marsh of Marathon' should be the Lesser Marsh. The descriptions in ancient literary sources point to this and not the Great Marsh, which was quite far away from Plasi and Vranas. Besides, the Great Marsh was within the borders of the *deme* of Trikorynthos, not Marathon. Thus, Aristophanes, *Lysistrata*, line 1032, records that the mosquito that throve in the area of Trikorynth – location of the Great Marsh – was called the 'Trikorynthian/Trikoryssian mosquito'. This reference gives us an indication that in antiquity the Great Marsh may have been known as the 'Marsh of Trikorynth/Trikoryssia'. Hammond deems that the entire area between the Lesser Marsh and the foot of Agrieliki close to the church of Saint Demetrios was dedicated to Athene, most probably (Athene) Hellotia. Hammond, 1968, 24–25, emphasizes, though, that the shrine of Hellotia cannot be identified with the remains of the shrine of Athene that Sotiriadis had excavated and its site was in the area of the Lesser Marsh. In the late-eighteenth – early-nineteenth centuries, foreign travellers to Marathon recorded the existence of ancient remains on dry land known as 'Nisi' within the Lesser Marsh. One of these visitors, Colonel Leake, considered that these belonged to the shrine of Athene Hellotia. Recent archaeological excavations, however, have revealed that the architectural remains in the Lesser Marsh belong to installations of a shrine dedicated to Egyptian deities dating to the second century AD and not of the Classical era.
151. SEGX 2 and IGI³ 3. Marathon Archaeological Museum cat. no. 21.
152. According to Souda, 'Herakleian', the Athenians honoured Herakles with athletic games at Marathon and Kynosarges in Athens.
153. Pindaros *Olympionikos*, 9.89–90, and *Pythionikos*, 8.78–79, mentions among the winners of the Herakleian Games of Marathon athletes from Opus, Aegina and perhaps Corinth.
154. Vanderpool, 1984, 296.
155. Vanderpool, 1942, 335–336. Bowie, 2013, 64.

156. Pausanias, 1.32.5.
157. Euripides, *Herakleides*, lines 31–32. Diodorus, 4.57.4.
158. Strabo, 8.6.19.
159. Bowie, 2013, 64, deems that the Herakleian Empylia were held at Marathon even before the battle but were upgraded after 490. Similarly, Jung 2006, 31, considers that the oldest inscription of the Herakleian Games indicates that they were upgraded after 490.
160. Pritchett, 1985a, 106–112, mentions that games in Athens honouring the fallen in battles included musical, athletic and equestrian events. Boedecker, 1995, 223, speculates that during the Herakleian Games at Marathon, Simonides of Keos and Aischylos competed for the best elegy in memory of the fallen Athenians of the battle. There is an ancient tradition that Simonides' elegy won the contest, something which embittered Aishylos to the point of him leaving Athens.
161. Cf. Vanderpool, 1942, 336–337, who interprets the phrase 'των επιδήμων' ('τον επιδέμομ') in line 5, the group from which thirty athlothete were chosen, as visitors 'temporarily at Marathon' during the Herakleian Games. Lewis, 2004, 299, thinks that they may have been new residents at Marathon who received land that had been confiscated as a result of Kleisthenes' reforms. However, there is no evidence of land confiscations at the time of Kleisthenes' reforms.
162. Herodotus, 6.120.
163. IGI³ 2. The specific inscription may be linked to Kleisthenes' judicial reforms. See Vanderpool, 1942, 333.
164. It seems that copies of public inscriptions relating to the Tetrapolis were placed at Marathon's shrine of Herakles. Lambert, 2000, 52.
165. Vanderpool, 1966a, 323: 'I would not claim that the finding place of the inscription marks the exact spot where the Herakleion was located, but I think it does indicate the approximate position.'
166. Vanderpool visited the spot with S. Kakaris, who had found the inscription in his field a decade earlier.
167. *Karten von Attika*, 'Marathon', Plate XIX, spot marked as 'Kapelle Theodoros'. The first to have described these marble relics was Lolling, 78, who connected them to the Byzantine church of Saints Theodore. Leake, 1841, 2, 102, records that at Valaria he saw ancient foundations and a Greek inscription, which was probably used as building material in a local church (Sts Theodore?).
168. Vanderpool, 1942, 330 and 1966a, 322.
169. When Vanderpool was doing research in Valaria in 1940, the biggest part of the Lesser Marsh had already been dried out. Nonetheless, its limits can be precisely traced even today.
170. Vanderpool notes in his 1942 publication that the inscription was found at Valaria without however referring to this fact as evidence that the shrine of Herakles may have been in the same area. In his 1966 article, however, Vanderpool reveals that he had had this suspicion since 1940 but refrained from publishing so as not to upset Sotiriadis who believed that he had located the site at Saint Demetrios at Vranas.
171. Pritchett, 1965, 90–91.
172. Vanderpool, 1966a, 323.
173. Robert, 486.
174. Pritchett, 1969, 7, n. 37.
175. IG I³1015bis. Marathon Archaeological Museum cat. no. 34. Marinatos, 1972, 6. According to Themelis, 236, the inscription was built in the wall of a late-Roman

building, very close to the northern edge of the Lesser Marsh. This is the same area where four decades earlier the first inscription of the Herakleian Games was found.

176. This view was accepted by many other scholars. Based on the discovery of the second inscription of the Herakleian Games, as well as ancient architectural parts, Themelis, 226–227, considers that the shrine of Herakles at Marathon was in Valaria in the area between the late-Roman building in the northern boundary of the Lesser Marsh where the specific inscription was found and the church of Saints Theodore. In 1985 Pritchett published two articles accepting Vanderpool's proposed location for the shrine of Herakles at Marathon. 1985a, 129, n. 129. 1985b, 115–116.

177. Matthaiou, 2003, 191.

178. Koumanoudis, 238, followed by (among others) Van der Veer, 315, n. 96. Travlos, 1988, 219. Petrakos, 1995, 50–51. Matthaiou, 2003, 193–194. Bowie, 2010, 207.

179. According to McCredie, 91–92, no Attic *deme* was fortified.

180. Koumanoudis, 237–242, followed by (among others) Van Der Veer, 315, n. 96, Matthaiou, 2003, 194. Goette and Weber, 65.

181. Koumanoudis, 238–240, followed by (among others) Pritchett, 1985a, 167 (with reservations). Humphreys, 169, n. 98. Krentz, 2010a,121. Lambert, 2014, 6.

182. Pindaros, *Pythionikos*, 8. 78–79. Van der Veer, 297, deems that this reference by Pindaros is in tune with the features of the narrow Brexiza pass, which can be characterised as a 'recess' (*mychos*).

183. IGI³ 503/4, Lapis AII. Koumanoudis, 239–240. Matthaiou, 2003, 200. Most scholars who have studied the specific inscription agree that it belonged to a group of three or four inscriptions of epigrams honouring the fallen Athenians at Marathon and perhaps other battles of the Greco-Persian Wars. Epigraphists thought in the past that these epigrams honoured the dead Athenians at Marathon and Salamis, while the specific verse referred to the former. During the early-twentieth century, Oliver 1933, 487–488, disagreed with this general admission and considered that all these epigrams honoured exclusively the fallen Athenians of the battle of Marathon and were placed on the walls of their cenotaph in Athens. Aggelos Matthaiou seems to confirm Oliver's theory by publishing evidence showing that the inscriptions of the epigrams belonged to a monument in the public cemetery of Athens that was the cenotaph of the fallen Athenians at the battle of Marathon. See Matthaiou, 1988, 118–122. Matthaiou's theory has been accepted by many scholars, for example, Keesling, 116–117 and Arrington, 2015, 45–46. Cf. Bowie, 2010, 207, who deems that this particular epigram honours the fallen at the battle of Marathon but the other epigrams honour those of Salamis. Jung 2006, 93–96, believes that all the epigrams honour the fallen of the battle of Salamis, based on the 'pan-hellenic' nature of their texts. He argues that if they had been dedicated to the fallen at Marathon they would have specifically referred to Athens. However, as we have seen, the Athenians claimed soon after 490 that at Marathon they had defended the freedom of all Greeks.

184. As claimed by Jacoby, 1945, 167, n. 35.

185. For example, Oliver, 492, and Hammond 1968, 27, believe that the phrase, 'in front of the gates' was figurative and referred to Athens and Attica in general. Raubitschek, 1940, 58 argues that the *gates* refer to Phaleron as the *entry gate* to Athens from the sea.

186. Matthaiou, 2003, 200.

187. See Onasoglou, 64. An indication that the shrine of Herakles of Marathon was in the southernmost point of that area may also be found in the 'Calendar of Sacrifices of the Tetrapolis', where this shrine is referred to together with Apollo *Apotropaios*. The inscription records an offer to the altar of this deity, which most likely was at Kynosoura, the most northeastern part of Marathon. Lambert, 2000, 65, postulates that thus the area of the Tetrapolis was demarcated in the inscription, with Kynosoura in the north and the shrine of Herakles in the south. If Lambert's theory is correct, then it is likely that the shrine of Demeter and Kore – the Eleusinion – could have demarcated the area of Tetrapolis in the west (see above, Lambert's view that this Shrine is in Koukounari, at the foot of Pentelikon) and the site of the Shrine of Dionysos – the most important shrine of Tetrapolis – could have been in the centre of the Marathon plain, between the points which designated the aforementioned shrines.

188. Hammond eventually rejected his own theory about the position of the shrine of Herakles – he had located it at Kotroni – in favour of Vanderpool's. Burn also did the same and his change of mind in accepting Vanderpool's proposed site of the shrine of Herakles – instead of Vranas – was emphasized by Van der Veer, 296, and Pritchett, 1985b, 115–116. Though Burn is one of the best-known scholars of the Median Wars, we consider Pritchett's change of mind more important regarding the position of the shrine of Herakles at Marathon. This is because he had done extensive archaeological research in the area trying to locate it and was the main opponent of Vanderpool's theory about Valaria. Pritchett's acceptance of Vanderpool's theory went unnoticed by certain younger scholars. Thus in 1998, Doenges, 8, n. 15, mentions that Pritchett advocated that the shrine of Herakles was located in Vranas. However, Pritchett had changed his mind many years earlier and accepted Vanderpool's proposed location of the shrine in Valaria. In actual fact, Pritchett himself recorded in 1999 this oversight by Doenges.

189. Finlay, 380

190. Themelis, 236.

191. Van der Veer, 295, postulates that the position of the shrine of Herakles is in Valaria at the spot where the map 'Marathon', Plate XIX of *Karten von Attika*, marked 'Unterbau und Baustucke' ('Foundations and Buildings'), close to the church of Saints Theodore. However, Van der Veer, 316, on map C of his publication has the indication 'Shrine of Herakles' at the base of Agrieliki, 200 m. southwest of the aforementioned point. We analyse this contradiction by Van der Veer below. Koumanoudis, 239, states that: 'Unfortunately, even though remains of the Shrine of Herakles have been found; no excavation has been carried out'. He does not clarify to which 'remnants' he is referring; most likely these belong to the church of Saints Theodore, as maps of Koumanoudis', publication, 240–244, figs. 1–4, have the site of this church marked as 'Shrine of Herakles'. Frazer, 435, does something similar with Koumanoudis: while making a reference to the Shrine of Herakles at Marathon, he points out that at his time (late-nineteenth century) there were in Valaria foundations of an ancient building of elliptical shape with inbuilt Ionian pillars and architectural remnants. The shape of the building that Frazer suggests may have been the site of the shrine of Herakles is similar to a Byzantine church, with the most likely candidate Saints Theodore.

192. For drawings of the specific architectural parts, see Themelis, 237–238, figs. 5α–5β.

193. Kromayer 1921, 11–14, was the first to point out that the Greeks could not have encamped at the Marathon plain, but on the highland, due to the fear the Persian

cavalry instilled in the Greeks. Hammond, 1968, 34, n. 96, Kontorlis, 20, and Fotiou, 202, also reject the possibility of the Athenian camp having been on the plain of Marathon plain (Valaria is on the southern part of the plain).

194. Nunnus, *Dionysiaka*, 13, 184.

195. Athenaios, 14.627D.

196. Herodotus, 8.52.1. The confrontation between Greeks and Persians at Marathon took place at the end of the summer of 490, when the conditions were optimal for forest fires. Just four years before the battle of Marathon, in 494, during a war between Sparta and Argos, the Spartan king, Kleomenes, set on fire a grove where Argeian soldiers were hiding and burned them all alive. See Herodotus, 6.78–80.

197. All archaeological publications record this spur of Agrieliki as 'height or spur 209m'. McCredie, 35. Vanderpool, 1966a, 320 and 321. Van der Veer, 291. Hammond, 1988, 509. This height has been copied from *Karten von Attika* των Curtius and Kaupert, 1889, 'Marathon', XIX. However, on the map of the Hellenic Military Geographical Service (Γεωγραφική Υπηρεσία Στρατού or Γ.Υ.Σ.), Φ Χ. ΚΗΦΙΣΙΑ, n. 6437/7, the maximum height of the spur is 205.80 metres, i.e. 206m.

198. McCredie, 35, records 206-metre spur as: '*the northernmost of the eastern ridges of Mt. Agrieliki*'.

199. Sotiriadis, 1927b, 121, 125.

200. According to Kromayer, 1924, 5, n. 1, Agrieliki is the 'mountain of wild olive trees': 'Wilder-Olbaum-Berg'.

201. Sotiriadis, 1927b, 121, n. 1, mentions that in 1927, shortly after his first visit to Agrieliki, all the olive trees burnt in a forest fire. Forest fires have also occurred at Agrieliki in 1939, 1977 and 1994.

202. Finlay, 380: '… some ruins in the pass, and an Hellenic wall running up the side of the mountain'. Finlay mentions in a letter to Leake dated 16–12–1836 that he had traced himself these remains during a visit at Marathon. See Hussey, 521, 527–528. Finlay was an expert of Greek art and archaeology and the fact that he was impressed by this wall means that he considered it to be important.

203. Finlay's publication about the battle at Marathon was known to Sotiriadis who refers to it. However, Sotiriadis did not realize that the fortification he found on 206-metre spur was the ancient Greek wall that Finlay mentioned in his article as having located at northeast Agrieliki, see below.

204. In Agrieliki there is only one ancient rampart and it is certain that Sotiriadis discovered what Finlay describes as 'Hellenic wall'. As we will see, Finlay has marked on two maps the position of the Athenian camp at the exact point where Sotiriadis located the fort. His observation that the wall was 'running up the mountain' also confirms that it is Sotiriadis' rampart; on the map of the Hellenic Military Geographical Service, Φ Χ. ΚΗΦΙΣΙΑ, n. 6437/7, heights 205.80 m. and 201.70 m. are recorded on parts of the wall showing that there is a difference in height over four metres between them. The co-ordinates of the top corner of the rampart are: N38°06'20.67", E23°57'38.40".

205. Sotiriadis' first publication of the rampart is 1927, 125–126, where he states that he made its discovery in 1926. In 1927 *The Classical Weekly* published, in English, an article by Sotiriadis about his discovery see Sotiriadis, 1927a, 83–84.

206. Sotiriadis, 1927b, 125–126.

207. Sotiriadis, 1927b, 126, is the first record of the Agrieliki rampart as the 'Mycenaean Acropolis of Marathon'. Between 1932–1935, Sotiriadis repeated this claim in several publications, see below.

208. Sotiriadis, 1927b, 126.
209. Sotiriadis, 1935, 156. According to Sotiriadis, the ceramics he found in the cavern in the perimeter of Agrieliki's rampart were lost when they were transferred from Marathon to Athens; thus, they cannot be re-examined.
210. Sotiriadis, 1935, 157.
211. Sotiriadis, 1934, 35–38.
212. Vanderpool, 1966a, 321, n. 8, highlights that this was one of the reasons why Sotiriadis believed that the Agrieliki rampart belonged to the Mycenaean era.
213. McCredie, 35: 'the construction can be seen to be rather more careless than usual among similar Attic fortifications […] it may well be that this fortification was rather a small temporary outpost in the Marathonian area […] it should probably be classed as a small fortified camp …". At this point we need to emphasise a contradiction by McCredie: He records that the rampart at Agrieliki was a small construction whereas in the same publication he mentions that its circumference was 300 metre; this is quite a large size for an average Greek fort.
214. According to McCredie, 91–92, there is no evidence whatsoever on the existence of fortified refuges for the residents of Attica during the Classical period. This applies even to Ramnous and Sounion, that had important fortifications next to their civic centres; their role was to defend Attica and not to protect civilians during a military crisis. Furthermore, the responsibility for their construction, maintainance and manning belonged exclusively to the Athenian state and not the local administration.
215. Thus, archaeologists were not able to date this structure based on its construction technique. Despite its careless appearance, the wall is compact and appears to have been constructed by skilled builders, something Sotiriadis, 1927b, 125–126, emphasizes.
216. Pritchett, 1960, 150: '…(The wall)… clearly did not enclose a building of any sort'. McCredie, 35: 'The wall does not seem to have had towers, and no gateway is now visible […] The interior of the enclosure is very rocky and uneven, and there are no traces of buildings'. Vanderpool, 1966a, 321, n. 8: 'The fort was certainly never permanently occupied and there are no buildings in it and no earth deposits'. Goette and Weber, 21, also record that the rampart has no towers or gate.
217. Pritchett, 1960, 150. McCredie, 35. Vanderpool, 1966a, 321, n. 8: 'the rough, irregular surface of the rock is the same inside the walls as it is outside'.
218. Pritchett, 1960, 150. Vanderpool, 1966a, 321, n. 8. McCredie, 35. Van der Veer, 293. Pritchett notes that despite the persistent research he conducted on the surface of the rampart in 1959, together with Vanderpool, then director of the American School of Classical Studies in Athens, they were unable to find a single dateable potsherd. Pritchett paid another visit to the rampart in the same year, in tandem with two members of the American School, and did more surface research to no avail. Potsherds are the most common finding on the surface of any ancient Greek site. Therefore, archaeologists who do surface research on a site try to find potsherds which can be identified with parts of dated vases.
219. McCredie, 35, n. 46. Based on McCredie's description, these pottery sherds may have come from large storage pots, like pithoi which were used to carry goods in large quantities.
220. Vanderpool, 1966a, 321, n. 8: '*but these sherds only date the occupation of the cleft, not the fort*'.
221. Langdon, 1982, 95–97.
222. Langdon, *op. cit.*

223. Between 1927–1935, the fort of 206-metre spur was researched by Sotiriadis, and during the 1930s by archaeologists of the German Archaeology Institute in Athens. After the war research at the rampart was taken up by archaeologists of the American School of Classical Studies in Athens. Dateable ceramics have been found on the surface of most ancient fortifications of Attica during archaeological research. Thus, Ober, 1987, 197–227, presents the ceramic findings from surface research of 19 fortification works in northern and western Attica. They date between the Classical and Roman times.

224. Sotiriadis records that even in his time some of his colleagues voiced reservations on his theory that the rampart of Agrieliki was Mycenaean. Nonetheless, in the bibliography, apart from Wrede's reference (see below), we didn't find any publication contemporary to Sotiriadis' criticising his theory about Marathon's 'Mycenaean Acropolis'.

225. According to McCredie, 35, about the rampart on 206-metre spur: 'There is, unfortunately, no evidence now on the site to determine its date'.

226. Pritchett, 1960, 150 and Vanderpool, 1966a, 321, n. 8. See also Hammond, 1988, 509, fig. 43, where height '209', i.e. 206-metre spur, is marked 'Hellenistic Fort'.

227. Wrede, 30. This theory was later adopted by Pritchett, 1965, 87.

228. McCredie, 92–93. Cf. Fotiou, 100, n. 47 and Hanson, 1998, 113, based on Xenophon's reference, *Poroi*, 4.43–4.48, believe that during antiquity refuges had been constructed in various places throughout Attica to protect locals during military crises. In the aforementioned reference, Xenophon suggests erecting a refuge to protect the population of Laurium, due to the importance for the Athenian economy of the local silver mines. This reference, though, does not ascertain the existence of such refuges in Attica. Besides, it is even doubtful whether Xenophon's proposal was ever implemented.

229. McCredie, 93: 'in places with such obvious strategic importance that they could not be overlooked by an army engaged in a serious attack on Attica [...] and Agrieliki controlled that [the road] between the Marathonian plain and the Mesogeia'. Sotiriadis, 1932, 40, refers to the strong and strategic position of 206-metre spur vis a vis the Marathon plain and Goette and Weber, 21, stress the strategic significance of the rampart in controlling the southerly end of the Marathon region: 'das zur Sicherung der bereits erwahnten Landenge am sudlichen Ende der Marathonia diente'.

230. Hanson, 1998, 112–114, and n. 17.

231. According to Hanson, *op. cit.*, during the Classical era the inhabitants of Attica would not have sought refuge in a fort, because they would have found themselves in the line of fire and their presence would also have caused problems to the defenders. Even if we accept that there were refuges for the inhabitants of Attica in case of a military crisis – which as we have seen, is unlikely – the inhabitants of Marathon would have built their own at a higher and more suitable spot in Agrieliki than 206-metre spur. The peak of the mountain at 557m is such a position; the ascent takes a long time and an enemy army would access it with difficulty. The inhabitants would certainly have felt safer if their – alleged – refuge had been constructed even higher than Agrieliki, on Pentelikon.

232. According to Pritchett, 1960, 150, during his surface research no potsherds were found either in the enclosure of the rampart in Agrieliki or in the wider northeast side of Agrieliki. Only a few ancient potsherds were recovered at the peak of spur 361m of Agrieliki. We discuss below the significance of these archaeological finds.

233. Finlay, 383.

234. Sotiriadis, 1932, 40.
235. McCredie, 93.
236. Sotiriadis, 1927b, 121 and 125.
237. Ober, who has researched the system of fortifications set up by the Athenians during the fourth century to protect Attica from external threats, has not found any evidence that Marathon was included in this system. The Agrieliki rampart could therefore not have been part of fortification works the Athenians erected at the time.
238. There was one more crisis in the area of Marathon during classical times, which has nothing to do with Agrieliki and its fort and should therefore be ruled out from our research. Demosthenes, *First Philippic*, 34, records that during operations by Philip II of Macedon's fleet in the Aegean, the Macedonians raided the coast of Marathon, where they came across and stole one of the two 'sacred' triremes of Athens. This action dates to 354/353, or two years later, see Harding, 152, and the trireme was on the Marathon shore either to carry to Delos the envoys of the Tetrapolis, or to receive the blessings of the priest of the Delion, Apollo's local shrine. It was a raid which surprised the Athenians but who didn't need to dispatch military aid to Marathon and built fortifications to defend themselves. In Kynosoura there are remains of roughly built walls next to which potsherds of various ancient periods have been found. Sotiriadis, 1935, 153–154, postulates that these walls belonged to the time of the Peloponnesian War and that they had been erected there to provide refuge for locals. Varouha-Chrystodoulopoulou, 346, speculates that these walls may have been erected during the Chremonidean War (267/261) by forces of Ptolemy II who were in eastern Attica at the time. McCredie, 46, dates their construction in the later-Classical or early-Hellenistic period, without ruling out the possibility of part of them having been constructed at the same time as Ptolemaic fortifications in Attica during the Chremonidean War. Even if the fortifications at Kynosoura were built during this war by Ptolemaic troops, the case of the rampart and the rest of the facilities in northeastern Agrieliki being connected to the Chremonidean War should be ruled out. The Ptolemaic camps of Attica are beside the sea as the power that used them relied on its maritime supremacy against an adversary, Macedonia, which was a land power. However, the Agrieliki rampart does not have direct access to the sea. It was therefore built by a power defending itself against a foe in the plain of Marathon. The force at Marathon had evidently disembarked there and thus had control of the sea; not the one which had occupied defensive positions at Agrieliki. Besides, McCredie, 107–115, in his thorough presentation on the forts which may have been erected in Attica during the Chremonidean War, does not include that of Agrieliki.
239. Herodotus, 1.62.1–1.63.2.
240. Finlay, 383.
241. Thucydides, 4.4–5.
242. Thucydides, *op. cit.*
243. Pritchett, 1974, 135.
244. Pritchett, *op. cit.*
245. Pritchett, *op. cit.* McCredie, 18–25 and 98, reached the same conclusion after realising that the *charax* of an ancient temporary camp on Patroklos' islet mentioned by ancient authors must have been the roughly-built wall that still exists today, which is of low height (less than 1m), considerable width (2.5m) and its stone structure has no adhesive material.

246. McCredie, 97–99 and Krentz, 2007a, 163–164.
247. Hanson, 1998, 26–27, mentions the example of the Athenian camp's fortification in Delion of Boiotia in 424, which Thucydides, 4.90.2, records that the Athenians built with wood as well as vines from vineyards they uprooted and stones from nearby houses which they demolished. A year earlier at Pylos, the Athenians picked up stones from the ground to construct their fortification wall. Thucydides, 4.4.
248. McCredie, 97, n. 27, points out that ancient camps in Attica didn't have a moat, as the rocky environment in which they were built made their construction difficult.
249. There is extensive bibliography on the Ptolemaic camps in Attica during the Chremonidean War which includes the finds of Greek and American archaeologists who excavated them.
250. McCredie, 99–100, records the characteristics of temporary camps in Attica, with references to the forts at Koroneia and Patroklos' island, which were camps of the Ptolemaic forces during the Chremonidean War.
251. According to Sotiriadis, 1927b, 125, the wall of the Agrieliki rampart has a width of two metres. In another publication, Sotiriadis, 1935, 148, he records them as two-and-a-half metres wide. Mazarakis-Ainian, 705, records a width of about two metres for the wall of the rampart.
252. McCredie, 35.
253. Sotiriadis, 1927b, 126.
254. The fort of Fylla is built on spur-130 metre, see Coulton et al., 1.
255. For this characteristic at the fort of Fylla, see Coulton et al., 25, and for the Agrieliki fort, see Sotiriadis, 1927a, 84.
256. Agrieliki: Sotiriadis, 1927b, 125. Fylla: Coulton et al., 45.
257. Coulton et al., 113–114.
258. J. Anderson, 1970, 62, postulates that the *tents* mentioned in connection to Greek camps may have been huts made of wood and bushes, not merely tents. Krentz, 2007a, 164, 31, disagrees with this idea, regarding them as proper tents made of leather. Even if Anderson is right, such constructions were built by the Greeks when they were encamped for a long period of time. The reverse was true for Marathon, where the short duration of the campaign makes it unlikely that there were any huts in the Athenian camp.
259. See Van Wees, 2011, 104.
260. In the temporary Greek camps of the Classical period, only the Spartan army had a special central space where all soldiers stored their equipment. This space was guarded, thus the Spartans were the only Greeks who had guards inside their camp as well as outside. Xenophon, *The Constitution of the Lacedaemonians*, 12.2.
261. For installations in a temporary Greek camp of the Classical era, see J. Anderson, 1970, 59–62. Krentz, 2007a, 162–167. Van Wees, 2011, 107. According to Herodotus, 9.44, the night before the battle of Plataia, in 479, Athenian soldiers were doing guard duty in designated posts (*phylakas*) in front of the Greek camp.
262. No known military operation took place in the region of Marathon after 490, so that the danger of an invader from the plain would have forced the defending army to fortify the part of Agrieliki above the Brexiza pass. Neither 206-metre spur nor its rampart seem to have been used again for military purposes. So, it didn't go through alterations which might have tampered with its original form.
263. IG I³ 503/4. Lapis C. For the epigram, see Matthaiou, 2003, 194–202, and Bowie, 2010, 204–212.
264. IG I³ 503/4. Lapis C, line 1.

265. Matthaiou, 2003, 200–201.
266. Herodotus, 6.134, uses the term '*herkos*' to describe the precinct of the Shrine of Demeter at Paros, and in 9.96–97, the rampart that the Persians erected around their temporary camp at Mykale before the battle of 479. For the various terms ancient Greek authors used to describe types of fortifications, see Pritchett, 1974, 134–139.
267. Finlay was the first and only researcher of the battle of Marathon, until the publication of this book, to identify the rampart on 206-metre spur of Agrieliki as part of the camp that the Greeks erected at Marathon just before the battle. In Finlay's lifetime, the great majority of scholars didn't accept his proposed location of the Greek camp at Agrieliki and it was put aside and forgotten. The reason for this was that they were convinced that the shrine of Herakles and the Athenian camp were at Vranas. This is especially true for scholars, such as Leake, who, as we shall see, had based their recontructions of the battle on this parameter.
268. 'The Northeastern Part of Attica, prepared from the French Surveys with the assistance of F. Aldenhoven, Athens 1838', published by *Aldenhoven*, Athens 1840, where the indication 'Athenian Camp' appears on ridge 206m. However, on the map in Finlay's publication entitled 'Plain of Marathon', the indication 'Greek Camp' covers the ridge and also part of the Brexiza pass. Finlay implies in his text that the Greeks had encamped inside this specific area.
269. Finlay, 383: 'The elevated position of the Greek camp gave the Athenians a perfect view of the camp and fleet of their enemy, and enabled them to seize instantly any advantage which might result from the movements of the Persians'.
270. Curtius, 1898, 301, highlights that the main way between Marathon and Athens is through the southern part of the plain, so his reference is certainly about the Brexiza pass. The environmental features of the area that Curtius deems the Greeks had chosen for their camp at Marathon are in tune with 206-metre spur of Agrieliki.
271. Meyer, 329, records his view that the Athenian camp was on the foothills of Agrieliki above the southern passage to Athens, i.e. the northeastern foothills of the mountain
272. Kromayer, 1921, 10–11, 12, 14, and 1924, 6.
273. Bengtson, 135: 'Die athener nahmen auf den Nordostabhangen des Agrieliki Stellung'.
274. Themelis, 236.
275. Koumanoudis, 240, fig. 1.
276. Dionysopoulos, 183 and fig. 63.
277. Berthold, 90.
278. Krentz, 2007a, 162,
279. Pritchett, who as we have seen recorded the general features of ancient Greek camps, had done surface research at the rampart on 206-metre spur. However, he didn't mention that this could have been a camp of such type. We postulate that this may have been so because Pritchett's research on 206-metre spur was conducted in 1959, before he acquired his expertise in Greek camps (his relevant publications appeared many years later). Only McCredie, 35, records that this rampart was an ancient Greek camp, thanks to the similarities of its construction with that of Ptolemaic camps in Attica. Therefore, he classified this camp along with other makeshift and roughly constructed camps as 'fortified camps in Attica'. At the same time, he notes that only through dating archaeological finds at these forts

would it be feasible to date them and establish their connection to some 'historical event'. However, in the case of the rampart of 206-metre spur, McCredie didn't explore the possibility – even in order to reject it – of the historical event which led to the erection of this rampart having been the battle of Marathon!

280. Finlay published his theory that the Greeks had lined up in the southern end of the Marathon plain close to the Brexiza pass in 1839. Nonetheless, this had little response in his time. As we shall see, only when Vanderpool published a similar theory during the 1960s did several scholars start accepting it.

281. Langdon did archaeological research during the 1970s on spur 361 of Agrieliki (see below) but not on the rampart of 206-metre spur.

282. Perhaps it is no coincidence that the only modern publication where the rampart on 206-metre spur is mentioned as part of the Greek camp of 490 is of spilaeological, not archaeological or historical content. A team of spilaeologists searched the caves in eastern Agrieliki in June 2005 and their findings were published by Tountopoulos, in the on-line periodical edition SPELEO NEWS (Issue 6. June 2005), 'Mission at Agrieliki': http://www.actiongr.com/speleonews/to6.htm#topic4. In his publication Tountopoulos makes a passing reference to the rampart on 206-metre spur describing it as an ancient Acropolis with a circumference of 300 metres. However, in his closing remark about this fort, Tountopoulos refers to it as the Greek camp of the battle of Marathon.

283. Apart from the Greek camp, traces of the shrine of Herakles may also be unearthed, provided it was at the spot where the Greeks encamped, not where they lined up for the battle. As we have seen, the latter is also possible

284. As this inscription is unpublished, we were granted permission by the Greek Archaeological Service to include this reference in our book. The *edition princeps* of the inscription is currently under preparation by Dr Charles Denver Graninger of the American School of Classical Studies to whom we are indebted for information he gave us relating to the inscription.

285. All literary and epigraphic references to the Herakleian Games at Marathon date to the first half of the fifth century. The games may have ceased during the Peloponnesian War due to the Spartan invasions of Attica. The last known reference to the shrine of Herakles at Marathon is in the inscription of the 'Calendar of Sacrifices of the Tetrapolis' dating to the early-fourth century. IG II^2 1358, Lapis A.

286. Athenian epheboi visited the graves of the fallen at Marathon in 138, as recorded in an inscription IG II^2 1006.26–27 where there is no mention of the camp. The same also applies for a visit by another group of Athenian epheboi at Marathon in 176–175 recorded in an unpublished inscription. See Matthaiou, 2003, 197.

287. Pausanias, 1.32.7

288. Leake, 1841, 2, 89–90.

289. Herodotus, 6.105.1.

290. Herodotus, 6.105.3

291. Petrakos, 1995, 86–91

292. Sotiriadis, 1935, 156–158, records that long before 1926, when he searched for the first time the cavern of 206-metre spur, Soutzos – a local land owner – had done illegal excavations at its entrance looking for 'treasure'.

293. Sotiriadis, 1935, 154–155. Vanderpool, 1966a, 321, n. 8.

294. Sotiriadis, 1935, 155.

295. Vanderpool made extensive researches in northeast Agrieliki but these did not include the altar at the peak of spur-361m. Pritchett, 1960, 150–151, who did

surface research there, states that he saw potsherds of the periods that Sotiriadis recorded in his publication, without adding any further evidence.

296. Langdon, 1976, 104–105, gives a description of the altar at spur-361m and agrees with Sotiriadis that it had been erected by local farmers. According to Langdon, the altars and shrines on mountain peaks in Attica were dedicated to Zeus. Sacrifices were made to him as Ombrios Zeus, who brings rain to the meadows below the mountains. The altar on peak 361m at Agrieliki affords a view over the Marathon plain and is an ideal spot to make sacrifices for that purpose.

297. The Greeks would have encamped at Agrieliki as a uniform unit without having been dispersed into smaller parts, as they would have to be ready to all rush in the battle in a flash. Literary sources clarify that during the Classical period the Athenians on a campaign encamped all together, in order to keep their coherence; they entered into the battle as one unit without keeping men in the reserves to be sent later in the battle. Dionysopoulos, 35.

298. The gully in northeastern Agrieliki, is large enough to have accommodated in 490 between 20,000–25,000 men, the estimated number of Greeks at Marathon. In our days such a large body of men could not possibly camp there, as its facilities would take up more space than that required in antiquity. The reason is the danger arising from the enemy artillery and enemy air-force, factors which didn't concern the commanders of troops in antiquity. Fotiou, 178, deems that Agrieliki was inappropriate for the Athenian force to camp there but does not corroborate this with evidence.

299. Finlay, 379: 'for these works must have been constructed before, and not after the arrival of the Athenian army at Marathon'.

300. Fotiou, 178, ascertains that the Agrieliki rampart could have held 100 to 150 hoplites. A conservative, but rather reasonable estimate.

301. Curtius 1898, 299–300, assumes that in the Athenian camp at Marathon, the generals would have had their own space to deliberate and to use it as their headquarters before the battle.

302. According to ancient literary sources, the Ten Generals conferred at the 'Strategion', a public building located in the Athen's Agora. The scant remains of a building excavated there, whose construction dates to the fifth century, have been identified by archaeologists with the 'Strategion', albeit with some reservations. See Camp, 1986, (2005), 147–149.

303. See below about the possible role of the rampart on 206-metre spur as an acropolis; that is, the most powerful defensive position of the Athenian camp. A similar camp formation is found at Koroni on the eastern Attica coast. This is where the main camp of the Ptolemaic army was in Attica during the Chremonidean War. It consists of a fort at the peak of the Koroni highland and various other remnants of fortification and facilities at a lower altitude. McCredie, 4–8, describes the fort at the peak as 'Acropolis' and that it stands out from the other structures.

Chapter 4

1. Whatley, 137.
2. Munro, 1926, 241–243. See also, Steinhauer, 2009a, 100–101,111, and 2010a, 60.
3. Munro regarded Artaphernes as the Persian troops' commander in Eretria, while Datis was at Marathon as Pausanias 1.32.7, records that Artaphernes commanded the Persian cavalry. According to Munro, the Persians intended to move their cavalry by sea from Euboia straight to Phaleron without disembarking at Marathon.

Therefore, Artaphernes, as commander of the cavalry, was most suitable to lead this operation against Athens while Datis would head the part of the Persian troops which remained at Marathon. However, it seems that Munro failed to notice that Pausanias records Artaphernes was at Marathon even before the battle, as he mentions that his tent was pitched there! Again, Munro might have claimed that Datis had carried Artaphernes' tent with him to Marathon, which he had borrowed from him in Eretria!

4. Nepos, *Miltiades*, 5, mentions that Datis wished to clash with the Athenians as soon as possible, before the Spartans had arrived at Marathon. If Datis really had known the arrival of the Spartan expeditionary force at Marathon was pending, he would have been even more eager to fight against the Athenians and the Plataians, before they were re-inforced by the Spartans. The fact that the Persians had disembarked their entire troops at Marathon can be deduced by Herodotus' narrative and is clearly recorded by Plutarch, *Aristides*, 5.1. Ancient literary sources aside, common sense indicates the Athenians would have known in 490 the exact number of ships in the Persian fleet, which would sail along the shores of Attica; either through military intelligence given by Greeks who had defected from the Persians or through observers who had seen the Persian fleet heading from Karystos to Eretria.

5. Whatley, 137: '*Delay is especially likely if, as probably at Marathon, the smaller army is the more strongly posted*'.

6. Finlay, 378–379.

7. Herodotus, 5.121.

8. For this estimate, various elements and parameters are combined: such as the phases of the moon before and after the battle, the alternation of the Athenian generals concerning the command of the day – see below – and the dispatch of Pheidippides to Sparta. Raaflaub, 2010, 221, hypothesises that between the disembarkation of the Persians at Marathon and their departure from Attica, ten days must have elapsed. According to Scott, 613–614, the Greeks and the Persians were at Marathon nine days before the battle. Isokrates, *Panegyric*, 4.87, and Souda, 'Hippias' (II), erroneously refer to the Athenians fighting the Persians on the very day they arrived in Marathon. The same goes for Nepos, *Miltiades*, 5.3–4, and Plutarch, *Ethics*, 350E, who claim that the Athenians fought against the Persians on the following day of their arrival in Marathon. According to a scholion on Aelius *Aristides*, Panathenaic (Dindorf, 1829, 3, 131–132), 'the generals were ten, and each day one succeeded the other as commander of the army; the day the Persians disembarked at Marathon, Miltiades was the commander'. Since Miltiades was 'commander of the day' when the battle was fought, ten days had elapsed since the Persian landing at Marathon.

9. Aelius Aristides, *Panathenaic*, 106, refers to the echoes coming from the Persians who were in the Marathon plain and heard by the Greeks who were encamped on higher ground. Due to the formation of the natural environment, Iphikrates, 205, 288, whoever is on 206-metre spur can distinctly hear the echo of sounds coming from the Marathon plain.

10. According to Pritchett, 1960, 172, n. 249, ships of the Persian fleet must have sailed between Marathon, Karystos, Eretria and other areas where they either did reconnaissance operations or carried supplies for their troops at Marathon.

11. Wallinga, 139–140, states that never before in history did the Greeks confront such a huge enemy navy as in 490.

12. Aelius Aristides, *Panathenaic*, 107.

13. Herodotus, 6.109.1.
14. Herodotus, op. cit. Aelius Aristides, *Panathenaic*, 106, stresses that the Persians were certain that merely through their presence – without even having to fight – they would force the Greeks to surrender.
15. Lycurgus, *Against Leokrates*, 104, claims that the Persian army at Marathon was from all over Asia. Plato, *Menexenos*, 240d, writes that the Athenians punished the arrogance of the whole of Asia. These are of course exaggerations but would have seem real in 490 for any Athenian soldier on Agrieliki looking down on the Persians in the Marathon plain.
16. Herodotus, 9.20.1.
17. Nepos, *Miltiades*, 5, refers here to the Athenian line-up just before the battle. Notwithstanding this, we deem that the features fit in with the spot where the Athenians had encamped. The issue with the wooden barricades arises from the translation of the term 'tractu arborum' which may mean either trees or pieces of wood. Cary, 206–207, suggests that Nepos' text does not refer to artificial obstacles, but to trees in front of the Athenians' positions; cf. Hammond, 1968, 39–40, 45–46, who considers that the Athenians had erected an abatis in front of their camp by positioning trunks of trees in the ground. The oldest known such construction in Greece was also erected in Attica and dates two decades before the battle of Marathon. When the Spartans, under Kleomenes I, campaigned against Hippias in Athens in 510, they built an abatis at Phaleron for protection against the Thessalian horsemen who were allies of Hippias, see Frontinus, 2.2.9. This appears to have been successful as Kleomenes defeated the Thessalians. If the Spartans had used such a defensive measure at Phaleron, the Athenians would have known from first hand that it could protect foot soldiers against a cavalry charge. Therefore, it would make sense to have built an abatis in front of their camp at Marathon.
18. Herodotus, 9.20–21, 9.52.1 and 9.60.
19. Kromayer, 1921, 14 and 1924, 10–15, located the Athenian camp in northeastern Agrieliki and speculated that Datis would have endeavoured to coerce the Athenians to come down from Agrieliki and fight him in the open plain; he suggests Datis did this by lining up his men in the plain beneath the mountain and challenging the Athenians with screams.
20. Herodotus, 9.60–63. What the Persians sought for at Plataia, by relentlessly using their cavalry, they achieved on day twelve of the two armies confronting each other in that region. Still, this happened only when the Greeks judged the time was ripe to fight. The battle at Plataia started with the Persian cavalry charging the Greek line-up and moved on with the opposing infantries clashing.
21. For Greek troops on a campaign in the Classical era, *maza* was a substitute of bread, which was a staple for the Greeks and other Mediterranean peoples during antiquity. References to it are frequent in ancient Greek literature. *Maza* was made of flour and looked like Arabic pie; contrary to bread, though, it was not necessary to bake at high temperatures, so it was easy to prepare by the troops on campaign, as building ovens in the camp was not essential. Krentz, 2007a, 165.
22. In fifth century Greece, only the Spartans followed a common, daily programme for the men who were on a campaign. They had a common wake-up call, ate and exercised all together, like a modern army. Xenophon, *The Constitution of the Lacedaemonians*, 12. 5–7.
23. For the Athenians playing dice in their military camps, see Herodotus, 1.61.

330 Who Really Won the Battle of Marathon?

24. In their camps the Athenians shared their tents with whoever they wanted and not necessarily men from the same *lochos* or even tribe. Conversely, in a Spartan camp men of the same unit ('moira') slept together and were forbidden to leave the designated area for their unit in the camp. Xenophon, *The Constitution of the Lacedaemonians*, 12.5.

25. Ancient literary sources make clear that Athenian soldiers circulated freely in their camp. A famous example is a reference by Plato, *Symposium*, 220c-d, that during the siege of Potidaia, men in the Athenian army would leave their sleeping quarters during nightime and go and watch Socrates whenever he was on guard duties in amazement that he stood still and did not move at all for a long time.

26. J. Anderson, 1970, 43–44. Krentz, 2010a, 108.

27. Krentz, 2007a, 162–163, remarks that Greeks on campaign encamped near shrines as there was water to be found and assumes that the same must have happened at Marathon. This is likely if the Athenians did in fact camp in the area of the local shrine of Herakles, but they may have lined up there and didn't camp.

28. Kromayer, 1924, 19, cites Veith's reference, who had visited Marathon in the early-twentieth century, according to which, farmers who had cultivated land near the foothills of northern Agrieliki claimed there was a source at the base of the mountain. Nonetheless, Kromayer and Veith highlight that – with the exception of that source – water was not to be found in northern Agrieliki. Nezis, 9, states that there are no water resources at Agrieliki due to the sedimentary rock there.

29. Despite many scholars' observation that the Greeks chose to camp near water resources being correct, this was not always feasible. For example, at Plataia in 479 there were no water resources near to the Greek camp; so water had to be carried from far away. When the Persian cavalry started assaulting Greek soldiers carrying water, there was a severe water shortage at their camp. In addition, McCredie, 99, notes that there was no water resources at the two main Ptolemaic camps in Attica during the Chremonidean War and the men had to get water supplies from elsewhere.

30. As we have seen, the only potsherds that archaeologists have found at the rampart on 206-metre spur – apart from the cavern in its enclosure – belong to rough, unpainted vessels. Those may have been used to carry water to the Athenian camp.

31. Krentz, 2007a, 151.

32. According to Krentz, 2010a, 107, an average ancient Greek needed an intake of at least 3,000 calories per day to be in good physical condition; this corresponds to 1–1.5kg of food. Aside from food, he also required water and wine.

33. We have estimated an average loading of 90.9kg for each course on a donkey, based on the ratio in Coulton et al., 97: 15 tons= 165 loads on a mule.

34. Krentz 2007a, 152, records that in antiquity two-wheel carts could have carried 500kg of supplies while four-wheel carts 650kg.

35. Herodotus, 9.39.2.

36. Herodotus, 9.50.

37. This road is unrecorded in the bibliography.

38. Diodorus, 10.27. Datis' ultimatum and its significance are analyzed by Raubitschek, 1957, 234–237.

39. Plato, *Laws*, 3.698d. This evidence makes it likely that Datis' message to the Athenians, which Plato refers to, might have been an ultimatum of surrender. Plato does not doubt if it was sent to the Athenians, only its reference on how the Persians caught all Eretrians. In any case, whether the latter was real or not, Plato

advocates that all the Greeks – especially the Athenians – were scared stiff as soon as they heard about it.

40. Raubitschek, 1957, 236–237. Sekunda, 41.
41. Herodotus, 7.133.1.
42. Dionysopoulos, 205.
43. Dionysopoulos, 201, emphasizes that the Spartans could have waived the ban and gone on a campaign provided they got permission from the seers; this didn't happen in 490.
44. Herodotus, 6.109.1.
45. Herodotus, *op. cit.*
46. Scott, 610, makes the logical assumption that not only half the generals but also most soldiers would not have been in the mood for clashing with the Persians in Marathon after seeing how numerous they were.
47. Souda, 'Hippias' (II).
48. Nepos, *Miltiades*, 5.
49. Sotiriadis, 1927a, 84, and 1927b, 125–126.
50. Finlay, 383. Sotiriadis, 1935, 126.
51. We postulate that the rampart at the peak of 206-metre spur of Agrieliki would function for the Athenian camp as an Acropolis of a city-state of that time; i.e. as the point of ultimate resistance if the enemy occupied the citadel, in this case the camp.
52. Nepos, *Miltiades*, 4.
53. Herodotus, 6.109. For this reference, see Hammond, 1968, 48, n.138. Lazenby, 57, n.28.
54. Evans, 1993, 284: 'If what they advocated was at all costs to avoid any engagement with the Persians before the Spartan contingent arrived, their policy seems eminently sound'.
55. Scott, 618.
56. Herodotus, 6.109.5.
57. However, there is evidence that after the battle of Marathon many Athenians believed that eminent citizens were ready to betray the city to the Persians. As we shall see, just after the battle Athenians started ostracising fellow citizens whom they suspected of being tyrannophiles. Among them there might have been some of the generals who in 490 were against clashing with the Persians, a view which after the battle may have been castigated as treacherous. The author of the *Constitution of the Athenians*, 22.6, mentions that the first ostracisms were against citizens the Athenians who were 'friends of tyrants'. These citizens must have been considered suspicious: labelled friends of the Persians, acting against their city›s interests and in favour of Darius. This assumption is borne out by the fact that on some potsherds of the first ostracizations (480s) the name of an Athenian etched on them is characterised as 'traitor' or 'Medos'. On one of these sherds, a design was etched showing a Persian archer and casting suspicions on Kallias as having co-operated with the Persians at Marathon. see Brenne, 174–175.
58. Fornara,1971,4.
59. Fornara, 1971, 4, n. 11, also speculates that through his personal influence the Polemarch may have taken on his side the majority of generals. This view stands to reason as the Nine Archons represented the supreme authority of the Athenian state and these high-ranking officials were influential even before their involvement in politics as members of the highest class. Being elected to the most important public offices increased their prestige and influence among their fellow citizens.

60. Miltiades' words to Kallimachos clearly show that the final decision on the clash with the Persians would have depended heavily on the latter by his own vote and not because he would convince a general into changing his negative vote. Herodotus, 6.109.6.
61. Gomme, 1952, 79–80.
62. Evans, 1993, 284. Both cases deal with the same scenario: a highly efficient person has made a plan which would lead to Greek victory against the Persians but he cannot bring this plan to fruition unless he convinces someone else in authority into implementing it. At Marathon Miltiades planned and Kallimachos executed. At Salamis in the respective roles were the Athenian Themistokles and the Spartan Euribiades. For the latter, see Herodotus, 6.109.3–4.
63. Plutarch, *Ethics*, 628E.
64. Herodotus, 6.110.
65. Plutarch, *Aristides*, 5.2.
66. Most scholars believe that the battle was fought either 11 September (Hammond, 1968, 40 and n.121. Holoka, 350), or the next day (Dionysopoulos, 91 and 98).
67. Herodotus, 6.110. Plutarch, *Aristides*, 5.2, wrongly records that all nine generals had given their day of command to Miltiades.
68. For possible reasons why the Athenians continued to avoid giving battle with the Persians even though they had decided to do this, see Macan, 1895, 2, 159–161. Hammond, 1968, 35–36. Shrimpton, 25–26. Hamel, 164–165.
69. Shrimpton, 25–26.
70. Aelius Aristides *Panathenaic*, 108, mentions that before the battle of Marathon, the Athenian generals held several debates among themselves but also with their men. If his reference is correct, the debates would have happened with a view to briefing the soldiers on Miltiades' plan concerning the tactics they would use against the Persians. This type of briefing was unusual in ancient Greece where men were quite familiar with the tactics of the hoplite phalanx and had little need to be briefed by the army commanders. We can therefore speculate that Miltiades' plan had some particularities compared to established tactics; that's why it was absolutely essential to explain the ins and the outs to the troops.
71. Leake, 1829, 183 and 1841, 2, 215. Burn, 1962 (1984), 246. Lazenby, 59. Hamel, 165.
72. Leake, *op. cit.* Scott, 618, claims that Miltiades attacked the Persians the day he was institutionally commander of the army in order to secure personal fame by the victory. Nonetheless, on p. 620, Scott claims that the Persians began the battle and on that day Oenis tribe, commanded by Miltiades, 'happened' to be the 'commanding' tribe. This way, though, he accepts that the day of the battle was not Miltiades›, but Datis› choice. Evans, 1993, 287, also hypothesises that the Persians triggered the start of the battle and Miltiades played no role in the choosing the day of the battle. However, on the previous page, 286, Evans claims that from Herodotus› text, it can be seen Miltiades had chosen that very day of his own command to give battle for his own glory.
73. According to Pritchett, 1974, 232–245, the lack of team spirit in military discipline was a typical characteristic of all troops in ancient Greece with the exception of the Spartans.
74. See Herodotus, 9.26–27, how the Tegeates and the Athenians almost came to blows on who would occupy the second most prestigious place in the Greek line-up after that of the Spartans at the battle of Plataia in 479. As for Marathon, a decade earlier, most recent scholars believe that the Athenian tribes were placed in

the hoplite phalanx according to their serial numbers, which had been laid down by the Oracle at Delphi in 508/7, when Kleisthenes set them up. Some ancient sources give the following number order: I Erechtheis, II Aigeis, III Pandionis, IV Leontis, V Akamantis, VI Oineis, VII Kekropis, VIII Hippothoöntis, IX Aiantis and X Antiochis. Most older commentators accepted this ordering, hence the Roman numerals that were later generally used. However, it appears that the ordering was changed during the fifth century, and hence the abovementioned one may not correspond to what applied in 490. In Roman times, Pollux, 8.110, gave a somewhat different ordering: I Erechtheis, II Kekropis, III Aigeis, IV Pandionis, V Akamantis, VI Antiochis, VII Leontis, VIII Oineis, IX Hippothoöntis and X Aiantis. Raubitschek, after studying the issue, concluded that the ordering mentioned by Pollux was made in the mid-fifth century and differed somewhat from that which applied in the battle of Marathon. His ordering was: I Erechtheis, II Kekropis, III Aigeis, IV Pandionis, V Leontis, VI Antiochis, VII Oineis, VIII Hippothoöntis, IX Akamantis and X Aiantis. Besides Raubitschek's sources, there is another piece of evidence that argues in favour of his ordering of the tribes. This is Plaque A10 from the Heroön of Trysa in Lykia which, as we have seen, features ten hoplites which could represent the ten Athenian tribes at Marathon, portrayed as the generals of each tribe, and in which the central figure is very likely Miltiades as portrayed in the wall painting of the Poikile Stoa in Athens. This figure is seventh in the line, which could tell us that Miltiades' tribe, the Oineis, had that position in the lineup. Raubitschek, 1956, 280–281, gives the Oineis the same position, assuming that the Aigeis was on the right of it. In both cases the Aiantis was on the left of the Athenian formation – that is, to the right of the Plataians. According to Plutarch, *Ethics*, 628E, however, the orator Glaukias maintained that the men of the Aiantis took up the extreme right of the Athenian line at Marathon. Glaukias was reported to have quoted an elegy of Aischylos, now lost, which tends to add weight to Plutarch's claim. Aischylos himself fought in the battle in the ranks of the Aiantis. Though this somewhat contradicts the abovementioned orderings, it could indicate that the Athenian tribes were numbered from left to right; this ordering would place the Erechtheis (I) on the left next to the Plataians and the Aiantis (X) on the far right. If this indeed was the case at Marathon, then the Aiantis would have been under the direct command of their tribesman, Kallimachos. The above evidence indicates how the Athenians could have formed up at Marathon. However, the study of a monument connected with the battle may produce evidence of a different ordering of the tribes, especially the position of the Aiantis. This is a complex of sculptures that the Athenians dedicated at Delphi just before the mid-fifth century to commemorate the victory at Marathon. The statues depict seven of the Eponymous Heroes of Athens, plus Athene, Apollo, Miltiades, Kodros, Theseus and Philaios. In the nineteenth century Mommsen (449–489) surmised that the three Athenian heroes must have replaced those three of the Eponymous Heroes who are missing on the monument, viz. Aias, Oineus and Hippothoön. According to this theory, the Aiantis tribe was honoured by a depiction of Theseus, while Philaios replaced Oineus and Kodros replaced Hippothoön as representatives of the tribes of that name. Mommsen believed that the order of the statues corresponded exactly to the order of the Athenian tribes at Marathon, which in his view was: I Erechtheis, II Kekropis, III Aigeis, IV Pandionis, V Akamantis, VI Antiochis, VII Leontis, VIII Hippothoöntis, IX Aiantis and X Oineis. The fact that the Oineis tribe is placed on the extreme right of the Athenian line would indicate that the formation lined up from left to right in numerical order; the indication is significant in that the Oineis tribe general, Miltiades, as commander of the day, had operational responsibility for the whole Athenian army on the day of the battle. Miltiades' position on the far right of the Greek line – the strongest but yet the most dangerous position – would appear to make sense, as it would enable him to supervise the tactics he had planned, working with the Polemarch, the supreme commander, who also occupied that spot. Miltiades could thus be in direct touch with Kallimachos about any problem that might arise in deploying the Greek formation, and Kallimachos would be in a position to order remedies. The placing of the Oineis at the far right of the line – the position of honour – cannot be ruled out, even though no ancient source mentions it. It is quite possible that the tribe of the commander of the day would be placed by custom at the place of honour. Yet against all this we must place Plutarch's explicit assertion (based on Aischylos' elegy) that the extreme right of the Greek line was occupied by the Aiantis tribe.

75. Meissner, 281: 'Thus, at Marathon, Miltiades did not actually prepare the army for action before his own turn came, despite the majority vote and the willingness of the other strategoi to submit to his command. However charismatic, the Athenian leader meticulously seeks to maintain military, social and political stability within the military arm of a fragile state system that has little in the way of developed decision-making capabilities'. Aelius Aristides, *To Plato, In Defence of the Four*, 163, points out the fact that Miltiades' obedience to the law was an example for his fellow citizens.

76. Diodorus, 10.27.

77. Krentz 2010a, 189, n. 1, postulates that in 490, Medos was not yet considered the pro-genitor of the Medes and therefore Datis could not have made that claim at Marathon. Cf. Evans, 1993, 290, who accepts as historically accurate Datis' ultimatum arguing that before the battle of Lade, in 494, the Persians dispatched an ultimatum of surrender to the Ionians, with a similar content to that of Datis to the Athenians on the eve of the battle of Marathon, according to Diodorus. In the ultimatum sent to the Ionians by the Persians, they mentioned that if they surrendered, they would forgive them for their revolt. If, however, they kept on resisting the Persians, they would give their land to foreigners, sell all of them as slaves, castrate their sons and sell their daughters as slaves to the far ends of the empire. Herodotus, 6.9.3–4. Persian commanders on other occasions, too, just before giving battle against the Greeks during the Ionian Revolt threatened that they would castrate their sons and deliver their prettiest girls to Darius. Herodotus, 6.32.

78. Diodorus, records that the answer given to Datis' ultimatum expressed the Athenian generals' view, without mentioning Kallimachos, which is wrong. Miltiades might have spoken Persian, so he could have undertaken to get across their reply to Datis' delegates. It is more likely, though, that this conversation was held in Greek, as the Persians had plenty of Greek-speaking administrative employees. Besides, the ultimatum could have been delivered by some of the Greeks who as we have seen were in the Persian camp along with Hippias. In 494 the Persians had sent their ultimatum to the Ionians with their former tyrants who had gone over to the Persians. Some ancient literary sources mention that Datis himself spoke Greek less than fluently, though. Raubitschek, 1957, 234–236, has collected these references deeming that Aristophanes, *Peace*, line 289, not only satirises the content of Datis'

ultimatum, but also makes fun of a grammatical mistake it seems he made while speaking Greek. Philologists named this mistake 'datism', after Datis.

79. Hammond, 1968, 49.
80. Harrison, 364. Based on Nepos' reference that Miltiades was depicted on the mural at the Poikile Stoa together with the other nine Athenian generals.
81. Harrison, *op. cit.*

Chapter 5

1. Evans, 1993, 300: 'It is hard to propose any reconstruction of Marathon that is original'. A century earlier, Munro, 1899, 185, had made a similar claim.
2. Van der Veer, 'Reconstruction A': 311–313. 'Reconstruction B': 313–315. 'Reconstruction C': 315–317.
3. For the Tumulus of the Athenians, see Appendix III.
4. J.-J. Barthelemy, *Maps, plans, views, and coins illustrative of the travels of Anacharsis the Younger in Greece, during the middle of the Fourth century before the Christian era.* London, 1806. Text by J.D. Barbie du Bocage, 'Critical observations on the maps of ancient Greece, compiled for the Travels of Anacharsis the Younger', 1–104, and 166 (map).
5. Enepikidis, 181–183.
6. Leake, 1829, 180–182, and 1841, Appendix I, 'The Battle of Marathon', 203–227.
7. Pritchett, 1960, 143. Burn, 1962 (1984), 244. Hammond, 1968, 19, map 2. Berthold, 94. Doenges, 8–13. Hammond adopted in a later publication Reconstruction 3 and Pritchett, Reconstruction 5. See below.
8. History Channel (television network), Arts and Entertainment Network and New Video Group, *Decisive Battles: Marathon* (New York: A and E Television Networks, 2004). And β) *Command Decisions: Battle of Marathon and Battle of Chalons* (New York: A and E Television Networks, 2004). See Krentz, 2010a, 218.
9. Finlay announced his theory in a speech he gave in 1838 and was published the following year.
10. Meyer, 329. Kromayer, 1921, fig. 1, and 1924, 10–15. Schachermeyr, 1–35. Hignett, 1963, 69. Kontorlis, 22–23, 26, 27. Lazenby, 65, n. 47. Steinhauer, 2009a, 103, Dionysopoulos, 183, fig. 63, 220–221, fig. 85–88.
11. Van der Veer, 313, who in the context of Reconstruction 2 regards Mesogaia in Herodotus' text as present day Nea Makri. But on maps of publications with this reconstruction – for example, Kromayer, 1921, fig. 1 – it is clear that few Athenians retreating during the battle – principally from the right wing – could have used this getaway. Finlay locates the retreat of the Greek centre towards Xylokeriza (Nea Makri). But it is obvious from the map in his publication that the Greek centre had in its rear the middle of the northern foot of Agrieliki making impossible the retreat from that spot.
12. For example, Lazenby, 65–66, who had adopted Reconstruction 2, presumes that during the battle the men of the Greek centre would have resorted to the foot of northern Agrieliki where the natural environment would have protected them from the pursuit of Persians and Saka. But in reality the opposite would happen; any Greeks there would have been trapped at the foothills of the mountain and would have been annihilated by the Persians.
13. Berthold, 90–91, presents the problems the Greek would have faced from the natural environment if they had lined up as in Reconstruction 2.
14. Hauvette-Besnault, 261–265 and map in p. 263.

15. Hammond, 1988, 509, 510–513.
16. Sekunda, 61–75.
17. Eschenburg, 152–156, 182–187 and 1889, 33–39.
18. For the Trophy of Marathon and the find of bones reputed to belong to the Persian dead of the battle, see Appendix III.
19. Eschenburg also considered that all phases of the battle of Marathon were fought beside the Great Marsh.
20. Thucydides, 2.34.5. Pausanias, 1.32.3.
21. Krentz, 2010a, 153–155.
22. Krentz, *op. cit.*
23. Krentz, 2010a, 172–175, analyzes the weaknesses and drawbacks of the battle tactics he considers that the Greeks used at Marathon.
24. Vanderpool, 1966a, 323, and 1966b, 103–105.
25. Themelis, 235–236. Koumanoudis, 237–243, fig. 1–4 (240–243). Burn, 1977, 90–91. Shrimpton, 31–32. Van der Veer, 317–318. Pritchett, 1999, 3. Matthaiou, 2003, 200–202.
26. IG I³ 503/4, Lapis AII.
27. Matthaiou, 2003, 200.
28. Matthaiou, *op.cit.*
29. Vanderpool, 1966a, 320, fig. 1, and 1966b, 104, fig. 3. Vanderpool, as all modern scholars, presumes that the Athenians had encamped at the Shrine of Herakles and not lined-up there.
30. Koumanoudis, 240, fig. 1.
31. Van der Veer, 316, Map C. In 295 and 315–317 he claims that the location of the shrine of Herakles is at the spot where map xix 'Marathon' of Karten von Attica indicates: However, the indication 'Herakleion' on Van der Veer's map is 200–300 metres southwest of the respective location on Karten von Attica.
32. Vanderpool, 1966a, 323.
33. Themelis, 232. Van der Veer, 320. Pritchett, 1999, 3, points out that *'Vanderpool's reconstruction of the battle is in conformity with the Herodotean record'*.
34. See Appendix III.

Chapter 6

1. Pausanias, 1.33.2.
2. Holoka, 334–335, argues that battle could not have commenced at dawn but early morning after sunrise.
3. In our reconstruction we adopt Vanderpool's view on the position of the Shrine of Herakles. However, this shrine might also be at Agrieliki where the Greeks encamped.
4. For the Greek line-up see Reconstruction 5.
5. Our reconstruction solves the query of some scholars of why the Persians did not attack the Greeks as they were forming their line-up – see for example, Delbrück, 1920 (1990), 87. The answer is rather simple: they too were preparing for battle. If the Persians were already lined up when the Greeks were forming their own line-up the former would have seized the opportunity and had attacked them.
6. Herodotus, 6.111.
7. According to Herodotus, 6.112, before the clash the Athenians carried out the ritual killing of the sacrificial animals, the last they would carry out before the battle. Conducting the actual sacrifice would be the supreme commander of the army,

whether king or Polemarch, in front of the line and in the neutral zone between the two opposing armies with the aid of a seer. Wheeler, 2007, 204. The sacrifice at Marathon would have been carried out, then, after the Athenians were already in position, which would corroborate Herodotus' account. This last sacrificial ritual was not designed to secure an omen of victory, as the previous such rituals were supposed to do, but to be a final attempt to secure the gods' favour. Jameson, 1991, 221. Its 'favourable' outcome indicates that it gave confidence to the Greeks for the imminent clash. Herodotus makes no mention of other such sacrificial rituals that must have been conducted before the battle, either before the army left Athens or at the camp on Agrieliki. A fourth century inscription, however, describes one such rite and the oath taken by Athenian soldiers on an expedition. Most scholars believe the oath to be modelled on what was sworn before the battle of Plataia in 479. Krentz, 2007b, 731–742, goes so far as to assert that it could refer to the oath taken by the soldiers before the battle of Marathon, and hence the whole ritual would have that origin. The inscription states that after taking the oath, the soldiers covered the slaughtered animals with their shields. It would follow that such an act could not have taken place if the soldiers were already in formation, prepared to meet the enemy. Therefore the ritual described, called the 'sacred' (*hiera*), must have been conducted shortly before the Athenians left their camp on Agrieliki to take up position in the plain below. In this ritual the head of the army, in this case Kallimachos, slit the throat of a small animal whose blood was collected in a concave shield. Then he cut open the animal's body to examine its entrails with the aid of a haruspex, or seer. If the signs were favourable the pieces of the animal would be placed where the whole army could see them. Over these pieces the soldiers would swear to obey their superiors during the battle, to fight bravely and if necessary give their lives, and to bury their fallen comrades afterwards. The ritual would conclude with a solemn curse on anyone failing to carry out the oath. The Greeks certainly would have carried out that ritual before the battle at Marathon, similar (according to Krentz) to that on the abovementioned inscription. In 490 the pieces of the sacrificial victim would have been placed where the whole army could see them, likely by the path from the rampart on Agrieliki to the plain of Marathon. The spot would have been on the left of the path so that the hoplites could hold their shields over the pieces, as their right hands would have been carrying their spears.

8. In ancient Greece, the commander of an army usually gave a short talk to his men in the line-up just before a battle, see Van Wees, 2011, 192. This was a final attempt to boost their morale before the fighting began.
9. Xenophon, *Anabasis*, 1.8.15–16, presents this tactic in skirmishes before the battle of Cunaxa. See Van Wees, 2011, 192.
10. Herodotus does not record what was the command Kallimachos gave to the Greeks to start charging against the Persians. According to Aelius Aristides, *To Plato: In Defence of the Four*, 174, on the mural of the battle at the Poikile Stoa, Miltiades is depicted the moment he gives the signal for the Greek attack by waving his arm towards the Athenians. Although at the start of the battle, Miltiades may have urged the Athenians either to line-up against the Persians or even to assault them, the starting signal for the battle must have been given by the supreme commander of the Greek troops, Polemarch Kallimachos. This he may have done by moving his arm, and his signal was passed straight away to the troops through a bugle call.

According to Thucydides, 6.69.2, the signal for advance in the hoplites' phalanx was through a bugle-call.

11. Kromayer, 1924, 13–14, presents this tactic of the Persian cavalry in the context of the battle of Marathon.

12. For the separatation of the cavalry and infantry in the Persian line-up, see Herodotus, 9.32.2.

13. Cavalry in centre: Xenophon, *Anabasis*, 1.7.11, 1.8.6. Kromayer, 1924, 13–16. Left wing: Shrimpton, 32–33. On both wings: Gaebel, 72, Lazenby, 65, Sekunda, 25.

14. Kromayer, 1924, 13–16.

15. Shrimpton, 29–30. Scott, 390. Farrokh, 73. Burn, 1962 (1984), 250, has the Saka in the centre of the Persian line-up as cavalry but with a question mark. Lazenby, 65, also mentions the possibility that the Saka at Marathon in the centre of the line-up were cavalry but concludes that they were infantry.

16. Shrimpton, 29–30. As we have seen Herodotus doesn't state that these forces at Marathon were cavalry or infantry. Additionally, all his references to combined forces of Persians and Saka at the battle of Plataia are for cavalry not infantry.

17. According to Shrimpton, *op. cit.*, all evidence shows that the Saka foot soldiers were not elite forces of the Persian Empire.

18. For the elite forces and the commander in the centre of the Persian line-up, see Xenophon, *Anabasis*, 1.7.2. He also states that the Persian commander – whether it was the king or a general – was always at the centre of the line-up for security reasons. At the same time, his presence there ensured that commands to either wing would have been given in half the time. Herodotus, 9.71.1, mentions that at the battle of Plataia, the Saka was the most distinguished of all the Persian cavalry forces. It is therefore certain that at Plataia, the Saka cavalry was an elite unit. It is logical that a decade earlier, at Marathon this also applied, and the Saka cavalrymen were in the centre of the Persian line-up with other elite forces, see Shrimpton, 30 and Scott, 390.

19. See Hammond, 1968, 35. In 479, the Persian cavalry attacked the Greeks at Plataia in groups during skirmishes before the main battle, see Herodotus, 9.20 and 9.22.1. On one occasion the Persian cavalrymen attacked all together against the Greek line-up when they tried to recover the corpse of their commander, Masistios, who had been killed during such a skirmish, see Herodotus, 9.23.1. According to Herodotus, 9.47.3, at the start of the battle of Plataia, the entire Persian cavalry attacked the left wing of the Greek line-up, see Shrimpton, 32, n. 29. Lazenby, 32, claims that the Persian cavalry never attacked *en masse*, but the aforementioned citations reject his view.

20. Herodotus, 9.49.1–3, describes vividly how the Persian cavalrymen attacked the Greek line-up at Plataia. As soon as they were close enough they threw a barrage of arrows and spears against the Greeks causing them many casualties. After that the cavalrymen wheeled back to their line. As Whatley, 133, states: 'The ordinary method was to ride up close to the infantry and shoot, then they wheeled and went back to prepare for another advance'.

21. When during a battle the Persian cavalrymen after an attack against the enemy, wheeled back to the rear of their line-up they probably rode next to its right wing. It is also likely that, as the Persian foot soldiers marched into battle, they opened gaps in their ranks through which their horsemen passed in order to get back as quickly as possible, see Shrimpton, 34–35.

22. Herodotus, 9.47.3. Shrimpton, 32, n.29.

23. For the *gerron*, see Barret and Vickers, 21–22. Sekunda, 25.
24. Krentz, 2010a, 26.
25. Shrimpton, 34.
26. Shrimpton, *op. cit.*
27. Euripides, *Herakles*, 190–194, describes how in the hoplite phalanx each hoplite depended on the men next to him. If a hoplite was killed or fled during the battle the lives of those beside him were put in peril. Conversely, an archer had no such problem as he depended on himself. Euripides, *Herakles*, 195–200.
28. Persian cavalrymen wielding long swords attacking hoplites are depicted on an early-fifth century sarcophagus from Klazomenai, see Greenhalgh, 143–144, fig. 77, and Evans, 1987, 102. Additionally, a wall painting of a tomb in Lykia of the same period shows a Persian cavalryman holding a spear and attacking a hoplite, see Krentz, 2010a, 28–31.
29. Aischylos, *Persians*, lines 240–241.
30. It was not unusual as the men in a hoplite phalanx marched to battle for gaps to appear in their front row, see Thucydides, 5.71, who writes that the reason for this was that not all hoplites held their shields in the same way as they marched and this created gaps in the front row.
31. Xenophon, *Cyropaedia*, 7.1.21
32. Dionysopoulos, 216.
33. In 'no man's land' between the two line-ups no archaeological remains have been found. It seems that there were no human structures that could inhibit the charge of the Persian cavalry. The *deme* of Marathon in 490 was probably at Plasi which according to our reconstruction was behind the Persian line-up. As we have seen, at the time of the battle trees seem to have been scarce in the Marathon plain.
34. This estimate is based on an average galloping speed of 30km per hour for the Persian horses. The spur was first used during the late-Roman period and helped to increase the galloping speed of horses in battle, see J. Anderson, 1961, 76. Vigneron, 238–239.
35. McLeod, 197–198.
36. Herodotus, 6.112.
37. Evans, 1993, 286
38. According to Evans, 1987, 101, the fact that the Persian cavalrymen did not possess saddles and spurs meant that it was difficult to stay mounted when they lost control of their horses.
39. See Vanderpool, 1966a, 323. Van Der Veer, 316–319
40. Herodotus, 6.113, notes that the Greeks on the wings let their adversaries escape without being pursued and concentrated their action against the Persians and Saka in the centre.
41. According to Herodotus, 6.114, it was during this phase of the encounter that polemarch Kallimachos, general Stesileos, Kynegeiros, and other 'notable Athenians' were killed. Kynegeiros is reported to have met his end on the beach while holding on to the stern of a Persian ship to try to stop it from sailing off, when a Persian cut off his hand with an ax. The implication is that Kynegeiros fought at the farthest Athenian advance from the Marathon plain where the main action took place. Herodotus employs different verbs to describe the fate of the leading fallen: thus Kallimachos is 'destroyed' Stesileos 'dies' and Kynegeiros 'falls'. Scott, 391, notes that these three men are cited in order of rank: first the polemarch, then a general and then a soldier. The different verbs used are considered to be nothing more than elegant variation, though it could be that Kallimachos perished first,

then Stesileos and finally Kynegeiros, as a result of his wounds. Thus, the different terms may reflect the time factor. Herodotus' description of the confrontation on the coast of Marathon beside the Persian ships is fraught with problems due to the lack of crucial details on how the action evolved during this phase of the battle. For example, his reference that the Greeks who fought the Persians on the coast asked for fire – from the rear? – to burn the enemy ships sounds weird. But this is exactly what the Trojans do in *Iliad* (O) while fighting next to the Greek ships on their coast. The Athenians who fought the Persians at Marathon may really have wanted to set fire to their ships and asked for fire for that very reason. It is evident, though, that Herodotus did not elicit this piece of evidence from a witness but borrowed it straight from Homer. The account of the fighting by the Persian ships at Marathon echoes the fighting between the Greeks and Trojans as narrated in the *Iliad*. This has led some researchers to conclude that Herodotus' account is more literary than historically accurate. However, the story of Kynegeiros hanging onto the stern of a Persian ship has the ring of authenticity. Herodotus' claim that 'the Athenians prevented seven ships from sailing' shows that Kynegeiros was not carrying out some foolhardy solitary act but was one of a number of soldiers who were doing the same, perhaps in coordination. It would not seem possible to have held onto more ships, especially if archers were on board. The rowers of the Persian fleet were not slaves but armed men skilled in the use of the spear, the bow and the axe. This could explain the high casualty rate of the Athenians in this sector, as they found themselves at a lower level than their enemies who could hit them from the ships.

42. Herodotus, 6.117. The same number of dead Persians is recorded by Xenophon, *Anabasis*, 3.2.12, According to Pausanias, 1.32.3, after the battle the Athenians erected stelae over the common grave of their dead at Marathon, bearing their names and tribes. Thus the number of 192 Athenian dead must be the correct one, as was inscribed on the stelae. A stele discovered during an archaeological dig at the Herod Atticus estate at Eva in Kynouria may be one of those erected over the grave of the fallen Athenians at Marathon. See Spyropoulos. It records the names of 21 men of the Erechtheis tribe and appears to corroborate Herodotus since such a number of dead from a single tribe would account for about one-tenth of the total Athenian figure he reports.

Chapter 7

1. Shrimpton, 25: 'what we are witnessing at Marathon must be recognized as the execution of a plan that was designed to meet and to cope with Persian cavalry'.
2. Krentz, 2010a, 143.
3. Hammond, 1968, 35. At this point we refer exclusively to battles where the hoplite phalanx fought with its usual tactics; not those which applied 'unorthodox' methods that we analyse below.
4. Herodotus, 5.63.3, and *The Constitution of the Athenians*, 19.5.
5. Herodotus, 9.69.2. The loss of 600 hoplites was a great blow to the Greeks considering that during the battle of Plataia all their other losses amounted to only 159 dead. Herodotus, 9.70.5.
6. Herodotus, 7.196.
7. Herodotus. 6.28–29.
8. Burn, 1969, 118, considers that the delay in the involvement of the Persian cavalry in the battle of Malene could have been either accidental or planned in advance by the Persians. Whatever the case, what matters is that the Persian cavalry dispersed the Greek hoplites and won victory for the Persians.

9. In 498 the Greeks were defeated at Ephesus by Persian troops who had cavalry with them. Herodotus, 5.102.2, gives the impression that the Persians followed the Greeks in hot pursuit from Sardis to Ephesus, where they defeated them, perhaps with their cavalry. Besides, the fact that in the mid-sixth century, the Persians had conquered the Greek cities of Asia Minor in a short time span indicates that their hoplite phalanges were unable to deal with the Persian battle tactics, especially their cavalry, see Briant, 539–540. Lazenby, 32–33, mentions that up to the battle of Marathon the Persians had won significant victories in battles against hoplites. Apart from Ionia, the Persians had also conquered the cities of Karia, that also had large numbers of hoplites.

10. Whatley, 134–136. Greenhalgh, 78. Hignett, 1963, 69. Shrimpton, 20. Evans, 1993, 283, n. 18.

11. Kromayer, 1924, 14.

12. According to Polyainos, 1.35.2, and Frontinus, 4.7.21, before a battle between Athenians and Thebans in the mid-fifth century, the Athenian general Myronides warned his men about the powerful Theban cavalry, telling them that if they didn't panic and remained in their line, they had high hopes of winning; if however they retreated, the enemy cavalry would wipe them out. Even though this reference belongs to the Roman period, it may conserve authentic historical evidence about Greek battle tactics during the Classical era.

13. Greenhalgh, 78. Van Der Veer, 299–300, n.34. Evans, 1987, 102: 'But we should remember that, though it might be an axiom of warfare that horses will not charge into a solid line that they can neither get through nor jump over, men also have a very strong natural impulse to get out of the way of a charging horse! The Persians knew […]: that a charge of sabre-wielding cavalry had a good hope of success, if the discipline of the infantry was imperfect…'.

14. Hammond, 1968, 35, analyses the successful actions of the Persian cavalry against the Greek hoplites at Plataia, which were performed before the main battle. Gaebel, 74–79, also makes extensive reference to the Persian cavalry's action at Plataia in 479.

15. Xenophon, *Anabasis*, 1.8.20 and 1.10.7.

16. Xenophon, *Anabasis*, 1.8.21.

17. According to Kromayer, 1924, 13–14, the fact that Greek hoplites in 490 were non-professionals leads to the conclusion that gaps could have easily been formed in the Greek phalanx at Marathon, where the Persian cavalry would have assaulted the hoplites.

18. The only success that the Greek hoplites had against the Persian cavalry at Plataia was the killing of its commander, Massistios. Herodotus, 9.22.1–2. Nonetheless, this occurred during a skirmish before the main battle; an Athenian archer shot an arrow against Massistios' horse, which dropped him to the ground and the Greeks were thus able to kill him. Therefore, this highly successful move was not the result of specific battle tactics of the phalanx but accidental.

19. Herodotus, 9.46. According to Plutarch, *Aristides*, 16, the Spartan commander: Pausanias by this move granted – unofficially – to the Athenians the command of the Greek troops, which he institutionally possessed. Herodotus does not overtly say that this move by Pausanias appointed the Athenians head of the Greek troops, but insinuates this. See Vidal-Naquet, 1983 (1986), 73, n. 7. Lazenby, 231, and Lendon, 346, n. 21, dismiss Pausanias having asked the Spartans to swap places with the Athenians in the Greek line-up but do not present evidence discrediting Herodotus' reference.

20. Herodotus, 9.46.2.
21. Shrimpton, 28–29.
22. Herodotus, 9.60.3.
23. Herodotus 9.68.
24. Herodotus 9.71.
25. The supreme commander of a Persian army had absolute power over his men and complete control over their moves. On the off chance he was killed during a battle, none of his inferiors could replace him. Therefore, Mardonius' death, during the Battle of Plataia, contributed to a large extent to the utter defeat of the Persian troops. Meissner, 293.
26. Tuplin, 2010b, 101–182, claims that the Persian cavalry didn't play such a significant role in the Greco-Persian Wars as is widely accepted. His arguments are not convincing though, and even this scholar acknowledges that in 479, the Persian cavalrymen were in full control at Plataia and exerted great pressure on the Greeks prior to the battle. See Tuplin, *op. cit.*, 173, n. 277.
27. Herodotus, 5.97. Hanson, 2000, 211.
28. For the equipment of Persian foot soldiers see Herodotus, 7.61.1. Krentz, 2010a, 23. Miltiades was the best expert in the Athens of 490 on the battle tactics of the Persian army, having fought with it as an ally but also against it. In addition, some Athenians, such as those who had re-inforced the Ionian rebels, would have known a few basic things about the Persian army. However, these Athenians had fought against second-rate troops in Asia Minor, and not the elite forces of the Persian Empire that were facing them in the plain of Marathon. See Scott, 389.
29. The sons of Persian aristocratic families were trained to become expert horsemen and archers who always told the truth. Herodotus, 1.136. The Persian ideal was the combination of these three characteristics; thus, the empire's ideal soldier was an 'honest' mounted archer.
30. Herodotus, 6.112. Waters, 192, is perplexed by Herodotus' claim that the sight of the Persian apparel instilled fear in Greek hoplites, considering the inferior equipment of the Persian army. However, Herodotus most likely made this comment having the Persian cavalry in mind, not their troops in general.
31. Aischylos, *Persians*, lines 103–106.
32. Tuplin, 2010b, 180–181, mentions that literary sources do not show that the Greeks were terrified by the Persian cavalry during the Greco-Persian Wars. Nevertheless, these sources are much later and are influenced by the fact that the Persians were eventually defeated by the Greeks and their cavalry didn't bring victory, despite its superb action at the battle of Plataia. However, in Aischylos' *Persians*, the use of the Persian cavalry against the Greeks is overemphasized. This may be due to the fact that Aischylos had had first hand experience of what it was like to have to face the Persian cavalry in the battlefield.
33. Gaebel, 69 and Bugh, 10–11.
34. Kromayer, 1924, 16, remarks that the Persians at Marathon had no reason to change their cavalry tactics, which had much contributed to the conquest of Asia Minor, despite the fact that they had never fought before Greek hoplites (in mainland Greece).
35. Our reconstruction of the Battle of Marathon is based on the fact that the principal concern of the Greek commanders was how to deal with the Persian cavalry. This is also the view of Krentz, 2010a, 1.

36. Hippias and his Thessalian allies may not have had a significant infantry force at Phaleron in 510 which could, in co-operation with the Thessalian cavalry, have coerced the Spartans to leave their abatis and fight against them in the open field.
37. See Krentz, 2000, 167–200, who presents 143 cases of battles in Greece of the Archaic and Classical periods which were won using cunning and deception.
38. Demosthenes, *Third Philippic,* 48–52. Polybius, 13.3.2–3. See Hanson, 2007, 204–205.
39. Out of the 143 cases of battles in Archaic and Classical Greece which were won using ambush techniques and other stratagems, 48 were Athenian victories. Krentz, 2000, 167–200.
40. Rawlings, 357. Vidal-Naquet, 1983 (1986), 110–111.
41. Wheeler, 1988, 5.
42. According to Detienne and Vernant, 35–39, this kind of intelligence in ancient Greece was represented by Odysseus among men and by the fox among animals.
43. Herodotus, 8.27, and Pausanias, 10.1.3. Herodotus writes that the war between the Thessalians and Phokians occurred 'not many years' before Xerxes' campaign, which shows that it was contemporary to the Battle of Marathon. According to Pausanias the war took place before the 'Persian invasion' against Greece, i.e. Xerxes' campaign. In most recent publications, the invasion of the Thessalians in Phokis and the battle of Hyampolis are dated about 500, see Hall, 143.
44. Just like in 511, Thessalian horsemen – perhaps the same who fought a few years later at the battle of Hyampolis – assaulted and vanquished the Spartans at Phaleron.
45. About the tactics at the Battle of Hyampolis, see Herodotus, 8.28, Polyainos, 6.18.2, Pausanias, 10.1.3. The best analysis of the battle is by Pritchett, 1982, 140–144, who claims that the same tactics were successfully applied by Robert Bruce, King of Scotland, at the Battle of Bannockburn. Klearchos also used the same tactics in 402/1 in Thrace, see Polyainos, 2.2.9.
46. Herodotus, 8.27. Pausanias, 10.1.11.
47. Herodotus, 6.39.
48. Herodotus, *op. cit.*
49. Scott, 453.
50. Herodotus, 6.140. The story also appears in Nepos, *Miltiades,* 2, who, however, says erroneously that Miltiades' stratagem led to the peaceful surrender of the whole island and not just Hephaisteia. Miltiades and the Athenians occupied Myrina – Lemnos' second city – after a siege.
51. For an assessment of such qualities in a military leader, see von Clausewitz, 100–112.
52. Wheeler, 1988, 15.
53. Miltiades may have been inspired in working out his Marathon tactics by what Herodotus refers to about the Persian campaign against Scythia in 513, when the Scythians resisted Darius' army by making use of the physical terrain in various ways (see Herodotus, 4.120, 128, 130). Though Herodotus does not provide details, Miltiades very likely was aware of the successful Scythian tactics as he participated in the campaign himself, and applied them later at Marathon (see Fotiou, 183).
54. Thucydides, 7.66.3.
55. Tarn, 62. See also Drews, 143.
56. It would have been exceptionally rare for Greek troops whose centre in the line-up had been occupied by the enemy during the battle to win at the end. Apart from the battle of Marathon, ancient literary sources record only one battle in ancient

Greece where that occurred: at Nemea in 394, the Spartans beat the Athenians and their allies even though the Spartan centre had been occupied by the latter.

57. Evans, 1993, 285–286. The Persian *gerrophoroi* didn't have time to raise their shields at Marathon. We gather this from almost all the depictions on Attic vases, where hoplites surprise Persian infantrymen who do not appear to have raised their shields for protection.

58. For an analysis of the 'charge at a run', see Krentz, 2010a, 143–152 and 219–220, who refers to older works. How and Wells, 112, and Schachermeyr, 28, speculate that the Greek hoplites charged at a run in order to get out of the range of Persian arrows, and for 1.5 kilometres. But Lazenby, 66–68, holds the logical view that the hoplites would have broken into a run only for the last 150 or so metres to get out of arrow range. Herodotus does not mention anything like that. Yet as we have seen, his description of the battle is skeletal and has many gaps. So the theory that the Greeks ran to get out of arrow range is quite plausible. Herodotus either didn't know the reason for the 'charge at a run' or considered it not worthy of inclusion in his narrative. His claim (6.112.3) that the Athenians were the first to use this tactic in battle is wrong, see Van Wees, 2011, 180.

59. Hanson, 1989, 197–198, provides several examples in which the dust raised by a battle in ancient Greece decisively affected the outcome. Plutarch, *Eumenes*, 16.6, describes how Antigonos Monophthalmus destroyed the camp of Eumenes during a battle by taking advantage of the dust raised by men and horses. In 362, Epaminondas used his cavalry at Tegea to blind the Lakedaimonians by clouds of dust, behind which he attacked the enemy rear and won the fight (See Frontinus, 2.2.12 and Polyainos, 2.3.14).

60. The following list contains representative examples of depictions on Attic vessels of the early-fifth century that appear to have been inspired by the action at Marathon, particularly the surprise attack by the Greeks on the wings. 1. Metropolitan Museum of New York, 1980.11.21. ARV² 417.4=Beazley Archive Database 204549; red-figure kylix by the 'Painter of the Paris Gigantomachy,' 490/80. Tuplin, 2010a, 257, dates this vessel to about 470, which raises the possibility that it could depict an incident of the battle of Plataia or no particular battle at all. 2. Metropolitan Museum of New York, Cat. No. ME07527; red-figure amphora, c. 480. 3. Boston Museum of Fine Arts, finding no. 13.196; a wine-jar by the 'Chicago Painter,' c. 460. 4. Athens, National Archaeological Museum: black-figure jar, Cat. No. 4691, 490/480. Tuplin, 2010a, 257, believes that the scene is from Marathon. 5. Edinburgh, Royal Museum of Scotland, Cat. No. 1887.213; red-figure Attic kylix by the 'Triptolemos Painter,' c. 480. 6. A vase that in 1932 belonged to the Grace private collection (see Macurdy, 27, and Sekunda, 22). Tuplin, 2010a, 256, regards this as a scene from Marathon. 7. Antikenmuseum Basel und Sammlung Ludwig Inv., BS 480, c. 460. According to Sekunda, 70, even though the vessel is dated to about thirty years after the battle, it may be connected to the battle of Marathon. 8. Louvre, G117, red-figure kylix by Duris, c. 490. Tuplin. 2010a, 257, dates the vessel at soon after 490 and relates the image to the battle of Marathon. 9. Archaeological Museum of Berlin, F.2331.

61. Herodotus does not describe exactly how this happened; but we may reasonably conclude from his account that the Greeks on the wings, after allowing the Persians on their fronts to escape, about-faced and, as a single unit, advanced in the opposite direction, towards where the Greek centre had fallen back at the start of the battle. This movement brought the Greek wings in the rear of the Persians and Saka who were still pursuing the Athenians in that sector, catching them in a

pincer. In Greek history there is only one other recorded case of a hoplite phalanx halting its pursuit of the enemy on its front in order to turn back and help another section of the line in danger. This occurred at the battle of the river Nemea in 394, see Van Wees, 2011, 191. At the battle of Koroneia, which took place a few weeks before that of Nemea, both rival right wing line-ups that had won stopped pursuing their defeated rivals, went back to the field and gave a second battle. See Xenophon, *Hellenica*, 4.3.16–19, who calls that battle *unique* in comparison with any battle fought in his time. However, at Koroneia the right wings did not return to aid their defeated comrades but to keep on with the battle. At both these battles (Koroneia and Nemea) Agesilaos, one of the greatest military geniuses of ancient Greece, was the head of the Spartan army and responsible for the tactics of his forces that won both battles. But the Marathon case, in which both wings turned back at the same time to rescue their embattled comrades in the centre, is unique in ancient Greece. On the basis of the above, some scholars speculate that the abrupt change of direction of the two Greek hoplite wings and their joining up into a single formation would have been so complicated that they could not have been executed in an organized manner. According to this school of thought, the movement must have succeeded purely by chance. For example, Van Wees, 2011, 180, postulates that the action described stems from Herodotus' imagination as the Athenians could not have performed such a move. If this view was correct, though, Herodotus would have been fiercely criticised in Antiquity – especially in Athens – as he would have recorded false evidence on the Greek battle tactics. On his part, Lazenby, 250, believes that the Greeks did not use any battle tactics at Marathon and 'what happened at Marathon was the result of a series of accidents'. Yet this observation raises the question of how such a complicated manoeuvre could have come together entirely fortuitously. Common sense dictates that it would not have been possible for every Athenian and Plataian hoplite to about-face at the same moment, on his own initiative, after the Persians had broken through the Greek centre. Neither would it have been possible for them, in the heat and confusion of battle, to hear their superiors' orders to turn back. At the time of the battle of Marathon the most common type of helmet was the Corinthian, which hindered the wearer's sight and hearing. The hoplites fighting hard at close quarters on the wings would not have been aware of what was happening in real time a few dozen metres around them, not to mention what was happening hundreds of metres in the rear and centre. We may also confidently rule out the picture of a senior officer, say Miltiades, running back and forth between the wings calling on the men to stop pursuing the Persians and turn their attention towards helping their comrades driven back in the centre. Even if some on the Greek wings of their own accord turned back to confront the advancing Persians and Saka in the centre, most can be presumed to have maintained the pursuit in their sectors. Hence the complicated manoeuvre by which the wings closed inwards to jointly attack the Persian centre from its rear could not have happened by mere chance; there had to be a specific plan. The tactics adopted at Marathon were not included in the typical training regimen of a Greek hoplite. Yet it is possible to theorize that the Greeks on the wings could have synchronized their inward movement on the assumption that they would have been previously instructed on exactly when to carry it out, and as long as they were in visual contact with one another, which appears certain. The actual manoeuvre would have been signaled by perhaps a horn blast. It would not have been necessary for the men to immediately format into a single straight line; all they needed to do was turn about and rush to where the Greek centre had been, straightening the ranks on the way. The units could have done this piecemeal, and not necessarily in a single coordinated action as a modern army would have been trained to do. The difficulty would not have lain in the tactic itself but in the excitement of just having repulsed the enemy on the wings and being psyched up to kill as many as possible; the Greeks had to rein in their impulse just as the adrenalin and stress of battle were at their peak. Thus the only way the manoeuvre could be successful was for the soldiers to have been briefed beforehand, not once but several times. The abrupt about-face and juncture of the two wings at the most critical stage in the battle, and their subsequent move towards the rear, are the strongest indication that the Athenians and Plataians executed a specific manoeuvre that had been previously worked out in detail and for which the men had been briefed in the days leading up to the battle. See Van Der Veer, 319-320. The distance separating the two wings being only a few hundred metres onto Marathon plain without any natural obstacles between them rendered this manoeuvre feasible. It is noteworthy that at the battle of Nemea in 394, four Athenian tribes defeated the Spartan divisions opposite them and pursued the retreating rivals. At the same time, though, the Spartans vanquished the men of the remaining six tribes of the Athenian line-up. The Athenians who were about to defeat the Spartans rather than go back to aid their comrades who were in jeopardy kept on pursuing the enemy: the result being the Athenians losing the battle, see Van Wees, 2011, 191. It is clear that in this case, the Athenians followed no battle tactics plan, but operated on the spur of the moment resulting in them not being able to take advantage of their victory on one spot of the front. Naturally, this did not happen at Marathon as the men had been analytically briefed beforehand about the jink of the turnaround they were to perform as soon as they saw the enemy ahead, with a view to ensuring victory. The Greek tactics at Marathon bore no relation to the general tactics employed in ancient Greece, a fact which argues for Herodotus' account of the actions of the Athenians and Plataians being historically accurate. If it were not, then the account would have sounded incredible to the Athenians as containing serious errors and absurdities. Yet not even the harshest ancient critics of Herodotus have cast the slightest doubt on his description of the battle tactics, and thus they can be considered to be in agreement with the basic elements.

62. Burn, 1962. (1984), 250; Hammond, 1968, 29; Shrimpton, 24–25; Van der Veer, 319–320; Green, 36; Meissner, 282–283; Dionysopoulos, 48.

63. Burn, 1962, (1984), 249–250; Meissner, 282; Dionysopoulos, 48.

64. In many battles in antiquity an army defeated in the centre would have casualties numbering in the thousands. At Marathon the Persians lost 6,400 men out of a total combat strength of some 25,000 troops. The great bulk of Persian losses were of men in the centre of the formation. Herodotus tells us that the Athenians suffered a mere 192 dead. Some of them, including Kallimachos, Stesileos and Kynegeiros, fell during the Greek pursuit of the Persians to the ship. During the fight on the wings, the Athenians and Plataians would also have suffered losses. According to Vanderpool, 1966a, 323, and Hammond, 1968, 46, and 1973, 246, the Athenians had the most losses in the centre of their formation. Even in the most improbable case that the 192 Athenians dead were all in the centre, the small number does not indicate that the Greeks were overcome in the centre. Rather, it argues strongly for a planned tactical withdrawal after battle had been joined.

65. Most scholars interpret Herodotus' (6.111.3) phrase 'few ranks' (τάξιας ολίγας) as fewer lines. But the correct meaning is fewer units, not ranks or lines. (See Van

Wees, 2011, 298, n. 59). In short, the men were lined up more loosely in the centre of the Greek formation.

66. On the problems of vision and hearing while wearing a hoplite helmet, see Hanson, 1989, 110. At the time of Marathon the most common Greek helmet was the Corinthian type which, however, hindered both vision and hearing.

67. As will be seen, it is conceivable that some hoplites were stationed at the rear to beef up the ranks of the light-armed troops who would have been placed there. But such a number of hoplites would not have been large.

68. Herodotus writes that during the pursuit of the Persians to the ships, many 'well-known' Athenians fell. Aristotle, *Politics,* 1303a9–10, employs that word that implies that the fallen were members of leading aristocratic families. It is curious that though Herodotus mentions the 'well-known' hoplites, he omits mention of those who fell at the start of the battle, when the Persians and Saka broke through the Greek centre. There would have been considerable casualties in that retreating sector (see Vanderpool, 1966a, 323, and Hammond, 1968, 46, and 1973, 246). But Herodotus names not one, as very likely those were light-armed troops of a lower social order, and hence not deemed important enough.

69. Thucydides, 1.106.2–8.

70. Thucydides, 3.107–108.

71. Krentz, 2010a, 60, sees the battle of Marathon as the first instance in ancient Greece of a phalanx made up solely of hoplites separate from the light-armed troops. Lendon, 65, believes that early-fifth century Athenian archers didn't fight alongside the hoplites.

72. For example, Van Wees, 2011, 196, writes that until the mid-fifth century, light-armed Athenian troops fought alongside the hoplites in the phalanx. He figures that the separation of the hoplites from the light-armed troops began about 500, but the process was still incomplete by the time of Xerxes' invasion of 480. A few years later the Spartans formed their own hoplite-only phalanges, to be followed by other Greeks, including the Athenians.

73. Herodotus, 9.60.3.

74. Aischylos, *The Persians,* line 460.

75. Herodotus, 9.28.

76. Most reconstructions of the battle assume that the Greek ranks were eight deep at the flanks and four deep in the centre (Pritchett, 1960, 144–145.) If the army had been composed entirely of hoplites, that would make sense. But the presence of light-armed troops could well upset that calculation.

77. Herodotus, 6.113.

78. Most modern scholars agree that the Greeks formed up in front of the Brexiza pass leading to the plains of the 'Mesogaia'. The meaning of this term, however, is in dispute. Hammond, 1968, 18, takes it to mean the Marathon plain near Vranas, far from the sea. Thus in his view the Greek hoplites formed up between Mounts Kotroni and Agrieliki, with the Persians in front of them, their backs to the sea (Reconstruction 1). The Greek centre then retreated to Vranas. But other scholars believe the Mesogaia to refer to the wider plain of Pallene beyond the Brexiza pass. Hammond later amended his view, agreeing that the Greek lines drew up in front of the pass.

79. Koumanoudis, 243, fig. 4, places the Mesogaia right at the entrance to the Brexiza pass, on the theory that the pursuit of the Greek centre stopped there. These Greeks would therefore have stopped at the Lesser Marsh, which according to Koumanoudis existed at the time of the battle. That is when, according to his

reconstruction, the two Greek wings joined up and moved on the Persians from the rear, ending up at the marsh (Koumanoudis, 244, fig. 5). But his conclusion appears to be arbitrary, as neither Herodotus nor any other writer explains how the Athenians could have halted their retreat and reorganized to meet the enemy advance. The halting of the Persian advance would have occurred in the Brexiza pass and within the boundaries of the Lesser Marsh.

80. Wheeler, 1988, 26, 47.
81. Mikroyannakis, 18–19.
82. Mikroyannakis, *op. cit.*
83. 'Here we need a return of high spirits that have vanished and which Herodotus referred to. That is exactly what the Pythia recommends to the Athenians (in an oracle of 480 before Salamis):'You fled, you quailed, but your fighting spirit will return. This spirit, like virtue, is necessary" (Mikroyannakis, *op. cit.*).
84. Plato, *Laches*, 190e–191c; Vidal-Naquet, 1983. (1986), 95. It was generally accepted in ancient Greece that the Spartans, the bravest warriors in Greece, had a high regard for stratagems in battle (see Powell, 173–192). One such Spartan trick was the 'feigned retreat' as practiced at Thermopylai. Plato probably had in mind Herodotus' (4.120, 128, 130) description of how the Scythians fought.
85. Scott, 390–391.
86. Pausanias, 1.32.7: 'Not knowing the paths, the barbarians fell while fleeing'. Fauvel in the late-eighteenth century makes mention of man-made paths through the Lesser Marsh uniting the 'Island' of Brexiza with the mountains (probably Agrieliki). Sotiriadis, 1927b, 125, a few years before the marsh was drained, noted the existence of narrow pathways 'after being told of them by an old shepherd who was a very useful guide'. At the time of the battle the Great Marsh, as we have seen, was mostly a lagoon with no paths inside.
87. Nepos, *Miltiades*, 5.5: 'Datis nonetheless saw that that the location was not suitable for his men'.
88. 'By nature rough, not good for horses, with marshes and lakes' (See Petrakos, 1995, 6.)
89. See above for evidence of geological studies that show the existence of the Lesser Marsh many centuries prior to 490.
90. Nepos points out that before the battle the Athenians feared that the Persian cavalry might threaten their camp.
91. Herodotus, 7.208.2–3, mentions a mounted Persian who reconnoitred the Greek camp at Thermopylai and reported to Xerxes.
92. A large volume of water flows through the place even today, nourishing a thick wetland.
93. Because of the great quantity of salt that encrusted the surface of the Lesser Marsh in summer, in the early-1930s when the greater part of the marsh – some 200 acres – was drained, additional work had to be done to ensure that the reclaimed land was cultivable (See Margoni, 49).
94. Exactly as happens today.
95. Finlay, 364. Also Leake, 1841, table III, notes on his map of Marathon that the Lesser Marsh was dry in summer. The Great Marsh, on the other hand, retained much water even in the hot months. When Sotiriadis examined the Lesser Marsh at the end of September 1924, he reported that 'because of the extended drought since February, the marsh was negotiable even where it normally would have been impassable' (Sotiriadis, 1927b, 124).

96. In 1959 Pritchett examined that part of the Lesser Marsh that had not been drained in 1933 and noted that most of the surface consisted of black silt (Pritchett, 1960, 154). At the close of the nineteenth century, Frazer, 432, found the marsh covered with vegetation and bushes. However, he had visited the location in November 1895, when the autumn rains had already begun.

97. As we have seen, Finlay, 379–380, writes that the Athenians had set up defensive works in the Brexiza pass in the form of an abatis and guard. It is possible that the Greeks could have assumed defensive positions besides 206m-spur on Agrieliki. These men could have used their javelins to ward off attempts by small Persian detachments to penetrate the pass.

98. The hooves of a horse are formed in such a way as to make it hard for them to move on a muddy surface, as the concave undersides have a sucker effect. That is why they are shod for difficult terrain. J. Anderson, 1961, 91–92, does not rule out that the technique of shoeing horses was known in the northern parts of the Roman empire. But it is certain that at the time of Marathon the Persians didn't shoe their horses.

99. Our contention that there could have been hoplites at the Lesser Marsh derives from Thucydides, 3.107–108, who relates how the Athenian general Demosthenes, during operations in Akarnania in 426, reinforced an ambush force of light-armed troops with 400 hoplites. On a black-figure Attic vase in the Metropolitan Museum of New York (No. 26.60.76) there is an image of an ambush by four hoplites and an archer who appear to be hiding in a marshy wetland; the archer has his arrow drawn and ready. Though the subject is mythical, the vase is dated to about 490, so it could well record an incident in the battle of Marathon, viz. the presence of hoplites in the ambush prepared at the Lesser Marsh.

100. Donlan and Thompson, 420, write that when a hoplite fought on sandy or wet ground, he required 20–25% more oxygen than he would if operating on solid ground. The need for extra oxygen would be greater in muddy terrain (Hanson, 1989, 120–121 and Holoka, 343).

101. IG I³ 503/4. Lapis C. Line 1.

102. Matthaiou, 2003, 200–201.

103. IG I³ 503/4. Lapis C. Lines 3–4. The line of the epigram 'at the edge of the plain' refers to where these particular Athenian soldiers fell, not to where they were subsequently buried.

104. Bowie, 2010, 208–209, believes that this epigram honoured those Athenians who perished in the battle of Salamis, and also Phayllos of Kroton. He suggests that the plain mentioned could be that of Kroton in southern Italy. But Bowie's assertion is problematic, as all other scholars conclude that the epigram is for those fallen in the Persian Wars, and most likely was set up at the *Demosion Sema* in Athens. Also, Phayllos and the crew of his trireme survived Salamis. On Phayllos' action at Salamis, see IG I³ 822; also Dillon and Garland, 210.

105. IG I³ 503/4.

106. Bowie, 2010, 207, does not rule out that the epigram may have referred to the warriors of Marathon, and that the 'island' was Euboia, which the Persians had ravaged a few days before the battle.

107. For example, Herodotus, 9. 51, calls 'island' a place in the Plataia plain encircled by the Asopos river.

108. Krentz, 2010a, 151, also believes that the light-armed Greeks and freedmen played a decisive role at Marathon. He argues that they joined the 'charge at a run' along with the hoplites on either wing. According to his theory, the hoplites, light-armed

350 Who Really Won the Battle of Marathon?

troops and dismounted cavalrymen attacking the Persians were armed with spears and swords.

109. Our reconstruction agrees with Krentz, 2010a, 60, that at Marathon the hoplite-only formation was adopted for the first time. This applies to the battle on the wings, when the light-armed troops in the centre had retreated and were at Brexiza. At that point only hoplites remained on the plain.

111. This epigram is attributed to Simonides of Keos (see Bach, 15 and Bergk, 961). But there is no agreement on whether it is genuine Simonides. The city referred to is most likely Athens.

112. Herodotus, 9.22.60.

113. All the votive offerings connected with the Persian Wars which ancient sources say were deposited on the Acropolis of Athens, derive from the battle of Marathon. Pausanias, 1.27.1, doubts the Athenian claim that a sword among the offerings belonged to Mardonius at the battle of Plataia. He says (1.28.2, and 9.4.1) that the statue of Athene Promachos on the Acropolis was made with booty seized at Marathon. This suggests that when the Athenians evacuated the city in 480, they must have taken with them the Persian booty with which Phidias later fashioned the statue.

114. For ancient references to Athenian archers, see Plassart, 195–204.

115. Pausanias, 1.15.3 and 1.32.7.

116. Aristophanes, *Wasps*, lines 1085–1090; Jeffery, 1965, 44, concludes that the scene was inspired by the fighting in the swamp during the battle of Marathon depicted in the Poikile Stoa wall painting. The text employs a term referring to tuna-fishing with harpoons and a net, where the trapped tuna would thrash against one another while being speared. This could have been a good analogy of what happened to the Persians. Jeffery, however, opines that the slaughter of the Persians occurred while they were in the Great Marsh fleeing towards their ships.

117. Herodotus, 6.113.1. Krentz, 2010a, 157, gives the longest time-frame for the battle, timing it at six hours in total.

118. Aristophanes, *Wasps*, line 1085.

119. Caspari, 104, n. 16, was the first scholar to publish queries on why the Persian cavalry was apparently absent from the battle and it could have boarded the ships after the Greek pursuit. These queries were given more complete form by Berthold, 94, n. 61.

120. Second century AD. Santa Giulia Civici Musei di Brescia.

121. Vanderpool, 1966b, 105; Krentz, 2010a, 141.

122. Nearly all modern scholars accept that the south frieze of Athene Nike depicts scenes from the battle of Marathon; it was built c. 427/4 just six decades after the battle. For the depiction of the battle between Persian cavalry and Athenian soldiers on the south frieze of the Temple of Athene Nike, see Harrison, 353–356.

123. Harrison, 353: 'Elsewhere in the south frieze, the Greeks who confront Persian horsemen appear to have been pursued by the cavalry rather than vice versa'.

124. Plate E, Harrison, fig. 75, picture 9 (Acropolis Museum, Athens).

125. Plate L, Harrison, fig. 76, picture 12 (Acropolis Museum, Athens). This is the most spectacular scene from the south frieze of the Temple of Athene Nike. Nunnus, *Dionysiaca*, 28.164–167, in his account of the legendary battle between Dionysos' men and the Indians, writes that during the battle one horse threw its rider, 'like Pegasus threw Bellerophon'. Nunnus included descriptions of the battle of Marathon in his mythical account, possibly having been inspired by the scene on the south frieze showing a Persian horse rearing up and throwing its rider.

126. Plate O, Harrison, fig. 75, picture 8 (British Museum, London). The second and third figures from the left depict light-armed Greeks.

127. Plate E, Harrison, fig. 75, picture 9 (Acropolis Museum, Athens) and Plate O, Harrison, fig. 75, picture 8 (British Museum, London), show Persian horses apparently trampling fallen Persian soldiers. Plate A, Harrison, fig. 75, picture 7 (Acropolis Museum, Athens) shows a Persian foot soldier being hit by the raised hooves of a horse on his left.

128. Harrison, 354–355.

129. Plate E, Harrison, fig. 75, picture 9 (Acropolis Museum, Athens).

130. Harrison, 354. It appears that the horse in Plate E might actually have had its legs broken in the swamp. The horse's shoulders are at a lower level than those of the Greek hoplite in front of it. This could happen only if the horse had both its forelegs broken.

131. Harrison, *op. cit.* More recently Krentz, 2010a, 142, put forward the view that the scenes of the south frieze of the Temple of Athene Nike could be a copy of the mural of the battle of Marathon in the Poikile Stoa.

132. Plate O, Harrison, fig. 5, picture 8 (British Museum, London).

133. Plate G, Harrison, fig. 73, picture 1 (British Museum, London). Palagia, though agreeing that the scenes on the south frieze depict incidents of the battle of Marathon, doubts whether we could identify some of the figures with known protagonists of the battle who had appeared in the Poikile Stoa (see Palagia, 184–185).

134. Images on the frieze reliefs of fifth century temples habitually are depicted on a straight line. The south frieze of the Temple of Athene Nike, however, is one of the few exceptions in which the ground of the clash between Greek infantrymen and Persian horsemen appears uneven. A surviving frieze from the Temple of Artemis Agrotera in Athens shows figures sitting on what could be outcrops of rock (see McNeill, 104).

135. Harrison, 355, fig 75, picture 7 (Acropolis Museum, Athens). This is the second image to the left of Plate A. A soldier is trying to protect a wounded comrade lying on the ground from the arrows of a Persian archer on the far right of Plate A by 'holding up his cloak as a shield'.

136. An Attic red-figure kylix dated to the first-half of the fifth century in Berlin's Antikensammlung in the Schloss Charlottenburg (Cat. No. F2295) shows a light-armed soldier fighting behind a hoplite and holding before him a piece of leather to protect himself from enemy projectiles. Euripides, in his *Iphigeneia in Tauris*, lines 310–314, describes how during a battle Pylades protects Orestes with his cloak from the attacks of stone-throwing shepherds. It appears that a cloak could stop arrows and other missiles, as some Attic vases from 480/70 show pieces of material hanging below shields to protect the soldiers' legs. Everson, 162, believes that these 'aprons' were the result of experience gained confronting the Persian archers in the Persian Wars. They often had an eye painted on them to ward off enemy arrows.

137. Plate O, Harrison, table 75, picture 8 (British Museum, London).

138. Harrison, *op. cit.* These figures of Athenians are not carrying shields, and therefore must be light-armed troops rather than hoplites.

139. Plate G, Harrison, fig. 73, picture 1 (British Museum, London).

140. Harrison, 370: 'The manner in which the Persian cavalry was used and what if anything had happened to put the Persian cavalry at a disadvantage before the Athenians decided to attack are not things which the painting could show, just as it could not show the phalanx formation of the hoplites as they moved to engage with the enemy. These matters must be left in the hands of the military historians'.

141. A diligent search of our sources reveals that only Shrimpton, 22–23, and more recently Dionysopoulos, 110, n. 390 and 121, have taken into account Harrison's observations on the south frieze of the Temple of Athene Nike. All other sources merely note Harrison as saying that the scenes are probably connected to Marathon.

142. Some scholars have queried why the south frieze depicts only the phase of the battle that occurred in the marsh and seemingly omits other phases portrayed in the Poikile Stoa and described by Pausanias, such as the start of the battle and the fight by the Persian ships. Harrison, 355, speculates that the scene was sculpted in honour of Kallimachos as the main protagonist, and not Miltiades or Kynegeiros, who are absent. That would be why the moment of Kallimachos' death in the fight by the ships is not represented, but the moments of his greatest glory earlier in the battle are. The subject of the south frieze is thus solely the fight in the marsh and the beginning of the Persian retreat.

143. No reconstruction of the battle claims that the Persian cavalry advanced in the direction of the Great Marsh. An exception is Dionysopoulos, 220, who believes that the Persian cavalry entered the fray where the church of Panaghia Mesosporitissa now stands at the edge of the marsh.

144. Lazenby, 14, asserts that there is no evidence that during the Persian Wars Athenian generals ever studied the tactics of earlier battles. We believe, however, that he errs.

145. See Herodotus, 8.84–93, for details on the Greek tactics at the battle of Salamis.

146. Herodotus, 8.95, writes that only Athenian hoplites disembarked at Psyttaleia. Yet Aischylos, in his *Persians,* line 460, says that light-armed Athenian archers and slingers fought at Psyttaleia as well.

147. Even if Themistokles had not been one of the ten Athenian generals at Marathon, and hence would not have known of the battle plan through personal experience, he surely would have been told about it in detail afterwards. According to Plutarch, *Themistokles,* 3.4, Miltiades' fame from the battle had become an obsession with *Themistokles* to the point that 'it didn't allow him to sleep.'

148. Thucydides, 1.106.2–8.

149. Thucydides, 1.105.4, writes that the Athenian expeditionary force that fought the battle of Megara included 'the eldest' conscripts, i.e. men up to sixty years old (see Rawlings, 358).

150. Aelius Aristides, *Panathenaic,* 131.

151. See Mikroyannakis, 18–19. An analysis of the Spartan battle tactics at Thermopylai can be found in Van Wees, 2011, 180–181.

152. At Thermopylai it was impossible for the Greeks to adopt the same tactics as the Athenians and Plataians had at Marathon, as the terrain was vastly different. There was no possibility of deploying forces in the plain in front of the pass, and of course, given the numerical superiority of the Persians, there was no way the Greeks could encircle them.

153. Katsimitros, 43.

154. We were unable to locate the source of Katsimitros' inspiration which runs against all other scholarship. It is likely that he personally inspected the field at Marathon and attempted a reconstruction on his own judgement.

155. Pausanias, 1.14.5.

156. Thucydides, 2.34.5.

157. Whitley, 228–229, supposes that the raising of the Tumulus of the Athenians linked the fallen at Marathon with the heroes of the *Iliad* who in similar fashion were cremated and their ashes interred under a mound. The same practice was common

with the Athenians of the early Archaic era, but stopped under the Peisistratids. In 490, however, the Athenian democracy brought back the old aristocratic method of interment for its heroes. Yet we don't know just when the Tumulus was raised, and it's quite possible that it was long after the battle. See Spyropoulos. G. Anderson, 2006, 151–153 and Krentz, 2010a, 63, believe that the first Athenian war dead to be honoured with a state burial and a stele on their tombs were those who fought the Chalkidians in 506. This is based on an epigram by Simonides. See Page, 1975, 9. Pritchett, 1985a, 125–235, 249–251, and Toher, 497–501, arrive at similar conclusions. Hence Thucydides is not quite correct when he writes that the practice was not known before Marathon. Yet that does not obviate the fact that the fallen at Marathon were considered *par excellence* heroes of the Athenian democracy along with the Tyrannicides.

158. Matthaiou, 2003, 197–200, has gathered records of funeral games held at the monument to the fallen at Marathon and at their cenotaph in Athens. A bronze vessel in the Kanellopoulos Museum that was found buried near the Tumulus of the Athenians seems to have been a prize for such a contest.

159. Pausanias, 1.32.4. Brown-Ferrario, 28, n. 59, has examined the bibliography on the worship of the Marathon fallen as heroes (see also Whitley, 216–217, and n. 13). Loraux, 29–30, 39–41, asserts that the Athenians generally worshipped as heroes all war dead. Some believe this practice at Marathon originated in the second or first century, when the first inscriptions appear (Ekroth, 76 and Whitley, 216–217). Others believe that it began in the Classical era: Jacoby, 1944, 39 and 47 (n. 49), places the beginning right after the battle of Marathon. Boardman, 39–49, says the 192 Athenian dead were honoured by being depicted as horsemen on the Parthenon. Dionysopoulos, 223, speculates that the 'de-heroized' figures on the Parthenon could have included Plataians and freedmen. There is no agreement on whether the figures were indeed those of Marathon warriors.

160. At that time a complex of statues commemorating Marathon was set up at Delphi (Pausanias 10.10.1–2). According to Kluwe, 21–27 and Vidal-Naquet, 1983, (1986), this monument was connected to Kimon.

161. Plutarch, *Kimon*, 15.1–2 (see Jung, 2006).

162. Jung, 2006, offers a lucid analysis of the importance that Kimon attached to the battle of Marathon as evidenced in his policies.

163. Krentz, 2010a, 151, also stresses the importance of the light-armed troops and freedmen for victory at Marathon.

164. Pausanias, 1.15.3 and 1.32.5.

165. The majority of researchers of the battle of Marathon regard Echetlaios as a supernatural being; some however think that he was a real person, one of the thousands of light-armed thetes who fought the Persians. Thus, Krentz hypothesises that Echetlaios must have been a farmer, who used the handle of a plough as a club during the battle. The first to make this view known was not a scholar, but the renowned English poet, Robert Browning. In 1876 he dedicated to him the poem, 'Echetlos'. There, Echetlaios is presented as a poor farmer, who during the battle slays the Persians with his plough at the centre of the Athenian line-up while hoplites around are either killed or lose their nerve.

166. Deities depicted in the mural of the Marathon battle at Poikile Stoa include Athene, Herakles, Theseus, Pan, Demeter and Kore, Marathon and others.

167. Herodotus, 6.105

168. There are extant a few examples of Attic vases whose illustrations are inspired by Marathon and show different phases than the clash on the wings. Two of the

vessels show what could be the destruction of the Persian cavalry: the first is a red-figure Attic kylix by the 'Triptolemos Painter' in the Royal Museum of Scotland in Edinburgh showing hoplites battling Persian cavalry; the second, dated shortly after 490, in the Faina collection shows a Persian horseman trying to flee. Krentz, 2010b, 183–204, speculates that a vessel by Duris showing a hoplite and archer running together could have been inspired by the 'charge at a run', though that remains uncertain.

169. Worthy of note is that even on the 'Triptolemos Painter' in Edinburgh, the Greeks fighting Persian horsemen are all hoplites and not light-armed troops.

170. The emphasis on the hoplites and cavalrymen rather than the light-armed troops on Attic vase paintings is not confined to the battle of Marathon but in all battle scenes from the late-Archaic and early-Classical periods. Osborne, 35, notes that the more expensive cups used in banquets depicted hoplites and cavalrymen. Light-armed troops and peltasts, on the contrary, appeared on cheaper ware affordable by the thetes.

171. Van Wees, 2011, 180, is one of the scholars who believes that light-armed Athenians played an active part in the Battle of Marathon and that their 'deletion' from historical memory occurred just a generation afterwards. Yet it must have taken somewhat longer, probably until the last veterans had passed on. The artist who painted the mural of the battle of Marathon of the Poikile Stoa about 460, as the first post-Marathon generation was growing up, knew who Echetlaios was, and hence would have known about the action of the light-armed troops.

172. On the basis of these ancient sources Vidal-Naquet, 1968, 167, concludes that the battle signifies the victory of the hoplite classes before the growth of the Athenian fleet which entailed the political rise of the thetes.

173. Sargent, 209–210, asserts that Herodotus' account of the battle promotes the hoplites at the expense of historical truth. Hunt, 1998, propounds a similar view, i.e. that the narrative was designed to ensure the fame and prestige of the Athenian upper classes. Though such an interpretation makes sense, it must be pointed out that Herodotus' narrative was informed by a general indifference towards the action of light-armed troops, i.e. thetes, on the battlefield. Dionysopoulos, 45, considers that Herodotus' account was based on the Athenian tradition that the hoplites were alone to be credited with the victory, and hence the light-armed troops' and freedmen's contribution was omitted. However, he believes that the thetes didn't fight at Marathon. Most scholars remain uncertain whether to fully trust fourth-century accounts of what had happened in the previous century (see Day, 47–48).

174. Were it not for Pausanias' writings we would know nothing about the clash in the marsh, as no other literary source mentions it. Aelius Aristides' reference to the importance of the marsh to the Greek victory is so brief as to be virtually useless.

175. Kynegeiros did not have an official rank in the Athenian troops who fought at Marathon. He was, though, Aischylos' brother, the most renowned play writer in Greece during the mid-5th century when Herodotus began work on his history. Therefore, he belongs to the 'famous' fighters at Marathon. It is possible that information on the heroic deeds and death of Kynegeiros may have been made known through Aischylos, whose position in the hoplites' phalanx would have been in close proximity to Kynegeiros'; as we saw, during the battle hoplites lined up near their next of kin. Therefore, Aischylos must have found himself among the Athenians who pursued the Persians to the shoreline and their ships. Even if he had not seen his brother getting injured, he must have found out what had occurred and may have spotted his brother critically wounded. Kynegeiros may

even have died in Aischylos' hands. A relief on a Roman sarcophagus at Brescia in Italy depicting the battle of Marathon has at its centre a young Greek soldier lying on the ground next to a Persian ship whose stern he seems to be clutching with his left hand. It is obvious that this man has been injured by the Persians and may have had his right hand cut off; a detail which is not clear since the image has been damaged. A Persian is standing on the stern of the ship, just about to strike him with an ax, while another older man – a bearded Greek hoplite – is trying to protect him behind his shield. Harrison, 359–360, identifies the injured Greek hoplite with Kynegeiros. Therefore, the man who is trying to protect him may have been his brother, Aischylos. In accordance with an ancient tradition, during the battle of Marathon, Aischylos received multiple injuries but kept on fighting till the moment when his fellow soldiers carried him away from the battlefield on a stretcher. Some scholars consider that Aischylos' reference in *The Persians*, lines 463–464, to mutilated soldiers, regardless of being Persians killed at Psyttaleia. during the battle of Salamis, may have been a conscious reminder of the fate of the dramatist's fallen brother 10 years earlier. In Herodotus' narrative it is Miltiades, Kallimachos and Kynegeiros who are the protagonists, the first before the battle and the last two during it. Of the other Athenian generals Herodotus mentions only Stesileos as the general who was killed. Of course, a great many Athenian and Plataian hoplites, as well as freedmen, fought bravely and with distinction. Herodotus focuses his attention on Epizelos, the son of Kouphagoras, whose action was interesting enough to be given special mention; as Epizelos was busy fighting hand-to-hand, he was struck blind without having been hit by any weapon and remained so for the rest of his life. He himself said that just before he lost his sight he saw in front of him a very large hoplite whose beard was so long that it covered the shield in front of him. This man sidestepped Epizelos and killed the man next to him. Herodotus, 6.117. We may speculate that as Herodotus refers to the apparition as a 'hoplite', it could be that Epizelos thought the man was fighting on the Greek side. It is likely that Epizelos became permanently blind having suffered a stroke during the battle and not as result of a phycological or neurological problem; if it had been one of the latter cases, he would have regained his sight at some point. See Scott, 396.

176. This is the tenor of Nepos' biography of Miltiades (see Koulakiotis), as it is of the depiction of Miltiades on an Athenian coin of the early-second century AD.
177. Berthold, 94, n. 61: 'The capture of the Persian horse would surely have made an impact on the tradition from which Herodotus drew'.
178. For example Demosthenes, in his *Third Philippic*, 48–52, ridicules Philip II of Macedon for using in his phalanx not hoplites but a melange of light-armed troops of various kinds, cavalry and mercenaries (see Hanson, 2007, 204–205).
179. Hanson, 1989, 45–46.
180. Reinforcing this picture of the battle of Marathon in the fourth century is Plato, with his references in *Menexenos* and *Laws*. The philosopher held no high regard for the later victory at Salamis, as he deemed it to have been the achievement of thetes rowers, which is probably why he didn't mention any thetes at Marathon. The picture of thousands of light-armed troops in the marsh picking off Persians with their projectiles and then attacking them en masse was not one that Plato wanted to promote. As Plato's work was hugely regarded in later centuries, his version of the battle became the prevalent one. Yet we know now that his accounts contain serious errors, even in their details.

181. One possible explanation of the Athenians' reluctance to make known their defensive plan at Marathon was the concern that they might have to apply it again – as indeed happened– and not necessarily against just the Persians. Marathon for the first time showed how the natural features of the terrain could be used to determine battle tactics; it would prove revolutionary for the technique of warfare in the Greek world.
182. Polybius, 13.3.2–3. See Whatley, 122, and Hanson, 1989, 43–44.
183. Xenophon, *Hellenica*, 4, 5.15.
184. Aischines, *Against Ktesiphon*, 243; Demosthenes, *On Syntax*, 22.
185. Incidentally, Thucydides considered it shameful that hoplites could be slain by light-armed troops (see Hanson, 2000, 228). Thucydides also undervalued the exceptional victory of the Athenian light-armed over Spartan hoplites at Sphakteria in 425. He saw fit to quote a Spartan prisoner who scoffed that the arrows of the Athenian archers were no better that women's distaffs, the implication being that the archers didn't have the manhood of the hoplites (Thucydides, 4.40. See Lendon, 47).

Chapter 8

1. Most scholars would agree that the victory at Marathon helped strengthen the democratic polity, though without presenting conclusive evidence. For example, Stathakopoulos, 43–44, connects the victory to the *zeugitai* who supposedly gained new political rights. Others assert that the victory lent new status to the *zeugitai*, thus buttressing the democracy. This class, though low in the scale, gave the hoplites most of their recruits. Yet there is no real historical evidence that it elevated its political status in 490, as its exclusion from the higher Athenian state offices continued for some years afterwards. Only in 458/7 did the *zeugitai* acquire the right to become Eponymous Archons, thanks to the reforms of Ephialtes and Perikles (*The Constitution of the Athenians*, 26.2).
2. G. Anderson, 2006, 80.
3. The reforms of Ephialtes and Perikles, by downgrading the authority of the Areopagus and granting allowances for all citizens to attend the Assembly and serve on juries in the courts, pushed along the trend towards an extreme democracy at Athens that had got started immediately after Marathon.
4. According to author of *The Constitution of the Athenians*, 7.3, it was Solon who had conferred the right of the thetes to vote in the Assembly. Under the tyranny, however, the Assembly was mere window-dressing to mask absolute rule. The right became real only after Kleisthenes' reforms (see G. Anderson, 2006, 52–57).
5. *The Constitution of the Athenians*, 22.3. Most scholars (e,g, Forrest, 41) accept this reference. Discoveries of potsherds show that the first ostracisms were conducted at Athens shortly after 490 and not before.
6. For the reasons why ostracism was adopted in 488/7, see Kagan, 393–401.
7. We note that Aristotle (*Politics*, 1290b, 39–1291b, 30) does not include members of the upper classes in the Assembly, but only the thetes.
8. *The Constitution of the Athenians*, 22.6. Excavations at the Agora and Kerameikos in Athens have turned up *ostraka* with the names of all the politicians we know were ostracized in the 480s (see Vanderpool, 1949, 408–409). There are also many *ostraka* of that time with the names of Athenians unknown to us.
9. Lang, 33, n. 14.
10. S. Forsdyke, 2006, 166: 'Ostracism was first used, and used most frequently, in the 480s. Between 487–2 no fewer than five persons were ostracized. The frequency of

the use of ostracism in this decade may itself indicate that the city was undergoing a particularly intense period of political strife'.

11. *The Constitution of the Athenians*, 23.1. The author of this work says that right after the Persian Wars the powers of the Areopagus increased. This logically would have been at the expense of the Assembly. However, the allegation in this work (25.1) that in the seventeen years between the end of the Persian Wars and Ephialtes' reforms (478–461) the Areopagus had the ascendancy appears to be wrong. Despite the considerable powers wielded by the Areopagus at the time, Athens never ceased being a democracy with the Assembly acting as the highest executive power in the city.

12. *The Constitution of the Athenians*, 22.5. The drawing of lots for the Nine Archons was done from five hundred candidates elected by the *demes* and known as the *prokritoi*.

13. Aristotle, *Politics*, 1294b.

14. As we have seen, the battle of Marathon was the last Athenian military operation in which the office of Polemarch was important in the Athenian command. That battle, in fact, showed up the value of the rank of general.

15. See below for the Athenian expedition against Paros of 489.

16. *The Constitution of the Athenians*, 8.4.

17. Miltiades was accused by the *main* Assembly (see details in Carawan, 167–208).

18. The second known legal proceeding by the Assembly against an archon was that involving Hipparchos, the son of Charmos. According to Lykourgos, *Against Leokrates*, 117, while awaiting the verdict on a charge of treachery he escaped, and was sentenced to death in absentia (see Scott, 364). The *eisangelia* aimed chiefly against generals was a common feature of Athens' democracy in the fifth and fourth centuries.

19. Plutarch, *Aristides*, 7.1.

20. Aristophanes, *Knights*, line 781. On this line see Sfyroeras, 93: 'Here the victory at Marathon earns the Athenian *Demos* bragging rights'.

21. *The Constitution of the Athenians*, 28.2.

22. As reported by Thucydides, 1.93.3, and Pausanias, 1.1.2, Themistokles fortified Piraeus, after which the Athenian fleet began to use its harbours. He seems to have done this as Eponymous Archon in 493/2 and not in the latter half of the 480s when he was a general. However, the creation of the fleet that would secure Athens' domination of the sea in the fifth century was Themistokles' work in 484/0.

23. Pseudo-Xenophon, *The Constitution of the Athenians*, 2.18.

24. Bowie, 2013, 69.

25. Bowie, 2013, 70. These comedies could have been inspired by the battle of Marathon. Though in the third century AD Athenaios considered the play *Paupers* (*Ptochoi*) to be a forgery, Bowie speculates whether it belongs to the same historical framework as other works by Chionides.

26. According to the author of *The Constitution of the Athenians*, 28.2, Miltiades was the political leader of the aristocratic faction at Athens, and quite understandably, his role at Marathon would have reinforced his position.

27. This offering was a statue of Pan, on the base of which the following epigram was inscribed, attributed to Simonides of Keos: 'Miltiades set up me, the goat-footed Pan, the Arkadian, foe of the Persians, ally of the Athenians'. Dubner *Anthology*, 2, 575, n. 232. See also Bowie, 2013, 62–63. Page, 1981, 195, believes it is a genuine epigram of 490, though with reservations. How and Wells, 108, believe this offering was the Pan statue in the cave on the Acropolis.

28. Plutarch, *Kimon*, 8.1. This reference is fully analysed by Evans, 1993, 304. Sophanes had served with distinction in the war against Aigina a few years before Marathon, killing Eurybates, the commander of 1,000 Argive volunteers fighting alongside the Aiginetans (Herodotus, 6.421 and 9.75). This war can be dated either to 493/2 or 492/1. Sophanes was the Athenian who distinguished himself also in the battle of Plataia. He was killed in 464 while serving as Athenian general in the battle of Drabiskos near Amphipolis (see Herodotus 9.73–75). For other ancient references to Sophanes, see Scott, 333.

29. This story may well be fanciful, as its protagonist, Sophanes, was one of Athens' greatest heroes, a contemporary of Miltiades.

30. Popular feeling on the subject was so intense that even a century after the battle of Marathon, Demosthenes (*Against Aristokrates*, 198) noted that the Athenians attributed the victory not to Miltiades but to the *Demos*. The comic poet Eupolis in a lost play also indicates the same feeling (see Storey, 136).

31. Meidani, 173, puts the time interval at twenty-three years at least.

32. Herodotus, 6.132.

33. The first known instance in which the Assembly worked out details of a military expedition was in 498, when it sent aid to the Ionian Revolt (see G. Anderson, 2006, 56). In the Classical era the number of men and ships for an expedition had to be approved by the Assembly (see Hamel, 5–14 and Scott, 432).

34. Aelius Aristides avers that on the eve of the expedition to Paros, the Athenians believed that nothing was impossible for an army with Miltiades in command. Miltiades himself may have underestimated the power of the thetes, but he well knew that all classes, especially the lower ones, looked first to their own self-interest. For all their distrust of him, the thetes would have had no reason not to believe his promise of bringing back wealth. Marathon had shown that he was able to act so as to bring about the best result. Develin, 1977, 574–577, believes that Miltiades lied to the Athenians about the wealth to be got in order to get them to approve his campaign.

35. On the reasons for the Athenian attack on Paros, see Herodotus, 6.132–136; Nepos, *Miltiades*, 7; Plutarch, *Kimon*, 4.4. Herodotus, 6.134, claims that Miltiades wanted to punish the Parians because one of their number named Lysagoras had slandered him to the Persian Hydarnes. This could be the same Hydarnes who had helped Darius seize power, or his son of the same name who, according to Herodotus, 7.135, was 'general of the coastal peoples of Asia' at the beginning of Xerxes' reign. During the campaign of 480 the younger Hydarnes was the commander of Xerxes' crack unit, The Immortals, (see Herodotus, 7.83). For more on Hydarnes father and son, see Scott, 434–435. Yet almost all recent scholars doubt that this was the real reason for the Parian expedition (cf. How and Wells, 120). The story could have been put about by Miltiades' political rivals the Alkmaionidai, as part of their propaganda against him after the failure at Paros. Nepos says that Miltiades wished to penalize Paros for helping the Persians against the Athenians the previous year. Some scholars connect the expedition also with an Athenian attempt to create a buffer zone in the Aegean to guard against any more Persian offensives (see Develin, 1977, 571–577 and Hammond, 1988, 518). Meidani, 177–178, speculates that another aim was to create a powerful Athenian fleet by possessing triremes of the Cyclades islands, a theory reinforced by Nepos' statement that Miltiades moved against other islands as well.

36. According to Ehrenberg, 137–142, and Wallinga, 144–148, the real purpose of Miltiades' expedition was not political or geo-strategic, but economic. He wished to bring inside the Athenian orbit not only the Cyclades but also the gold mines at Thasos and Mount Pangaion. Develin, 1977, 574–577, however, doubts whether Paros could have influenced its colony Thasos to submit to Athens. On the economic power of Paros in the Archaic and early Classical eras, see Kouragios *et. al.*, 166, n. 310. The Parians did very well out of shipping, trade, small industry and exploiting the mines at Thasos. Its fabled white marble was especially prized.

37. Herodotus, 6.133. This account appears to say that Miltiades wanted to make a show of Athenian strength before giving the Parians an ultimatum. Herodotus says nothing of negotiations between the two parties. He also concentrates on the resistance of the Parians to the besiegers after the Athenian ultimatum was refused, describing how they built up the weaker parts of their wall at night.

38. Casson, 84, judges that Nepos' account of the Parian expedition is more realistic than that of Herodotus, whose story that Miltiades' actions against the priestess of Demeter Thesmophoros led to his defeat, seems more rumour than fact. Herodotus, however, quotes the Parians on that. They, of course, would have had every reason to blacken Miltiades' reputation. Herodotus' pointing out his source for the story could mean that he realized his readers might have a problem with it.

39. Kouragios, 76–86; Kouragios et. al., 166.

40. Kouragios *et. al.*, *op. cit.* Herodotus, 6.135.1, reports that Miltiades ravaged the island before departing. At Despotiko, however, there is evidence not only of looting hut the deliberate destruction of sacred objects such as *kouroi*.

41. Herodotus, 6.135.

42. See Herodotus, 6.134, who writes that Miltiades was wounded either in the thigh or the knee. The location of the shrine to Demeter Thesmophoros remains unknown, though Kouragios has excavated an area in the present town of Paros and found a statue connected with the deity. Herodotus' report that the shrine was located on a hill in front of the town indicates that Miltiades received his wound during a reconnaissance to determine the location's strategic value and not to steal or desecrate sacred objects as the Parians alleged. Nepos, *Miltiades*, 7, says Miltiades was wounded during the siege of Paros, but does not say where or how. According to Aelius Aristides (quoted in Dindorf, 1829, 3, 572), Miltiades was wounded in the thigh by an arrow shot from the walls of Paros, and as the shrine to Demeter stood next to the walls, Miltiades thought the goddess had done it. The Brescia Sarcophagus shows a Persian biting an Athenian hoplite in the leg. Could this have been a depiction of Miltiades? Harrison, 359, n. 49, is not convincing when she writes that this scene symbolizes Kynegeiros, who gripped the stern of a Persian ship by his teeth after a Persian cut off both his hands.

43. Nepos claims that Miltiades raised the siege of Paros when a clump of trees far from the town caught fire and he feared it might be a signal for the Persian fleet to come and help the Parians. Herodotus' claim, on the other hand, that Miltiades had to leave because of his wound sounds more realistic, as he was to die from that wound soon afterwards.

44. Bowie, 2013, 60, makes the observation that if Miltiades had not died in 489, quite possibly he would have become the first victim of the ostracism process, as the *Demos* considered him a greater enemy than Hipparchos, the son of Charmos.

45. The trial was conducted in the Assembly and not in some courtroom (see Scott, 441). Miltiades was charged with 'deceiving the Athenians'. Carawan, 194,

suggests it was the same charge as those of the *eisangeliai* of the fourth century. Nepos asserts the specific charge as being that Miltiades accepted a bribe from Darius to lift the siege of Paros, though we have no confirmation of this from any other ancient source.

46. In the Classical era the accused undertook his own defence, as there were no trial lawyers. We know, however, from reports of fourth century trials in Athens that accused women, minors or invalids would be defended by friends (see Scott, 441). Miltiades himself was a very capable speaker, but the fact that he was unable to defend himself must have weighed heavily on his spirit.

47. Plato, *Gorgias*, 516 E, says that when the presiding judge saw that Miltiades would be condemned to death and thrown into the *barathron*, he intervened to save him. This, however, does not seem realistic (see Berve, 101). The fine of fifty talents imposed on Miltiades was extremely high, and even he, one of the wealthiest men in Athens, could not pay it. According to Herodotus, 6.136.3, the fine was eventually paid off by his son Kimon. Diodorus Siculus, 10.30.1, adds that Kimon consented to being jailed until the fine was paid in order to receive his father's body. The same writer claims that Kimon was freed only after marrying a wealthy Athenian woman with a large dowry, and that the matchmaker was none other than Themistokles! Plutarch's story in *Kimon*, 4.7, is that the wedding in question was that of Miltiades' daughter Elpinike, with whom Kallias, the son of Hipponikos – the richest man in Athens in the fifth century – fell in love and promised to pay off her father's fine to get Kimon's permission to marry. These tales must be considered fanciful. Kimon may have paid off the fine twenty years later, in 467 , when he donated to the *Demos* part of the rich booty he had amassed from the Persians at the battle of the Eurymedon river. That would have been unprecedented, as war booty until then was shared among the soldiery, with a portion going to the divinities.

48. Miltiades was put on trial after the expiry of his annual term as general, probably in August 489. We know that trials in Classical Athens, even the most important ones, took just a few days. After his conviction Miltiades was jailed until he could pay the fine. He may well have been denied medical attention, and thus the jailing would have been in reality a death sentence. Herodotus, 6.136.3, writes that he probably died of gangrene ('a rotting of the thigh'). Scott, 444, estimates that he died five weeks after suffering his leg wound, that is, in August or September 498, on the first anniversary of the battle of Marathon. Herodotus does not specify whether Miltiades died in jail, and so some speculate that he could have been moved to house arrest.

49. Nepos, *Miltiades*, 7.

50. For example, Cicero, who in *Pro Sestio*, 141, claimed that his fellow-citizens had behaved ungratefully to him, as had happened with Miltiades (see Koulakiotis, 154). As Miltiades had saved Athens at Marathon, so Cicero figured that the Romans had rewarded his services to the Roman Republic with exile. A Roman stele of the Imperial period in the Ravenna Archaeological Museum bears this quote: 'Qui Persas bello vicit Marathonis in arvis civibus ingratis et patria interit' ('He who beat the Persians at Marathon died because of the ingratitude of his compatriots and his country') (See Schefold, 532).

51. These six Byronic lines are perhaps the most flattering words that have been written about Miltiades, the man who saved Greek liberty at Marathon. The poet wishes that a 'tyrant' like that of 'the Chersonese' could give Greece its freedom again. (Lord Byron, *Don Juan, Canto the Third* – LXXXVI, 'The Isles of Greece', 12).

52. Nepos, *Miltiades*, 8.
53. Figueira, 1986, 275–279, theorizes that Xanthippos was 'head of the fleet' responsible for Athens' ships, and hence having the power to accuse Miltiades of mismanaging the abortive Paros campaign.
54. *The Constitution of the Athenians*, 28.2.
55. See Bowie, 2013, 61. According to the author of *The Constitution of the Athenians*, Xanthippos was the first politician to be ostracized who was not considered a 'tyrannophile'.
56. A view shared by many, see Hignett, 1952, 188–189, and Dillon, 148.
57. Ober, 1996, 35: 'Democracy in Athens… was not a gift from a benevolent elite to a passive *demos*, but was the product of collective decision, action, and self-definition on the part of the *demos* itself…'. G. Anderson, 2006, 79, considers that even after Kleisthenes' reforms the thetes had only a minor political role and that the climax of Athenian democracy came only with the reforms of Ephialtes on 461/0, when all who attended the meetings of the Assembly were paid for it.
58. Aristotle, *Politics*, 1304a20–31.
59. We would concur with Ober's comparison of Athens after Kleisthenes' reforms with the French revolutionary regime after 1789.
60. G. Anderson, 2006, 213, avers that in 490 Athenian politics assumed the form it would retain until the end of the Classical era, but does not explain his reasoning. But the consequences of the political reforms triggered by the victory at Marathon, thanks to the decisive contribution of the lower classes, determined the subsequent life of the city. There are dramatically fewer luxury monuments to aristocratic families after about 500, and virtually no new ones after about 480 (see Morris, 128–149 and 1998, 64–65; Osbourne, 313). The production of *kouroi*, those symbols of Athenian aristocratic culture, also came to a halt about 490, the 'Aristodikos Kouros' being the last known example. We know of no other similar sculpture in subsequent years. The 'Kritios Boy' of about 480 was a modestly-sized memorial rather than a proper *kouros*. According to G. Anderson, 2006, 113, even between 508 and 490 *kouroi* and other elaborate statues continued to go up on the Acropolis, before measures to restrict the display of aristocratic wealth were taken.

Index

Istros, 303
Italy, 349, 355
Italian, 200

Jeffery, 221, 263, 350
Julius Caesar, 281
Justin, 6, 86, 222, 255, 296, 298, 306, 308

Kainourgios, 98
Kallias, 207, 331, 360
Kallimachos, 40, 73, 79–80, 82–3, 85–6, 90–1,
    125, 129, 133–5, 137–40, 143, 158–9, 169,
    196, 201, 203, 208, 215, 217, 221, 235, 261,
    272, 282, 284, 301–302, 305–307, 332–4,
    337, 339, 346, 352, 355
Karia, 5, 127, 253, 341
Karians, 5, 127
Karneia, 42
Karten von Attika, 106, 119, 155, 317, 319–20,
    336
Karystians, 21
Karystos, 1, 15, 19, 21, 86, 228, 254, 266, 308,
    328
Kathygros, 272
Katsimitros, 200, 352
Kato Souli, 96, 151
Kaupert, 106, 155
Keos, 261, 317, 350, 357
Kephisodotos, 308
Kerameikos, 227, 356
Kifissia, 91–2, 311–12
Kilikia, 5, 17, 263–4
Kimon, 75, 77, 80, 201, 287, 298, 303–306,
    353, 358, 360
Kineas, 258
Kir-Ab, 271
Kissia, 24
Kithairon, 101, 130–1
Klearchos, 313, 343
Kleisthenes, 38, 46, 49, 67–73, 76, 79,
    207–208, 210, 215, 273, 281, 289, 291, 301,
    317, 333, 356, 361
Kleomenes, 42, 262, 282–3, 320, 329
Kleon, 292
klerouchoi, 21–2, 35–8, 60–2, 67, 97, 117, 124,
    127, 130, 156–7, 266, 268, 277–8, 291,
    294–5, 309, 313
knights, 46–8, 58, 75, 206, 208–209, 221,
    234–6, 286, 292, 298, 307, 357
Kodros, 333
Kontorlis, 10, 256, 258, 313, 320, 335
Kopais, 200, 236
Koroneia, 324, 345
Koroni, 327
Kotroni, 27–8
Kotylaion, 269
Koukounari, 275, 310, 319
Koumanoudis, 107, 120–1, 152–3, 173,
    318–19, 325, 336, 347–8
Kouphagoras, 355

Kouragios, 211–12, 359
Kratinos, 32, 277
Krentz, 21, 57, 64–5, 85, 151–2, 224, 253, 255,
    258–60, 263–7, 269, 272–3, 283–5, 287,
    290, 292–3, 295–8, 300–301, 303, 307–308,
    310, 313, 315, 318, 324–5, 329–30, 334–7,
    339–40, 342–4, 347
Kromayer, 119–20, 148, 160, 231, 312, 315,
    319–20, 325, 329–30, 335, 338, 341–2
Kroton, 276, 349
Ktesias, 218, 259, 270
Kybele, 13, 23
Kynegeiros, 169, 201, 203, 215, 221, 339–40,
    346, 352, 354–5, 359
Kynosarges, 99, 217, 316
Kynosoura, 27, 96, 138, 272, 319, 323
Kynouria, 340

Lacey, 291, 296
Lade, 19, 254–6, 334
Lakedaimoniai, 301
Lakiades, 304
Lakrates, 227
Lambert, 273, 275, 317–19
Langdon, 113, 123, 321, 326–7
Lazenby, 8, 77, 148, 224, 230, 253, 256–8,
    263–4, 269, 290, 304, 308, 331–2, 335, 338,
    341, 344–5, 352
Lampros, 298
Laurion-ium, 46, 52, 322
Leake, 7, 9, 58–9, 64, 146, 230, 256–8, 273–5,
    277, 292–3, 296, 298, 305, 310, 312, 315–17,
    320, 325–6, 332, 335, 348
Lelantine, 117
Lemnians, 279
Lemnos, 76–7, 180, 210, 212, 279, 302–303,
    343
Leonidas, 63
Leontis, 67, 81, 306, 333
Lesbos, 270
Lesser Marsh (Brexiza Marsh), 27, 94,
    106–107, 131, 155, 158–9, 166–73, 181, 184,
    187–95, 197–200, 202–205, 215, 272–3, 312,
    316–18, 347–9
Lewis, 12, 255, 259, 276, 285, 304, 317
lexiarchike grammateia, 68–9, 300
Libanios, 296
Lindos, 18, 264
Linear B', 272
lochagos, 82
lochos, 68, 82, 299–300
Lokrians, 63
London Illustrated News, 225
Lucian, 219
Lydia, 12–13, 19
Lydians, 13
Lykeion, 301
Lykia, 5, 100, 314, 333, 339
Lysagoras, 358
Lysias, 6, 227, 255, 261, 301